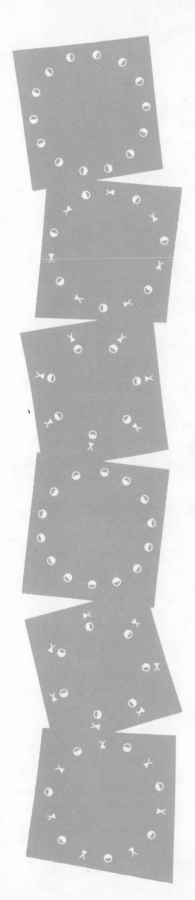

Fitness for Elementary School Children

Through Physical Education

Victor P. Dauer, Ph.D.

School of Education
Department of Physical Education
Washington State University
Pullman, Washington

Burgess Publishing Company

Minneapolis, Minn. 55415

Preface

This guide for elementary school physical education is the result of the author's experience in both public school teaching and teacher-training work. He has taught the course in Elementary School Physical Education for the past fourteen years at Washington State University and has participated in extension courses and workshops in this field. His experience as a committee chairman in compiling and assembling the first state curriculum guide for elementary school physical education for the State of Washington provided a broad viewpoint covering many aspects of the program. Some firm convictions have prompted this guide.

The first conviction pertaining to elementary school physical education is that a successful program occurs only through planning. Each teacher must have a curriculum blocked out into areas with enough detail so that the year's work is outlined. It is recognized that planning takes time, but a program of merit will only be secured through adequate planning.

The second is the author's feeling that it is too much to ask the elementary school teacher, with a limited background in physical education, to select from an overall list those materials which the teacher feels should be experienced by the children. Much of the material in this work is presented in a sequential form rather than in alphabetical listings. This certainly makes for better progression. It is recognized that activities are more easily found in a guide when listed alphabetical. But--do we teach physical education in alphabetical order?

The third firm conviction is that materials in physical education should be allocated to different grade levels, rather than just to the primary or intermediate grades. There are some types of activities, like rope skipping, which are presented in toto, but the majority of the activities in this guide are allocated to particular grades.

A fourth belief is that the material and experiences would determine the best method of approach to secure desirable learning experiences for children. At times experiences can be presented by the direct approach, while at other times movement exploration methods will offer better results. Within the framework of curriculum experiences for any grade level, the teacher should make good use of the indirect or problem solving approach to widen and broaden the learning potential of the material. This new and effective approach can do much to enrich the experiences for the children. Many suggestions and illustrations are included in the revised edition pertaining to movement experiences and the problem solving approach.

A fifth point of conviction is that there are enough materials in physical education so that a variety of activities can be presented on each grade level. New and interesting experiences should face the children in their physical education programs as they move from grade to grade. Teachers should review materials from previous grades and be cognizant of what is in store for the child in the grades ahead. Undoubtedly, some of you will differ with the placement of activities. This is natural and expected, but the important point is that they are placed.

A sixth conviction is that physical fitness values come only from a program which is planned and administered with that end in view. The attainment of good fitness is not happenstance or casual. The child must be placed in a program which has the development of physical fitness as an important goal.

Seventh, there is an attempt to make this book as complete as possible. Few activities are of the type wherein the teacher is referred to other sources. If the activity is recommended for the program, it is described in this guide. However, it is not to be inferred that the teacher should not compile adequate reference and supplementary materials. In fact, the recommendation is that the teacher collect all materials possible for enriching the program.

Efforts made toward good planning and execution in the program of physical education will pay off dividends in the attainment of good physical development, as well as other qualities, for our children.

The illustration with regard to good and poor posture was adapted by permission from one of the curriculum guides from the Seattle Public Schools. The material on Rope Skipping is also from the Seattle Public Schools as developed by Dennis Meyer. This material was adapted from original material compiled by Paul Smith, Director of Physical Education for Shoreline Public Schools, Seattle, Washington. The author is also indebted to many other teachers and consultants too numerous to mention for the many ideas which were incorporated in the book.

The Oregon State Motor Fitness Test Battery is used by permission of the Oregon State Department of Education.

The author would like to express his appreciation to Dr. James Sweeney, Assistant Professor and Gymnastics Coach, of Washington State University for his help in the many areas of the book and, in particular, the stunts, tumbling, and apparatus sequences.

The illustrations for the first edition were done by John Friel of Pullman, Washington. The additional illustrations, for the present edition, mostly in the stunts, tumbling, and apparatus areas were done by Roger L. Miller, Walla Walla, Washington.

Contents

Chapter 1

Introduction

The Child and the Elementary School

Health, vitality, and vigor are a basis for excellence in living. Physical education is concerned about physical welfare and vigor as basic for a balanced life. From a broader viewpoint--physical education provides an important educational medium which can make a significant contribution to the growth and development of children physically, mentally, morally, and socially. Basically, it makes use of the activity drive of children because they are active creatures and enjoy movement --any kind of movement. The aim of each teacher should be to assist each child to attain the maximum development possible for that child.

Another viewpoint in the growth and development picture is important. The body reacts directly to the demands of the environment in which it is placed. Physical education can provide an environment of activity which will make demands on the individual during his six growth years in the elementary school. Bones become stronger, muscles undergo good development, and ligaments and tendons are strengthened to meet the demands of activity. A child who is deprived of or who has an insufficient amount of activity fails to reach the growth potential he should. The cardio-respiratory system, as well as other systems, derives benefit from activity demands. The concept of the benefits of regular and systematic exercise in relation to the prevention of heart disease should be established early in the child's education.

A child seeks status through activity. Hear the youngster say, "Watch me," or "I can do that." A wide choice and range of appropriate challenging activities will allow each student to realize a measure of success in activity, contributing to pride

of performance. The challenge of excellence can be presented early to the child in that he comes to realize that success in the physical world demands a dedication and concentration on the task at hand. Children certainly enjoy testing strength and skill and experiencing the "feel" of new activities. The basic drives for activity are used by physical education to promote and guide these potential learning experiences into channels of proper growth and development of the individual.

When the child comes to school, he is associated with other children. This leads to experiences of social adjustment, emotional problems, and self-discipline. His wants and desires are reflected in the light of his association with his classmates. Kindness, thoughtfulness, and consideration need to be learned early.

Physical education gives the teacher an excellent opportunity to observe the child in an active social setting and to become more familiar with the characteristics of the children in light of this experience. How does he move? Awkward children often approach physical education classes with misgivings because of the fear of failure and, more important, the fear of rejection by their classmates. Physical education can help children to become more skillful, accept their limitations, and gain status in the eyes of their playmates.

How does he act? Is he getting along with other children? Does he share and take turns? Does he take unfair advantage? Is he easily discouraged? In the normal classroom setting, the child has few opportunities to make conduct choices which have bearing on the social qualities listed.

Is he progressing satisfactorily in physical qualities? Is his posture satisfactory? How strong is his endurance? Does he recover from fatigue readily? Many physical attributes are tested through the medium of physical education activities.

One unfortunate flaw in the concept of physical education is that anyone with a good book of games can teach physical education in grades one to four. If children are to be skillfully guided toward the attainment of desirable growth and development objectives, a carefully planned and directed program is essential. Values are not automatic in physical education. A child may learn how to cheat successfully in contrast to the desirable goal of cooperation with other children. Neither is physical education to be regarded as an unsupervised period of recreation, nor is it a time primarily when the child will rid himself of the "energy drive" so that he will sit quietly through classroom work. The teacher has a vital role in physical education as in other learning activities. The learning potential in play activities is high. Not to use the medium fruitfully would be to deprive the child of a valuable part of his educational heritage.

Physical Fitness

Physical fitness is a unique and important contribution which can be made by physical education as contrasted to other subject matter fields in the curriculum. If physical education cannot and does not provide fitness, no other area of curriculum ever will.

Why have our children gone soft? The youth of our nation are affected particularly by the existence of press-button gadgets and other devices tending toward habits of inactivity. The school and home need to compensate for this immobility imposed upon our children by increased mechanization and material wealth. The lack of walking, working, and using bodies for exercise are contributing factors toward soft living. With increasing population, there are fewer places where a youngster can play. He becomes a sitter and not an active participant. The impact of the television is high. Many youngsters, who would be better off in the open air playing, spend three and four hours each day in front of the television set. How many youngsters have chores to do before or after school? The ranch type home with its lack of stairs makes for easy walking and practically no climbing. Man, by nature, is a dynamic not sedentary creature. But the lack of opportunity can stifle this drive for activity.

Total Fitness and Physical Fitness

There is some confusion between the terms "total fitness" and "physical fitness." Physical fitness is actually an attribute of total fitness. Physical fitness refers to those physical qualities needed so that the individual can function efficiently and happily in his environment. As children grow in self-discipline, self-direction, inventiveness, creativity, and group adjustment, they are exhibiting qualities important in total fitness. It follows then that a person could be physically fit but not totally fit. The reverse does not hold true, as a person lacking in physical fitness would lack an important component of total fitness. In physical education we look toward total fitness through the medium of acquiring physical fitness.

A program that stresses the physical and skill developmental phases of physical education taught in an educationally sound manner will tend to achieve such other qualities as social and psychological adjustment, leadership training, and emotional stability. These can be achieved through an environment that provides feelings of security, of being wanted and included, pride in a strong and healthy body, and the attainment of skill in an activity. A good program in physical education would stress not only the physical but would include adequate consideration for the intellectual, social, and emotional development of each individual. The goal of the entire educational program, and physical education, is total fitness. The unique and important contribution of physical education is its ability to develop and maintain physical fitness.

Skills

How important are skills? A child who likes to move and has been taught to use his body skillfully and effectively usually becomes an active adult who seeks activity in his adult life. Likewise, he will tend more to support, encourage, and even supervise activities of his children and others in the neighborhood if he has skill and background in an activity.

Skills have a direct relationship to participation. A person who is skillful in an activity enjoys his participation more and is likely to continue this participation. Skills make for purposeful movement and economy of movement.

Physical Education — A Modern Viewpoint

Physical education is that phase of general education which contributes to the total fitness, growth, and development of the child primarily through physical activities. Physical education has the same goals as other subject areas, that is, the development of an effective citizen, one who can take his place in a democratic society. Physical education helps satisfy certain age-old needs of individuals, primarily physical, mental, emotional, and social. Physical education is both a means and end. It is a means in that it provides a medium for optimum growth and development of the child. It is an end in itself because physical fitness and the acquisition of desirable skills are needed for full living. More people have leisure time today than ever before. It is a purpose of physical education to provide guidance in using these leisure hours wisely and constructively.

Collectively, the fitness of our citizens is a most important resource and is indispensable in times of emergency. The late President John F. Kennedy, himself an advocate of good fitness, feels that "the physical vigor of our citizens is one of America's most precious resources. If we waste or neglect this resource, if we allow it to dwindle or grow soft, then we will destroy much of our ability to meet the great and vital challenges which confront our people."*

The Purposes of Physical Education

While the goal of physical education - well-rounded development of our children and youth as responsible citizens - is of a general nature, it can be expressed in the following specific purposes or objectives:

1. The development of physical fitness
2. The development of useful physical skills
3. The acquisition of socially desirable traits
4. The acquisition of safety skills and habits
5. The enjoyment of wholesome recreation

*John F. Kennedy, "The Soft American," Sports Illustrated, Dec. 26, 1960, p. 57.

The Development of Physical Fitness

WHAT IS PHYSICAL FITNESS? A person who is physically fit possesses the strength and stamina to carry out his daily tasks without undue fatigue and still has enough energy to enjoy leisure and to meet unforeseen emergencies. This definition can be broken down into a number of concepts.

1. A person should possess enough strength, power, endurance, flexibility, agility, coordination, balance, and speed to do easily and effectively the routine duties and maximum tasks that the day may bring.
2. He should be free from disease and removable handicapping disorders.
3. He should possess a sturdy physique which means a well-developed body with proper proportions of bone, muscle, and fat tissue. His posture should be acceptable and evidence of good nutritional habits should be present.
4. At the end of the day he should be sleepy, but not overly tired. He should be able to sleep well and feel recovered in the morning from the activities of the preceding day.

The development and maintenance of physical fitness are covered in Chapter 2.

Movement Excellence - Useful Physical Skills

Every boy and girl of the elementary school should have an opportunity to develop skills so they can enjoy activities and develop a desire to participate in them. This would include:

1. Basic Movement Skills and Patterns. These are the fundamental skills relating to body movement which are useful for the basic activities of living and playing. A child should become proficient in walking, running, jumping, dodging, throwing, kicking, lifting, catching, and gauging moving objects. In addition, he should have opportunities to explore and reach an understanding of his body, its movement patterns, and possibilities. He should know and appreciate simple postural skills.
2. Special and Sports Skills. Included here are the more specialized skills of rhythmics, sports, stunts and tumbling, and similar activities. These

are useful to the child in his present day living and point to the future as avocational and recreational interests for better living. Such activities as basketball, volleyball, track and field, softball, soccer, and flag or touch football are introduced in the elementary school in a modified form and on a skill level commensurate with the ability of the youngsters.

Desirable Social Traits

Physical education is concerned with the development of desirable standards of social and moral conduct and emotional control. Many terms such as good citizenship and sportsmanship can be used to describe this goal. A child needs to be able to get along with others, take turns, win and lose gracefully, work for the common good, and respect the personality of his fellows. He should learn to exercise self control in activities which are often emotionally intense. He can be helped to act wisely with courage and resourcefulness in situations of stress.

Since successful living demands the ability and willingness to lead skillfully and to follow intelligently, the child should be afforded opportunities to develop these capacities. One can develop the powers of judgment, observation, analysis and decision through the medium of complex physical activities.

Physical education can aid the child in developing respect for facilities and equipment and an appreciation of the opportunity that is his through physical education. He needs to learn to be at ease in a variety of social situations and to accept the consequences of his own actions. He can learn to appreciate the concept of competition as life itself is competition.

The relief from tension and anxiety through activity is important to his future well-being. The relationship of recreational activities to mental well-being has been established.

Nowhere in the curriculum are the opportunities for give and take as high as they are in physical education. As life itself is governed by social rules, customs, and traditions, so are the activities on the playfield and gymnasium floor. Fair-play, honesty, and conformance with the rules can be stressed through physical activities.

Proper attitudes of boy-girl relationships can be furthered through properly conducted co-educational activities. Par-

ticularly, in rhythmic activities can there be promoted courtesy and consideration between opposite sexes. The group method, so often used in Physical Education, provides numerous opportunities for social and emotional growth.

Safety Skills and Attitudes

In the child's world today, attention to safety factors is of utmost importance. The capacity for safe living is not an automatic value but must be sought. The ability to use equipment safely, to consider oneself and fellow students in the light of safety, and to handle one's body efficiently in times of stress are attributes which are important for safe living. The teacher needs to explain the techniques of an activity in the light of the consequences from unsafe procedures. While all necessary precautions should be taken to develop habits of safety, consideration also must be given to avoid fear and overcautiousness in activity. Rules are needed to eliminate unsafe procedures, and children need to understand and recognize the importance of these practices.

It needs to be emphasized that the teacher should be so familiar with the activities that the program can be carried out in a safe environment and the youngsters learn safe procedures.

Water safety is an important facet of physical education. Although few elementary schools provide opportunity for aquatic instruction, students should be encouraged to seek instruction in this area. Private groups, like the Young Men's Christian Association and public recreation agencies, can provide the needed proficiency and background in water safety practices.

Recreational Activities

Since children will play many hours beyond the opportunity afforded them in physical education, consideration should be in the program to make this a fruitful experience. Part of this prepration can be met by teaching a variety of skills well enough so that the child has the tools for his leisure time activities. In addition, the youngster should develop knowledges, attitudes, and appreciations which will guide him in his free play. Some of the ways physical education can contribute to the recreational ideal are:

1. Give the child an understanding of

physical fitness, its importance, and how to develop and maintain this important body attribute. This would imply an appreciation of the values of physical activities for healthful living.

2. Provide him a wide variety of activities which are of use to him in his play time. This should include active games and movement experiences suitable for the home and backyard.

3. See that he knows the rules, regulations and strategies of various games, together with ways of modifying and improvising these for use with small groups and spaces.

4. Give children experience in playing with and accepting other children in physical activities. Children should not play alone and should seek the company of others of their ages and interests.

5. Permit them to study the sources and origins of activities. In the rhythmic program, for example, a dance becomes more meaningful if the children know the origin and can acquire an appreciation of the culture of the people.

A second approach would be the effect of the program on the leisure-time activity in his future years. While few adult activities of carry-over value are taught in the elementary program, habits of and an interest in purposeful activity can be established. An appreciation of beauty in physical skills and in the human form can be motivating factors for further participation.

How Can These Objectives Be Attained

Basically, to attain the objectives, physical education must be a planned developmental program which takes into consideration the needs and interests of each child in the school. The following attributes characterize such a program:

1. There must be movement. There must be something happening. Movement is the basis of physical education, and one way to judge the quality of a physical education program is to evaluate the degree of movement which each child experiences. Children learn by doing and skills are taught by repetition. If there is practice, for example, in bouncing a ball, a child profits in direct relationship to how many times he is able to handle and bounce the ball. It is of importance what the child does to the ball, but it is more important what the ball does to the child.

Physical education implies activity. The child profits little from an experience which is characterized by too much standing around, waiting for equipment to be arranged, lengthy explanations by the teacher, and domination of activity by one or two children.

2. The selection of the activities must be based upon the needs and interest of the youngsters and geared to their level. This means pre-planning and not just a "what-shall-we-do-today" type of program. If desirable learnings are to result, the activities must be suited to the developmental level of the child.

3. The activities need to be conducted in a manner that the objectives of physical education will be attained. The values of physical education are not gained automatically nor accidently. Physical activities need to be skillfully taught by understanding teachers who like children and have faith in their own ability to help children develop through this medium. This implies the application of educationally sound methods of teaching and the evaluation of the teaching process in terms of progress to the goals. Values in activity are not inherent in the activity but rather in the method of presentation. If a child is to achieve his potential in skilled movements, he must have quality teaching.

Mere participation does not mean that the child will attain the developmental level he should. The activities must be planned and directed by qualified leadership.

The Role of the Teacher

Just as a good physician treats the patient and not the disease, the teacher teaches the child and not the activity. It might be success for one skillful youngster in a class to hit a home run while it might be just as successful for another child merely to meet the ball with his bat.

It would be difficult to set the same standards of success for all youngsters in a class. Children differ greatly in their progression and values they get from activity. However, in some ways they are very much the same and travel a common path of growth and development. This allows the teacher to select activities of a central core for the class but consideration for individual differences is important.

A major problem in physical education is the sub-par group. These youngsters lack maturity, strength, endurance, and skill for successful and enjoyable participation. They are much more of a problem than the highly skilled, athletically inclined group. The unskilled need help and encouragement in the form of special aid and attention. Goals for this group are not the same as for all children.

In physical education, the teacher has an opportunity to observe the whole child in the interchanges with other students. Fruitful knowledge about children can be garnered from their conduct in physical education and in free play.

The role of the teacher is that of a leader, not a dictator. Helpfulness and friendliness are qualities needed to assist youngsters in their physical development. The democratic process can be an instrument of direction in physical education.

Nor can the school absorb the entire responsibility for the development of physical fitness. Certainly this problem extends into the community and to the parent. The school, with its emphasis on proper methodology and background, can promote habits and dispel some of the false notions which exist about fitness.

The teacher should be a reasonable example of the health and physical fitness dictums that the school is attempting to promote. Elderly teachers may feel that this would be a difficult standard to meet. However, the teacher should be free of glaring departures from what is considered good healthful practices. An example might be of the teacher who requires his students to change to rubber shoes for the physical education class period and then conducts the class wearing street shoes himself.

Children tend to imitate those whom they admire and respect. The teacher needs to be certain that the personal example that he holds forth to the children will not lay the basis for improper habits or attitudes.

The Approach to Physical Education

Some physical education people hold that modern educational theory has relegated the traditional approach to elementary school physical education to the side lines. The rigid traditional (or sometimes called the direct) approach, specifying conformance of all children to the same manner, is now considered by some to be an inferior approach. Little attention was given to creative aspects, the varied interests of children, the difference in capacity, and the opportunities for movement exploration.

On the other hand, in the opinion of the author, the pendulum has swung too far the other way in some cases in complete use of what is termed the indirect approach. This approach has had good success in England and in parts of Canada, and has a number of advocates in the United States. This is a fresh approach of child-centered education in which the child has complete opportunity to explore, create, and move according to his desires and capacities. There are those who feel the term "Physical Education" is not longer apt and should be replaced by "Movement Education," since movement is the key to the new methodology. It takes a skilled and resourceful teacher to make the most of the indirect approach so that objectives are met and the result is not merely a variety of free play.

This source recommends that teachers use methodology which combines the good features of the old and the new. This is a middle-of-the-road approach, one of which would take advantage of the best of both the traditional and the indirect.

There should be opportunity for free choice at times, and certainly creativity and exploration should be the right of each child in the program. At times creativity and exploration will be within definite limits set by the teacher. The direct approach would occur when the teacher feels specific items should be presented to the class as a whole. If in the mind of the teacher the instruction should follow a specific pattern in which children learn, for example, a complex skill, then the traditional (or direct) method would present the best route of achieving the learning. A good illustration of this is in the teaching of sports skills or a dance step wherein a particular pattern of skill is desired. However, even within such structured teaching, children should be permitted and encouraged to try different patterns in accordance with good practice so that each child can adopt and adjust for himself the pattern to fit his capacity. Some types of fitness developmental activities, where the child is required to follow a definite routine of vigorous activity, certainly qualify as the direct method.

The enterprising teacher will teach the child by the most suitable method, either direct or indirect as the case may be. Even within a single lesson, part of the activities can be presented by one means and the remainder by the other. It would seem to be inconsistent logic for some to hold that one method is entirely suitable to the exclusion of the other. No matter what the method, the child should be the center of the lesson.

Chapter 2

Physical Fitness

The New Physical Fitness Emphasis

Basically, physical fitness has always been an important consideration in physical education. There have been periods when particular stress has been placed on fitness, particularly when published statistics have indicated deplorable physical conditions among American citizenry. Draft rejection figures from both World Wars I and II received wide publicity. In each case, measures were proposed and changes were made to put more "physical" into physical education. While there were some lasting effects, the uproar died down after a period of time, and programs were back on a business-as-usual basis.

In 1954 a study of far reaching influence was made. Dr. Hans Kraus, Doctor of Physical Medicine in New York City, compared certain strength and flexibility measurements of 4000 New York City children with the same number of Central European counterparts. He was interested in finding out why his own patients, mostly middle aged or older, had so many physical ailments, particularly in the lower back. Could there be causal factors among children? According to his test, consisting of five strength items and one of flexibility, 57 per cent of the American children failed one or more of the items. In contrast, among a similar number of Austrian, Swiss, and Italian children, he found only 9 per cent failure.

The comparisons in themselves do not seem earthshaking, but the American Press raised a national hue and cry over the weaknesses of American children, and the new fitness movement was on. The first important result was the creation of President Eisenhower's Youth Fitness Council. Since its continuation by Presidents Kennedy and Johnson, the work of the Council has had far reaching effects on the quality of school physical education programs. With the aura of national authority and the endorsement of many leading professional organizations, the recommendations of the Council have been received by administrators on almost an authoritarian basis. In particular, during the year 1961, the publication of the Council entitled Youth Physical Fitness - Suggested Elements of a School Centered Program provided an important set of directives for school programs. A national physical fitness test with appropriate norms was included in the publication.

Fitness programs for adults have become fashionable. In 1962, there appeared a publication of the Royal Canadian Air Force called Exercise Plans for Physical Fitness, which provided individual exercise plans for adults, both men and women. The President's Council countered with Adult Fitness, a similar publication. Vim and Vigor also were published. Vim presents a program of individual exercises for girls of high school age, and Vigor a similar plan for boys. These publications have had an incredible sale. Naturally, the effect on the public support of school fitness programs was tremendous.

The results of this new emphasis on fitness have been evident in elementary schools. Programs are of improved quality, and programs have been established where none existed formerly. Administrators have been made increasingly aware of the important contributions that physical education can make to the growth and development of children. Other apparent effects noticed are increased time allotment for physical education, better facilities and equipment, and provision for consultant service and special teachers in physical education programs. In addition, much experimentation has occurred bringing in new and unique approaches in the development of fitness.

On the other hand, there has been some misunderstanding about the new emphasis. In the minds of many laymen, fitness is a totally new area of emphasis and concern for educators. This is in error, as the movement can be more realistically terms a re-awakening of the "physical" in physical education. The movement is gaining in strength, and it appears that the effects will be highly beneficial and lasting, not only to children but to people of all ages.

A program for physical fitness includes two important considerations. The first is an emphasis on the health of each individual child. This is basic. A physically sound, emotionally stable, and socially adjusted child provides a good basis for the development of physical fitness. On this framework, physical fitness values can be built.

To be assured that a child has a desirable level of health, programs for physical fitness should begin with an adequate and comprehensive health examination given periodically. Among other things, this should determine the child's capacity for participation in physical education. It is axiomatic that measures should be taken to remove any disorders or detrimental conditions which would respond to treatment.

The second consideration is a sound program of physical activity in the daily living of each child so that each ideally can attain an optimum degree of fitness (for himself) and maintain it during life. The school physical education program can lead the way by providing vigorous activities, establishing habits, developing attitudes, and promoting knowledge in the fitness picture. On the other hand the school cannot assume the entire responsibility for the development of physical fitness. The home and community must be brought into the picture if good fitness values are to result.

The development of favorable attitudes is an important part of the program. A sound and enjoyable program of physical fitness in the public schools is a first step in this direction. A person will be fit or unfit depending upon the value that physical fitness occupies in his personal thinking. Fitness is a transitory state, and the physically fit person of the mo-

ment can be unfit tomorrow if he fails to keep up the habit of regular exercise. Teachers should strive to impress on young children that regular exercise and activity are necessary throughout life.

Values of Physical Fitness

While not all children derive the same benefits from a program stressing physical fitness, the important values which may be forthcoming from such a program are many.

1. Regular activity stimulates growth and development and can give the body an efficient and suitable musculature. Muscles are the basis for all body action. They increase in strength with activity and deteriorate with lack of it. Since we are creatures of movement, good musculature makes movement more efficient and enjoyable. Fit muscles use less energy to perform the same tasks, leading to an increase in that body factor called vitality.
2. Strong and well-developed lower back muscles can be an aid to preventing lower back pain in later life, provided the development started in the elementary school is continued. Fitness programs can promote the development of strength, suppleness, endurance, and flexibility of the lower back needed to give proper support in good postural alignment.
3. A physically fit person is able to maintain his postural alignment better than one with weak musculature. Good fitness programs stress the development of anti-gravity muscles which maintain good postural alignment. In particular, the muscles of the abdominal wall and those of the arm and shoulder girdle are singled out for specific development. Exercise, if sufficiently intense, is the only way to prevent muscles from sagging in their fight to maintain body position against the forces of gravity.
4. Fitness improves general health and is essential for full and vigorous living.
5. The physically fit child feels more alert and eager to do things. He is able to move about with ease and confidence.
6. Fitness is a factor in weight control. Diet alone is not the best method of maintaining proper body proportions. A combination of diet and exercise is generally the best approach.
7. The efficiency and capacity of organic

systems, particularly the heart and lungs, are increased through regular vigorous exercise. There is growing conviction that regular exercise can play a major role in the prevention of degenerative heart disease in later life.

8. If one is to develop and use his mental powers fully, he must have a good abundance of physical and mental health.

9. Good physical fitness can be a factor in good peer relationships. Children respect achievement, and personal satisfaction results from the acquisition of fitness.

10. Regular physical exercise contributes to the ability to relax and is a factor in reducing tension.

Considerations in the Development of Fitness

Physical fitness, as an overall body condition, can be broken down into a number of specific physical components. The terms stamina and vitality are mentioned prominently in connection with physical fitness. These attributes are a little difficult to describe and more difficult to measure. Stamina implies staying power and good resistance to fatigue. Vitality refers to the quality of having physical vigor and an abundance of energy. Both of these qualities certainly are important, but not measurable. The most important measurable components of physical fitness are strength, power, and cardio-respiratory endurance. Agility and flexibility rate only slightly less in importance, followed by such qualities as speed, balance, and coordination. The development of each component is discussed in turn.

1. STRENGTH DEVELOPMENT. There must be sufficient big muscle activity over a wide range of activities done regularly and with enough intensity to develop strength. The improvement of strength is a basic necessity to the development of physical fitness. Muscles can be developed only through stress and the tension applied during exercise. A physiological principle important in this process is that of loading the muscle. This principle holds that as the limits of the demand (load) for muscular work are increased, the development of strength also increases. We need to make our children work if strength is to be developed.

Many of the usual physical education activities involve primarily the use of the legs, lower back, hands, and arms. The program should include hanging and arm-support activities, which are not generally used enough in many programs.

The inclusion of rope climbing, ladder work, horizontal bars, and similar hanging activities is important in making sure that the upper torso is developed proportionately to other parts of the body.

Since few physical education activities contribute to the development of strength in the abdominal wall, special selected developmental activities leading to such development are needed in the program.

Beginning on the intermediate level, a carefully selected fitness developmental program should be instituted. This should include, among other things, specific activities for strengthening the abdominal wall and the arm-shoulder girdle area.

Isometric type activities should receive some consideration in the program.

2. THE DEVELOPMENT OF POWER. Power implies the process of using strength to apply force for effective movement. Power is based on strength and its application to movement. Teaching youngsters how to move effectively in situations demanding an application of force will develop the ability to apply powerful movements when needed.

3. THE DEVELOPMENT OF ENDURANCE. Endurance refers to the ability to carry on muscular effort over a period of time. It has a basis in strength in that the stronger person is able to keep up muscular effort longer than one without adequate strength. However, there are other involvements in the body. Primarily, this is a postponement of the stages of fatigue so that muscular work can be carried on. A person with good endurance has a conditioning involving the cardio-respiratory system and other deep body mechanisms.

To achieve endurance, the program must make demands on the individual in the form of muscular effort which causes accelerated breathing. Generally, this involves running or other rapid movement. No activity should be carried on to the point where the participants are breathless. The latter is an over-stimulation and should be avoided. However, the children need to push themselves beyond the first inclination to cease. If the activity is interesting and stimulating, this presents little problem. Otherwise, as in exercises, or rope climbing, the child needs to push himself.

The conditioning for endurance connotes increased dosages. Most coaches practice this by gradually increasing the dosages of activity until the athletes can participate in a full length game. Teachers are cautioned that this process takes time. If considering playing an active game (like soccer), thought must be given to bringing the children up gradually to the level of endurance through increased dosages of activity.

4. AGILITY. Agility refers to the ability to change direction swiftly, easily, and under good control. A particularly agile person is one who is hard to catch in a tag game. He can dodge and change direction well.

Agility is a needed safety quality. Many persons today are alive and free from injury because they were agile enough to get out of the way of a moving object.

Agility can be developed in many games, relays, and similar activities. The development is not automatic, however, and children need to be taught how to stop, start, and change direction properly.

5. FLEXIBILITY. Flexibility is in terms of range of movement at the joints. A flexible child can stretch farther, touch his toes, reach farther, etc. In apparatus work, hanging exercises stretch the upper torso. Stunts and tumbling activities contribute much to flexibility. Movement exploration involves good opportunity to increase flexibility of the body. Youngsters need activities where they can stretch, reach, hang, and otherwise force the joints into good ranges of movement.

6. SPEED. The ability to move quickly and effectively is a needed skill in many physical education activities. Youngsters should be taught proper running techniques, including fast starts.

7. BALANCE. Balance refers to the ability to maintain body equilibrium in a variety of positions. Stunts and tumbling, movement exploration, and similar activities give practice in maintaining balance.

8. COORDINATION. Coordination means the harmonious functioning of muscles in producing complex movements. Generally, a movement of high skill well done needs a high degree of co-ordination. By giving practice and instruction in various movement patterns, coordination can be an expected outcome. The application of basic principles important in skill movements should be a part of the instruction.

Principles in Acquiring Physical Fitness

Physical fitness can be acquired only through the medium of muscular effort and is maintained only through continued activity. It follows then that this activity must be carried out regularly throughout life, and that the type of activity must be geared to the age, sex, and physical condition of the individual. A child who enjoys movement and has been taught how to use his body effectively usually becomes an active individual who can maintain his fitness throughout his life.

However, youngsters must face the fact that muscular development does take effort and is not always fun. To raise the level of fitness, students must be pressed, they must expend energy, and this must be done regularly. Activities selected must have the potential to develop fitness and must be conducted in such a manner that fitness is an outcome. Strength, power, endurance, and the other physical characteristics are developed best through a variety of vigorous activities.

The President's Council on Physical Fitness has proposed the following specific recommendations which should be applied to physical education programs so that the goal of physical fitness can be realized.

1. Programs to improve physical fitness must provide vigorous activities that will develop the physique, increase the efficiency of the cardio-vascular system, and contribute to the developmen of skills.
2. Progressive resistive exercises involving increased work loads for longer periods are essential to increase the level of fitness.
3. Endurance develops in proportion to the total work done over a period of time.
4. Strength is increased through activities requiring more than 50 per cent of the total strength capacity.
5. Organic efficiency is improved where rhythmical muscular activity is continued over long, unbroken periods.
6. Physical fitness is directly proportional to the levels of strength, power, and endurance achieved.

7. The school physical education program should include a core of developmental and conditioning activities, appropriate to each grade level. These activities should be carefully identified and stressed in progressive order.

8. The school health education program provides knowledge and understanding based on scientific facts and principles in order to develop desirable health attitudes and behavior for the promotion of physical fitness. *

To this list, two other principles can be added.

9. The school program should include activities which are not only functional now but can be used in later life to achieve fitness.

10. An attempt must be made to inculcate an attitude that physical fitness is desirable and important for wholesome adult living.

It would seem important, too, that the health instruction include units on different levels which would stress the importance of fitness and how fitness can be achieved and maintained. Instruction should include the relationship to fitness of medical and dental supervision and care, immunization and other protection against disease, proper nutrition, adequate rest, relaxation, good health practices, sanitation, and other aspects of healthful living. ** Vigorous exercise is important to fitness, but a program that relies on exercise alone to solve fitness problems falls far short of its mark.

To attain good physical fitness benefits, a daily program of physical education should be the right of every child on every grade level in the public schools. A part of the daily program should be given over to vigorous activity.

The substitution of band, chorus, play practice, and athletic programs for physical education is certainly not a recommended procedure. Teachers, too frequently, take the physical education period for practice for special events for part or all of the children. Neither should health instruction be counted as a part of the physical education requirement. The practice of alternating health and physical education is another departure from good practice. Health instruction is an important area in its own right and should be so treated. Confusion exists often because the terms health and physical education are often coupled together in literature

* Youth Physical Fitness, pp. 5-6.

** Ibid., p. iii.

and discussions. The practice of teaching health during inclement weather when the children cannot go outside certainly leaves a bad taste for health instruction. The motivation to better health is doubtful when taught under these circumstances.

Sufficient time is needed for physical education. A minimum of 30 minutes of activity on a daily basis is the goal. The teacher needs to organize the lesson plan in such a fashion that maximum use of the class period can be made for activity.

Class size should not exceed the normal limits of one class. The practice of sending out two or more classes with one teacher for physical education results in little more than a supervised play period.

Activity is measured on an individual basis. The activities must be taught so the children get many turns. Groups for any one activity should be as small as possible consistent with the activity. Sufficient supplies should be available so many children can be active.

Intramural sports should be available to all children with the goal of participating and using the skills learned in the physical education class program. The program should be broadened to include many sports, more teams, and more participants. It should be stressed equally for boys and girls. Out of this program can grow a limited amount of inter-school experiences. These may result from an intramural program but are not the goal of such a program.

Club work can be encouraged. Clubs like those for tumbling, hiking, swimming, skiing, skating, and other activities increase the motivation for activity. Opportunities for informal physical recreation in the school should be encouraged and sponsored at all available periods.

Cooperation with the community in recreation programs is a desirable adjunct of the physical education program. School facilities form the basis for many fine recreation programs in hours of non-school use.

Special attention must be given to the physically underdeveloped child. Any program for physical fitness which omits this consideration falls short of attaining good fitness for all children. Too often the concentration of effort is on the so-called normal and physically gifted children. In extreme cases, the emphasis is only on the strong and skilled with the view of developing future varsity athletes for the high school program.

Testing for Physical Fitness

A testing program is an absolute essential in any fitness program. Testing should uncover low-fitness students, measure status of the remainder, determine needed areas for improvement, provide motivation for the students, and provide material for public relations. Certainly, much of the effectiveness of the physical education program can be measured with respect to how it meets the challenge of fitness. While physical education should be justified on the broad basis because of its contributions to the growth and development of the youngster, fitness statistics provide for parents and administrators an understandable justification of the program.

As a minimum, testing should be done at beginning, middle, and end of each school year. The progress of low-fitness students should be checked more often.

A valid, reliable, and accepted test should be used. Probably the most widely used test, and one this source recommends strongly, is that of the Blue Book of the President's Council for Physical Fitness. This is a national test with national norms and is presented in Chapter 17. For purposes of convenience, another test is also included in this manuscript. This test is simpler and less time-consuming and has been developed and adopted in the State of Oregon. The directions and norms for this this test are presented in the Appendix. * Teachers should note that few tests are considered reliable below the fourth grade and most test norms begin with that grade level.

The fitness of primary children can be evaluated on the basis of subjective judgment. Further discussion of this is made in Chapter 5.

Test results for each individual should be a matter of school record and a consideration in his overall school evaluation. Since fitness is a good indication of the health of the child, his fitness scores should be a part of his health record, to follow him throughout his school career. Testing for physical fitness is covered in detail in Chapter 17.

The Low Fitness Program

After the low-fitness children have been identified, a plan of action for them is needed. Any plan of action should con-

sider three approaches to the problem. The first is a determination of the causes of the low fitness level.

A professional approach to this diagnosis is needed. A scrutiny of the health status of the child is a first consideration. Available health records should be consulted and, if needed, a special examination by a physician should be scheduled. Next, through consultation with the parents and the child, the health habits of the child should be evaluated. After all information has been sifted and checked, the recommendations for each child can be established.

The second step is to impose corrective measures growing out of the analysis of the child's basic causes for poor fitness. Corrective steps for possible health conditions amenable to correction should be taken. If health habits need adjustment, these changes should be made.

The third step would be a matter of a program of developmental exercises and activities designed for the individual to raise his physical performance to his desired level. The students should be tested periodically to determine progress.

An excellent procedure to handle low fitness problems is on a committee basis. Each case can be reviewed and remedial procedures prescribed. Such a fitness committee could be composed of the school nurse, a physician, the principal, the physical education consultant or teacher, and teachers from the elementary school.

Stressing Physical Fitness in the Program of Activities

A child profits and gains in physical fitness in relation to the activity demands which he experiences. Certainly, a wide variety of big-muscle activities which extend and challenge the child should be included. In addition, the inclusion of special developmental activities is important. These are activities which can be carried on for short periods of time and provide fitness developmental values. Calisthenics, circuit training, running, other endurance activities, and rope skipping are examples of special activities included in the program because they can develop fitness. It should be recognized that, while activities of this nature have good potential in developing fitness, sound methodology is important in reaching this potential.

* See Appendix, page 325.

Further discussion of specific activities to develop fitness is included in the primary and intermediate sections.

While occasionally games and other activities can be used where the child is eliminated from the activity, these should be used with caution. This is a particular consideration if the child is eliminated on the basis of skill or some other fitness component. A child gets no value from an activity where he watches the skilled and strong take over and finish. It is better to count points against an individual instead of eliminating him. If elimination games are played, do not play them too long. After a portion of the children (say 4, 5, or 6) have been eliminated, then reform and play the game or continue the activity.

Chapter **3**

Organizing for Effective Teaching

There are a number of considerations which affect the kind and quality of the physical education program. In the last analysis, it is the school administration which determines the quality and kind of an educational program which is carried on in the elementary school. The administration through policies sets the basis for the program in physical education. Decisions with respect to consultant service, staff competency, equipment, supplies, finances, facilities, and similar matters are made first on an administrative level. It is vital that the administration accept the concept that physical education is an instructional program which is an important part of the child's educational experience, and that this teaching area merits suitable consideration in planning. Whether or not physical education is a teaching program or merely a glorified recess period, where children just let off steam, is determined largely by the administrative viewpoint.

It must be recognized that the regular classroom teacher needs help to do an adequate job in physical education. Generally, teachers are well trained in overall elementary school teaching, but lack adequate preparation in physical education. Perhaps one course through the undergraduate preparation is the extent of this background. In addition, some teachers, mostly on the intermediate level, feel inadequate in teaching skills which they, themselves, cannot do well. If satisfactory teaching in physical education at the elementary level is to result, the administration must accept the premise that some form of aid for the classroom teacher is necessary whether it be in the form of consultant service, special teachers, or other arrangement.

The Patterns of Teaching Physical Education

The patterns of teaching physical education with respect to staff assignments vary from school to school. Some of the plans by which physical education teaching is organized are listed.

1. Full responsibility by the classroom teacher with no supervisory or consultant aid. Often, in this administrative arrangement, there isn't even a curriculum guide available. The average elementary school teacher left on his own does not do an acceptable teaching job in physical education.

2. Major responsibility by the classroom teacher with consultant aid. The consultant under this plan works primarily with the teacher, aiding in the planning of an overall program and in the individual lessons.

3. Major responsibility by the classroom teacher with part time teaching by a special teacher. Under this arrangement, it is important that the efforts of the classroom teacher, who has to teach the majority of the time, and the special teacher be coordinated. The specialist teacher presents usually the more difficult skill instruction, and helps the teacher with plans for teaching the remainder of the week. The teacher should be with the children during all physical education classes, even those taught by the special teacher.

4. Full time teaching by special physical education teachers. Research shows that this plan produces the best results in terms of child progress toward the objectives of physical education. The

majority of this type of teaching, however, is confined to the intermediate grades, with the primary teacher still responsible for her own teaching. The chief administrative objection to this plan is that it requires extra teachers. However, if the school system is given to a program of special teachers (art, music, language, home economics), it should include the area of physical education. A second objection to this plan is that the classroom teacher loses contact with the students during the physical education class and loses a valuable opportunity to work with and observe them in this setting. However, some of this can be overcome by having the classroom teacher observe the physical education lessons.

5. Departmentalized Teaching. This plan involves a rotation of teachers and subject matter fields among classes, on much the same plan as used in the high school scheduling. The teachers usually work with the self-contained classroom type of teaching during the morning (or afternoon), and the other half of the day is given over to departmentalized teaching by the same teachers on a rotating class schedule. Here is one way such a plan could work utilizing two fifth and two sixth grade classes and subject matter fields of music, social studies, language arts, and physical education. This plan could also be adapted to separating the sexes for activity. The plan could work equally well with two or three classes; although with only two classes, it would amount primarily to a teacher exchange of classes.

Periods	5th - 1	5th - 2	6th - 1	6th - 2
1st	Teacher A Music	Teacher B Social Studies	Teacher C Language Arts	Teacher D Physical Educ.
2nd	Teacher D Physical Educ.	Teacher A Music	Teacher B Social Studies	Teacher C Language Arts
3rd	Teacher C Language Arts	Teacher D Physical Educ.	Teacher A Music	Teacher B Social Studies
4th	Teacher B Social Studies	Teacher C Language Arts	Teacher D Physical Educ.	Teacher A Music

Advantages of the plan are specialist type teaching by instructors with good background in respective fields. For the children, it would mean a better and more profitable experience in physical education. Since this plan demands only a time arrangement, it represents no additional staff expense to the administration.

6. Trading or combining classes. A practice which has merit is to have a man and woman teacher combine for physical education with two classes, usually on the intermediate level. With two sixth grade classes and two teaching stations available, the male teacher could take the boys of both classes, and the woman teacher handle the girls. This arrangement should not rule out coeducational activity, but is a convenience in activities where the sexes should be separated. The teacher exchange of classes could function on any level where one teacher has special talent in physical education or in a particular type of activity.

The Time Factor

How much time is available and how much time can be allotted for physical education are other administrative decisions affecting the program. While the recommendation is that each child have a daily experience in physical education, there are situations which do not permit this schedule. It may be a shortage of outdoor space, indoor facilities, or both. It may be that the principal in setting up the program feels that he cannot allot more than three periods per week, for example, to a program of physical activity. Competition for time for various subject interest groups poses a problem to the administrator and continual pressure is put upon school officials by vested interest groups. Physical education should be a daily experience wherever possible. If the schedule calls for less than a daily period, the length of the class period should be increased to compensate.

Climate and Geographical Conditions

It is recognized that the weather is an important factor in planning. Whereas, physical education should be an outdoor experience when possible, the vagaries of the weather in some sections of the country have a profound effect on planning an adequate program. Where the weather is consistent, few alternate programs are needed. Where the weather is uncertain, teachers are faced with the prospect of modifying from day to day their overall plans.

The length of the seasons would determine the emphasis within the program. In more temperate climates, children can play outdoors until well into December and are then able to be on the playground again in late February. This would mean mean an indoor program of only eight to ten school weeks as contrasted to the possibility of perhaps double this figure in other localities.

Consideration by the administration of adequate facilities would involve such items as covered outside areas (shed types) and hard-surfaced areas which dry quickly. In addition, thought should be given to the installation of basketball goals and volleyball standards in sufficient areas to sustain a wide number of children where the climate permits.

For those who lack facilities, inclement weather means that the teacher must provide physical experiences in the classroom setting, with its attendant problems.

Staff Competencies

Because of the basic nature of physical education on the primary level, the classroom teacher is generally asked to assume this responsibility. The types of activities and the skills to be taught are within the grasp of most teachers. Background and training are important and necessary, but it is the feeling that the most important attribute of a good program on this level is the desire of the teacher to make the most of the opportunities in physical education for the youngsters under her charge.

On the intermediate level, the character of physical education changes into a more specialized program of activities and skills. This demands a higher degree of training and skill for teaching than on the lower level.

How can a teacher become proficient in the area of physical education? A number of suggestions follow:

1. In undergraduate preparation, most teacher-training institutions require at least one course for credential requirements which proves little more than an introduction. Teachers would do well to enroll in specialized physical education courses beyond this experience. Courses available that have merit are those particularly in the skill areas including tumbling, body mechanics, rhythmic activities, sports skills, and fundamental movements. Undergraduates could not only acquire skills, but would be able to observe professional physical educators in the conduct of activities. Another area which could provide aid to the undergraduate teacher candidate is that of the physical education activity courses required of all students. While these are not conducted in the professionalized manner like the teacher-training courses in physical education, the courses in sports skills, folk and square dancing, aquatics, and individual activities offer opportunities for acquiring skill and knowledges in different areas.

2. A second area for additional course work lies in graduate preparation. Most education degrees on the graduate level will accept one or more courses in physical education as meeting the requirements for the degree. After teaching experience, teachers should be able to select courses of value to themselves.

3. Many state institutions of higher learning provide extension services in physical education with academic credit. In some states, the administration is allotted funds which can be used to finance such courses or workshops.

4. Consultant services are available upon request from most universities. These may take the form of personal visits, workshops, and responses to help solve problems which have arisen.

5. A fund of literature is available. This includes texts in elementary school physical education, game books, how-we-do-it articles, magazines, and pamphlets. Of particular value are the card systems which have games, rhythmic activities, and stunts printed on convenient cards. The teacher, as a time saver, should consider a card system for his activities. Teachers

should also develop a personal library of physical education materials for a varied program.

6. Most states provide guides in physical education which can be used as the basis of the program. In addition, state consultants will interpret the guides for teachers.

7. Within the school system, in many cases, are specialists in physical education retained for the purpose of providing service to teachers in physical education teaching.

It would appear that, if the teacher is genuinely interested, enough material, course work, and consultant service are available to provide the needed background for an individual to become adequate in physical education.

Available Facilities, Equipment and Supplies

It is essential that sufficient facilities for physical education be present so that an adequate program can be conducted. This would include sufficient outdoor playing space in the form of play fields, hard surfaced areas, and other needed areas. Indoor facilities include the gymnasium, the all-purpose room, and other indoor areas used for physical education.

Equipment refers to those items of a more or less fixed nature. Supplies include those physical education materials which have a limited time of use. To illustrate the difference--a softball is listed under supplies while the longer lasting softball backstop comes under the category of equipment. Equipment needs periodic replacement, and budgetary planning must consider the usable life span of each piece of equipment. Supplies are generally purchased on a yearly basis.

It is important not only to have adequate financing for equipment and supplies, but it is of equal importance that these funds be wisely expended.

Equipment and Supply Policies

If the objectives of physical education are to be fulfilled, there must be sufficient equipment and supplies. It is difficult to envision children learning skills or acquiring physical fitness when they handle objects only occasionally or are limited to an occasional turn on the mat. Since physical education is activity, there must be sufficient materials to keep the children

active. Special attention to policies involving purchase, storage and issue, care and maintenance, records and inventory are necessary if maximum use and return from the allotted budget is to be realized. It is important to decide what the boys and girls need in the program, and then base the purchasing plan upon this list.

Purchasing Policies

Purchasing of supplies and equipment involves careful study of the school's needs, prevailing prices, the quality of workmanship, and satisfactory materials. Safety and protection of the participants are also of vital concern.

Quantity buying by pooling the needs of the entire school system generally results in better use of the tax dollar. However, there may need to be compromise on the type and brand of materials in order to satisfy different users within a school system. If bids are asked, there is need to make careful specification for materials. Bids should be asked on only those items specified, and "just as good" merchandise should not be permitted as as substitutes. Otherwise, the school may be supplied with inferior and unsuitable materials.

Generally speaking, one individual within a school should be designated as responsible for the keeping of records of equipment and supplies and for the purchase of these items. The principal might assume this duty or appoint a teacher to this chore. Needs vary from school to school, and it becomes practical for the school district authorities to deal with a single individual within a school. Prompt attention to repair and replacement of supplies is more likely under this system.

Storage and Issue

The following plans are generally used in the elementary school for storage and issue of supplies ofr phyical education.

1. STORAGE IN THE CLASSROOM. This plan keeps a sufficient supply of physical education materials in each classroom to meet the needs for participation of that class. Advantages of the plan are: (1) Less time wasted. (2) The supplies available are known, (3) Definite responsibility may be fixed for loss or damage, (4) Children

18

have a sense of responsibility for "their" materials, (5) There is no competition or overlap in demands for supplies by different classes.

Disadvantages given for this plan are that it is initially expensive, storage facilities are needed for each classroom, and that equipment must be marked carefully to insure it being returned to the right classroom.

2. STORAGE IN A CENTRALLY LOCATED SUPPLY ROOM. In this plan, the teachers may check out materials needed for the class period and return after use. Advantages listed are lower initial cost, availability to the teacher of all materials, assurance of materials in a well-run system, and sufficient material.

In opposition to such a plan would be the following reasons: (1) Classroom responsibility is lost, (2) Equipment may not be repaired promptly, (3) Someone must take charge of the supply room, (4) The room needs to be kept locked, which makes the availability of the key a problem, (5) With so many using the supplies, good controls are necessary.

3. A COMBINATION OF THE TWO METHODS. Such a plan would provide sufficient equipment in each classroom for the conduct of free play and recess. This is to be supplemented by an additional supply of materials for physical education available from the supply room.

If a central supply source is used, there should be adequate room for the supplies. Currrent supplies should be placed in such a fashion that there is an easy count available. Off-season items should be moved to a "dead" area for storage. If there is to be a check-out system, a form with the names of the items available would be of help. This would save laborious writing. Care in the central supply room is needed, or the place will become disorderly and a dumping ground.

For checking out supplies from the central source, a monitor in each class can be appointed. Sufficient time should be allowed so that the monitor cañ have the materials ready for the class when it is to start. In case problems arise then adjustment can be made. Check out forms should be prepared in the classroom by the monitor, a practice which would save time at the supply room. The same child who checked out the equipment should check it in.

The principal or physical education supervisor should inspect the central supply room at regular intervals. An established routine of taking care of the repair and replacement of supplies must be instituted.

Recommended Equipment

Two criteria are important in selecting equipment for the outdoor setting for physical education. The first is that the piece of equipment must contribute to the development of the child. For this reason such items which involve only "sit and ride" experiences as swings, teeters, and merry-go-rounds are not recommended. In addition, the slide is questionable but some feel that there is value in the climbing part, and that the slide is a challenge to overcome fear. The second criterion is the safety factor. Many of the circular, hanging types like the giant stride are accident prone.

OUTDOOR EQUIPMENT

Climbing Structures. There are many names and many good varities. Various types such as jungle gyms, castle towers, and similar items have good value in physical fitness.
Horizontal Ladder
Horizontal Bar Combinations. The set of three horizontal bars together at different heights is a valuable piece of apparatus for physical education.
Basketball Goals. These may or may not be combined with a court. Youngsters play a great deal of one-goal basketball, and a regulation court is not needed for this game. These should be in a surfaced area, however.
Volleyball Standards. The outdoor volleyball court is useful for many activities.
Softball Backstops
Tether Ball Courts.

INDOOR EQUIPMENT

Balance Beams. A wide beam (4") is recommended for kindergarten and first grade children. For older children, a beam 2" wide and 12' long is suitable.
Chinning Bar. This is especially useful in testing for physical fitness. A substitute for this is the portable

doorway gym bar.

Climbing Ropes. In order to provide for sufficient activity, at least four ropes should be considered. These may be supplemented by climbing poles.

Volleyball Standards. The standards should allow for various heights for different grades and also for other games.

Mats. At least four are needed. These should be 4' x 6' and preferably be the newer foam plastic type. The newer types can be cleaned with soap and water and can be moved easily by grade school children.

Portable Climbing Structures. These are portable sets usually based on wooden horses and include supported bars, ladders, and other equipment for climbing. (See diagram on page 135).

Parallel Ropes. These consist of two ropes at a height of 5 to 6 feet 6 inches from the floor. The ropes are strung parallel to each other about 20 inches apart. They are attached between walls or across a room. A span from 15 to 25 feet is considered best and some method of keeping tension on the ropes is necessary. A large turnbuckle or other device for maintaining tension will provide suitable means of control. A set of pulleys also can be used.

Benches. Ordinary benches have good use in the program. Small wooden horses are also useful so that an inclined bench may be set up. Both benches and horses should be of sturdy construction. Special benches for physical education are available and can be used for balance beams by turning them over.

Horizontal Ladder Sets. Horizontal ladders which fold against the wall make an excellent addition to indoor equipment. The ladder may be combined with other pieces of apparatus in a folding set.

Climbing Sets. Climbing sets which fold flat against the wall are valuable for the program. These generally combine ropes, ladders, chinning bars, and other climbing devices on which a number of children can work at one time.

SUPPLIES

The following are the supplies and the tools for learning in physical education.

Bean bags - 6" x 6"
  Filled with dried beans, peas, wheat, or sand.
Balls
  Softballs - 12"
    Regular and the Soft Variety
  Fleece Balls
    Similar in size to softballs but filled with fleece
  Playground Balls - various sizes
    These are rubber balls of various sizes and colors
  Soccers - Rubber covered
  Volleyballs - Rubber covered
  Basketballs - Rubber covered - Junior size
  Footballs - Rubber covered - Junior size
  Cage Ball - 24" in diameter
  Tether Balls
  Tennis or Sponge Balls
Ball Inflator with Pressure Gauge
Softball Equipment
  Bats
  Bases
  Catcher's Masks
  Batting Tees
    Either adjustable or in different sizes
Track and Field
  Stop Watch - 1/10 second
  Jumping Standards
  Cross Bars
  Broad Jump Board
    Tape - 50'
Volleyball Nets
Rhythmic Needs
  Phonograph - with variable speed
  Records
  Tom-Tom
  Microphone
Jumping Ropes
  Individual - 8' or 9'
  Long Ropes
Game, Relay, and Stunt Items
  Wooden paddles - for paddle tennis and similar games
  Jump-the-Shot Rope
  Rope Rings - for tossing
  Indian Clubs
    Could use old bowling pins
  Wooden Blocks
    Small for relays
    Larger for balancing stunts
  Wooden line Markers - 1" x 4" about 4' long, painted white. Used to mark boundaries of various games
  Wands or Broom Handles
  Tug-of-War Rope
  Individual Tug-of-War Ropes
Squad Cards

Lining Materials
Dry liner
Marking lime
Cord
Shuffleboard sets
Targets
For throwing
For pitching
Hurdles
For jumping by primary children
Sizes 12, 16, 20, and 24"
Hoops

Recommendations for Supplies

Some of the supplies are designed especially for children in the intermediate grades. Junior size footballs and basketballs are available and should be used. Rubber covered balls generally prove more satisfactory than the leather variety for use in the elementary school, particularly during wet weather.

Smaller children can use playground balls for volleyball type games. When playground balls are used for soccer skills, they work more satisfactorily when slightly deflated.

When children are working with simple bouncing skills, it is desirable for each child to have a ball. The supply of balls can be augmented by tennis or sponge balls. Discarded tennis balls from the high school tennis team are a good source. Sponge balls are inexpensive and with care last indefinitely.

For jump ropes, 3/8 inch sash cord is suitable. The ends should be whipped or dipped in some type of hardening solution in order to prevent unraveling. Adhesive tape may also be used to bind the ends of the ropes.

Another good source for jump ropes is 3/8 inch yellow plastic (not nylon) rope of a hard weave variety. The ends can be melted with a match or burner.

Bean bags can be easily made. Good quality bright colored muslin is suitable. Some prefer a bean bag with an outer liner which snaps in place. This allows for washing. Another idea is to sew three sides of the bean bag permanently. The fourth side is used for filling and has an independent stitch. For washing, the beans can be removed through this side. Bean bags should be about 6 by 6 inches and can be filled with dried beans, peas, wheat, rice, or even building sand.

Batting tees can be constructed using a wooden or metal base similar to a high jump standard and a piece of radiator hose.

If it is to be adjustable, then two pieces of hose can be used so that one will slide (adjust) for different heights. However, this adjustment takes time and isn't always satisfactory. An alternate suggestion would be to make tees of various sizes.

For games which need boundary markers, pieces of rubber matting can be used. In addition, small sticks or boards, painted white, are excellent. A board 1 by 4 inches, 3 or 4 feet in length makes a satisfactory marker.

Tether balls should have a snap-on fastener for easy removal at night.

Softballs can be purchased without stitching (concealed stitch) which eliminates the problem of broken stitches and consequent repair.

A jump-the-shot rope can be made by using an old completely deflated ball tied on the end of a rope.

Old tires can be used for throwing targets, even those from bicycles.

Schools in and near ski areas may contact lift proprietors for discarded tow ropes. These make excellent tug-of-war ropes.

Barbells can be constructed for use in elementary school programs. These have use particularly in the circuit training programs. A four-foot piece of 3/4 inch pipe is needed for each barbell. A light barbell can be made using two one-pound coffee tins with the bar. A heavier piece of apparatus will result if two-pound tins are used. A sack of Readi-Mix Concrete is needed. Both ends of the pipe should be flattened somewhat to prevent them from being pulled out of the concrete. Water is added to the concrete mix to the desired consistency. The coffee tin is filled and the pipe end centered in the wet concrete in the tin. The pipe should be supported upright until the concrete has set. The second tin is affixed to the other end of the pipe in the same manner.

Indian clubs can be turned in the school woodshops. However, many substitutes can be made. Lumber of size 2 by 2 inches cut off in short pieces (6 to 10 inches long) will stand satisfactorily. Lumber companies generally also have available round poles from 1 to $1\frac{1}{2}$ inches in diameter. Sections of these make satisfactory Indian clubs. Broken bats also can be made into good substitute clubs.

Schools should consider the use of the fiber glass or aluminum cross bar for high jumping. Although initially the expense is high, these may prove to be the most economical in the long run. The bars will last indefinitely with reasonable care.

Bases can be constructed from heavy canvas. It should be folded over three or four times and then stitched together. Bases may also be made from outdoor plywood and should be painted. Heavy rubber matting also is suitable material for bases.

Handles from old brooms or mops can provide the needed wands and sticks. These come in various diameters, but this is not an important factor.

Deck tennis rings can be made from heavy rope by splicing. However, the ends can be joined rather satisfactorily with adhesive tape binding.

CARE AND REPAIR. There needs to be established a definite system for repair of supplies and equipment. If the central storage system is used, the repair materials can be kept in this location. Children and teachers tend to become discouraged if the repair process is lengthy and, rather than be deprived of the use, may continue with the item until it is no longer worth salvaging.

An important objective for children under the social area is the respect for and care of school property. Proper development of attitudes and habits in the care of physical education materials will help achieve this goal.

Balls need to be inflated to proper pressures. This means an accurate gauge and periodic checking. The needle should be moistened before it is inserted into the valve. Children should not sit on balls and should kick only balls made specifically for this purpose (soccers, footballs, and playground balls).

Softball bats and wooden paddles should not be used for hitting rocks, stones, or other hard materials. Neither should bats be knocked against fences, posts, or other objects that will cause damage. Broken bats should be discarded as they are not safe for use even if taped around the break. Children should learn to keep the trademark up when batting. Bats should be taped to prevent slippage.

Cuts, abrasions, and break in rubber balls should be immediately repaired. Some of this repair can be handled by a vulcanizing patch similar to tire tube repairs. In others, the use of a hard setting rubber preparation is of value. However, some repairs are byond the scope of the school, and the ball needs to be sent away for repair.

STORAGE AND MARKING. For off season storage, balls should be deflated somewhat leaving enough air in them to keep

their shape. Leather balls should be cleaned with an approved ball conditioner.

For small items, clean ice cream containers (2 gallon) make good storage receptacles. Most school cafeterias have these and other containers which may be used in the storage room to provide order.

An area for the equipment needing repair should be established. This means that, at a glance, the articles needing repair are evident.

Equipment that will warp should be laid in a flat place.

All equipment and supplies should be marked. Particularly, this is important for equipment issued to different classrooms. Marking can be done with indelible pencils, paint, or stencil ink. However, it needs to be recognized that few marking systems are permanent and that remarking at regular intervals is necessary. Sporting goods establishments have marking sets available for this purpose.

An electric burning pencil or stamp is also useful but needs to be used with caution against possible damage.

Rubber playground balls come in different colors, and an assignment to classrooms can be made on the basis of color. A code scheme can also be used with different color paints. It is also possible to devise a color system by which the year of issue can be checked which offers research possibilities into equipment.

Health Policies Affecting Physical Education

Optimum health of the child is a primary objective of modern education. If the school is to make the greatest possible contribution to health and physical fitness of its pupils throughout their lifetime, it should formulate and apply health policies in keeping with the best thought and practice in this field. Policies, based on the health needs of children and the objectives of education, give direction to efforts designed to protect and improve the health of children.

Healthful Environment for Physical Education

A healthful environment for physical education requires attention to standards for school safety, hygiene, and sanitation. The child has a legal and moral right to a safe environment. In addition, the physical education setting should emphasize good standards in cleanliness, ventilation, and heating. Ventilation should be sufficient to remove objectional odors. Temperatures, depending upon the extent of the activity, should range from 65 to 68 degrees. Generally, a temperature comfortable for an elderly teacher is too high for active youngsters.

Healthful environment also includes attention to mental hygiene factors. Proper student-teacher relationships in activity areas are important. Students should be able to relieve tensions through activity. Physical education should be a period where students lose rather than acquire tensions.

The Periodic Physical Examination

The periodic health examination should be the basis of determining the extent of the child's participation in physical education. Ideally, each health examination should be yearly and include all factors having a bearing on the child's educational experience. However, in practice, examinations are given about every three years and can be scheduled at the beginning of the first, fourth, seventh, and ninth or tenth grades.

The teacher must have access to the records and should be familiar with the health conditions of each of her charges, or the examination is of little value.

Excuses and Readmittance

If a child is to be excused from physical education activity for any length of time, it should be done by the recommendation of a physician. Caution needs to be observed when a child has been absent due to an illness and returns for activity. If a school nurse is present, all such cases should be routed through her for recommendation. In the absence of both a physician and nurse recommendation, consultation with the principal and the parent is probably the best solution. Students who have been ill should be observed closely by the teacher for signs which might suggest that they are not ready to participate in the regular activity.

Girls should not be required to participate in vigorous activity during the early part of their menstrual periods.

General Health Practices

Schools should move toward the practice of having all students change clothing for physical education. A class that changes to appropriate gym or play clothing will have a better experience in activity. It is recognized that this is not an easy problem to solve as few schools have adequate facilities to provide privacy for a change of clothing. Not only should children change clothing, but, ideally, every child should shower after a class in physical education. More and more schools are adopting this practice and designing schools with this in mind.

Even if showers are not available, there should be a change of clothing. For children, this usually involves only the outer garments, but could be a complete change. The change is particularly necessary for stunts and tumbling and activities where modesty is a problem in mixed groups. The chief stumbling block is finding places in the school where the children can change. It can be pointed out that most Canadian, Australian, and European children are required to change for activity, and facilities in these countries make space to provide for this. An extra room, the stage in the all-purpose room, and even wash rooms are used for changing.

Children should, as a basic minimum, wear appropriate gym shoes for the activity period. The practice of allowing children to "skate" around in stocking feet is certainly not desirable. Sufficient time for clean up should be allowed after the activity period.

An efficient system involving first aid and care of emergencies needs to be established and followed. Further discussion of this will be made under the topic of safety.

Screening by the Teacher

Teachers can make good use of the physical education period as part of their daily health screening of youngsters. Teachers are in good position to note changes in appearance, behavior, and reaction to acitivity which may prove indicative of changes in the child's health. Children who are listless, tire easily, lack interest, and possess unusual skin colors should be subject to additional investigation or referral examinations for determination of possible health conditions. A child who is inept in catching may have vision defects.

Operational Policies

Coeducational Activity

This term is used to refer to activity in which boys and girls participate together. If the social and emotional objectives of physical education are to be realized fully, boys and girls should have the opportunity to play together in at least some activities on each grade level.

On the primary level, there is little need for separation of sexes in any activity. Boys and girls of these ages are very much alike in development that almost all activities may include both sexes together. However, there is need to separate boys and girls in some activities beginning in either the fourth or fifth grade. The types of activity where separation is recommended are the contact and rougher sports. Certain other activities must make due allowance for modesty. If stunts and tumbling are held together, children must be properly attired.

Scheduling

Children should be scheduled in a daily period in physical education. This is exclusive of recess or free play. For the primary levels there should be a teaching period of at least twenty minutes. For the intermediate grades, this figure is raised to thirty minutes. Not included in this time specification is going to and from class, changing shoes, and the time for visiting the washroom and cleaning up.

Where there is sufficient outdoor space, the scheduling of the period is not a serious problem. However, where equipment needs to be shared and facilities are limited, a definite time schedule should be worked out by the principal.

Teaching Responsibility

The regular teaching staff should be responsible for the conduct of the physical education program. If others assist in the program, like student teachers, the regular teacher should retain the control and supervision.

If the instruction is handled by a physical education specialist, then defi-nite policies regarding the relationship and responsibilities between the specialist and classroom teacher should be established.

The Supervised Play Period

Commonly called recess, the supervised play period provides a time for relaxation and relief of tensions for youngsters. Adequate superivision is necessary to insure that safety practices are being followed and that youngsters have proper consideration of each other. Rules need to be established and children made cognizant that they are under self-discipline.

Supervision should be positive and in terms of helping youngsters make the most of their free play. Intermediates can develop and carry out their own plans of organization based on equal opportunities for grades and sex and on good standards of play conduct. Teachers need to recognize that supervisory duties of this type are a regular and important part of the teaching duties. Assignments are generally handled on a rotation basis.

The Noon-Hour Play Period

The noon-hour period can be both educational and recreative. The first part must be devoted to a supervised, happy, restful lunch. After this, the children should be allowed to play, in the main, in quiet games. There should be plenty of time allowed for attending to personal needs.

Each child should have an opportunity to enjoy an activity of his interest. Individual games, quiet games, table type activities, and semi-active sports are recommended. While some adult supervision is needed, older children can plan and carry out an adequate noon-hour program.

For children who eat lunch at home, a time should be set before which they cannot return to school.

Intramurals

The intramural program is an important part of the physical education program and is an outgrowth of the activities offered in the physical education program. The emphasis in program should be on competing and participating and not the determination of champions. Generally, the program is carried on after school, but some schools find it feasible to use other times. Adult leadership is an essential ingredient but students should have an important part in the planning and execution of the program.

Teams may be chosen on the basis of classrooms, by a classification system, or by lot. Equitable competition is needed to maintain interest. The program should be an opportunity for all boys and girls and not just the more skilled. Since the program is primarily for the intermediate level, competition should be separate for boys and girls. This does not rule out the possibility of suitable co-education activities, but these should be in the minimum.

The program should be under a teacher who should receive special compensation for this duty. To ask a teacher to assume this responsibility in addition to regular duties seldom produces the desired results.

Extramurals

The term "Extramural Program" is felt to be more appropriate than other terms connoting inter-school activities. While there is value in students from one school competing against students from another, the competition should be of an informal type and not involve the common high school pattern with its concentration on a few highly skilled individuals. Such other attributes of interscholastic athletics as yell squads, pep rallies, distant travel, emotional partisanship, ornate uniforms, emphasis on the winning team through district and league championships, publicity exalting individual performance, and all-star teams have little place in the elementary program.

The inter-school program should be an outgrowth of the physical education and intramural program and should not be a substitute for either. It should be limited to the 5th and 6th grades and not include younger children. There is common agreement among medical and educational authorities that neither boxing nor tackle football should be included in an elementary school program.

Playdays

A playday is a festival-type setting where children of a school or different schools meet together to take part in physical education activities. The emphasis is on the social values rather than com-

petition. Yet competition is important in that teams made up from different participating schools play against each other.

A play day may be entirely within a particular school. The usual pattern is for a play day between schools or on a district basis. It may be carried on during the school day on an afternoon, for example. Or, the play day might be scheduled after school or on a Saturday.

The program may be made of sports type activities or it may include the more simpler games, relays, and contests. Stunts, individual athletic events, and even rhythms are the basis of activities in some meets. The programs vary with respect to the size of the schools and the grade level of the children. They usually involve both boys and girls and may include some coeducational activities on the intermediate level.

Play days which attempt to determine champions or which emphasize the star performers from each school are considered undesirable. The real purpose of a play day is to have "everyone on a team and a team for everyone."

Children should have a large part in the planning, and the experience gives them a fruitful opportunity to act as hosts or as guests in a social situation. The program emphasis may be on activities which have been previously practiced or rehearsed, or it may include new and unique events broadening the scope of the physical education experience.

Pageants, Demonstrations, and Assembly Programs

Classroom teachers are asked at times to organize demonstrations for assembly programs, parents, and other groups. This is an excellent medium of public relations and dispels some of the false notions regarding physical education. If such programs are requested, the following may be helpful:

1. The activities should grow out of and be typical of the physical education program.
2. The activities should not require a long period of preparation so that the physical education period becomes a training period for the demonstration.
3. Children should be properly dressed or costumed for the activity, but elaborate and intricate costuming should be avoided. Simple costumes that can be made by the children are most acceptable.

4. The demonstration should generally include numbers of children. Programs can be designed where all children participate in some phase of the exhibition. However, recognition can be given to superior ability by specialty numbers.

5. It is important to avoid tests of strength and skill which would lead to embarrassment of those defeated.

6. While a high degree of performance is not needed, the activities should be done reasonably well with respect to the level of the children.

7. The program should be fast moving and contain activities of good audience appeal. Music is indispensable and a well-balanced program will contain several numbers with music.

8. The program should call attention to physical fitness, and some elements should be devoted to this area. A demonstration of physical fitness testing is always a well received presentation.

Chapter 4

Program Planning for Optimum Fitness

In selecting the content of the program for elementary school children, a most important consideration is that the selection be based upon the capacities, needs, and interests of the youngsters.

Certain basic urges of young people should be given utmost consideration in program planning. These may vary in degree among children, but for the child are important reasons for living and being.

1. THE URGE FOR PHYSICAL FITNESS AND ATTRACTIVENESS. Every teacher should understand how eager boys and girls are to be physically fit and to possess bodies that are agile and attractive. To be strong is both a joy and a glory. It gives dignity and confidence. Teachers also need to understand the humiliation suffered by the youngster who is weak, fat, crippled, or abnormal in any way.

2. THE URGE TO CONTEST. This is tied up with the first urge and refers to the child's desire to match physical skill and strength with one's fellows. It means the urge to wrestle, to hit a ball, to pit one's skill, to overcome the other, to take joy in competition, and be successful in situations of stress.

3. THE URGE FOR SOCIAL COMPETENCE. This is related to both of the previous urges. The child would like to be accepted, respected, and liked by others. He doesn't want to feel awkward at games or contests. He wants to do well so he will not be embarrassed. He wishes to appear to an advantage not only with his peers, but also among the world of adults.

4. THE URGE FOR ADVENTURE. This is the urge to participate in something different, romantic, or unusual. This is the desire to climb to the heights, to be able to do something different, and to participate in activities which of themselves are interesting. It means a change from the "old stuff" to something new and exciting.

5. THE URGE FOR CREATIVE SATISFACTION. Children like to try out different ways, experiment with different materials, and to see what they can do creatively. Finding different ways of expressing themselves physically satisfies the urge for creative action.

6. THE URGE FOR RHYTHMIC EXPRESSION. Every boy and girl basically likes rhythm. The program should offer a variety of rhythmic activities which every boy and girl should learn well enough to give them many pleasant, satisfying hours of leisure living. Rhythm is movement and children like to move. Dancing, rhythmic movements, rope jumping skills, ball bouncing and dribbling routines, and similar activities are pleasing and exciting experiences under good leadership.

7. THE URGE TO KNOW. Young people live in a world of curiosity. They are interested not only in what they are doing, but they want to know why. The "why" is a great motivator. Lasting habits are established only if the individual is convinced they are worthwhile.

An examination of the characteristics of children at any given grade level will reveal many important needs and implications which can be used in planning an effective program. For purposes of discussion the following grade combinations have been chosen: (1) Kindergarten and first grade, (2) second and third grade, and (3) the intermediate level of grades four, five, and six.

Kindergarten and first grade children exhibit similar characteristics. Children are imitative, imaginative, individualistic, and lacking in good hand-eye coordination so necessary for handling bats, balls, and other objects. Development in the simple skills of handling objects, throwing and catching, and simple team games begin to appear during the second and third grade. A noticeable difference over the first grade capacities appears in the development of agility and the ability to run and maneuver. A few simple athletic skills are introduced on the third grade level. The increased efficiency with which the body is handled is apparent in the rhythmic and stunt area. The child is beginning to find himself here.

By the fourth grade, both boys and girls are able to apply the play skills of throwing, catching, kicking, and batting to sports type activities like soccer, softball, basketball, flag football (boys), volleyball, and track and field. A stable basis for these activities is generally laid in the fourth grade with consideration for progression through the fifth and sixth grades.

Characteristics, Interests, Needs of Elementary School Children Important as Considerations in Program Planning in Physical Education

Kindergarten and First Grade

CHARACTERISTICS	PROGRAM NEEDS AND IMPLICATIONS
Noisy, constantly active, ego-centric, exhibitionist. Imitative and imaginative. Wants attention.	Vigorous games and stunts. Games with individual roles--hunting, dramatic activities, story plays. Few team games or relays.
Large muscles more developed, game skills not developed. Naturally rhythmical.	Fundamental skills of throwing, catching, bouncing balls. Attention to simple locomotor skills. Use of music and rhythm with skills. Creative rhythms. Simple stunts.
No sex differences in interest.	Same activities for both boys and girls.
Short attention span. Fatigues easily.	Change activity often. Short explanations. Use activities of brief duration. Provide short rest periods or include activities of moderate vigor to allow for recovery.
Sensitive and individualistic.	Needs to learn to take turns, share with others. Learn to win, lose, or be caught gracefully.
Is interested in what his body can do. Curious.	Movement exploration. Attention to fundamental movements.

Second and Third Grades

CHARACTERISTICS	PROGRAM NEEDS AND IMPLICATIONS
Still active but attention span longer. More interest in group play.	Active big-muscle program including more group activity. Begin team emphasis in activity and relays.
Likes physical contact and belligerent games.	Dodgeball games and other active games. Rolling stunts.
Enjoys rhythm.	Continue creative rhythms, singing games, and folk dances.
Developing more skills and interest in skills. Wants to excel.	Organized skill practice. Continue basic skills of throwing, catching, moving, etc. Introduce sports skills. Provide challenge in stunt activities.
Becoming more social conscious.	Learn to abide by rules and play fair. Learn social customs, particularly in rhythmic areas.
Becoming more sports interested.	Introduce simple lead-up games and sports skills.
	Continued work in movement exploration and the development of basic skills.

Fourth, Fifth, and Sixth Grades

CHARACTERISTICS	PROGRAM NEEDS AND IMPLICATIONS
Steady growth--girls more rapidly than boys. Boys better in game skills.	Continue vigorous program. Separate sexes for some activities. Stress correct movement fundamentals and posture.
Enjoy team and group activity. Competitive spirit.	Include many team games, relays, combatives.
Sports interests.	Sports in season with emphasis on lead-up games. Good variety.
Muscular coordination improving and skills are better. Want to know how and why. Interested in detailed techniques.	Continued emphasis on the teaching of skills through drills and practice. Emphasis on correct form.
Little interest in opposite sex. Some develop sex antagonisms.	Need coeducational activity. Stress social customs and courtesy through folk and square dances.
More acceptance of self responsibility.	Need safety controls. Need leadership and followership opportunity. Include students in evaluation procedures.
Differences in capacity.	Flexible program and standards so all may succeed.
Great desire to excel both in skill and physical capacity.	Stress physical fitness. Include fitness and skill tests to provide both motivation and check progress.

Guides in Planning the Program

It is axiomatic that if the program is to realize its objectives, there must be effective planning. Too often an unplanned experience for children is based on the "what-do-we-do-today" concept. The following suggestions are guides for effective planning in physical education.

1. The program selected must have the potential of developing physical fitness and, in addition, should give due consideration to the other objectives in physical education. Activities should be selected for their potential contributions to the objectives of physical education.
2. Basically, a positive school-wide approach in planning is needed. This means an overall school physical education curriculum with content for each grade level specified. Included would be a schedule for the use of facilities and consideration for the sharing of equipment and supplies.
3. After allocations of activity have been made to specific grade levels, the classroom teacher should begin his planning with a yearly outline. This would indicate the kinds of things (objectives) to be accomplished, the program content to meet the objectives, and the approximate time allocations to the various program areas. The yearly plan should be completed before the opening of school. The yearly plan should then be broken down into seasonal plans.
4. Weekly and daily plans can now be developed with the aid of the children based upon the acitivities for a parti-

cular season.

5. A daily period in physical education should be scheduled and a part of this period should be devoted to vigorous activity.
6. The program should be broad and varied. It should include a wide selection of activities. There should be balance among the types of physical education activities.
7. There should be progression in the activities for physical education. Progression should occur within activity divisions, from grade to grade, and during any one particular school year.
8. Repetition, particularly in the skill area, is important in motor learning. The program must allot sufficient practice time to perfect skills. Repetition can be done through the use of drills or through the use of the skill in a game or other activity.
9. While a teacher may wish to expand or enrich his program in physical education, he should avoid taking materials from future grade levels. Sufficient materials exist in physical education and are available to the enterprising teacher without "robbing" the grades ahead of their substance. An example is in an activity like square dancing. It is felt that the sixth grade is a good level in which this activity should be introduced. Teachers in the grades below the sixth then should not include square dancing in their programs. Rather, they should look for materials to expand within the framework of the allocations to their grades. Many interesting folk dances can be found us using varied movements, formations, and rhythms.

Grade Level Emphasis and Suggested Yearly Percentages

	ACTIVITY TYPES	GRADES AND YEARLY PERCENTAGES					
		1	2	3	4	5	6
1.	Movement Exploration and Body Mechanics	25	20	10	5	3	3
2.	Rhythmical Activities	25	25	20	15	15	15
3.	Stunts, Tumbling, and Apparatus	10	10	15	15	15	15
4.	Fitness Activities and Testing				10	10	10
5.	Relays		5	10	10	5	5
6.	Simple Game Activities	35	30	30	15	15	10
7.	Athletic Skills and Games	5	10	15	30	37	42
8.	Swimming and Water Safety				*	*	*

* Swimming and Water Safety is a recommended area of instruction for elementary school children. The amount allocated to this area would depend upon the facilities and instruction available. If swimming is included in the program, it should reduce proportionately the percentages of time allotted to the other activities.

Developing Weekly and Daily Programs

How does the teacher begin to translate the suggested emphasis from the percentage chart into an effective program in physical education? A step by step procedure is presented by which this can be accomplished.

STEP 1. Take from the chart, the activities and percentages for the grade level involved. Thus, the year's activities have been selected, and the proportionate amount of time to be devoted to each has been determined.

STEP 2. The second step is to calculate the number of whole class periods which would be devoted to an activity based upon the percentage allotment. This gives a unit of measurement which is the basis of planning. It is recognized that the entire class period may not be devoted to an activity type but the use of the class period offers a handy unit for planning the seasonal programs.

An illustration will help clarify this procedure. The example used is third grade planning. Steps one and two are given together. Planning is based on a school year of 180 days.

The chart is to be read that for Movement Exploration and Body Mechanics, 18 days (periods) out of the school year of 180 days will be devoted to this area. Similarly, 36 periods will be devoted to Rhythmical Activities and so on in other areas.

STEP 3. Seasonal planning begins with the selection of the seasons. For purpose of convenience, it is felt that four seasons of equal length--fall, early winter, late winter, and spring--are better than the traditional seasons of fall, winter, and spring. If the school year comprises 36 school weeks, then each season would cover 9 weeks or 45 school days. The problem now is to allocate 45 periods of the kinds of activities desired to each of the seasons. Indoor activity types can be scheduled heavily during the two winter seasons, and the outdoor activities reserved for spring and fall.

The next move is to take the allocated periods to each of the activity types and spread them over the four seasons in such a fashion that each of the seasons will have 45 periods as has been done in the following illustration.

THIRD GRADE PROGRAM

Activity Type	Percentage (year)	Periods per year
Movement Exploration and Body Mechanics	10%	18
Rhythmical Activities	20%	36
Stunts, Tumbling, Apparatus	15%	27
Relays	10%	18
Simple Game Activities	30%	54
Athletic Skills and Games	15%	27
Totals	100%	180 days

THIRD GRADE PLANNING FOR SEASONS

Activity Type	Year's Periods	Distribution to Seasons			
		Fall	Early Winter	Late Winter	Spring
Movement Exploration and Body Mechanics	18	1	8	8	1
Rhythmical Activities	36	0	16	20	0
Stunts, Tumbling, Apparatus	27	5	9	9	4
Relays	18	6	2	5	5
Simple Game Activities	54	23	5	3	23
Athletic Skills and Games	27	10	5	0	12
Total	180	45	45	45	45

From the table, it can be seen that the fall and spring programs would feature simple game activities with good emphasis on athletic skills and games. In addition, there would be tumbling and relays in about the same proportion. The winter programs would stress rhythmics, movement exploration, and tumbling with some allocation to the other areas.

SEASONAL THIRD GRADE WEEKLY PROGRAM

Season	Monday	Tuesday	Wednesday	Thursday	Friday
Fall	Games 30 min.	Athletic Skills 20 min. Relays 10 min.	Games 15 min. Stunts, Tumb. 15 min.	Athletic Skills 20 min. Relays 10 min.	Games 30 min.
Early Winter	Move. Explor. 10 min. Folk Dance 20 min.	Stunts, Tumb. 15 min. Athletic Skills 15 min.	Move. Explor. 10 min. Folk Dance 20 min.	Stunts, Tumb. 15 min. Relays 5 min. Games 10 min.	Move. Explor. 10 min. Creative Rhy. 10 min. Games or Athletic Skills 10 min.
Late Winter	Move. Explor. 10 min. Folk Dance 20 min.	Stunts, Tumb. 15 min. Relays 15 min.	Move. Explor. 10 min. Folk Dance 20 min.	Stunts, Tumb. 15 min. Relays 10 min. Game 5 min.	Move. Explor. 10 min. Creative Rhy. 10 min. Free Choice 10 min.
Spring	Games 30 min.	Athletic Skills 30 min.	Games 15 min. Stunts, Tumb. 15 min.	Athletic Skills 15 min. Relays 15 min.	Games 30 min.

STEP 4. For each of the seasons, the teacher should make a weekly program guide which, in essence, would present the activities for a week in about the same proportion that they are scheduled during a season. Thus, in the fall program, if the seasonal schedule shows about one-half the periods to be in the games program, the weekly program should reflect the same emphasis. It follows that if the program distribution were the same for all the seasons, there would be need for only one weekly schedule which would do for all four seasons.

The illustration is continued and the weekly program for each of the seasons is presented for the third grade based upon an assigned thirty minute period for physical education.

It is apparent that the fall and spring programs are quite similar and also the two winter schedules. However, there are minor differences and this is reflected in the weekly schedules. During the fall and spring, there is an allotment for movement exploration and body mechanics (one period or 30 minutes). No definite time is set in the weekly programs but this must be taken from other activities by special arrangement.

STEP 5. The actual activities to be taught in the program are chosen next. In the absence of sufficient research data, selection is generally made on an empirical basis, the potential of the activity for physical fitness, and the contribution the activity can make to the other objectives and needs in the program. This guide will present lists of suggested activities which can be used as the basis of the program for the individual teacher. The activities of this guide will show progression within activity, within grade, and from grade to grade. The activities must be selected and the order of presentation determined.

STEP 6. Lesson plans can now be made for the week using the lists in step five as the basis. The teacher can discuss with the children on Friday after the last physcal education class for the week what needs to be accomplished for the coming week. The daily lesson plan grows out of the weekly plan.

STEP 7. The daily lesson plan can follow the suggested outline.

A. Vigorous big-muscle activity -- 3 - 5 minutes. This could be in the form of movement exploration activities, fitness oriented activities, exercises, running, or stunt movements.

B. Review of previous material. The progress of the children will determine how much time is needed here.

C. Introduction of new material.

D. Closing activity. This can be a fun activity or one the children know well. It should provide for a slackening off of activity to give the children a chance to cool down. The teacher can have the children sit down for a moment or two and discuss what they have learned today.

E. Visiting the lavatory, changing clothes and shoes, cleaning up, and water fountain permission. It should be emphasized that lavatory and cleanup time should not be taken out of the designated activity period, but is done after the period is over.

The Block System of Teaching

The block system is defined as unit teaching. Under this system of scheduling, activities (the unit) are carried on for consecutive days until the instruction is completed. There is merit in this type of scheduling as progression is apparent and can be emphasized. It lends itself well as a method of presenting sports, folk dancing, stunts and tumbling, and other activities of a progressive nature. It is not a good method to use for activities which are carried on for only a short duration of time and are not suitable to fill the whole class period, much less consecutive days. Reference is made to relays, combatives, exercises, simple games, and basic skill work.

The weather is also a factor in block teaching in outdoor activities. Alternate plans to take care of inclement weather are needed. However, block teaching is a consideration in the physical education program and can be used as deemed desirable and efficient.

Planning with the Individual Teacher

Teachers are busy people and have many different areas to cover in the year's work in addition to physical education. Some school administrators find it helpful to provide each teacher with a chart of activities to be covered for the respective grade. This enables the teacher to check off the materials as they are covered and assures the children of being introduced to the activities and materials in physical education which the school system has allocated to the respective grade level. Some consultants find it helpful to divide the year further, that is, into the seasons. A chart with seasonal divisions would emphasize activities for each of the major divisions of the year.

Another plan has met success in some systems. These systems list the basic essentials to be covered in each of the respective areas of physical education. They go one step further and list the elective or choice activities which can be used after the basic essential elements have been covered.

Planning is excellent and is in line with that done in other school areas. Planning also assures progression from one grade to the next. How much flexibility a teacher should have would depend upon local viewpoint. In some cases, the charts are quite detailed even down to specific activities.

In the process, however, we must not lose sight of the fact that the goal of the physical education program is the development of the child and that the planning process is only a means toward this end. Based on child progress and interest, plans need to be modified to give the child the best educational experience.

Chapter 5

Class Management for Better Physical Fitness

Useful Directives for Physical Education Based on Educational Laws and Drives

Since physical education is to be an educational experience, it should make use of pedagogical drives which can promote efficient learning. Important applications in the form of directives to physical education teachers can be derived from these basic education drives.

1. Include in instruction the reason for doing things. Children learn more rapidly when they know the "why" of a procedure or activity. Teach not only the "how" but also the "why".

2. Consider the readiness of the children for any particular activity. Maturation is an important concept, particularly so in the teaching of skills. If children are introduced to an activity for which they are not ready, a frustrating learning situation develops.

3. See that each child has an opportunity to be active in the learning situation. Self-activity is the basis of physical learning -- and for that matter -- all learning. A child must participate to learn. The child should have an opportunity to explore, try out, and experiment with different ways of performing skills as opposed to the autocratic "this is the way you do it" teaching.

4. See that children derive enjoyment and satisfaction from the activity. Learning is facilitated when children find joy and satisfaction in the learning situation.

5. Provide a measure of success for each child. Each child can succeed in some fashion in physical education. Children progress at different rates and attain success in different fashions.

6. Set reasonable goals and use measurement procedures to assess progress toward these goals. Children are stimulated when they have an attainable goal and measurement toward this goal is a part of the program.

7. Provide effective demonstrations and visual aids. Children learn by example and effective demonstrations can show youngsters how to perform skills. Many techniques lend themselves to slow motion demonstrations. Selected children, properly directed, can provide suitable demonstrations if the teacher is unable to do so. In addition, from different sources, slides, film strips, motion pictures, pamphlets, posters, and other visual aids can be obtained.

8. Techniques of evaluation should be a part of the program. Only through evaluative procedures can the degree of progress toward the objectives of the program be ascertained.

9. Include the children in both planning and evaluation. Based upon the democratic principle that those who participate in the planning are more likely to support the activities, the teacher should include the youngsters in the planning of the program. While planning may be introduced in the primary grades, it is a more useful tool on the intermediate level. To be able to plan suitable play activities is, in itself, a desirable goal for the children.

10. Provide opportunity for creative activity. Children need an opportunity to try out their own ideas, solve some of their own movement problems, and bring forth movement of their own origin. Teachers need to take advantage

of this drive in providing opportunity for the child to come up with his own movement ideas.

Teaching Procedures

Teaching methodology applicable in general to all activities is presented here. Procedures for handling activities are treated under the specific activities.

Working with Children

1. The child who does not participate, who is not accepted by the group, or whose ineptness does not allow him much success needs special consideration to help him find himself. Give him tasks in which he can succeed or can achieve status in the eyes of his fellow students.
2. Beware of activities which tend to eliminate slow or unskilled children from activity. Those eliminated usually are the ones who need the activity the most. Use this type of organization sparingly.
3. Divide the children into small enough groups so there is little waiting for turns. Make arrangements for sufficient equipment from other classes or use methods of rotation so equipment can be sufficient for the group concerned.
4. Use methods of choosing partners so that the children are not embarrassed by being the last chosen.
5. If children are assigned as leaders, give them an actual opportunity to lead.
6. Include all children in program -- the handicapped, the overweight, the unskilled.
7. Children love to run, at times, for the sheer zest of activity. Provide time in the program for this basic drive.
8. If facilities permit, children should change to gym clothing for activity. This, in practice, is not too common a procedure. Better health practices result when children can also shower and clean up properly.
9. In the interest of safety, rubber soled shoes or sneakers should be a requirement for indoor play. For children, in the first grade, instruction and practice may need to be given in tying shoe laces. Shoes also may need to be marked so children can distinguish right from left. One suggestion is to place the shoes flat on the floor with the inside edges together. A mark can be placed on each shoe such that the marks will come together when the shoes are placed properly alongside each other. This avoids the right shoe being on the left foot and vice versa.

Consideration for proper storage for the gym shoes is important. The child's name should be on the shoes, preferably on the outside where it can be read easily. Also, a routine for orderly arrangement of street shoes should be established, so that the child after the class can find his own shoes quickly without unnecessary scrambling.

Directing Activities

1. Devise ways of moving children easily and efficiently from one activity to another.
2. Many activities lend themselves to modification through small changes which increases the interest and provides variation. Teachers should be alert for these changes and allow children to make suggestions for variations.
3. Use the whistle sparingly. Give one sharp blast and insist on the courtesy of attention. Early attention to this will pay off later in dividends of time saved.
4. A physical education class needs to be a happy medium between quiet and boisterousness. Youngsters should be able to let off steam but be under control.
5. Use the more formal methods of organization only when needed. Stunts and tumbling are examples of activities in which good control in the form of formations is needed in the interest of safety and good teaching.
6. A sanitation problem is present when children share whistles for officiating. Enough whistles are needed to each referee may have one to himself. Provisions for washing and sanitizing whistles emphasize good health procedures. A thorough washing and immersion in alcohol is a solution.
7. Rules should be clear and boundaries definite. It is difficult to enforce an out-of-bounds penalty when the location of a boundary line is vague and indefinite.
8. Each activity needs to be considered from the safety standpoint. Considered are the possible hazards inherent in the activity, the measures to eliminate

the hazards, and what the children should be taught and follow regarding the safety factors.

9. In order to make maximum use of the allotted time for activity, much of the explanations and directions should be given to children in the classroom. Rules can be explained, procedures outlined, and formations illustrated on the blackboard.

10. Teachers need to analyze each activity from the standpoint of how maximum activity and movement can be a part of the activity. Teachers need to realize that activities are a means of development through movement and as much movement must be "milked" out of them as possible.

11. Avoid too rigid an approach. At times allow for experimentation and exploration by the children. The teacher may find it appropriate to give basic instruction in the topic or skill and then allow for exploration and creative activity based upon the material just presented.

Other Considerations

1. The teachers need to use caution so that their own interests do not rule the program. Generally, adults drift toward those activities which they know and can do successfully.

2. Develop an equipment consciousness among the children. Respect for and acceptance of responsibility for equipment are most desirable outcomes.

3. Occasionally allow a choice time or day. There might be many choices which can mean small group play at different activities.

4. While desirable learnings can result under proper learning atmosphere, these are not automatic for activities but are the result of planning. Relays can be used as an example. Under a good learning atmosphere, a child can learn to cooperate, to observe rules, and to abide with the capacities of his teammates. On the other hand, in a poorly conducted class, he can learn to cheat, to become intolerant of the shortcomings of the members of his team, and to put winning over all other goals.

5. Since life itself is competition, learning to "give a good try" and accept the results is a concept to be emphasized in physical education. Children need to learn to be good winners or losers,

as the case may be.

6. Ventilation should be sufficient indoors to remove the objectionable "athletic" odors of activity. The temperature should be between 65 and 68 degrees.

7. The development of courtesy, fair play, and honesty are important goals to be achieved by elementary children. In discussion and evaluations, children need to bring out what constitutes proper conduct in various situations.

Safety Considerations

It is often said that safety is no accident. Teachers of physical education have both a legal and moral responsibility to set up precautions to prevent accidents and to develop habits of safety. Despite all precautions, accidents will occur. The possibility of serious injury is always present in physical education. Dealing with youngsters also adds an emotional factor because parents cannot look impartially upon injury to their children.

Legal Responsibility

Since the child is subject to compulsory attendance laws, the school has the legal responsibility of providing a safe environment. Teachers, as individuals, share this responsibility. While the teacher cannot be held responsible for all accidental occurrences in activities under his supervision, he can be held legally for the consequences of his negligence which has proven injurious to one of the children.

Liability occurs when the teacher is held responsible for a given situation. It is always a court action, and negligence by the teacher must be established. Negligence is a basic factor involved in all liability. A person is deemed negligent when he has failed to act as a reasonably prudent person would act under the circumstances. Foreseeability is the key to whether or not there is negligence. If the teacher should have foreseen the causes leading to the injury and failed to take action as a prudent person would, then a ruling of negligence can result.

Each teacher needs to ascertain that the child is in an environment that meets all the criteria of safety. In addition, it would be well to consider liability insurance which is available quite reasonably in conjunction with memberships in some educational societies.

The discussion which follows emphasizes the various aspects of safety procedures for the teacher.

Safety Procedures

Provision for a Safe Teaching Place. Safety begins with this consideration. There must be sufficient room, and the area must be suitable for the intended activity. It should be free of obstructions, holes, and other hazards. The presence of broken glass, protruding nails, tin cans, fruit skins, junk, and other articles are sources of accidents. Holes, sprinkling taps, and pools of water can cause leg injuries. The character of the activity would determine the amount of space necessary for safe play.

Safety in Equipment and Supplies. It is the responsibility of the teacher not only to provide the right kinds of equipment and supplies for each activity, but to instruct the children in the proper safe use of these. Adequate instruction is important. Close inspection of all equipment is an essential.

Inherent Hazards in Activity. It is prudent and vital that the teacher study the safety elements involved in the activity to be taught. Consideration and elimination of the unsafe features of each activity are paramount. For example, a teacher should not allow children to slide into bases during softball games. Aside from the wear on clothing, sliding is most hazardous. Safe practices should be taught along with any game or activity.

Health Status. Make sure that the health status of each child is known in order to permit no child to participate beyond his capacity. It could be negligence for the teacher to fail to observe a health restriction which is a part of the student's school records. It is also considered good practice to secure a physician's note regarding the status of a child returning after a period of illness or injury.

Supervision of Activities and Play Periods. Only qualified personnel should supervise physical education classes. Turning the class over to high school students, for example, would violate this fundamental precept. If children are permitted to be in activity during class, recess, or lunch hour, then proper supervision procedures are in order.

Proper Selection of Activities. The activity selected should not provide hazards because it is unsuitable for the group involved. Teachers should avoid highly specialized or difficult games beyond the ability of the pupils. The scheduling of tackle football, for example, is a most questionable procedure for the elementary school.

First Aid Procedures -- Emergency Care. Since accidents will occur in all phases of the school program, but more so on the playground or in the gymnasium, some system of emergency care is mandatory. The teacher should administer only first aid and call a doctor, if there is any question. First aid procedures could follow this plan.

1. The administration of first aid is the first step. Generally, one teacher or nurse in the school should have first aid certification and be available to be called in case of an accident. If the child is to be moved, it must be done only with proper first aid procedures.

2. After proper first aid procedures have been carried out, the parent should be notified unless the injury is such that the child must be taken to a doctor without delay. Teachers should have on hand the telephone numbers of the parents both at home and at work. In addition, it would be well to have written permission from the parent listing the doctor to be called in case of need. Parents need to be informed that the financial responsibility for treatment is theirs. If a parent can be reached, then arrangements should be made to release the child to his custody as soon as possible.

3. The child is referred to the doctor, preferably his family physician.

4. A report of the accident is filled out promptly. This can be made on a form adopted by the school system or could be informal in nature. One copy should be sent to the principal, and one retained by the teacher. The report should list full name of the child together with the names of witnesses. Details of the accident should give the place, the time, the circumstances, the possible causes, and the necessary measures to prevent a reoccurrence of the accident. Whether the child was referred to parent or doctor should be noted.

5. Follow-up procedures be instituted to eliminate the causes of the accident and prevent future occurrences.

6. A properly filled medicine chest should be a part of every school. The chest

should contain only medicines and materials approved by a physician or group of physicians. A county or city medical society could establish the content of such a chest. In addition, specific directions for the use of the medical preparations should be prominently posted. These, also, should have medical approval.

7. School accident policies for individual children are available and provide some measure of compensation in case of accident. If a parent rejects the option of school accident insurance for his child, he has little basis for objection to expenses of an accident which could have been partially or fully covered by such a policy.

Other Safety Considerations. Dogs and other animals should be kept from the school yards. Children can trip over the animals and also, the possibility of being bitten is always present. Whenever the skin is broken from an animal bite, the possibility of rabies must always be considered. The animal must be caught and held for the authorities. Only by observing the animal for a period of two weeks or so can the possibility of rabies be rejected.

The rubbish burning area should be protected from the children. Fire has an intrinsic attraction to children, and they love to handle burning materials.

Throwing stones and snow balls needs to be controlled. Other habits of rowdyism having possibilities of injuries need to be controlled also.

Special rules need to be established for procedures in various areas, particularly in the various pieces of apparatus on the playground. These should be discussed with the children and posted.

Leadership Experiences

If the goals of leadership and followership are to be realized, the program must provide social situations wherein the students have real opportunities to lead. The very nature of the physical education program provides many jobs which can be distributed among students to give them real opportunities to assume responsibility. This training, on one hand, results in an understanding of the nature of authority and responsibility, and on the other, an acceptance by the children of the leadership authority so designated. If social goals are to be achieved, then the ability to lead or follow, as the situation demands,

must be developed in our public schools. It should be noted that this is a gradual assumption of responsibility, and the process begins in the elementary schools generally about the third grade.

Guides for the Leadership Program

1. The leadership program is not to be regarded as a time saving device for the teacher. Furthermore, it is unfair to ask children to assume responsibilities without adequate guidance. The teacher must give due consideration to the training of the leaders and provide sufficient supervision. This takes both time and effort.

2. The jobs assigned should be realistic and definite, and should be assigned over a designated time period. Job descriptions aid in orienting the child to the proper performance of duties. A list of duties avoids overlapping and designates definite areas of responsibility.

3. If leadership is considered a fine developmental opportunity, then it follows that it is good for all children. Jobs should be rotated at specified periods so that all children are given some type of responsibility during the year. It is recognized that jobs require different levels of ability and that the teacher must assign carefully on the basis of the capacity of the child. It would be unwise, for example, to ask a relatively unskilled or inept child to demonstrate a skill beyond his capacity.

4. The student should be held to a reasonable standard of job performance. He should be brought to the realization that to be a leader requires planning, and he must allot sufficient time to plan and discharge his duties.

5. The use of leaders should actually improve the efficiency of the class. It should be emphasized that leadership is not the important element but rather the quality of the physical education experience. A class should not suffer through an inferior experience because of the emphasis on leadership training. This is particularly true when physical fitness outcomes are expected.

Types of Leadership Experiences

1. Equipment Manager. He obtains, arranges, and returns equipment for the day's activities.

2. Area Supervisor. The duties of this individual include marking fields, setting up boundaries, and, in general, seeing that the area is ready for the activity. Indoors, this would entail duties like setting up mats or getting the public address system ready.

3. Squad Leaders. The possibilities in this area are numerous. Responsibilities vary from simple tasks like keeping the squad in proper order for relays or taking turns in stunt activities, to supervisory responsibilities in the teaching of skills. Routine record keeping in individual performance and in test scores can be a part of the duties.

4. Officials. Officials need to have a thorough knowledge of the rules of the game. Enough officials can be assigned so that each one would get a chance to play in the activity and still hold his responsibilities.

5. Game Leader, Demonstrator, Exercise Leader. Children can be assigned to choose and lead a game. If the activity or situation makes pupil demonstration desirable, the teacher can assign these duties to selected and properly directed students. Trained students may also lead exercises.

6. Monitors. Special responsibilities can be assigned to monitors. Turning lights on and off, supervising the wash-up after class, and making safety inspections are duties which can be assumed.

Some consideration can be given to a leader's club which would include all the leaders for a given period. Such a club can be organized in a class, or on an all-school basis. Leader's clubs can meet during the club period in the regular curriculum, or could be scheduled for an after-school session or on Saturday morning. The club organization provides for good discussion of duties, an improved esprit d' corp, and definite discharge of duties.

While children gain from leadership experiences, care must be taken that the leaders are not kept too busy to participate in the regular program. Also, where practical, assistant leaders might be appointed with the principle of assuming head duties for the next period. Continuity can be preserved in this manner.

Teaching Aids in Physical Education
Film Strips, Motion Pictures, Slides

In addition to the regular class work in physical education, the teacher should consider enriching the program demonstration with the use of motion pictures, film strips, slides, and the opaque projector. Good audio-visual procedures need to be followed.

1. Proper room darkening with consideration for ventilation.

2. Suitable seating arrangements.

3. Before the showing set up and check the equipment. Place speaker in good position, and center projection beam on screen. Check film for proper winding and thread the projector. Warm up amplifier, test run with suitable adjustments for focusing, volume, and tone.

4. Introduce the film. Give a short resume of the film. Direct attention to the critical points to be observed. This can be in the form of questions to be answered.

5. Show the film with attention to volume, tone, focusing, and framing.

6. After the showing, re-emphasize the points of importance. A discussion will bring out what the children feel is of value in the film.

Visual aids are available from a number of sources. Most schools provide a budget and have an arrangement with a state college or university visual aid center for obtaining films. If the film desired is not in stock, it usually can be secured by these agencies from other sources.

This visual aid should fit in with the learning situation and be appropriate for the level of the children. Since the rental charge covers the use of the film for a period of time, coordination with other classes should be arranged for additional showings. Programs need to be projected far enough ahead so films may be scheduled for correct placement in the program.

Visual aids emphasizing skill techniques should be shown early in a skill learning unit. Those illustrating strategies and game situation probably can come later.

Sound films and sound strips generally need to be shown completely through without interruption. Discussion can be permitted in a slide presentation or with a film strip without sound.

Teachers should give some thought to the use of the 35 mm slide as a teaching tool. Critical skills probably cannot be too well illustrated, but formations, game boundaries, and field layouts lend themselves to the home slide projector.

Loop films should also be considered. They are excellent in the area of stunts and skills, since they repeat over and over again the same technique. Schools can make their own films using 8 mm film. A box like arrangement for projection with a transparent screen allows for viewing in a lighted gymnasium.

The Opaque Projector

Another useful tool to consider is the opaque projector. This device, like the old magic lantern, will throw on the screen an enlarged version of the material. A teacher who uses a card system for games, rhythms or other activities, will find this an effective and useful time saver. If a new game is scheduled, the teacher can flash the card on the screen or blackboard before the physical education period and go over the details with the children.

Bulletin Boards

The class bulletin board should devote a proportionate time to physical education. It is well to select a theme for the board and change it often. A theme could illustrate fitness, a unit, a sport, physical education in other areas, posture, or health practices. A particular skill can be selected for illustration. Pictures from magazines, newspapers, and other sources can be used for illustrations.

The board can be constructed of wall board or beaver board which will hold thumb tacks or staples. A backdrop made of colored paper or colored muslin makes a nice display. The color scheme can be tied up with the theme and changed with the display. Some materials that can be used are listed.

1. Pictures and diagrams lend life to the display. Snapshots also can be included. Newspaper materials should be pasted or stapled to sturdy paper for better display.
2. Colored paper of all kinds and colors is needed. Construction paper pro-

vides an excellent source for these materials.
3. Stickmen can be made from pipe cleaners. These are interesting and provide an outlet for creative talent.
4. Yarn or string can make field outlines or provide borders for the displays.

The character of the bulletin board is limited only by the imagination of the children. The responsibility for the board could be assigned to groups of children on a rotative basis. A good bulletin board program also offers good possibilities for integration with other subject matter fields.

Displays

Displays offer similar possibilities to bulletin boards. However, the display is generally one in three dimensions. The display should have a theme around which to organize the material.

A display may be put in a show case in the school hall. It could be arranged on a table in the classroom.

Bibliographical Materials

Physical education is not static and the collective written materials provide a wealth of ideas for enriching a program. Materials can be classified as follows.

1. Texts in Elementary School Physical Education. Works offering an overall treatment of physical education in the elementary school are available in considerable number. It seems that each year, one or two new manuscripts are offered. While there is considerable duplication among text in the basic material presented, each text emphasizes certain ideas and activities.
2. Curriculum Guides in Physical Education. Curriculum guides have been assembled on a number of different levels. Many states, counties, cities, and school systems have developed guides for their own situations. The guides are not generally advertised but are available reasonably from the various agencies.
3. Specialized Subject Area Books. For more intensive treatment in a particular area of physical education, a number of good books are on the market. These treat only a portion of the physical education program, but develop the area to a much greater extent than the written works covering the entire program. Books dealing with games,

sports, rhythmics, posture, class-room activities, testing, and similar topics are available from different publishers.

4. Magazines and Periodicals. There are magazines devoted to physical education in general, but no periodical which gives its entire emphasis to the elementary school physical education program is on the market. The Journal of the American Association for Health, Physical Education and Recreation is probably the one best source for up-to-date materials in physical education on the elementary level.

5. Card Files. Available today are card files for various physical education activities. Card files* can be secured in the area of games, rhythmics, relays, and stunts. These are convenient teaching aids and good time savers. Cards include the description of the activity, teaching suggestions, safety considerations, and variations.

6. Miscellaneous Materials. Posters, pamphlets, mimeographed material, convention reports, and research reports are indicative of the vast amount of material which is available to the teacher today. Some system of filing is necessary for the teacher. Materials can be filed under the general topic (like rhythmics) and be available for handy reference.

A successful and enterprising teacher will keep up-to-date in his materials.

The Adapted Program

In many classrooms there will be children who cannot participate fully in the regular program in physical education. Frail children, those often absent due to illness, and others with identified handicaps need special consideration. The restriction may be permanent or it can be on a temporary basis as for children who have not fully recovered from injury or recent illness. It needs to be emphasized that a physician should be the determining factor in the recommendation for limited activity. Parents, at times, are given to a tendency to be overly protective and set restrictions which are not in the best interests of the child.

A basic principle for children with restrictions is that they participate within the limits of the restrictions in the regular program. They need to be in-cluded in the group and minimize the concept that they are "different."

However, there will be times when it is desirable for a special activity or groups of activities to be organized while the remainder of the children are participating in the regular program.

It is important that the physically handicapped child develops an optimum degree of physical fitness for his particular condition. This would mean a selection of individual activities which the child can do on his own or with the aid of another student. It is particularly important that the child learn to live with and within his physical condition. If there is some knowledge or skill which can be developed in handicapped individuals which will give them status and advantages both in school and adult life, then every effort should be made to promote this.

Unless the school has unusual facilities, the teacher will probably need to develop special activities which can be carried on while other children are in the regular program.

Suggested activities from which selection can be made are listed.

Aerial Darts
Archery (suction cup arrows)
Bean Bag Tossing
Bowling Games
Box Hockey
Croquet
Darts (suction cup)
Horseshoes (rubber for indoors)
Lawn Bowling
Shuffleboard
Table Tennis

If the restriction is major, then quiet games should be utilized. Chess, checkers, and other table games are available.

The attitude of the other children toward those with handicaps is important. Children should invite and urge the handicapped child to participate within the limits of his handicap. They can take turns working with him in special activities. Tolerance and understanding are excellent social values which can be an outgrowth of such a program.

Teachers need to remember that physical education has values for everyone, not just the skilled or the so-called normal child. The wants and desires of the restricted child are the same as that of the normal child. His needs are realized in different ways.

* Card files may be secured from the Burgess Publishing Company, 426 South 6th Street, Minneapolis 15, Minnesota.

Evaluation

Evaluation is the process of determining the extent a program in physical education meets its stated objectives. It would be fine if all progress toward these objectives could be determined by measurement techniques. However, we have to use many different devices to determine what is happening to children through their physical education experiences. It is true that certain objective procedures are available and should be used. These include fitness tests, posture tests, skill or achievement tests, pencil and paper tests, and the medical examinations. But many of the most important outcomes in physical education cannot be measured by such devices. Reliance on other techniques is necessary. Techniques of evaluation can be divided into four areas. These are (1) general standards for the program, (2) observation by the teacher, (3) pupil opinion and expression, and (4) accepted tests.

General Standards

Because research has indicated that better progress toward objectives, particularly physical fitness, has been made with a program that needs good standards, the evaluation process should begin with an examination of the program in light of these standards.

Time Allowance. Is there a daily allotment of at least 20 minutes of activity for primary children and 30 minutes for intermediate classes for instruction in physical education?

Facilities, Equipment, and Supplies. Are these sufficient for the particular situation so that they do not provide detrimental limitations for the experiences for the children?

The Program. Does the program meet good education standards? Is it geared to the needs, interests, and capacities of the children?

The Direction. Is the instruction in the capable hands of a trained and interested teacher? Does the teacher keep up-to-date through current literature and in-service or college workshops or courses?

Health and Safety. Are there good standards of health and safety? Is the participation based upon a regular medical examination? Is there proper provision for emergency care?

Is there consideration for the child who cannot participate fully?

Observation by the Teacher

The teacher can make reasonable judgments of the progress toward the goals of physical education by observing certain signs of desirable progress.

Physical Fitness. How well does a youngster meet the strength and endurance demands of activity?

How smoothly and adequately can he handle his body?

How does he respond physiologically to the demands of activity? Is there dizziness, nausea, shortness of breath, unusual paleness or redness, weakness, depressed mental or emotional states, or anxiety states?

How well does the child recover from activity? After ten minutes, is there return to normal pulse? Is he still overly tired? Is there marked stiffness or soreness that evening or the next day? Has he recovered the next day from the activity?

Is his posture and bearing satisfactory?

What about arm and shoulder girdle development? Can he perform on the ladder and horizontal bar with reasonable success?

Does he enjoy and thrive on vigorous activity?

Useful Skills. Has he mastered the basic skills of locomotion? Can he do these successfully to rhythm?

Does he show good form in specialized skills? Is he making satisfactory progress for his size and maturity?

Has he mastered throwing, kicking, and batting skills well enough to take part successfully in game type activities?

Can he perform on apparatus the activities appropriate for his age?

On the intermediate level, can he integrate dance steps into dances?

Does he know and apply the appropriate mechanical principles to skill learning? Does he have the desire to practice for better performance?

Does he have a wide appreciation of skills rather than concentration in a narrow area?

Social Learnings. Does he act democratically by entering wholeheartedly into activities chosen by group process?

Does he approach challenging activities with confidence? Is there evidence of fear?

Do children play together well and comfortably as boys and girls with wholesome boy-girl relationships? Are social graces the rule in the rhythmic program?

Is there evidence of good leadership and followership patterns? Do the children accept the proper decisions of the leader?

In competitive games, is there evidence of good sportsmanship in observing the rules, accepting the decisions of officials, and following the captain's suggestions? Can the youngsters win or lose in a sportsmanlike manner?

Can the child share with others and not try to dominate the play?

Safety. Have the students developed a safety consciousness?

Are they considerate of other children in safety situations?

Do they spot hazards and unsafe conditions and tend to correct them?

Recreational Objective. During free play, can he organize his own play either individually or with other children?

Does he learn the rules of activities so he can enjoy these on his own time?

Can he play with assurance on various pieces of apparatus?

Does he know modifications of rules so that he can adapt games to small-group play and places?

Is he motivated to take part in activity for activity's sake -- that is, the maintenance of fitness?

Student Opinion and Discussion

After a class period or the completion of a unit, the teacher can organize an evaluating session with the children for the purpose of critical discussion of the merits of the experience. Discussion should be terms of what was accomplished and how well they enjoyed the activity. Suggestions can be made on what needs to be done and how it can be accomplished.

A technique that can be used with intermediate children is the Buzz Group procedure. The class is divided into four to six small groups, each with a chairman and a recorder. The questions for discussion should be written on the board, and each group would be assigned to a section of the room to discuss these. The procedure gets its name from the buzzing that goes on while groups are discussing values. After a specified period (there should be a preliminary warning), the class is brought together again for the reports from the recorder. Further discussion can be expanded on the class level.

Testing

Measurement is important in physical education because it provides an objective means by which a student can be made aware of his progress. Children like to know where they stand in relation to other students and standards. Good motivation is a result of effective testing.

Tests can point out the strengths and weaknesses in terms of achievement toward standards or specified goals. The measurement program can re-emphasize to the school administration and parents the importance of the goals of physical education and what progress the children are making in terms of these outcomes.

The tests should be used in counseling and can be a part of the child's periodic report to the parents.

Measurement in physical education on the elementary level should consist of physical fitness testing, skill testing, and pencil and paper tests on knowledges and attitudes.

Tests covering knowledges have an important place in the program as they emphasize to both children and parents the importance of these learnings. Attitude tests are not as frequently used in the elementary program in physical education. Tests of this nature can provide important clues for progress in social learnings.

Skill tests are many and varied. Discussion in this text of skill tests has been placed with the activity in which the skill occurs. Testing in physical fitness will be covered on pages 169 to 173 in the Intermediate Program. Few, if any, fitness testing programs are carried on in the primary grades. Most of the fitness programs in the country begin with the fourth grade in listing the standards for the various tests.

Chapter 6

Movement Education

Posture and Body Mechanics
The Skills Instruction Program
Basic Principles Important in Skill Performance and Movement
Patterns of Skill Organization
Movement Exploration

Movement education is concerned with providing experiences so that the child can learn how to move effectively and efficiently. A child needs to be able to move effectively to express himself, carry out skills, and manage his body in a meaningful and productive way.

Movement education can be divided into three areas:

1. Posture and Body Mechanics. This is defined as the application of the laws of physics to the human body at rest or in motion. Correct use of the body is called body mechanics and it has its basic in good postural practices.

2. The Skills Instruction Program. Motor skills patterns of both simple and complex skills are an important area of learning experiences. The emphasis is on the "how" and "why" with drills and repetition of specific activities as the basis of motor learning.

3. Movement Exploration. Sometimes termed "Basic Movement," this program offers the child an opportunity to move effectively with spontaneity and creative imagination. It is unstructured as far as the individual child is concerned and is movement carried on for its own sake. It can be on a broad basis, or it can be within certain problem limits.

Posture and Body Mechanics

Posture refers to the habitual or assumed alignment and balance of the body segments while standing, walking, sitting, or lying. In good posture, these parts are in proper relation to each other and by good balance reflect ease, gracefulness, poise, and efficiency of carriage and bearing.

Correct use of the body is called good body mechanics and has its basis in good posture. How to lift and carry objects, open windows, go up and down stairs, climb ladders, and pull or push are examples of simple activities which need application of good principles of body mechanics.

Posture is dependent primarily upon the strength of the muscles which hold the body in balance against the force of gravity. These muscles work continually and require sufficient strength and energy to hold the body in correct alignment.

It needs to be recognized early by both the teacher and child that the maintenance of good posture is a positive act and has its basis primarily in the practice of good postural habits. The teacher needs concern not only with faulty posture, but also with the causes underlying this condition. Physical abnormalities such as poor vision and hearing, deformities, and even disease cause postural problems. Children who lack energy and fatigue easily become prone to postural slumps. Proper clothing and shoes are a consideration for good carriage. Emotional factors are important as the bearing of an individual is reflected in his emotional outlook.

Anatomical and Physiological Principles Affecting Posture

A better understanding of postural conditions can be established with an examination of some basic physiological facts which have bearing on posture problems.

The body, the wonderful mechanism

it is, adjusts itself to the exterior forces applied to it. Unfortunately, this is true with regard to poor posture. With elementary school children, poor posture may just be a habitual position. But, as the child matures, this now becomes a growth characteristic. Postural strain results when body segments are out of good alignment. The resultant effect is that the muscles which activate these joints, of necessity, adapt both in length and function to the faulty positions of the body segments.

Further breakdown occurs when the body is slumped continuously. The vital organs are compressed and crowded out of position and bones are forced out of alignment. Postural conditions, which were once remediable in the elementary school, now become structural with more difficult correction. Early attention to posture will yield large dividends.

For every set of muscles having a specific movement, there is another group with an opposite action. There must be balance in the power of these antagonistic muscle groups particularly in those keeping the body in alignment. If one set of muscles is markedly stronger than the other, the resultant elastic pull and possible shortening causes an imbalance at the joint concerned. An example of this is in the muscle groups governing the position of the shoulders. The chest muscles exert force to pull the shoulder blades forward, tending to round shoulders, and the upper back postural muscles must counteract this influence with sufficient development. A second example concerns the lower back curve which can be kept in check with a strong abdominal wall working against the lower back muscles.

In addition to the opposing muscle pull, the postural muscles have the force of gravity to overcome. If posture is poor, this gravitational force becomes stronger, and coupled with the opposing muscle pull; causes the muscles holding body alignment to weaken and stretch.

Muscles exhibit another characteristic important in postural considerations. This is the development of muscle tone, defined as a slight degree of tension or contraction. It is important because muscle tone aids in holding the body in correct skeletal alignment. If muscles are weak, flabby, and underdeveloped, then tone is lacking and posture suffers. Good muscle tone is a characteristic of a healthy, conditioned muscle.

From the standpoint of body struc-

ture, the slope or tilt of the pelvis is a critical point. The backbone is composed of a column of small bones, called vertebrae, which has a number of natural curves governing body contour. The foundation of the vertebral column rests on the pelvis forming a joint with very little movement. With correct tilt of the pelvis, the body contours can be natural and graceful. If the front of the pelvis is tilted down, the lower back curve becomes exaggerated causing sway-back which can vary from slight to pronounced. A slight curve in the lumbar region (lower back) is natural. Correct tilt will aid in flattening both a protruding abdomen and a prominent seat. Incorrect tilt has a tendency in standing position of an individual to force the upper legs back with attendant hyper-extension of the knee joint.

What the Teacher Can Do

Teachers must include in their lesson plans and administrative practices specific attention to good body mechanics and posture. Careful planning is needed if good posture is to result. But, in this area, teachers are not to regard themselves as corrective specialists. They can, however, help children form desirable postural patterns and acquire good habits in the many postures assumed. There are a number of factors to which the teacher can give attention in working with youngsters for better posture and body mechanics.

1. The first and most important objective is to provide motivation for good posture. There must be a development of understanding and appreciation of good posture through pictures, posters, demonstrations, and other media so the youngster consciously develops within himself the desire for a body in good alignment.

2. A program of vigorous physical activity to strengthen muscles that hold the body correctly is needed. The program should include a variety of active games, hanging and climbing activities, and selected calisthenics.

3. A planned program of instruction in the basic skills of locomotion, work, and play should be instituted as a part of the physical education program with definite time apportionment and definite goals on each grade level.

4. A healthful school environment is needed with particular attention to

proper seating, good lighting, avoidance of over-fatigue, and elimination of tension.

5. The removal and correction of health conditions which contribute to poor posture are a necessity. Cooperation between home, school, and physician in this program is essential.

6. The teacher must give attention to such emotional factors as discouragement, feelings of inferiority, consciousness of an unattractive appearance beyond the power of the individual to change, and severe acne. Children with fears, timidities, and other feelings of insecurity often reflect these inner states in postural positions. Another factor to be considered in the intermediate grades is the girl who feels that she is "overly tall." Since girls reach their growth more quickly than boys, there will be girls who are as tall as, if not taller than, any boy in the class. Feeling that they are conspicuous in their tallness, some girls react by slumping and trying to make themselves smaller. In contrast, boys want to be tall and usually are proud of their growth attainments.

7. The teacher needs to accept the concept that good posture is a practice and not a subject. Even, in the most simple movements and position, postural problems are continuously present. At times the teacher should introduce and teach good postural habits particularly as it would be related to activities the children are learning. At other times, children should be giv-

en a word of encouragement or advice as reminders for good practice. The teacher needs to be able to recognize good posture and deviations from the normal.

8. The rigid military type of posture is not the goal of normal living. While the service academies at West Point, Annapolis, and Colorado Springs find this useful, it has little part in the posture picture of the elementary school child.

9. The teacher should be a good example of good body mechanics and posture. It is not only important that the children have a good example to follow, but the teacher is able to endure the demands of classroom teaching with less fatigue.

10. The teacher should refer the student to the nurse, physical education specialist, principal, or other appropriate agencies for help in problem posture cases. After a corrective program has been set up, the teacher's part is in cooperating with the program and guiding the youngster in fulfilling his prescribed corrective work.

What is Good Posture?

Posture varies with the individual's sex and body type, and what is proper posture for one individual may not be suitable for another. However, the basic components for posture are much the same for all children. These are illustrated by the following chart.

GOOD POSTURE   FAIR POSTURE   POOR POSTURE

GOOD POSTURE	FAIR POSTURE	POOR POSTURE
Head up, chin in, head balanced above the shoulders with the tip of the ear directly above the point of the shoulders Shoulders back and easy with the chest up Lower abdomen in and flat Slight and normal curves in the upper and lower back Knees easy Weight properly placed with toes pointed forward	Head forward slightly Chest lowered slightly Lower abdomen in but not flat Back curves increased slightly Knees back slightly Weights a little too far back on heels	Head noticeably forward, eyes generally down Chest flat or depressed Shoulder blades show winged effects Abdomen relaxed and prominent Back curves exaggerated Knees forced back in back-kneed position Pelvis noticeably tilted down Weight improperly placed

DIRECTIONS FOR ASSUMING GOOD POSTURE IN STANDING POSITION

Feet. Toes are pointed straight ahead, weight evenly distributed on balls of feet and the heels. Cue by saying "Feet forward! Point feet straight ahead! Feet parallel! Weight off heels!" The feet should be parallel and from two to four inches apart.

Knees. Knees should be relaxed and easy. Avoid the back-kneed position where the knee joint is held forcibly back as far as it can go. Remind the children: "Knees easy! Knees relaxed!"

Lower Back and Abdomen. The abdominal wall should be flattened but relaxed. The lower back curve should be natural and not exaggerated. Children can be told: "Tuck your seat under! Flatten your tummy! Push the body up, tummy in! Flatten lower back! Hips under!"

Upper Body. The shoulders should be back and relaxed and the shoulder blades flat. Chest should be up and raised. Give them directions like: "Shoulders easy! Shoulder blades flat! Lift chest! Chest high!"

Neck and Head. The head should be up and chin in. Neck should be back. The ear should be directly over the point of the shoulder. Say: "Chin in! Head high! Stand tall! Stretch tall! Chin easy!"

LATERAL DEVIATIONS IN POSTURE

The discussions of posture to this point have been concerned mostly with the forward-backward plane of movement. The body must also be in balance in the lateral plane. From a structural standpoint, when viewed from the front or rear, a perpendicular line should divide the body into two symmetrical or equal halves. If parts of one-half of the body cross over this line, there is an unnatural curvature. Again, habit plays a part. The position may be due to faulty practices. A shift of the head may be caused by either visual or hearing problems or both. Uneven shape or size of the bones, particularly the leg bones, will cause the pelvis to tilt laterally with a compensating curvature of the spinal column.

The presence of lateral curvature can be determined by a check on the level of the pelvis, whether or not the shoulders are even, or if the head has a tilt to either side. It is estimated that about 50 per cent of the population have a lateral tilt to some degree. The teacher needs to be observant to screen for referral those cases meriting attention.

Faulty habits contributing to this condition are standing on one leg, leaning against a support, and improper sitting habits.

GOOD WALKING POSTURE

Good walking posture begins with proper use of the feet. It is vitally important that the feet point forward and are kept nearly parallel for best functional use. A person who walks with toes pointed out is subject to considerable strain in the arch and lower ankle leading to a breakdown of the arch and lower leg structure. The heel should touch first in a step with the weight transferred quickly to the balls of the feet and to the toes for a push-off.

The legs swing freely from the hips with the knees bent enough to clear the feet from the floor.

The arms swing in opposition to the legs, the body retains the properties of good standing posture and the eyes are focused on a level ahead. If the eyes are looking down, the head will follow suit.

PROPER SITTING POSTURE

The knee should form a right angle with the feet flat on the floor and pointed generally forward. The hips should be back against the chair and the body erect. Forward movement in a working position should occur from the hip joint, with the head, upper body, and pelvis remaining in good balance.

Evaluating Posture

Since it is a responsibility of the elementary school teacher to detect and refer bodily conditions needing attention, some program of posture evaluation must be established. Evaluation can be done through observation, both formal and informal, and measurement devices. The discussion will cover only those methods which classroom teachers can find practical and useable.

Formal Observation. Posture screening can be accomplished through a rating device which would allow the teacher to check segments of the body and note the condition with respect to postural standards. The following simplified rating sheet is useful for making checks.

POSTURE CHECK

Name_____Grade_____School_____

Date_____ Check made by_____

Side View

Head
    Erect, chin in _____ Somewhat forward_____ Markedly forward_____

Upper Back
    Shoulders back_____ Slightly rounded_____ Round shoulders_____

Lower Back
    Slight natural curve_____ Moderate curve_____ Hollow back_____

Abdomen
    Flat_____ Slight protrusion_____ Protruding_____

Knees
    Relaxed_____ Slightly back_____ Hyper-extended_____

Feet
    Pointed ahead_____ Somewhat out_____ Pointed out_____

Front and Back View

Shoulders
    Level_____ Slightly uneven_____ Considerably
                                                 uneven   _____

Hips
    Level_____ Slightly uneven_____ Considerably
                                                   uneven   _____

Back of ankles and feet
    Heel and ankle   Turned out
       straight   _____   somewhat_____ Pronated_____

Remarks

It may be that the teacher would prefer a single sheet to include all the numbers of the class. Such a sheet could be organized as follows.

POSTURE CHECK SHEET

Class_____ School _____

Date_____Teacher_____

Code
Meets good postural standards	1
Slight but definite deviation	2
Marked deviation	3

| Name | Side View | | | | | | Front and Back View | | | Remarks |
	Head and Neck	Upper Back	Lower Back	Abdomen	Knees	Feet	Level of Shoulders	Level of Hips	Feet and Ankles	
1.										
2.										
3.										

The individual form lends itself to better interpretation to parents and administrators. The class form is more adaptable for class analysis and comparisons. By averaging the rating numbers, it is possible to come out with a mean rating for each child.

Some formal type of organization is needed. Children can be examined five or six at a time. While it does present some difficulties, a better posture evaluation can be made if the children are in gymn clothing or swim suits. It needs to be recognized that any formal posture evaluation is an analysis of an assumed posture and not necessarily the one the child uses in daily living.

Informal Observation. Postural checks can be made of young people when they are participating in classroom and physical education activities. How does he walk, stand, or sit when he is not conscious of an observer? The teacher can make notes and supplement the formal posture check.

The Plumb Line Method. A plumb line can be used for a practical check of body alignment. The plumb line should hang freely. The student stands so the plumb line is between him and the observer, positioned so the line bisects the instep. The plumb line should go through the tip of the ear, the point of the shoulder, the point of the hip, just back of the knee cap, and the middle of the instep. Divergencies from the line can be checked and noted.

The Ear-Shoulder Method. Based on the plumb line method and the principle that if one part of the body is out of line, another part compensates in the opposite direction to provide body balance. This would mean then that if the head were forward, there would be other parts of the body protruding to counterbalance the first poor alignment. If we measure, then, the degree the head is forward, then we have an estimate of general posture.

The degree the head is forward can be measured by the use of a straight stick or a blackboard pointer. Hold the pointer vertically so the bottom portion is even with the tip of the shoulder. The teacher can then measure how many inches the ear tip is forward from the vertical line.

This method also lends itself well to observational practices as the child is in activity. The teacher merely needs to observe the tip of the ear in relation to the center of the shoulder, which is the approximate location of the point of the shoulder.

<u>Other Methods</u>. The use of pictures or silhouettes to check posture is expensive and time consuming, but is effective. It has more use on the high school and college level because of the availability of specialized physical education personnel and facilities.

The Feeling of Good Posture

Every child needs to "feel" when he is in good posture. The wall or door method provides an easy check which the child can use at home. The child places himself with his heels against a flat wall which has no floor molding. A flat door can also be used. The child stands with his heels, calves of the legs, seat, elbows, shoulders, and back of the head touching the surfaces. He walks away maintaining this position without tenseness or strain. The wall position is exaggerated but has value in aiding the child in getting the feeling of proper alignment.

A posture walk can be done using the wall position. A tom-tom can give the signals. When the tom-tom begins to beat, the children walk away from the wall in good walking posture. On a loud thump the children abruptly change direction, continuing the walk. When the beat is changed to a fast beat, the children shuffle fast to the nearest wall and stand in the wall posture position.

A second method of providing a kinesthetic feel is to have the child take a deep breath lifting up his chest while at the same time tucking the pelvis under. Have him release the air but maintain the lifted chest position without tenseness.

A method to aid the shoulders to be back in proper position is to rotate the thumbs outward (arms at the sides) as far as they will go at the same time bringing the shoulders back and flattening out the abdominal wall. Release the contraction in the arms but keep the shoulders back and the abdomen flat.

Exercises for Posture

A rounded program of vigorous activities coupled with hanging, climbing, and other activities which use the arms to support the body weight are helpful in strengthening the anti-gravity muscles of the body. However, at times, the

teacher may wish to use special exercises which strengthen areas which generally need attention from the standpoint of body alignment.

HEAD-SHOULDER-UPPER BACK DEVELOPMENT

1. SWAN EXERCISE

Position: Prone lying (face down), arms extended sideward with palms down.

Movement: Raise upper back, head, and arms in an exaggerated swan dive position. The chin is kept in and the movement is limited to the upper back. Hold for two counts. Repeat 8 or 10 times. Confine movement to upper back <u>only</u>.

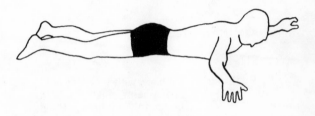

2. HOOK LYING

Position: Lie on back with the feet flat on the floor with the knees bent and arms out in wing position, palms up.

Movement: Press elbows and head against the floor, keeping chin in. Hold for 4 to 6 counts. Repeat 6 to 8 times.

3. TAILOR EXERCISE

Position: Sit tailor fashion (cross-legged) with trunk erect and locked hands on middle of back of head.

Movement: Force head and elbows back slowly against pressure. Repeat 10 to 15 times. Be sure that there is no change in the erect body position.

2. ROWING

Position: Lie on back with arms overhead.

Movement: Sit up, bringing knees to chest and holding firm. Arms are parallel to the floor and pointing beyond the knees. Repeat 10 to 15 times. This is a strenuous exercise. Use slow rhythm.

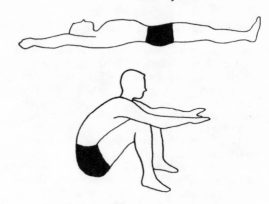

ABDOMINAL MUSCLES

1. SIT-UP

Position: On back with feet flat and knees bent. Instep should be held by a helper. Hands are placed at side with palms down.

Movement: Rise to sitting position with arms extended at shoulder height. Keep head well back. Hold for four counts. Repeat 10 to 15 times.

3. CURL-UPS

Position: On back with feet flat and knees bent. Toes should be held by a helper. Arms are clasped behind the head.

Movement: Curl-up and touch the right knee with the left elbow. Repeat alternating elbows. Repeat 8 to 12 times. The movement should be in the abdominal region.

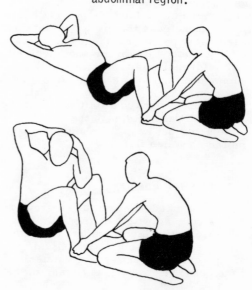

FEET

1. FLOOR SCRATCHING (Sand Scraping)

Position: Sitting or standing, feet flat on floor.

Movement: Using the toes, scratch the floor by bringing the toes toward you forcibly on the floor. Repeat 10 to 15 times.

2. MARBLE TRANSFER

Position: Sitting on a chair or bench. A marble or a wadded piece of paper is needed.

Movement: Pick up the marble with the right foot and bring it up to the left hand. Transfer the marble to the right hand and bring up the left foot to put the marble back on the ground. Repeat 8 to 12 times.

The Skills Instruction Program

Skills in physical education can be divided into two general categories. The first comprises the basic skills for locomotion and play. These have application in a variety of situations. The basic skills of locomotion are walking, running, leaping, hopping, jumping, galloping, skipping, and sliding. Basic game and play skills applicable to a variety of activities are throwing and catching various kinds of balls, kicking a rolling ball, striking a ball with the fist, bouncing balls, and similar skills.

The specialized skills have applications usually to a particular activity. Examples are trapping and passing in soccer, batting and fielding softballs, and shooting baskets.

Basic skills are taught in the primary grades through movement exploration, fundamental rhythmics, game play, and drills. Specialized skills are generally taught through planned drills.

Skills should be based upon sound mechanical skills previously discussed. It is important to avoid simply exposing the child to a skill and trusting to luck for results. A skill should be practiced and learned well enough for good retention and application. Instructors need to teach skills well and expect good performance. A concomitant of this process would be the development of a regard for good performance and an appreciation that in order to be skillful, one must pay the price.

Time and effort spent in learning game skills pays dividends in a lifetime of enjoyment which comes from being proficient in an activity.

Skill has a relationship to fitness in that proficiency in skill becomes a great motivator to continuous, habitual participation. The satisfaction in an activity rests partially in the ability to perform with a reasonable degree of personal skill.

In the teaching of skills, there are three groups which can cause problems. The first is the player of superior skill, who is often a problem. Ofttimes he is a member, and perhaps a star, of outside athletic groups like the Little League or YMCA basketball. He can be intolerant and impatient of his fellow students, particularly the unskilled. The pace of the skill teaching may be much too slow to interest and challenge him.

The second group is on the opposite side of skill ability scale. He is the player with poor skill and, likely, poor coordination. He has difficulty in achieving success and loses interest fast. For him very little progress seems to occur, and he is quite often embarrassed because of his ineptness, particularly if he is put in situations of comparison and competition with the more skilled.

Then, too, skill is a measure of acquiring status. Often young people who lack skill and who have a distaste for organized games are frequently ridiculed and shunned by their age group.

The third group is the withdrawal group, those children who do not want to do anything. They are simply not interested, go through the motions if necessary, and would prefer to sit out if this were permitted.

Even for the enterprising teacher, the solution to these problems is not simple. Several suggestions can be made. First of all, there should be sufficient equipment and supplies so many children are active and involved. Secondly, ability grouping can be considered. A third solution is in a rotation system based on a number of activities. Probably some attention to ability grouping would be of aid in establishing the groups for rotation. Certainly the objective that every child should achieve some measure of success is an important one to be emphasized. That the activities should be exciting and interesting is important. With those children having difficulty, the teacher needs to make individual diagnosis to determine the source of the difficulty and attempt to make corrections.

Basic Principles Important in Skill Performance and Movement

Although the elementary school child does not reach a high degree of skill when compared to high school and adult performances, he can set the basis for good future skills by observing the basic principles governing the execution of skills. It is important, first of all, that he is made aware that there are such principles, and secondly, how to apply them to his skill learning program. If good patterns are established early in the learning process, the child will have little need to make a difficult change later of an undesirable habit which has become established in his general skill pattern. For elementary school children, the following principles in the performance of skills should be considered.

Body Position

The feet should generally be at shoulder width. If the hands support the body as for the push-up position, the hands also should be at shoulder width's distance apart. For some skills, one foot may be forward of the other.

Knees should be slightly bent, toes pointed forward, and the weight on the balls of the feet. The legs are ready for movement in any direction.

The back should be straight, the head up, and the hands in a ready position (as for catching).

If a fast start is needed, then an adjustment is made in that the feet are brought closer together, the body leans in the desired direction, and the child can lower his center of gravity somewhat so he can be ready for the quick start.

Concentration

Visually, the eye should be focused on some fixed or moving point in keeping with the skill. In catching, the child should watch the ball. In batting or other skills striking a moving object, the child should see the ball hit the bat. In shooting a basket or bowling, he should fix his eye on the point of aim. In kicking, he should keep his head down and watch the ball.

Principles of Movement

1. There should be good follow-through.

This means a smooth projection of the already initiated movement. In kicking, kick through the ball, not at it. In batting, punch through and finish the swing. This principle is vitally important in throwing skills.
2. The child should be relaxed. Relaxing means using just enough muscular energy to perform the skill but avoiding an overuse, "tightening up," and distorting the results. Particularly, in target skills, like shooting a basket or pitching, the principle of relaxation is important.
3. Opposition refers to the use of the arms and legs. When throwing right handed, step with the left and vice versa.
4. Most skills require the coordination and use of the entire body. A child, while throwing primarily with his arm, should be taught to bring his entire body into play to help with the skill. By starting with his shoulder forward, the child used the rotation and movement of the body for adding power to the throw. Many other skills use this principle.
5. Weight transfer is important in throwing and batting skills. The child must learn to transfer his weight from his back to his front foot while executing the skill.
6. Visualization in complex skills is important. The performer thinks through what his body and its parts should do and are doing. He concentrates on the key points which make for success in the skill.
7. In almost all ball activities, the ball should be handled with the pads of the fingers.

The Teaching of Skills

Methods of teaching depend upon the level of the children and the skill being taught. Some considerations in teaching skills on the elementary level are given.

1. There must be sufficient repetition to establish good retention. This involves the principle of overlearning. Correct form must be practiced until it becomes a retention. The more complex the skill and the higher the performance level, the more need for practice to maintain the level.
2. Children should understand and apply common mechanical principles. Transfer of learning becomes an important

concept and is more likely to occur when students understand underlying principles and methods in a number of experiences. There are many common elements and mechanics in all throwing movements. The more thoroughly the skill and the principles have been learned, the more effective will be the transfer in learning a new skill.

3. Mimetics have a place in skill teaching. Students can be in mass formation and follow the directions of the leader. Many can practice at one time, good form is emphasized in a short time, questions can be answered, and gross errors discovered at the earliest period. Since the student can concentrate on the skill without the implement (ball, bat or object), kinesthetic feeling for the skill may be acquired. The child gets the feel of the movement.

4. Whether to teach by the whole or part method must be decided. The whole method is the process of learning the entire skill at one time. The part method is to learn parts of the skill separately until all parts are learned and the parts can be combined into a unified whole. This would depend upon the complexity of the skill. The teacher needs to decide whether or not the skill is simple enough to be taught wholly or if it should be broken down into parts. Batting could, for example, be taught by the part method. Practice could proceed in this fashion. First, the batting position could be analyzed and practiced. Next, the weight shift from back to front foot could be practiced. Children could swing the bat back and forth to get the feel of the swing. After these have been practiced, the parts could be put together.

5. A goal should be set which is within the attainment of the student. The instructor should help each individual set goals consistent with his power of attainment. Otherwise, the student never reaches the pinnacle of success. He needs to be able to say, "I did it!" Learning proceeds faster if the child is acquainted with the end in view.

6. Praise and positive directions are more effective than negative comments. With students who have emotional problems in activity participation, this becomes increasingly important. Encouragement often helps students make progress more rapidly and overcome the fear of failure.

7. The utilitarian value of the skill should be established early. The child should be made to understand where this skill fits into an activity. A game, relay, or activity using the skill can effectively put this across if it follows the skill practice period.

8. Teachers should not assume that the youngsters will learn the skill elsewhere. While some may learn from parents, brothers, sisters, and older children, repetition and practice will improve the level of performance. If errors in execution are present, the skill session can provide correct form.

9. A teacher should emphasize that there is a "best" way to do things. What constitutes correct form in a specific skill needs to be emphasized. However, he needs to have the students understand that there are performers who are successful even when using what is considered the poor form. These should be regarded as exceptions which have been developed only after a long period of practice and participation.

10. Children should follow sound mechanical principles, but to expect all to perform skills in an identical manner is in error not in keeping with the principle of individual differences.

11. Speed should not be introduced too early in skills. A hurried, sloppy performance in a relay or game prevents correct progress in the skill.

12. Teachers need to analyze and make corrections. Students will ask and expect an intelligent answer to the question, "What am I doing wrong?" The teacher needs to draw good word pictures and talk the student into good form.

13. Audio-visual aids are of profitable use in illustrating the fundamentals of skills. One needs to be sure that the technique shown is in keeping with the movement patterns the teacher is attempting to get across.

14. Teachers should be able to verbalize skills. This means to break a skill down verbally into its component parts so the children can follow the pattern of instruction.

15. Skills should be practiced with as small a group as possible consistent with the skill and the equipment available.

16. Early participation in an activity using the skill is desirable so that the children can visualize the use of the skill and also note areas of skill deficiency which need attention.

17. After a period of skill practice, the teacher can have the children in a comfortable position for an evaluation based on "What did we learn today?" This technique emphasizes the important points of the lesson.

Patterns of Skill Organization

There are a number of ways or organizing a class for learning and practicing skills. Let us assume that the class is divided into squads or groups.

EACH SQUAD PRACTICES THE SAME SKILL. This lends itself to mass teaching and group control over the same type of activity. It demands facilities which are adequate and supplies which are sufficient so that children do not have to wait unnecessarily for turns. A central demonstration group can be used from which other squads take their cue.

EACH SQUAD PRACTICES A DIFFERENT SKILL AND SQUADS ARE ROTATED ON SIGNAL. With different skill activities being practiced, considerable reliance on squad leaders is necessary. The teacher cannot feasibly provide explanations and directions for the different activities at the same time. The skills practiced also must have a similarity in accomplishment with respect to the time limit. It would be a poor learning situation for the rotation signal to be given when one group "was just getting started" and another "finished a long time ago."

SEPARATE GROUPS FOR DIFFERENT SKILLS ARE ESTABLISHED AND CHILDREN ARE ASSIGNED TO THESE ON THE BASIS OF NEED. Rotation, if any, would be on the basis of signal. The child's need for skill practice in an activity would determine his assignment. Care is needed to secure a balance of groups. However, if the need for practice in one type of skill is large, then more than one group for this practice could be organized. Children could change groups when they feel they have practiced sufficiently on a skill.

EACH GROUP PRACTICES SEPARATE SKILLS, BUT THE ASSIGNMENT TO A GROUP IS VOLUNTARY. Students should be allowed to move from one group to another when they feel the need. This is a more informal organization than the other three and needs good supervision and group leaders to make it work properly.

The Teacher Who Cannot Demonstrate

It needs to be recognized that there are teachers who, because of physical limitations, cannot demonstrate effectively. Few teachers, who are not physical education specialists, can do everything well. Even the relatively skilled teacher will, at times, need to devise substitutions for an effective demonstration. For the teacher who has difficulty in demonstrating activities, the following suggestions should prove helpful.

1. Through reading, study, analysis of movement, and other devices, arm yourself with an understanding and knowledge of the activities which you have difficulty demonstrating. Even if you cannot perform, know how the activity is to be done.
2. Select skillful children to help demonstrate.
3. Be able to verbalize the skill so you can coach the students and correct their errors.
4. Secure and use effective visual aids at appropriate points in the unit of teaching.
5. Place more reliance on the squad leaders and use the squad formation in skill drills.

Formations Useful in Teaching Skills or Relays

While there are exceptions in teaching specialized sports activities, the following formations are useful in teaching a wide variety of skills. Many of these formations are also used in games and relays.

1. Mass or Scatter

```
X  X  X  X  X  X  X

X  X  X  X  X  X  X

X  X  X  X  X  X  X
```

2. Small Group

```
 X     X     X     X     X
XX    XX    XX    XX    XX      (by 3's)

XX    XX    XX    XX    XX
XX    XX    XX    XX    XX       (4's)
```

3. Lane or Squad

```
X  X  X  X
X  X  X  X
X  X  X  X
X  X  X  X
X  X  X  X
X  X  X  X
```

4. Squad with Leader (or plus one)

```
X  X  X  X
X  X  X  X
X  X  X  X
X  X  X  X
X  X  X  X

L  L  L  L
```

5. Spoke

```
   X              X
     X          X
       X      X


      X      X
     X        X
   X            X
```

6. Line and Leader

```
X  X  X  X  X  X
         L
```

7. Semicircle and Leader

```
         X  X
      X        X
   X              X
      L
```

8. Circle

```
      X  X
   X        X
   X        X
      X  X
```

9. Circle and Leader

```
      X  X
   X        X
       L
   X        X
      X  X
```

10. Double Line

```
X  X  X  X  X

X  X  X  X  X
```

11. Zig-Zag Double Line

```
X     X     X     X     X

   X     X     X     X     X
```

12. Shuttle

```
⟨X X X X _____ X X X X⟩
```

13. Shuttle Turn-back

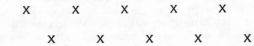

```
⟨X X X X         X X X X⟩
```

Movement Exploration

Within the framework of skills instruction, it is important that children have an opportunity to try out different ways and approaches to skills. Children should be encouraged and directed to explore with different methods and ways within the design of good skill performance. A teacher can instruct with, "See what happens if you try it this way." Or, "Which of the ways we are practicing is best for you?" A good instructor will set up skill drills and situations so that the child can explore realistically the skills in a modified or fragmented game situation.

In still teaching, if the child is violating good form, he should be corrected even if what he is doing seems (to him) to be the best way of performing. Children need to become aware that excellence in skill is not happenstance but rather the result of proper practice consistent with good principles. However, exploration is inherent in this process and should be included as an important part.

Chapter 7

Integration with Other Subject Matter Fields

Arithmetic
Art, Health and Safety, Geography, History, Language Arts, Music
Projects

Many physical education experiences and learning situations provide opportunity for the use of and combination with other subject areas for the purpose of broadening the learning environment. Physical education materials can make important contributions to other areas, and, conversely, other subject mediums can be of use in broadening and enriching the physical education program.

Even in the unit-of-work study program, physical education should be considered for its contributions. Take the example of the class which is studying the Oregon Trail as its unit of work. Combining with the geographical, historical, home economics, health, music, and social study approaches, the unit can include study of the recreational life of the pioneers. Games and dances used by the Trail youngsters as well as Indian games and dances could be a part of the study.

The opportunities for integration of physical education activities with other subject media are numerous and limited only by the ingenuity of the teacher and the interests of the children. Some suggestions with regard to the ways that physical education can be related to and complement other subject areas are presented. These merely introduce the topic and provide some examples. Many other integrations can be devised.

Arithmetic

Concepts of numbers can be strengthened. Practical application for the processes of addition, subtraction, division, multiplication, percentage computation, and measurement can be made through selected physical education applications.

Ways in which number concepts can be related to physical education are:

1. Measuring performance--distance, time, height.
2. Working out averages--from tests and other measured performances.
3. Working with percentages--batting, team standings, other comparisons.
4. Geometric principles--layout of fields and areas.
5. The metric system--comparison of European records (metric system) and American performances. Measurements taken with metric system.
6. Number perception--In games where numbers are called for signals, different combinations could be used. For example, instead of calling out "8," the teacher could say, "36 divided by 3 minus 4."

Art

Children like to make things for their own programs. Posters, decorations, and costumes bring together art and physical education areas. Others are:

1. Art work for games--toss games, clown faces, etc.
2. Movement pattern--forming triangles, squares, circles, and other figures.
3. Bulletin boards and displays--offer numerous possibilities.

Health and Safety

Like music, it is difficult to separate health and safety from physical education. Physical education should be carried on in a healthful and safe atmosphere. Many opportunities for incidental teaching of health concepts arise. Safety considerations for each activity are important in the planning. Other examples are:

1. Fitness concepts--knowledge of basic understandings, the development of fitness, and its relationship to the health of the individual.
2. Exercise and health--the part exercise plays in our health.
3. Safety campaigns--playground and gymnasium safety.
4. Recreation and health--the importance of recreation in our living.

Geography

Closely allied to history is the geographical approach. Emphasized would be the areas or countries from which the activities originated. Some ideas that can be used are:

1. Climate in different areas--how this affects the play habits of the people.
2. Games of different countries--how others play.
3. Folk Dances--origins, characteristics of the country, and of the people.

History

Physical education is rich in historical background. Practically all activities have a historical aspect with regard to origin and background. Many activities done today have a traditional basis. The historical aspects of physical education offer many possibilities of historical study and should be developed. Appreciations and favorable attitudes can be furthered if children understand the background of an activity. Some suggestions for incorporating history are:

1. The origins of activities--events like the discus throw, shot-put, and the pole vault are with us today only because of the tradition behind them. The origins of such games as baseball, basketball, and American football are equally interesting.
2. Dances--ethnic background, historical period emphasis, meanings.
3. Fitness of other peoples--the ancient Greek, Persian, and Roman civilizations. Modern emphasis on fitness-- the Russians, and other countries.

4. The Ancient and Modern Olympics-- the ancient games and how the modern games became into being.
5. Knighthood and the tournaments.

Language Arts

Physical education materials make useful subjects for both written and oral expression. The world of sports and games provides many examples of outstanding individuals who can serve as topics for presentations. Additional suggestions follow.

1. Reading--children can read game descriptions, rules, and related materials.
2. Writing--biographies, summaries of game programs.
3. Oral expression--pupil demonstrations, explanations, announcing events, speaking at evaluation sessions.
4. Spelling--new words in the coming physical education lesson, difficult sports terms.
5. Creative expression--working out story plays for the story periods.
6. Word origins--study of physical education terminology. Terms like gymnasium, calisthenics, and exercise have special origins.

Music

Rhythm is an integral part of physical education, and much of the program makes use of music and rhythm. Since music provides the basis for much movement in physical education, it is extremely difficult to isolate music from physical education. The two areas overlap and should cooperate in the experiences of the children. Examples of cooperative action are:

1. Understanding rhythm--learning the characteristics of the music and rhythm while physical education provides the interpretation through movement.
2. Singing games--the words and music can be taught by the music teacher, and the movement patterns later in the physical education class.
3. Learning about music--learning the names of different musical selections, becoming familiar with the heritage of music.

Projects

Class projects in physical education or related areas form excellent educational opportunities. The teacher and the children should plan the project together. Many ideas for these projects can be found with a little reflection. Playdays form an excellent area. A playday could be organized with one or more classes in the same school, with a class in another school, or just among the children of the class itself. Demonstrations and exhibitions for parents are fruitful projects. A convocation program or demonstration in the gymnasium before other children merits consideration.

Other projects could be a study of games of other lands, the Olympic Games, a sport, or other physical education activity. Another suggestion is to have a rhythmic party inviting another class.

The program can be planned, invitations written, committees formed, and all the necessary details arranged.

The enterprising teacher will think of many other ideas which can be used as projects for the children. The project could be on a yearly basis or could be one for each season.

Chapter 8

The Physical Education Program for the Primary Grades

The First Grade Program
The Second Grade Program
The Third Grade Program
Fitness for Primary Children

The general features of the physical education program for the elementary grades has been presented in Chapter 4. Only the general activity types were outlined. In this section a detailed review of the program for the primary grades will be given. Each of the primary grades is analyzed and presented in turn. The percentage allotments for the activity types will be given, and the recommended divisions under each of the types will be made.

The First Grade Program

The first grade program consists of five activity types. Two of the activity types--rhythmical activities, and game-type activities--are subdivided into component parts, the total of which makes up the general type. The chart on the following page lists the activity types and the recommended percentage allotments for the type and the subdivisions.

From the chart, the following features of the first grade program can be emphasized. The largest portion of the first grade program is devoted to simple game-type activities (35%). Rhythmics (25%) and movement exploration (25%) follow in quantity with the two together totaling a little more than the games program. One-tenth of the program is centered on

the area of stunts, tumbling, and apparatus, and a portion of time (5%) is given over to game skills.

Movement exploration is divided into two categories, with an equal amount of time devoted to each. Movement exploration and body mechanics make up one of these, and the other is the instruction in fundamental locomotor skills, of which a major portion is done to rhythmic accompaniment. Since only a portion of the work in fundamental skills is done with rhythmics, it is included here because of its close relationship to the program of movement.

In the games program, over one-half is devoted to running, tag, and circle games, and the remainder is given over to simple ball games with a small portion of time allotted to story type activities.

Singing games and folk dances make up most of the rhythmic program with the area of creative rhythms comprising the remainder.

In the skills area, the first grade child should have instruction in simple ball skills, primarily throwing and catching. Five per cent of the program is devoted to this practice.

Simple stunts and apparatus play make up 10 per cent of the program. The activities consist of floor stunts and simple maneuvers on the exercise bar, the horizontal ladder, and the balance beam.

ACTIVITY TYPE	RECOMMENDED PERCENTAGES		CLASS PERIODS PER YEAR*
Movement Exploration and Body Mechanics		25%	45
Rhythmical Activities		25%	45
Singing Games, Folk Dances	15%		
Creative Rhythms	10%		
Stunts, Tumbling, Apparatus		10%	18
Simple Game-Type Activities		35%	63
Running, Tag, Circle Games	25%		
Simple Ball Games	5%		
Story-Dramatic Play	5%		
Basic Skills and Skill Drills		5%	9
Total		100%	180 Class Periods

The Second Grade Program

The program for the second grade is similar to that of the first grade, with some exceptions and shift of emphasis.

Relays are introduced as an activity. The other activities are retained from the first grade with lesser emphasis on games and movement exploration, and a greater emphasis on the skills program.

ACTIVITY TYPE	RECOMMENDED PERCENTAGES		CLASS PERIODS PER YEAR*
Movement Exploration and Body Mechanics		20%	36
Rhythmical Activities		25%	45
Singing Games and Folk Dances	15%		
Creative Rhythms	10%		
Stunts, Tumbling, Apparatus		10%	18
Simple Game-Type Activities		30%	54
Running, Tag, Circle Games	22%		
Simple Ball Games	5%		
Story-Dramatic Play	3%		
Relays		5%	9
Basic Skills and Skill Drills		10%	18
Total		100%	180 Class Periods

As in the first grade, the majority of the physical education program rests in simple games, rhythmics, and movement exploration. The emphasis on stunts remains the same. Increased time is allotted to the skills program.

*Based upon a 180 day school year.

The Third Grade Program

The third grade program of activities provides the transitional bridge between the simplified activity program of the first two grades and the skills emphasis on the intermediate level. Third grade children are beginning to mature in skills and interests, particularly in the sports areas.

ACTIVITY TYPE	RECOMMENDED PERCENTAGES		CLASS PERIODS PER YEAR*
Movement Exploration and Body Mechanics		10%	18
Rhythmical Activities		20%	36
Folk Dances, Mixers	15%		
Creative Rhythms	5%		
Stunts, Tumbling, Apparatus		15%	27
Game-Type Activities		30%	54
Running, Tag, Circle Games	15%		
Simple Ball Games	15%		
Relays		10%	18
Athletic Skills and Games		15%	27
Skills and Skill Drills	10%		
Lead-up Games	5%		
Total		100%	180 Class Periods

One area no longer appears in the program of the third grade as compared with that of the two previous grades. Singing games are no longer a part of the percentage allotment chart. The emphasis on rhythmics is concentrated in folk dance and mixers. Creative rhythms are still retained as a minor part of the rhythmic program.

Lead-up games make their appearance in the curriculum. There is increased allotment to the skills, relays, and stunts areas.

Fitness for Primary Children

The emphasis for physical fitness for primary children should be placed upon learning the fundamentals of movement and building a foundation for physical fitness. A program to develop and improve physical fitness must provide vigorous activities that will develop the attributes of fitness--strength, endurance, agility, flexibility, organic power, explosive power, speed, and balance.

Activities for primary children which are important in developing fitness are:

1. Fundamental Activities--walking, running, hopping, skipping, balancing, jumping, sliding, catching, climbing, hanging, throwing.
2. Elementary Rhythmic Activities
3. Creative Movement Experiences
4. Simple Games and Relays
5. Simple Stunts and Tumbling
6. Apparatus Play
7. Movement Exploration
8. Fitness activities involving running, i. e., free running, running and stopping, running and falling, running in combination with jumping and leaping, etc.
9. Beginning on the third grade level, selected exercises can be given with the provision that the children do them properly.
10. Selected circuit training routines can

* Based on a 180 day school year.

be organized based on activities within the children's capacities.

Active participation and vigorous movement should be promoted and encouraged. A part of each class period should be devoted to vigorous activity.

Activities need to be selected and organized in such a fashion that many children are active at one time. Sufficient supplies and equipment are important factors in meeting the criterion of vigorous activity.

Activity selection should consider the development of the back, chest, shoulders, and arms. The demands of modern living provide insufficient load for these muscle groups. In addition, special activities for the development of the abdominal wall should be a part of the program.

All pupils should be motivated to achieve high levels of physical fitness commensurate with their age levels and capacities.

Chapter 9

Basic Skills and Movement Exploration

Movement Exploration
Bean Bag Tossing and Throwing

The development of skills is a major objective in physical education. It is of vital importance that a good basis for the realization of this objective is laid in the primary grades. It is at this level that the motor skill patterns are initiated which form the foundation for the specialized skills required in daily life, in work and play. Skills in each grade should be based upon those of the previous grade. The first grade, of course, is an exception. The teacher of the first grade class must begin with whatever skill patterns the children have. Other grade levels should first review the recommended skills for the previous grade before proceeding with the program for the grade level concerned.

The skills for the first graders are basic in type and utilitarian for the youngsters. By the time the child reaches the third grade, he should have mastered the fundamental skills of movement and locomotion, simple game skills, and introductory skill patterns for sports.

Skill teaching should begin with shortened distances, easy throwing, and emphasis on techniques. The children should understand and make use of good principles of movement in keeping with their level of learning. It is better to concentrate on fewer skills and learn them well than to be exposed to many skills taught poorly.

The following skill standards are suggested for the grades at the primary level. The lists do not include rhythmic or stunts and tumbling skills. Discussion of the elements to be achieved in these programs is presented under the separate topics.

Skills to be Developed in the First Grade

By the end of the first grade, each child should be able to perform in reasonable fashion the skills listed below. Due allowance must be made for individual differences.

Running. Be able to run in proper form with other children without falling down or running into another child.

Throwing and Catching. Be able to throw and catch bean bags and large balls to self. Be able to catch a ball on first bounce from on fly or against a wall. Be able to roll a ball.

Bouncing. Be able to bounce a ball and catch it using various combinations.

Jumping. Be able to jump over low objects or a low rope.

Kicking. Be able to kick a stationary ball for a distance of 10 to 15 feet under control.

Leaping. Be able to leap the brook.

Skills to be Developed in the Second Grade

By the end of the second grade, the child should be able to do the following skills commensurate with the ability of a second grade child.

Running and Stopping. Be able to run, stop, and dodge. Be able to use these skills in running games. Be able to run around a circle under control.

Throwing and Catching. Be able to throw and catch from distances beginning at 10 feet. Be able to handle and toss bean bags with good accuracy. Begin to throw and catch grounders with softballs and small balls.

Bouncing. Be able to bounce a ball with good skill, using various combinations. Begin to dribble in place and while moving.

Jumping. Be able to jump or hurdle objects about knee high. Be able to jump lightly in good rhythm.

Kicking. Be able to kick a rolling ball moving toward the kicker.

Striking. Be able to strike a volleyball from the hand for short distances. Be able to bounce a ball and strike it.

Skills to be Developed in the Third Grade

The third grade introduces some sports skills patterns which are built upon the skill instruction in the previous grades.

Running and Dodging. Be able to run and dodge in tag games. Be able to dodge a ball in dodge ball games. Be able to make changes of direction while running.

Throwing and Catching. Be able to throw and catch different size balls at varying distances with a partner. Be able to catch a ball thrown in the air.

Begin to learn softball techniques of the overhand throw, catching, batting, and pitching.

Dribbling, Passing, and Shooting. Be able to dribble in a straight line. Be able to dribble without looking at the ball. Be able to dribble, stop, and resume the dribble.

Begin to learn the chest pass and the chest shot. The chest shot is to a basket or to each other.

Soccer Skills. Continued practice in kicking skills. Be able to kick with the toe of the foot with some control.

Jumping. Be able to jump a single and double rope, using different combinations of turning at different speeds (slow, medium, fast).

Running. Be able to run 30 yards in good form and finish well.

Striking. Be able to strike a volleyball from the hand for a sufficient distance to play Bat Ball.

Fundamental Game Skills

1. Rolling a ball. The child stands with his feet well spread, knees and legs almost straight. Bending over, he places the ball between his feet and grasps it firmly with his hands. The arms are swung forward and up without bending them as the ball is released. The body remains in the forward bending position during the rolling.

2. Rolling a Ball--Bowling. To bowl right handed, the child stands with his left foot forward with his body bent over, knees bent slightly. The ball is held in both hands with the right hand behind the ball. With the weight on the back (right) foot, the ball is swung back with both hands and then rolled forward with the right hand. The weight is transferred to the front foot with the roll.

3. Tossing the Ball. The child takes a wide position with his feet, with the ball held firmly with the hands between his legs. He bends over and then brings the ball up with a tossing movement, keeping the arms straight. Later, the child can be taught to bring the ball up and out quickly.

4. Two Handed Toss. For a right handed child, the toss is done from the right side. The ball is at the right side grasped firmly by both hands with the fingers spread. The left foot should be slightly ahead of the right. The ball is brought alongside the thigh and then forward with a quick forceful motion, with the hands and arms pointing in the direction of the throw. At the toss, a step is taken with the left foot and the weight is transferred to it.

5. Chest Pass. The feet are together and the child faces the target. The ball is held against the chest with the ball gripped with the fingers. The thumbs are about two inches apart.

The pass is made with a forceful forward push with the hands and arms, while at the same time stepping with the left foot. The fingers and arms are straightened and pointing at the target for good follow-through.

6. Bounce Pass. The bounce pass is made the same way as the chest pass except that the ball is pushed downward for the bounce. It should be bounced a little over half way to the target.

7. Two-Handed Overhead Throw. The two-handed overhead throw begins with the child erect, feet even, and the ball held overhead with the fingers. The hands should be more behind the ball than at the sides. The ball is carried

back with the hands and arms and then
brought forward, finishing with a good
wrist snap. At the same time, a step
is taken with the left foot, and the
weight is shifted to this foot.

8. Bouncing a Ball. The child should
lean forward slightly, feet apart. The
ball is held with the fingers, the
thumbs being about an inch apart.
The motion is downward with both
arm motion and wrist snap. As soon
as the ball is released, the child
should get ready to catch it.

9. Dodging. Body comes to a slight
crouch with the weight dropped and
the knees bent. The child can feint
one way and side step in another.

10. Soccer, Softball, Basketball, Football,
Volleyball, and Track Skills. The instructional units in these sports found
in the Intermediate Level program
give detailed descriptions of different
skills. The teacher is referred to
these to supplement the game skills
listed above.

Movement Exploration

The word explore means to examine,
to investigate, to delve into the unknown.
With movement exploration, the child
through guidance uses movement as a
way of expressing, exploring, interpreting himself, and developing his capacities.
While it is recognized that all physical
education activities can be classed as
movement experiences, the term movement exploration will apply to experiences
organized so the child can learn about his
movement possibilities.

Movement exploration thus is a medium for helping children understand what
their bodies can do. Invention is its key.
The teacher does not demonstrate or instruct, but guides the learner to the solution of the problem. Occasionally, children may show to the class a particular
movement they have originated. However,
conformity is not a goal of movement exploration. The children interpret and react each according to his own feelings.

The child can benefit from an effective movement program, more so than
from other areas. Movement is explored
through many mediums such as literature,
teacher's directions and comments,
sports, play equipment, and dramatic
activities. In movement programs, generally all the children are active at one
time. Each child has an area or space
on the playground or in the gymnasium

which is his own.

While many of the activities are
done on an individual basis, others may
require partners or groups. How the
partners solve their movement problems
or how a group responds would come from
the children. Original responses should
be encouraged.

The movements will be of a great
variety and, in the main, will be gross or
big muscle types. The child should be encouraged to make complete movements to
the fullest extent. Only then can good fitness values accrue. The inept and un-
skillful child needs approval and encouragement. Since the quality of movement
varies, children can find succes in many
ways.

Purposes of Movement Exploration

What are the objectives of the movement exploration program? There are
four that are considered basic and important.

1. The program should offer a wide experience in movement, so that chil
dren will move with ease, coordination, fluency, and versatility.
2. The program should seek individual
creative responses and should be so
structured that the children have the
opportunity to be creative.
3. The children should be made aware of
their movement possibilities, so that
in time they can move skillfully with
sureness and confidence in a variety
of situations.
4. The children should develop a "movement vocabulary" of basic skills to
serve as a foundation for the more
complicated sports and dance skills.

Basic Elements of Movement

1. Time. Time is a characteristic of
all movement. Movement may be
slow or fast, or someplace in between.
Children should have movement experiences related to time, utilizing both
extremes of time. They should understand and sense the effect of time on
the quality of movement. They should
learn how to control movement slowly,
and to handle it when the pace is rapid. Changes in the time or in the
character of the time (even or uneven)
should be a part of the child's experiences.
2. Force. All movement involves the

application of force, since the contraction of the muscle in itself is force. The effective use of force is an important factor in efficient movement. Movements can be performed lightly or heavily or in between. A movement can be characterized as strong or weak. Controlling force through different movement patterns is important. Effective ways of stopping, starting, pushing, pulling, lifting, striking, kicking, throwing, and batting are needed areas of exploration.

3. Space. Since movement occurs in space, children to move well must be aware of space and use it freely, intelligently, and completely. Space can be analyzed from two standpoints:

   a. Space in relation to the whole area in which the children are working. This refers to the whole gymnasium, playground, or room. Children need to consider other children and manage themselves in the area in relation to them. They need to adjust movements to other individuals and objects moving in space. Space in this sense is explored through the medium of locomotor movements.

   b. Space in relation to themselves. The child in his own space may move in different directions--forward, backward, sideward, in various figures, obliquely, etc. He may work at different levels--high, medium, low. He may make full or limited use of his space by being big or small. In developing an understanding of space, he can experience different shapes--round, narrow, big, wide, different patterns. He can explore the range of body movements in his space by reaching, swinging, stretching, twisting, turning, and similar movements. He can confine his movements to one or more parts of the body. This brings in the need for axial movements--movements performed by the child without changing his space.

The resourceful teacher can devise numerous combinations from the above basic ideas. In addition, creative response can be encouraged by having the children identify themselves with or act out roles of many characterizations.

It can be recognized that maximum activity is possible in a class in movement exploration. There is little waste of time in getting started and all children are active.

Methodology

The teacher must set the framework for movement. Through comments, questions, and directive statements, the teacher leads the child through his movement patterns. The teacher begins by having the children in a scattered pattern in the play space so that each has sufficient room to solve his movement pattern. Each child can have a special place on the floor which he would take every time.

The problem solving technique is used in teaching basic movement. Great care should be exercised in phrasing the problems so each problem will bring out variety and multiple responses. The problems should be phrased to challenge the creativity of the students. Limitations given by the teacher for the movement patterns should not stifle, but should set limits within which the children can give responses. There should be more of "Let's try it this way," or "See if you can do it by - - ." Children should have the opportunity to explore, try out different ways of moving, and experiment using equipment.

It is important that as many variations and different ideas be explored by the children centered around the basic problem to be solved. Variations of a movement can be made by doing it at varying directions; at different speeds; with or without different parts of the body; with the body in different positions of shapes; over, under, or around different pieces of equipment. On the basis of these changes, guiding questions or directives can be used. Some examples are:

"Show me how you can go in different directions or changes of direction."

"How can you do the same movements at different speeds; in different combinations of speed?"

"How many other parts of the body can you bring in to help this movement?"

"What different levels can you use for this movement?"

"How many different ways can you . . . ?"

Simple Basic Challenge Movements

The most basic type of movement exploration is to set different bases of support and let the children work within these limitations.

Each child assumes some designated position. Positions could be standing, sitting in various positions, lying, on hands and knees, etc. Children do not learn by instruction and lecture, but are guided to meaningful movement by the questions and comments of the teacher. Questions like the following provide a good basis for the children.

1. CAN YOU - -
    Make circle with your right hand? Left hand? Both hands?
    Make yourself as small as possible? As big as possible?
    Run to the nearest wall and back without bumping anyone?
    Jump back and forth making a cross? A triangle? A square?
    Run around in a circle? Figure eight?
    Go faster and higher? Slower and lower? In zig-zag fashion?
    Hop on one foot five times? Change every third hop?
    Change feet often in the gallop?
    Show me how a ball bounces? Ball rolls?
    Bicycle standing up? Sitting down? On your back?
    Reach way back? Way out in front? To the side?
    Turn around quickly? Turn the other way? Turn over?
    Go sideways with one foot following the other? Go forward? Backward?
    Touch the floor in front? Behind you? On either side?
    Use big wide movements to imitate a . . . .
    Walk or move like a . . . .
2. LET'S TRY - -
    Kicking in front. Behind. High in the air. High to the side.
    Touching your left foot with the right while sitting on the floor.
    Paddling a canoe. Rowing a boat.
    Climbing a stair. A pole. A ladder. Over a fence. Under a fence.
    Rocking back and forth like a tree.
    Running lightly increasing speed. Decreasing speed. In place.
    Stretching way up. Way back. Way down. Way around.
    Turning over quickly using one hand. Not touching one foot.
    Lifting a heavy object.
    Jumping in place. With a full turn.
    Pushing against a partner. Pulling against a partner. Pushing and pulling.
    Looking through our legs at the person behind us. Around to the side.
    Making one hand follow the other around and around. With the feet.
    Bringing your toe to your forehead. To the back of your neck.
3. SHOW ME HOW - -
    A top spins. Falls down. Is wound up.
    To move slowly and carefully. Rapidly and lightly.
    To throw a ball. Bat a ball. Catch a ball.
    To balance on your seat.
    To build a bridge.
    To take giant leaps.
    To touch three different walls and back to place without bumping anyone.
    To be a giant. A dwarf. A witch.
    To swim overhand. Breast stroke.
    To bounce up and down in different positions.

The freedom to move and the chance to achieve mean much to the child. This movement, however, must be directed. It is not to be inferred that the teacher can conduct such an informal activity as movement exploration without adequate planning. Many of the previously mentioned statements and cues can be utilized. There are many others that can aid children to move naturally and easily. For use, a lesson plan should be made for each class.

From the beginning, it is necessary to establish and keep a sense of order. While the children must be kept busy in a gay and companionable atmosphere, they must also be under control. Otherwise, the activity can descend into a period of uncontrolled emotions. A balance of freedom of action with control and order is needed.

Each child is given a starting position and after the movement interpretation should again assume this position. Many different positions as a basis for initiating movement experiences are possible.

A child can be standing in various positions with his feet together, apart, at stride, toed in, toed out, or heels together.

Sitting positions that can be assumed are with legs outstretched, legs apart, feet up with knees bent, legs crossed, and arm support in several positions.

The child could be kneeling, on hands and feet, lying on back or prone, on front leaning rest, side leaning rest, and many other positions.

General Movement Patterns

Patterns allowing for more general movement can be structured for the children. A challenge or directive is issued to the children, the working of which allows individual and a variety of response. The objective for each individual is to have the opportunity to develop movement as stipulated by the wording of the directing statement or challenge. There should be contrasting and a variety of activities which the children can do, with the objective in mind of getting the children to move effectively and efficiently.

The pattern can be accomplished by each child working alone or in pairs. The use of small hand equipment can be utilized such as balls of various sizes, hoops, wands, ropes, and similar items. The problems could be set around different pieces of equipment such as climbing ropes, stall bars, horizontal ladders, exercise bars, balance beams, sets of climbing apparatus, and the like.

Children should be given a period of time to explore for a variety of responses. After a variety of activities have been experienced, the teacher could ask the children to select one or more activities which they would practice until they felt that they had reached some proficiency. Discussions can be held with the children volunteering information with regard to the best and most efficient ways of movement based on the experiences just undergone.

In using the indirect approach, the class could be working with a variety of apparatus, or they could be given the same movement problem to solve. In other words--there could be choice of activity on different pieces of apparatus or the entire class could be following the same pattern. This latter should not be interpreted as all children conforming to the same responses, but rather all children may respond creatively to the movement problem structured by the teacher.

Examples of how movement problems may be structured follow.

1. "Let's see how many different ways you can balance on two supports-- i.e., two hands, one hand and one foot, both feet."
2. "Can you show me the different ways you can move across the room?"
3. "What different shapes can you make your body into to represent different types of buildings?"
4. "Put your jumping rope in the form of a circle. What are the ways you can move in and out of the circle?"
5. "Let's see you carry a ball around the room without using your hands."
6. "Show me how many different parts of the body you can have moving in a circle. What different combinations can you make up?"
7. "How many different ways can you show me to bounce a ball across the room?"
8. "What are the different ways you can go over a bench without touching? What shapes can you make in the air?"
9. "What different ways can you twist the different parts of the body? What combinations of twisting can you show me?"
10. "Let's explore the different ways you can stretch the body to full limits."
11. "What are the different ways you can move along a bench?"
12. "What are the different ways you can find to roll across a mat?"
13. "On the horizontal ladder, what are the ways you can move along the ladder carrying a bean bag in some fashion?"

It is evident that there are many other types of problems that can be structured.

It is essential that the teacher bring out and stress the important points with respect to the movements demonstrated. The approach is, "What is good?" "How can we do better?" "Are the different parts of the body being used?" The children can be then sent back to the movement areas and explore further based on suggestions.

In the beginning stages of the activity, demonstrations and ideas widen the children's perspective. Contrast should be brought in. A heavy movement followed by a light movement, or a light walk followed by a leap provide examples of contrast. Thus the pattern of the problem can follow in this fashion: (1) a variety of movements by the children, (2) selection of contrasting movements, (3) narrowing the field for repetition of selected types of movements, and (4) improving the quality of the selected movements.

Keys to the child creating a variety of responses and contrasting movement lie in the following:

Body	Movement	On Equipment
Shape	Locomotor	On and off
Speed	Transfer objects	Over
Direction	Roll	Through
Level	Twist	Across
Size	Turn	Under
Part of	Spin	Around
the body	Balance	In and out
	Imitate	

In summary,

Movement exploration using the broad problem approach has the following characteristics:

1. Children move about freely on their own initiative in the playing area.
2. Children are individually creative and inventive finding out everything they can do within the limits of the movement problem.
3. Children are guided by the teacher to show contrasting qualities of movement within the scope of the problem.
4. An opportunity to become more proficient in movement patterns selected by the child should be the right of each child.

Exploration Using Running, Leaping, Stopping, and Change of Direction

A partially structured exploration activity can be done using running as the basic activity. The formation should be by squads in squad column with the stipulation that the squad members follow each other when the person in front is half way across the area. The children run across an area 20 to 30 yards wide, depending upon the age level of the children. When the children have completed a run across the area, the squads are reformed on the other side awaiting directions to come back.

The following running variations can be done as the children run across the area.

Run as lightly as possible
Run high on the toes
Run on the heels
As you run, bounce as high as you can
Run with tiny, fast steps
Run with giant strides
Run with high knee action
Mix in giant leaps with your run
Run backward
Run forward half way and backward the rest
Run backward half way and forward the rest
As you run across, turn around (right) completely and continue across
The same, but turn to the left
Run slowly and then suddenly fast
Run with an exaggerated arm movement
Run with a goose step movement

Cross your feet over each time as you run
Run low touching the ground on either side alternately
Run low touching the ground with both hands as you go along
Run forward looking back over your right shoulder
The same, except look back over the left shoulder
Run zig zag, that is--changing direction every few steps
Run to the center, stop and continue
Run forward, stop with the right side forward, then another stop with the left side forward
Run forward and stop. Come back three steps and stop again. Continue in original direction
Try a two count stop with a definite "one, two" slap on the ground with the feet.
Try a hop, step, and a jump and then continue
Run sideways. Run sideways with the other side

The children can devise other combinations to try out. Be sure that the children understand and use good running form. Skipping, galloping, and other locomotor movements can be included in the combinations.

Exploring With Balls, Wands, and Other Objects

Many different play objects lend themselves to movement exploration. Balls, bean bags, wands, ropes, hoops, and other play tools offer good possibilities.

Balls. Proper techniques should be stressed in handling various kinds and sizes of balls. Children should be encouraged to explore and seek understandings about handling balls by catching, throwing, bouncing, rolling, and dribbling. Different ways of batting a ball with the hand can be investigated. Children may combine walking, bouncing, and other locomotor movements. A child can clap, turn, jump, or use other movements while exploring the range of ball bouncing possibilities.

Music is excellent to stimulate ball bouncing possibilities and to provide a basis for dribbling skills.

Bean Bag Tossing and Throwing

Activities using bean bags are excellent exploratory activities for primary children. They provide good opportunity for throwing and catching skills, promoting good hand-eye coordination. All activities should be bi-lateral, developing both the right and left sides or limbs. There should be enough bean bags so that each child may have one for his exclusive use. Activities should consider the use of all parts of the body including the arms, legs, head, and trunk.

The following suggested routines will provide for the teacher and the children ideas upon which other activities can be developed. The activities are classified into the following categories:

1. Individual activities
2. Activities with a partner
3. Relays using bean bags
4. Suggested games

Individual Activities

1. Toss upward and catch. One hand, both hands, back of hands
   Toss overhead, turn and catch
   Toss upward, turn completely around and catch
   Toss upward, touch the floor and catch
   Toss forward, run and catch
   Toss overhead from one side to the other
   Toss from hands behind back overhead to front
   Toss overhead, catch with hands behind back
   Toss around the body, under the leg, back hand behind back, etc. and catch
2. Balance bean bag on instep. Walk, hop
   Swing leg forward and back with bag balanced on instep
   Toss to self from toe. From knee. From heel
   Place bean bag on both feet and toss to self
   Place bean bag between feet and toss to self
   Place bean bag between feet and jump several times
3. From lying on back position--
   Toss to self from various arm positions
   Toss bag to self from toe. From both feet
   Using both feet, bring bean bag overhead and deposit back of head. Try

bringing it up and depositing to the side.
4. With bean bag on head, walk, run, skip, hop, jump without losing bag
   Toss bag forward from head to hands. Toss sideways and catch. Toss backward.
   Toss bean bag forward for distance from head
5. Pick up with bare foot, using the toes, and set down
   Pick up with the bare foot and throw to self. Use right and left
   Throw overhead with the bare foot and catch
   Pick up with the bare foot and hop
   Throw into the waste basket with a bare foot hold
6. From a standing position, throw bean bag into the air. Sit down quickly and catch
   Begin with sitting position, throw and stand up and catch. Repeat with a lying down sequence.
7. Try juggling with 2 bags. Try with 3 bags
8. With bean bag balanced on head, sit down, get up. Lie down, get up.
9. With the bean bag pressed between the knees, hop like a kangaroo

Partner Activities

1. Toss back and forth using different types of throws--right hand, left hand, under leg, around the back, etc. Center as in football.
2. Toss to partner with feet--toe, both feet (on top and held between), heel bare foot.
3. Toss with bean bag balanced on head, elbow, knee.
4. With back to the partner, take Bunny Hop position. With bag held between feet, kick bag back to partner
5. Use two bags at a time. Each with a bag, throw back and forth at the same time.
   Try tossing both bags at the same time, using various means of throwing
   Try keeping three bags moving between two people.
6. Stand facing away from each other, 4 to 5 feet apart. Toss overhead and catch
7. Toss out in various directions so as to make partner move and catch
8. With one partner standing still, have the other partner run around him in

a circle tossing the bag back and forth between them.

9. Have partners sit tailor (cross-legged) fashion about 10 feet apart. Throw and catch with various styles. Toss from various other sitting positions with the bag balanced on the toes or instep.

Relays and Games

There are many games and relays using bean bags which can be used to round off a session of practice in bean bag activities. The teacher is referred to the sections on these activities.

Chapter 10

Rhythmical Activities Primary Grades

Fundamental Rhythms
Creative Movement and Rhythm
Singing Games and Folk Dances
Games Using Rhythmic Background

Rhythmic movement should be a part of each child's school experience. Children have a natural love for rhythmic movement and for using the body in expressive movement. For a child, such movement is both a need and a delight. Not only are dance activities a tool for self-expression, but inherent in rhythmics are excellent possibilities for physical development. Progress toward the perfection of simple skills is enhanced by the accompaniment of rhythm.

Through gross body movements and locomotor patterns, children gain better appreciation and understanding of the use of their bodies. Several other important objectives grow out of the program of rhythmics. Certainly, it is an important goal for each child to be able to keep time --to be able to move in keeping with the rhythm. An appreciation of the place that rhythmic activity has in our lives is another important immediate goal. This probably will be gained in proportion to the pleasure and satisfaction which children derive from dance activities.

Developmental possibilities for fitness are high in a well-conducted rhythmic program, particularly in the types of activities stressed on the primary level. Vigorous movements and gross body activities make up many of the rhythms for primary children. Rhythmic activities offer a maximum of participation for children as an entire class or a good portion of it can be active at one time. Stimulated by the desire for imitation and self-expression, movement experiences are carried sufficiently to the point where good fitness values can accrue.

Movement expression through rhythm offers good opportunities for incidental and direct teaching in body mechanics and posture. The proper carriage of the body and the most efficient ways of moving should be included in the teaching of rhythmics. With the encouragement of an appropriate rhythm, children accept naturally postural coaching and correction as a part of the teaching procedure.

The program of rhythmical activities for the primary grades is divided into three general areas. These are:

1. Fundamental rhythms
2. Creative movement and rhythm
3. Singing games and folk dances

Fundamental Rhythms

Fundamental rhythms include those rhythmic activities which provide experience in the fundamental forms of locomotor and non-locomotor movements. The following movement patterns are basic to such a program:

LOCOMOTOR MOVEMENTS
Even types--walking, running, hoping, leaping, jumping
Uneven types--skipping, galloping, sliding
NON-LOCOMOTOR MOVEMENTS
Simple movements--bending, turning, twisting, swinging, swaying, falling
Mimetics--pushing, striking, lifting, throwing, pulling

The fundamental rhythm program sets the basis for rhythmic movement in all forms of dance activities. Essentially, it is movement education using the medium of rhythm. Good fitness values are present as children learn to move efficiently and rhythmically. In addition, the big muscle and gross body movements stimulated by background rhythm offer good developmental possibilities.

In practice, the program depends much upon the teacher to initiate and guide the simple patterns. That the rhythms be conducted in an atmosphere of fun and enjoyment is important. Furthermore, the accompaniment should be suitable and proper for the movement to be experienced. For accompaniment, three sources of rhythm are generally found suitable.

The first of these is the tom-tom or drum. Commercial varieties are available but reasonably satisfactory substitutes can be made from simple materials. Using a #10 tin can with both the top and bottom removed, a piece of sheet rubber, plastic, or parchment can be stretched on both ends tight enough for a striker to make the beat.

The second source of accompaniment is the record player. From many sources* specialized rhythm record sets are available. The sets are excellent, and the records contain short selections (3 to 4 on a side) marked with the type of movement for which the music was designed. In addition, many standard records such as polkas, marches, dances, fox-trots, schottisches, and other music selections with good accent and rhythm are useful. Many of the latter can be secured at used record sales for small amounts. The teacher should consider building up a personal collection.

Third source of rhythm is the piano. The piano offers excellent possibilities but does demand a reasonable degree of skill or the program will suffer. It has a second drawback that if the teacher plays and follows the music visually, it is difficult to observe the progress of the children.

Methodology

The element of creativity must not be stifled in a program of fundamental movements. The instruction can be directed toward a specific movement (like walking), and a reasonable range of acceptability can be established. In other words--we are practicing walking, but we can walk in many different ways. The following pattern can serve as a guide in a lesson using fundamental rhythms.

1. With the children comfortable, let them listen to the music. Discuss with them such elements present as:
   Tempo--the speed of the music
   Meter--the way the beats are put together in measures. Common meters are 2/4, 3/4, 4/4, and 6/8.

* See list of sources in the appendix.

Intensity--the force of the music, the loud, soft, light, or heavy quality of the music.
Accent--the notes which carry the heavier emphases.
Beat--the even or uneven quality.
   As the children listen for phrasing, they can note any special changes or effects which are present in the music.
2. To gain a sense of the beat, the children can clap hands to the rhythm. Other simple rhythmic movements done with the hands, arms, legs, or feet can help get the feel of the music.
3. The children should now move about the room, using the basic movement selected. Movement should be free, informal, and in every direction instead of around the room in a circular pattern. Children should be encouraged to experiment with directional changes and other variations. Often the teacher can call a halt and have one of the children demonstrate a novel and interesting movement which the child employed.
4. Many variations and combinations can be used to lend variety and reinforce the learning potential of the lesson.
5. Discussions can be held with the children concerning the performance with respect to the right and wrong ways of moving and what they should remember about the skills.

IDEAS TO UTILIZE DIFFERENT MOVEMENT FUNDAMENTALS. In exploring the range of ideas to use movement, the following suggestions should be of value. The resourceful and imaginative teacher together with the aid of the children can make use of these ideas and others of their own fabrication to make up interesting lessons in movement.

The Natural Movement. For each of the movements, there is what might be termed the "standard" or "natural" movement. This means that there is, for example, a correct way to walk and children should recognize and learn the correct fundamentals. Variations and ideas should proceed from this base.

Body Variations. The different positions of the arms and legs can provide many ways of moving. One can perform high on the toes, with toes in or out, on the heels, with stiff knees, kicking high in front or rearward, with knees brought up high, in a crouched position, and many other positions.

Arms can be swinging at the sides or held stiff, held out in front or overhead, moving in circles or different patterns, and in other poses. The body can be bent forward, backward, sideward, twisted, or turned. By combining different positions of the arms, legs, and body, many interesting variations of position can be assumed by the children.

Space Patterns. The child can interpret the music in terms of space patterns and directions. He can pretend to be big or little, wide or narrow, up or down. In directions, there can be frequent and regular (or irregular) changes of direction. The individual in moving on the floor or surface can form pathways of geometric or other figures. By tracing circles, zigzags, triangles, squares, figure eights, lines and other patterns by his movement, he has a more interesting and educational experience.

Time Factors. Movement can be done at different speeds and using different time combinations. He may move rapidly or slowly. His speed can be increased or decreased. Movements may be in even or uneven time.

Intensity. The force of the rhythm can be interpreted with a light, moderate, or heavy emphasis. The movement of the individual can be strong or weak depending upon the quality of the rhythmic background.

Fundamental Movement Patterns

In working with fundamental rhythmic patterns, a good rhythmic beat pattern is basic. The tom-tom is especially valuable in working with children in basic rhythm teaching. The tom-tom provides an easy way to vary the tempo, accents, and other characteristics of the basic beat. Stops and starts, changes to different rhythms, and many other innovations are possible with skillful handling of the tom-tom. Combinations of different rhythms can be put together easily and effectively with this instrument.

Appropriate records, particularly those which are designed especially for fundamental movements, should be a part of the equipment for every school. On the commercial market, records set for fundamental movement work are available in a variety of approaches.

The teacher should consider at times having the children provide the rhythmic background. While it is of value in having children have this experience, it needs to be recognized that a poor rhythmic accompaniment can nullify much of the effectiveness of a good rhythmic lesson.

In the sections which follow, movement fundamentals are analyzed, and some ideas are presented based on a particular fundamental movement or combination of movements.

WALKING. The weight of the body is transferred from the heel to the ball of the foot and then to the toes for the push-off for the next step. The toes are pointing straight ahead with the arms swinging freely from the shoulder in opposition to the feet. The body is erect and the eyes are focused straight ahead at eye level. Legs are swung from the hips with the knees bent only enough to clear the foot from the ground.

Some ways that walking can be used as an activity are:

1. Walk forward one phrase (8 counts) and change directions. Continue to change at the end of each phrase.
2. Use high steps during one phrase and low steps during the next.
3. Walk forward for one phrase and sidewards during the next. The side step can be a draw step or it can be of the grapevine type. To do a grapevine step to the left, lead with the left foot with a step directly to the side. The right foot crosses behind the left and then in front on the next step with that foot. The pattern is a step left, cross right (behind), step left, cross right (in front), and so on.
4. Children can be partners in movement patterns, facing each other with hands joined. One child pretends to be pulling and walks backwards, while the other child walks forward and pretends to push.
5. Walk slowly and gradually increase the tempo. Begin fast and decrease.
6. Walk in various directions while clapping hands in front and behind alternating. Try clapping hands under the thighs at each step or clap hands above the head.
7. Walk forward four steps, turn completely around in four steps. Repeat.
8. While walking, bring up the knees and slap with the hands on each step.
9. On any one phrase take four fast steps (one count to each step) and two slow steps (two counts to each step).
10. Walk on heels, toes, or with a heavy tramp.
11. Walk with a smooth gliding step or walk silently.

12. Gradually lower the body while walking (going down stairs) and raise yourself again (going up stairs).
13. Use a waltz with good beat and walk to it accenting the first beat of each measure. Add a sway of the body to the first beat of the measure.
14. Walk high on tip-toes, rocking back and forth.

RUNNING. Running should be done lightly on the toes. It should be a controlled run and not a dash for speed. Children may cover some ground on the run or they can run in place.

Running should be done with a slight body lean. The knees are bent and lifted. The arms swing back and forth from the shoulders with a bend at the elbows.

Many of the suggested movements for walking are equally applicable to running patterns. Some additional suggestions are listed.

1. Walk during a phrase of music and then run for an equal length of time.
2. Run in different directions turning at times.
3. Lift the knees as high as possible while running.
4. Run and touch different spots on the floor or on the wall.

SKIPPING. Skipping is actually a series of step-hops done with alternate feet. To teach a child to skip, ask him to take a step with one foot and then take a small hop on the same foot. He now takes a step with the other foot and a hop on that foot. Skipping should be done on the balls of the feet with the arms swing to shoulder height in opposition to the feet.

Almost all of the combinations suggested for walking and running are useful for skipping movements. Combinations of skipping, walking, and running can be devised in many different fashions.

HOPPING. In hopping, the body is sent up and down by one foot. The body lean, the other foot, and the arms serve to balance the movement. Hopping on one foot should not be sustained too long. Children should change to the other foot often.

Some variations and combinations for hopping include:

1. Hop as a bouncing ball. Hop very high gradually reducing the height. The procedure can be reversed.
2. Hop in the direction used by a line, crossing back and forth over the line each time.
3. Draw a small circle (about 18 inches across) on the floor. Hop across, in

and out of the circle.
4. Hop in different figures like a circle, triangle, square, etc.
5. Trace out numbers by hopping. Try writing short words by hopping.
6. Alternate big and little hops. Form other combinations.
7. Hop on one foot a specific number of times and change to the other foot.
8. Turn around hopping in place.

JUMPING. Jumping, as the term is used in fundamental movements, means to take off with both feet and land on <u>both</u> feet. The arms aid in the jump with an upswing, and the movement of the body helps lift the weight along with the force of the feet. A jumper lands lightly on the balls of his feet with his knees bent.

The suggestions listed for hopping can be applied to jumping. In addition, the teacher can devise other movment patterns such as these:

1. Jump with the body stiff and arms held at the sides.
2. Jump and turn in the air. Quarter, half, and even full turns can be done to rhythm. Work gradually into full turns.
3. Combine jumping in combination with hopping, walking, running, and skipping.
4. Increase and decrease the speed of jumping.
5. Land with feet apart or crossed. Alternate feet forward and back.

LEAPING. Leaping is an elongated step and designed to cover distance or go over a low obstacle. Leaping is usually combined with running as a series of leaps is difficult to maintain. Leaping can be included in a running sequence using the music phrase as the cue. An excellent piece to use for leaping is Pop Goes the Weasel. The youngsters can take a leap on the "Pop" part of the piece.

SLIDING. Sliding is done usually to the side. It is a one-count movement with the leading foot stepping out to the side and the other foot following quickly. A novel way to use sliding is to head in a direction with a definite number of slides and then do a half turn in the air and continue the slides leading with the other foot but retaining the original direction.

GALLOPING. Galloping is similar to sliding but the progress of the individual is in a forward direction. One foot leads and the other is brought up rapidly to it. The hands can be in a position as if holding the reins of a horse. The leading foot can be changed frequently. Since later in the rhythmic program the gallop is used to teach the polka, it is important that the children learn to change the leading foot. The leading foot can be changed after a series of eight gallops with the same foot leading. Later, the changes can be reduced to four gallops and finally changing after two gallops.

DRAW STEP. The draw step is a two-count movement to either side. A step is made directly to the side and on the second count the other foot is drawn up to it. The cue is made by "left (or right); close; left, close; left, close; etc."

OTHER MOVEMENTS. Non-locomotor movements like swinging, bending, turning, twisting, circling, stretching, flexion, and extension offer many possibilities. The dramatic element appealing to the child's imagination should be exploited. A child should not just bend--he should bend like a tree in a heavy wind. Similarly, he should spin like a top, turn like a soldier, etc.

Creative Movement and Rhythm

The creative rhythm program is generally divided into two categories. The first is called identification rhythms, while the second is the dramatic type. In either case, the basic feature of the creative rhythm program is that ideas and thoughts can be interpreted through movement. An atmosphere of creative freedom must be a part of each lesson. Children need to be encouraged to explore, interpret, and express themselves in movement as they react to the rhythm.

For both types of rhythms, there are many sources of ideas in the child's world. The home, zoo, farm, industry, city, make-believe world, and literature provide a rich source of material.

Identification Rhythms

The basis of this rhythmic type is imitation or the idea of "becoming something." The child in his own mind has taken on the identity of one of the following objects and proceeds to interpret this identity to the accompaniment of the rhythm used.

1. Animals--elephants, ducks, seals, chickens, rabbits, cats, etc.
2. People--soldiers, Indians, clowns, firemen, sailors, workers, etc.
3. Play Objects--see-saws, swings, rowboats, balls, toys, etc.
4. Make-believe World--fairies, dwarfs, witches, giants, dragons, pixies, etc.
5. Machines--trains, planes, automobiles, elevators, tractors, etc.

Many modern record sets have excellent music for the many characterizations.

Dramatic Rhythms

In a dramatic rhythm, the children act out an idea, a story, a familiar event, or an ordinary procedure.

An example of how an idea can be exploited for a rhythmic lesson of creativity is in the "Wind and Leaves." One or more children are chosen to be the "Wind," and the remainder of the children are the "Leaves." Two kinds of rhythm are needed. The first indicates the blowing of the "Wind." The second rhythm is quieter and stimulates the "Leaves" to flutter to the ground after the wind has stopped. Thus, the story divides itself into two parts, each of which offers many possibilities of creativity.

Rhythm 1. Fast, high, shrill -- indicating the blowing of the "Wind." The intensity and the tempo would illustrate the speed and force of the wind.
Rhythm 2. Slow, measured, light beat to match the "Leaves" fluttering in the still air and finally coming to rest at various positions on the ground.

During the first rhythm, the children representing the "Wind" can show how they would represent a heavy blow. While this is going on, the "Leaves" show what they feel it means to be blown about.

During the second rhythm, the "Wind" is still and the "Leaves" are fluttering to the ground.

Other characterizations could be added. "Street Sweepers" could come along and sweep the "Leaves" up.

Other ideas useful for dramatic rhythms are:

1. Building a house, garage, or other project.
2. Making a snow man. Throwing snowballs. Going skiing.
3. Flying a kite. Going hunting or fishing. Going camping.
4. Acting out stories which include Indians, cowboys, firemen, engineers.
5. Interpreting familiar stories like the Sleeping Beauty, The Three Bears, Little Red Riding Hood, and others.

6. Building from household task ideas like chopping wood, picking fruit, mowing the lawn, cleaning the yard.
7. Celebrating holidays like Halloween, Fourth of July, Thanksgiving, Christmas.

Methodology

Both identification and dramatic rhythms have in common the basic purpose that the child reacts creatively and rhythmically to the selected rhythm. However, the approach differs. In an identification rhythm, the child should listen to the music, determine its quality and characteristics, and then act creatively as he feels. As the children listen to the music, they can look for answers to questions like these. What does the music tell us to do? What does the music make us think of? How can we move in keeping with the music? These are some of the important questions to be answered by the activity of the children.

In a dramatic rhythm, the idea may be expanded and the basic pattern set. Next, the children can devise a suitable rhythmic pattern for the plan of action. This could take most any form. Record selections, piano selections, a drum, or a rhythm band would provide suitable rhythmic background.

The teacher aids in setting the stage, and the children carry the activity to its point of fulfillment in the event or story selected. The teacher should be careful of setting preconceived standards for the children and attempting to hold to these. An idea may be expanded in many directions, and success in the activity can be judged by the degree the children have been able to interpret freely and creatively.

Creativity Using Balls and Ropes

A fruitful area for creativity for primary children is found in the application of rhythm to ball skills and individual rope jumping. To have the children get full value for such activities, a sufficient number of ropes and balls is needed. While the schools normally have a complement of volleyballs and playground balls, the supply can be augmented by small balls of various types. Ideally, each child should have a ball. Sponge balls or other balls that can be used for bouncing are

relatively inexpensive. Discarded tennis balls from a tennis team can be had in some localities where tennis is a varsity sport. The children themselves generally have a ball or two at home. These could be contributed to a central supply for the class or could be kept on an individual basis.

BALL SKILLS. The following ball skills lend themselves well to rhythm:

1. Bounce and catch. Bounce a number of times and then catch. Various combinations.
2. Throwing against a wall and catching. Volleying against a wall.
3. Bouncing continuously (dribbling). Dribble in place.
   Dribble under the legs. Also, dribble behind the individual.
   Dribble and move. Form circles, triangles, and other patterns. Dribble forward, backward, sideward, stop and go.
   Dribble using different locomotor movements--hopping, jumping, and sliding.
4. Passing the ball from one child to another in rhythm. Vary with bounce passes.

A selected polka with a definite beat makes a suitable selection for dribbling. If the record player has a variable speed control, a finer adjustment can be made coordinating the tempo of the record with the dribbling skills.

For the other bounce and catch skills, a little experimentation by the teacher with various selections will uncover suitable music. A number of firms now produce music especially made for various bouncing, dribbling, and catching skills. The sets of records for basic rhythms usually have numbers suitable for various skills using balls.

ROPE JUMPING SKILLS. Rope jumping skills lend themselves well to rhythmic accompaniment. A polka, fast march, or fox trot provides a suitable rhythm. The speed is critical, and the record player should have a variable speed control.

Selected rope jumping stunts and directions for instruction are found in Chapters 18 and 29.

COMBINING ROPE JUMPING AND BALL SKILLS. Children can be paired off around the room. A circle formation could be utilized or the pairs placed in a scattered formation so each child has enough room for the activity. One partner in each pair has a rope and the other a ball. After a period of participation on an individual basis, each performing with the assigned object, the children exchange. This has some advantages in that rope jumping is a strenuous activity. By alternating with the less active ball skills, the children welcome the change and recover for another period of jumping.

Singing Games and Folk Dances

Singing games and folk dances are considered by some as distinctly different rhythm activity types, but sometimes this difference is difficult to distinguish. A singing game is described as a dance where the children sing verses, and the words give direction to the movements. A folk dance is defined as a traditional dance of a given country. There may be considerable variation in the movement patterns in a singing game depending upon how the children follow and interpret the action picture of the words. In a folk dance, a definite pattern of dance routine is usually set up and followed. From a strict sense, little variation is permitted from the traditional dance pattern, but the practice in the elementary school has been to use many variations.

None of the folk dances for primary children involve special dance steps. Rather, the simple fundamental locomotor movements are the basis for the dances. The more specialized steps as the two-step, polka, schottische, waltz, and others are a part of the intermediate level program.

METHODOLOGY. Children should be organized into the activity as soon as possible. The teacher should proceed from the familiar to the unfamiliar, from the simple to the more complex, from dancing alone to with a partner. Tempo should be set as slow as possible for learning consistent with the activity, later moving to the faster speed.

The teacher needs to consider the parts relationship to the whole. A few simple dances can be taught as a whole, but usually the dance should be broken down into a number of workable parts. Particularly, this is true when there is a number of verses in a singing game. The teacher should select the largest workable part which the children can handle at one time. After this is learned satisfactorily, instruction proceeds to the other parts.

In some cases, it may be necessary to practice or review a locomotor movement that is important to the dance. Appropriate music for the movement should be selected or the music from the dance selection used.

The teacher should have definite starting and stopping signals for the children such as "ready and begin," "with the music," "and stop."

In the lower grades, the teacher need not be too concerned with strict mechanics. Children should be held to reasonable standards for their ages. To hold to standards which are too high breeds frustration and kills some of the enjoyment in the activity. The dance and practice sessions, however, should be repeated often enough so that the movements and the activities are reasonably learned. Individual help should be given where needed, but the majority of the class should not be held to the pace of the slow learner.

A balance of activity and rest should be provided. The children can sit in place on the floor to make analysis and carry on discussions about the dance, the music, or the movements.

Where a number of verses are to be learned for singing games, preliminary study can be done in the classroom before the activity period. The teacher can write the verses on the blackboard and discuss with the children the actions to be followed by the dancers.

Time is saved if a monitor can be sent into the dance room or area to warm up and try the machine before the other children come in. When the class comes in, the activity can then begin without undue delay. Third graders are quite capable of handling this assignment and younger children with training can be of aid.

In presenting a particular folk dance or singing game, the following steps provide a logical sequence of progression.

1. Background. Name the activity, give something of its background, and discuss the nature or the meaning of the dance. If pertinent, bring in the life and customs of the people from whom the dance originated.
2. Analyzing the Music. Have the children listen critically to the music and analyze it with respect to its tempo, mood, rhythmic qualities, and major parts.
3. Learning the Music and the Verses. The children can clap to the beat with heavier claps for the accents or first beat of each measure. In a singing game, the children should learn the

words and sing the song. If the words can be on a blackboard or on a cardboard poster, learning is faster and time is saved. Generally, it is better to learn only one verse a time and put this to action before proceeding with the others. However, if the learning of the verses is done in the classroom before the activity period, then all should be learned.

4. Learning the Dance by Parts. Select and teach the largest part of the dance that can be learned by the children at one time. The children should move into formations quickly and naturally by word directions. To secure partners easily on the primary level two suggestions are offered. Have the boys form a line on one side of the room and the girls on the other. They now face the same end of the room, move in column formation toward each other, and then walk down the center with a partner. The line of partners can now be directed around into the proper formation. The majority of the dances on the primary level using partners are in a double circle formation, boys on the inside, and all facing counter clockwise. A second method of getting partners is to have the girls form a single circle, facing counter clockwise. The boys form another circle inside this one, also facing counterclockwise. The teacher can have the boys walk forward in a circle in line of direction until told

to stop. Boys now pair off with the girls nearest to them.

If steps are done with a partner, it may be feasible to have the children practice the movements alone first. After sufficient skill is mastered, the movement is done with a partner. Enough drill and practice are needed so the children can derive satisfaction and enjoyment from the activity.

5. Combining the Parts. After the parts have been mastered, the dance or singing game should be put together in proper sequence. If necessary, the instruction may need to retrace and practice the more difficult parts. Skills can be polished up as the children repeat the dance.

6. Variations. The teacher should be alert to possible variations of the dance. Partners should be changed often. An easy way is to ask the boys to move ahead one partner.

Formations for Singing Games and Folk Dances for Primary Grades

The illustrated formations presented below cover almost all of the singing games and dances used in the primary grades. The teacher should be able to verbalize the formation, and the children should be able to take their places in formations without confusion. The formations are listed under single circle, double circle, or longways (double line) categories.

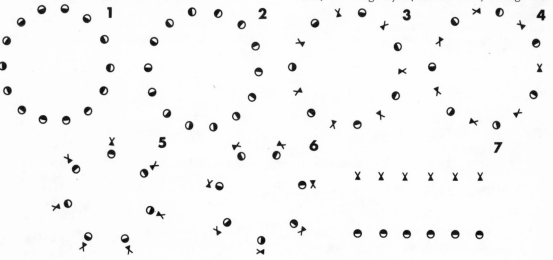

Single Circle
1. All facing center
2. All facing counter clockwise
3. By partners, all facing center
4. By partners, with partners facing

Double Circle
5. Partners facing each other
6. Partners side by side, facing counter clockwise

Longways Set
7. Double line, partners facing

*First Grade--Singing Games and
Folk Dances*

The first grade singing games and folk dances are introductory in nature and involve simple formations and uncomplicated changes. The movements are primarily walking, skipping, and running. Only a few of the dances are done with partners so the problem of getting the boys and girls paired off as partners is not important. Most of the activities are quite flexible in nature, and the children can interpret the words and music in various ways.

The following list of activities are suggested for the first grade. They are placed in sequence for instruction, but this is not to be regarded as a rigid order. The teacher may wish to vary according to the needs and interests of the children. The skills needed for the dance are listed.

DANCES	SKILLS
Farmer in the Dell	Walking
London Bridge	Walking
The Muffin Man	Skipping
Baa Baa Blacksheep	Stamping, walking
Oats, Peas, Beans, and Barley Grow	Walking, skipping
Looby Loo	Skipping
Pussy Cat	Walking, draw step, jumping
The Thread Follows the Needle	Walking
I See You	Skipping, two-handed swing
Sing a Song of Sixpence	Walking
Dance of Greeting	Running, bowing
Hickory Dickory Dock	Running
Twinkle, Twinkle Little Star	Tiptoe steps
Chimes of Dunkirk	Sliding

FARMER IN THE DELL

Records: Victor 21618 and 45-5066 (Album E 87)
Folkraft 1182

Formation: Children are in a single circle with hands joined and facing the center. One child is chosen to be the farmer and stands inside the circle.

Verses:
1. The farmer in the dell
    The farmer in the dell
    Heigh-O! the dairy-O!
    The farmer in the dell

2. The farmer takes a wife
3. The wife takes a child
4. The child takes a nurse
5. The nurse takes a dog
6. The dog takes a cat
7. The cat takes a rat
8. The rat takes the cheese
9. The cheese stands alone.

Directions
Verse 1. The circle players walk to the left with hands joined while the farmer is deciding on a child to be selected for his "wife".
Verse 2. The farmer chooses another child who is led to the center and becomes his wife. The child selected joins hands with him, and they walk around the inside of the circle in the opposite direction the big circle is moving.
Verses 3 to 8. Each child in turn selected joins with the center group.
Verse 9. All children in the center with the exception of the child who is the "cheese" return to the outside circle. The circle stops and the children face the center clapping hands during this verse.

Suggestions: The game should be repeated until all children have had an opportunity to be in the center.

Variations:
1. Several farmers may be chosen to start. When the outer circle gets smaller, the children no longer can join hands.
2. Verse eight can be: "The cat chases the rat." During this the cat does chase the rat in and out of the circle with the children raising and lowering their joined hands to help the rat and hinder the cat. If the cat catches the rat, he gets to be the farmer for the next game. If not, the rat becomes the farmer. The rat must be caught during the singing of the verse.

LONDON BRIDGE

Records: Victor 20806

Formation: Single circle moving either clockwise or counter-clockwise. Two children are chosen to form the bridge. They face and join hands holding them high in the air representing a bridge ready to fall.

Verses:

1. London Bridge is falling down,
   Falling down, falling down.
   London Bridge is falling down
   My fair lady.

2. Build it up with iron bars, etc.
3. Iron bars will rust away, etc.
4. Build it up with gold and silver, etc.
5. Gold and silver I have not, etc.
6. Build it up with pins and needles, etc.
7. Pins and needles rust and bend, etc.
8. Build it up with penny loaves, etc.
9. Penny loaves will tumble down, etc.
10. Here's a prisoner I have got, etc.
11. What's the prisoner done to you, etc.
12. Stole my watch and bracelet too, etc.
13. What'll you take to set him free, etc.
14. One hundred pounds will set him free, etc.
15. One hundred pounds we don't have, etc.
16. Then off to prison he (or she) must go, etc.

Directions: All children pass under the bridge in a single line. When the words "My fair lady" are sung, the bridge falls and the child caught is a prisoner. He or she must choose either gold or silver and must stand behind the side of the bridge which represents his choice. No one must know which side is gold or silver until after he or she has made his choice as a prisoner. When all have been caught, the game ends with a tug-of-war.

Variation: Using more bridges will speed up the game.

THE MUFFIN MAN

Record: Folkraft 1180

Formation: Children are in a single circle, facing the center with hands joined. One child, the Muffin Man, is in the center.

Verses:

1. Oh, do you know the muffin man
   The muffin man, the muffin man?
   Oh, do you know the muffin man,
   Who lives in Drury Lane.

2. Oh, yes we know the muffin man, etc.
3. Four of us know the muffin man, etc.
4. Eight of us know the muffin man, etc.
5. Sixteen of us know the muffin man, etc.
6. All of us know the muffin man, etc.

Directions:

Verse 1. The children in the circle stand still and sing, while the Muffin Man skips around the circle. He chooses a partner by skipping in place in front of him. On the last line of the verse, "Who lives in Drury Lane," the Muffin Man and his partner go to the center.

Verse 2. The action is the same except two people now skip around in the circle and choose two partners.

Verse 3. The action is repeated with four skipping and four partners being chosen.

The verses continue until all children have been chosen. When all have been chosen, the last verse is sung while the children skip around the room.

BAA BAA BLACKSHEEP

Records: Folkraft 1191
Russell 700A
Victor E-83

Formation: Single circle, all facing center.

Verse:

Baa Baa Blacksheep, have you any wool?
Yes sir, yes sir, three bags full.
One for my master and one for my dame,
And one for the little boy who lives down
the lane.

Directions:

Line 1. Stamp three times, shake forefinger times.

Line 2. Nod head twice and hold up three fingers.

Line 3. Bow to the person on the right and then to the left.

Line 4. Hold one finger up high and walk around in a tiny circle again facing the center.

OATS, PEAS, BEANS, AND BARLEY GROW

Record: Victor 20214
              Folkraft 1182

Formation: Single circle with a "farmer" in the center.

Verses:

1. Oats, peas, beans, and barley grow,
   Oats, peas, beans, and barley grow
   You and I, or anyone else know
   Oats, peas, beans, and barley grow.

2. First, the farmer sows the seed,
   Then he stands and takes his ease,
   He stamps his foot and claps his hands
   And turns around to view his lands.

3. Waiting for a partner,
   Waiting for a partner,
   Open the ring and choose one in
   While we all gaily dance and sing.

4. Now you're married, you must obey
   You must be kind in all you say
   You must be kind, you must be good,
   And keep your wife in kindling wood.

Directions:

Verse 1. The children walk clockwise around
   the farmer.
Verse 2. All stand in place and follow the actions suggested by the words of the verse.
Verse 3. Circle players again move clockwise
   while the "farmer" choose a partner, which
   should be done before the end of the verse.
Verse 4. Everyone skips during this verse.
   The circle continues in the same direction
   it has been while the "farmer" and his partner (wife) skip in the opposite direction.

LOOBY LOO

Records: Victor 20214
               Russell 702
               Folkraft 1102

Formation: Single circle, all facing center
with hands joined.

Chorus: A chorus is repeated before each
verse. During the chorus all children skip
around the circle to the left.

   Here we dance looby loo
   Here we dance looby light
   Here we dance looby loo
   All on a Saturday night.

Verses:

1. I put my right hand in
   I take my right hand out
   I give my right hand a shake, shake,
      shake,
   And turn myself about.

2. I put my left hand in, etc.
3. I put my right foot in, etc.
4. I put my left foot in, etc.
5. I put my head way in, etc.
6. I put my whole self in, etc.

Directions: On the verse part of the dance,
the children stand still facing the center and
follow the directions of the words. On the
words "And turn myself about" they make a
complete turn in place and get ready to skip
around the circle.

   The movements should be definite and
vigorous. On the last verse, the child jumps
forward and then backwards, shakes himself
vigorously, and then turns about.

PUSSY CAT

Record: Russell 700B

Formation: Single circle, all facing center
with hands joined. One player, the "Pussy
Cat", is in the center. If desired, more than
one "Pussy Cat" can be in the center.

Verse:

   Pussy Cat, Pussy Cat, where have you been?
   I've been to London to visit the Queen!
   Pussy Cat, Pussy Cat, what did you there?
   I frightened a mouse from under her chair!

Chorus: The chorus is a repeat of the same
music but the children sing tra, la, la, la, etc.,
instead of the words.

Directions:
Line 1. Sung by the circle children as they
   walk counter-clockwise around the circle.
Line 2. Sung by the "Cat" as the children
   reverse the direction and walk around the
   other way.
Line 3. Sung by the children as they drop
   hands, walk toward the center, and shake
   a finger at the "Cat".
Line 4. Sung by the "Cat" who on the last
   word "chair" jumps high into the air, and
   the others pretend fright and run back to
   the circle.

Chorus:

    Line 1. Children take two draw steps (one to each measure) to the right followed by four stamps.

    Line 2. Repeat to the left.

    Line 3. Four steps (one to each measure) to the center.

    Line 4. Three steps backward in the same time as line three followed by a jump.

A draw step is made by stepping directly to the side and bringing the other foot in a closing movement. It is a step with one foot and a close with the other.

Variation: Have more than one "Pussy Cat" in the circle or have a number of smaller circles each with a "Pussy Cat".

THE THREAD FOLLOWS THE NEEDLE

Records: RCA Victor 22760 (Album E87)
              Pioneer 3015

Formation: A single line of about eight children is formed. Hands are joined and each child is numbered.

Verse:

The thread follows the needle
The thread follows the needle
In and out the needle goes
As mother mends the children's clothes.

Directions: The first child (#1) is the needle and leads the children forming stitches until the entire line has been sewn. When the music starts, the needle leads the line under the raised arms of the last two children (#7 and 8). When the line has passed under their arms, they turn and face the opposite direction, letting their arms cross in front of them. This forms the stitch.

The leader now repeats the movement and passes under the next pair of raised arms (#6 and 7). Number 6 is now added to the stitch when he reverses his direction. This is repeated until the entire line has been stitched, with the leader turning under his own arm to complete the last stitch.

To "rip" the stitch, children raise their arms overhead and turn back to original positions.

The game can be repeated with a new leader.

I SEE YOU

Records: Victor 20432
           Russell 726
           Folkraft 1197

Formation: The boys and girls stand in two longways sets as follows.

  (1) x x x x x x x boys
  (2) o o o o o o o girls

  (3) x x x x x x x boys
  (4) o o o o o o o girls

Lines 1 and 2 are facing lines 3 and 4. The space between the two middle lines (2 and 3) should be from ten to twelve feet.

Directions: Lines 1 and 4 are the active players. Each active player's partner is directly in front of him and stands with hands on the hips.

Measure:

1   The active players look over the partner's left shoulder in a peekaboo fashion.

2   Look over partner's right shoulder

3,4   On the "tra, la, la's" the tempo of the peekaboo is doubled so the child looks over left and right in each measure.

5,8   Repeat measure 1-4.

9,12   All children clap at the first note of the measure and the active players, passing to the left of their partners, meet in the center with a two-handed swing, skipping around once in a circle, clockwise.

13-16 All children clap again on the first note and the active player now faces his own partner and with a two-handed swing makes a clockwise turn with his partner. Partners now have changed places, and a new set of active players is ready for the next dance.

SING A SONG OF SIXPENCE

Records: Folkraft 1180
           Victor 22760
           Russell 700

Formation: Players are in circle formation facing the center. Six to eight players are crouched in the center as blackbirds.

Verses:

1. Sing a song of sixpence, a pocket full of
      rye,
   Four and twenty blackbirds, baked in a
      pie,
   When the pie was opened the birds began
      to sing,
   Wasn't that a dainty dish to set before
      the king?

2. The king was in his counting house,
      counting out his money,
   The queen was in the pantry, eating
      bread and honey,
   The maid was in the garden, hanging
      out the clothes,
   And down came a blackbird and snipped
      off her nose!

Directions:
Verse 1.
   Line 1. Players walk around in a circle.
   Line 2. Circle players walk with shortened
      steps toward the center of the circle with
      arms outstretched forward.
   Line 3. Players walk backward with arms
      now up. The blackbirds in the center fly
      around.
   Line 4. Circle players kneel as if present-
      ing a dish.
Verse 2. (blackbirds continue to fly around)
   Line 1, 2, and 3. Patomime action of words
      counting out money, eating, and hanging
      up clothes.
   Line 4. Each blackbird snips off the nose
      of a circle player who now becomes a
      blackbird for the next game.

DANCE OF GREETING

Records: Victor 45-6183
         Folkraft 1187
         Russell 726

Formation: Single circle, all facing center.
Each boy stands to the left of his partner.

Measures:

1. All clap, clap, and bow to partner (girl
   curtsies)
2. Repeat but turn backs to partner and bow
   to neighbor.
3. Stamp right, stamp left.

4   Each player turns around in four run-
      ning steps. (Measures 1-4 are re-
      peated)
5-8 All join hands and run to the right for
      four measures with a light running
      step (16 steps)
5-8 (repeated). Run with light steps in
      the opposite direction.

         Use a light slide in place of the
running step of measures 5-8.

HICKORY DICKORY DOCK

Record: Victor 22760

Formation: Children are in a double circle,
partners facing.

Verse:
   Hickory Dickory Dock, tick tock,
   The mouse ran up the clock, tick tock.
   The clock struck one, the mouse ran down
   Hickory, Dickory, Dock.

Directions:
Line 1. Stretch arms overhead and bend the
   body from side to side like a pendulum, finish with two stamps on "tick, tock."
Line 2. Repeat action of line one.
Line 3. Clap hands on "one." Join hands with
   partner and run to the right in a little circle.
Line 4. Repeat the pendulum swing with the two
   stamps.

TWINKLE, TWINKLE LITTLE STAR

Record: Childcraft EP-C4

Formation: Children are in a single circle,
facing in.

Verse:
   Twinkle, twinkle, little star.
   How I wonder what you are.
   Up above the world so high
   Like a diamond in the sky
   Repeat first line
   Repeat second line

Directions: Children are in a large enough
circle so they can come forward seven short
steps without crowding.
Line 1. Children have arms extended overhead
   and fingers extended and moving. Each
   child takes seven tiptoe steps toward the
   center of the circle.

85

Line 2. Continue with seven tiptoe steps in place making a full turn around.
Line 3. Each child makes a circle with his arms and hands, rocking back and forth.
Line 4. All form a diamond with the fingers in front of the face.
Line 5. With the arms overhead and the fingers extended, move backward to original place with seven tiptoe steps.
Line 6. Turn in place with seven tiptoe steps.

CHIMES OF DUNKIRK

Records: Victor 45-6176
Folkraft 1188

Formation: A single circle with boys and girls alternating. Partners face each other. Hands are on own hips.

Measures:
1-2 All stamp lightly left, right, left.
3-4 Clap hands overhead, swaying back and forth.
5-8 Join hands with partner and make one complete turn in place clockwise.
9-16 All join hands in a single circle facing the center and slide to the left (16 slides)

Second Grade--Singing Games and Folk Dances

The second grade includes many activities similar to those taught in the first grade. In addition, there is more emphasis on partner type dances and change of partners. The dance patterns tend to become more definite, and more folk dances are included. The movements are still confined primarily to the simple locomotor types with additional and varied emphasis in more complicated formations.

DANCES	SKILLS
Mulberry Bush	Walking or skipping
Did You Ever See a Lassie	Walking
Go Round and Round the Village	Walking
Shoemaker's Dance	Skipping
Jolly is the Miller	Marching
Shoo Fly	Walking, Skipping
Ach Ja	Walking, sliding
A Hunting We Will Go	Sliding, skipping

How D'ye Do, My Partner	Bowing, skipping
Rig-a-jig-jig	Walking, skipping
Broom Dance	Marching, skipping
The Popcorn Man	Jumping, skipping

MULBERRY BUSH

Record: Victor 20806

Formation: Single circle, facing center, hands joined.

Chorus:
Here we go round the mulberry bush
The mulberry bush, the mulberry bush
Here we go round the mulberry bush
So early in the morning.

Verses:
1. This is the way we wash our clothes, Wash our clothes, wash our clothes, This is the way we wash our clothes So early Monday morning.

2. This is the way we iron our clothes, (Tuesday morning)
3. This is the way we mend our clothes, (Wednesday morning)
4. This is the way we sweep our floor, (Thursday morning)
5. This is the way we scrub our floor, (Friday morning)
6. This is the way we make a cake, (Saturday morning)
7. This is the way we go to church, (Sunday morning)

Directions: The singing game begins with the chorus which is also sung after each verse. As each chorus is sung, the children skip (or walk) to the right. On the words "so early in the morning" each child drops hands and makes a complete turn in place.

During the verses, the children pantomime the actions suggested by the words. Encourage the children to use big and vigorous movements.

DID YOU EVER SEE A LASSIE

Record: Victor 45-5066
Folkraft 1183

Formation: Children are in a single circle, facing half left with hands joined. One child is in the center.

Verse:

Did you ever see a lassie, a lassie, a lassie?

Did you ever see a lassie do this way and that?

Do this way and that way, and this way and that way.

Did you ever see a lassie do this way and that.

Directions:

Measures:

1-8   Children with hands joined walk to the left in a circle. Since this is fast waltz time, there should be one step to each measure. The child in the center gets ready to demonstrate some type of movement.

9-16   All stop and follow the movement suggested by the child in the center.

As the verse starts over, the center child selects another to do some action in the center and changes places with him.

The word "laddie" should be substituted if the center person is a boy.

GO ROUND AND ROUND THE VILLAGE

Record: Folkraft 1191

Formation: Single circle, hands joined. Several extra players stand outside and scattered around the circle.

Verses:

1. Go round and round the village,
   Go round and round the village,
   Go round and round the village,
   As we have done before.

2. Go in and out the windows, etc.
3. Now stand and face your partner, etc.
4. Now follow me to London, etc.

Directions:

Verse 1:   Circle players move to the right and the extra players on the outside go the other way. All skip.

Verse 2:   Circle players stop and lift joined hands forming the windows. Extra players go in and out the windows finishing inside the circle.

Verse 3:   Extra players select partners by standing in front of them. Should select opposite sex.

Verse 4. The extra players and partners now skip around the inside of the circle while the outside circle skips the opposite way.

Variations:

1. All chosen players can continue and repeat the game until the entire circle has been chosen.

2. An excellent way is to have the boys in the circle and the girls as extra players. In this way, everyone will select and be selected as a partner. Reverse and put the girls in the circle and leave the boys as the extras.

SHOEMAKER'S DANCE

Record: Victor 20450
             Victor 45-6171
             Russell 750
             Folkraft 1187

Formation: Double circle, partners facing, boys on the inside.

Verse:

See the cobbler wind his thread,
Snip, snap, tap, tap, tap.
That's the way he earns his bread,
Snip, snap, tap, tap, tap.

Chorus:

So the cobbler blithe and gay,
Works from morn to close of day,
At his shoes he pegs away,
Whistling cheerily his lay.

Directions:

Measures:

1-2   Clenched fists are held in front about chest high. On "see the cobbler" one fist is rolled forward over the other three times. On "wind his thread" roll the fists over each other backwards three times.

3   Fingers of the right hand form a scissors and make two cuts on "snip, snap."

4   Double up fists and hammer one on top the other three times.

1-4   (repeated). Same action, except finish up with three claps instead of hammering fists.

Chorus: Partners join inside hands, outside hands on hips. All skip to the left around the room. Near the end of the chorus, all slow down face each other. All children take one step to the left to secure a new partner.

JOLLY IS THE MILLER

Records: Victor 45-5067 or 20214, E-87
Folkraft 1192

Formation: Double circle, partners with joined inside hands facing counter clockwise. Boys are on the inside. A Miller is in the center of the circle.

Verse:

Jolly is the Miller who lives by the mill;
The wheel goes round with a right good will
One hand on the hopper and the other on the sack;
The right steps forward and the left steps back.

Chorus: The children march counter clockwise with inside hands joined. During the second line when the "wheel goes round" the dancers should make their outside arms go in a circle to form a wheel. Children change partners at the words "right steps forward and the left steps back." The "Miller" then has a chance to get a partner. The child left without a partner becomes the "Miller."

SHOO FLY

Record: Folkraft 1102

Formation: All are in a circle with hands joined facing in. Boy stands with his girl on right.

Verse:

Shoo fly, don't bother me
Shoo fly, don't bother me
Shoo fly, don't bother me
I belong to Company G
I feel, I feel, I feel like a morning star
I feel, I feel, I feel like a morning star.

Directions: The dance is in two parts and finishes with a change of partners.

Measures:

1-2   Walk forward four steps toward the center of the circle swinging arms back and forth.

3-4   Walk four steps backward to place with arms swinging.

5-8   Repeat all of above

9-16   Each boy turns to the girl on his right, takes hold of both hands and skips around in a small circle, finishing so this girl will be on his left when the circle is reformed. His new partner is on his right.

        The dance is repeated with new partners.

Variation: For the second part of the dance to take the place of the two-handed swing, the following is interesting.

    Designate one couple to form an arch by lifting joined hands. This couple now moves forward toward the center of the circle. The couple on the opposite side move forward, under the arch, drawing the circle after it. When all have passed through the arch, the couple forming the arch turn under their own joined hands. The dancers now move forward to form a circle with everyone facing out. The dance is repeated with all facing out.

    To return the circle to face in again, the same couple again makes an arch and the lead couple backs through the arch, drawing the circle after them. The arch couple turn under their own arms.

    In this version, there is no change of partners.

ACH JA

Record: Evans, Child Rhythms, VII.

Formation: Double circle, partners facing counter clockwise, boys on the inside.

Verse:

When my father and my mother take the children to the fair,
Ach Ja! Ach Ja!
Oh, they have but little money, but it's little that they care
Ach Ja! Ach Ja!

Tra la la, tra la la, tra la la la la la la
Tra la la, tra la la, tra la la la la la la
Ach Ja! Ach Ja!

Directions:

Measures:

1-2   Partners walk eight steps in line of direction.

3   Partners drop hands and bow to each other.

4	Each boy now bows to the girl on his left, who returns the bow.
5-8	Measures 1-4 are repeated.
9-10	Partners face each other, join hands and take four slides in line of direction (CCW)
11-12	Four slides are taken clockwise.
13	Partners bow to each other.
14	Boy bows to girl on his left who returns the bow. To start the next dance, the boy moves quickly toward this girl who is his new partner.

A HUNTING WE WILL GO

Records: Folkraft 1191
Victor 45-5064
Victor E-87

Formation: Longways set with the children in two lines facing each other, boys in one line and girls in the other.

Verse:
Oh, a-hunting we will go,
A-hunting we will go,
We'll catch a fox and put him in a box
And then we'll let him go!

Chorus:
Tra, la, la, la, la, la, la,
etc.

Directions: Everyone sings.
Lines 1 & 2. Head couple with hands joined slides between the two lines to the foot of the set.
Lines 3 & 4. Head couples slides to original position.
Chorus. Couples join hands and skip in a circle to the left following the head couple. When the head couple reaches the place formerly occupied by the last couple in the line (foot couple), they form an arch under which the other couples skip. A new couple is now the head couple and the dance is repeated until each couple has had a chance to be at the head.

Variation:
1. On the chorus, the head couple separates, and each leads his own line down the outside to the foot of the set. The head couple meets at the foot and forms an arch for the other couples. The other dancers meet two by two and skip under the arch back to place.

2. The first two couples slide down the center and back on lines 1, 2, 3, and 4. Otherwise the dance is the same.

HOW D'YE DO, MY PARTNER

Records: Victor 21685
Folkraft 1190

Formation: Double circle, partners facing, boys on the inside.

Verse:
How d'ye do, my partner?
How d'ye do today?
Will you dance in the circle?
I will show you the way.

Directions:

Measures:

1-2	Boys bow to their partners.
3-4	Girls curtsey.
5-6	Boys offer right hand to girl who takes it with her right hand. Both turn to face counter clockwise.
7-8	Couples join left hands and are now in a skaters' position. They get ready to skip when the music changes.
1-8	Partners skip counter clockwise in the circle slowing down on measure 7. On measure 8 the girls stop and the boys move ahead to secure a new partner.

RIG-A-JIG-JIG

Record: Ruth Evans, Childhood Rhythms, Series VI

Formation: Single circle, all facing center, boys and girls alternating. One child is in the center.

Verse:
As I was walking down the street
Heigh-o, heigh-o, heigh-o, heigh-o,
A pretty girl I chanced to meet
Heigh-o, heigh-o, heigh-o.

Chorus:
Rig-a-jig-jig, and away we go,
away we go, away we go
Rig-a-jig-jig, and away we go,
Heigh-o, heigh-o, heigh-o.

Directions: While all sing, the center player

walks around the inside of the circle until the words "a pretty girl" and then stands in front of a partner. Girls choose boys and vice versa. He then bows to her on the last line of the verse.

He takes her hands in skaters' position and on the chorus skips around the inside of the circle while the circle players clap hands in time.

The dance is repeated with the partners separating and choosing new partners until all have been chosen.

On the second time the verse is sung, the words "a nice young man" or "a handsome man" can be substituted for "a pretty girl."

Variation: The dance can be done by alternating boys and girls and using the appropriate verses. Select four or five boys to begin in the center. They choose partners and after the skip return to the circle. The girls continue the dance choosing five more boys, and so on.

BROOM DANCE

Record: Victor 20448

Formation: Double circle, partners facing counter-clockwise with boys on the inside. An extra boy with a broom is in the center.

Verse:
One, two, three, four, five, six, seven,
Where's my partner, nine, ten, eleven?
In Berlin, in Stettin,
There's the place to find him (her) in.

Chorus:
Tra la la, etc.
(repeats the music)

Directions: The record has three changes of music and then a pause. The verse is sung during the first change and repeated during the second change. The chorus is the third change. During the verse, which is repeated, all march counter-clockwise. The boy in the center hands the broom to another boy and takes his place in the inner line. The boy with the broom then in turn hands the broom to another inner line member and takes his place, and so on. The one who has the broom after the two verses are sung (on the word "in") takes the broom to the center. He then pretends to sweep while the others skip with inside hands joined. If there are extra girls, the dance can be done with the girls exchanging the broom by making the direction of the march clockwise.

Variation I
The first verse is sung during the first music change and the children march as in the original dance. During the second music change, the following routine is done. Note that in this routine the broom may only be exchanged when the boys move to a new partner.
Routine for the second music change.

Measures

1-2	Beginning with the outside foot, take seven steps forward and pause on the eighth.
3-4	Beginning with the inside foot, take seven steps backward and pause as before.
5	Beginning on the outside foot, take three steps away and pause.
6	Beginning with the inside foot, take three steps in and pause.
7-8	Swing once around in place with a right elbow swing. As the boy comes back to place, he moves forward to the next girl. During the exchange of partners, the broom man gives the broom to another boy and takes his place.

Variation II
This routine is used during the first change of the music.

Boys and girls form separate lines facing each other about twenty feet apart. The broom man is in the center. The teacher holds the broom to one side.

Measures:

1-2	Lines advance toward each other with seven steps.
3-4	Lines retreat with seven steps.
5-6	Lines again advance seven steps.
7-8	Lines retreat seven steps until the word "in!" All, including the broom man, rush for a partner and get ready to march around the room. The player left goes to the center to become the new broom man. The new broom man now takes the broom from the teacher and the dance proceeds in the second and third changes of the music as in the original dance. Note that the broom should not be given to the broom man until after the first music change.

90

THE POPCORN MAN

Record: Folkraft 1180 (The Muffin Man)

Formation: Children are in a single circle, facing the center with hands at sides. One child the Popcorn Man, stands in front of another child of opposite sex.

Verses:
1. Oh, have you seen the Popcorn Man,
   The Popcorn Man, the Popcorn Man?
   Oh, have you seen the Popcorn Men,
   Who lives on - - - Street?

2. Oh, yes, we've seen the Popcorn Man,
   The Popcorn Man, the Popcorn Man.
   Oh, yes, we've seen the Popcorn Man,
   Who lives on - - - Street

Directions:

Verse 1. The children stand still and clap hands lightly with the exception of the Popcorn Man and his partner. These two join both hands and jump lightly in place keeping time to the music.

Verse 2. The Popcorn Man and his partner now skip around the inside of the circle individually and near the end of the verse each stands in front of a child, thus choosing new partners.

Verse 1 is now repeated with two sets of partners doing the jumping. During the repetition of Verse 2, four children now skip around the inside of the circle and choose partners. This continues until all the children are chosen.

Boys should choose girls and girls should choose boys for partners. The children should choose the name of a street which they would like to put into the verses.

Third Grade--Singing Games and Folk Dances

Most of the emphasis in the third grade shifts to the folk dance. A few singing games are included. Simple locomotor skills are still the basis of the movement patterns. Continued emphasis on the simple skills is made with more attention to sliding and draw steps. The formations tend to be more of the partner type with partner changes included in many of the dances. Some basic formations are introduced which are later used in more advanced dances in the intermediate grades.

DANCES	SKILLS
Paw Paw Patch	Skipping
Yankee Doodle	Marching, turning
Three Blind Mice	Skipping
Jump Jim Joe	Jumping, running draw steps
Carrousel	Draw steps, sliding
Children's Polka	Draw steps, running
Bleking	Bleking step, step-hops
Crested Hen	Step-hops, turning under
Hansel and Gretel	Bleking step, skipping
Gustaf's Skoal	Walking, skipping, turning
Csebogar	Skipping, sliding, draw steps, elbow swing

PAW PAW PATCH

Records: Victor 45-5066 Folkraft 1181

Formation: Children are in sets of four to eight couples, boys are in one line and the girls are in another on the boys right, all facing forward.

Verse:
1. Where, Oh where is sweet little Nellie,
   Where, Oh where is sweet little Nellie,
   Where, Oh where is sweet little Nellie,
   Way down yonder in the paw paw patch.

2. Come on, boys, let us find her, etc.
3. Pickin' up paw paws, puttin' in your basket, etc.

Description:

Verse 1. Girl at the head of her line turns to her right and skips around the entire group and back to place. All other remain in place and sing.

Verse 2. The first girl turns to her right again and follows the same path as in verse one. This time she is followed by the entire line of boys who beckon to each other.

Verse 3. Partners join inside hands, and skip around in a circle to the right following the head couple. When the head couple is at the foot of the line, they make an arch under which the other couples skip back to original formation, with a new head couple.

The entire dance is repeated until each couple has had a chance to be the head couple.

Instead of using the name "Nellie," the name of the girl at the head of the line can be sung.

YANKEE DOODLE

Record: Victor 22760
             Victor 45-5064

Formation: Children are in sets of threes. The sets are a line of three with a boy in the center and holding to a girl on either side of him. The sets are facing counter clockwise in a large circle formation.

Verse:

> Yankee Doodle came to town
> Riding on a pony,
> Stuck a feather in his hat
> And called it macaroni.

Chorus:

> Yankee Doodle keep it up,
> Yankee Doodle dandy;
> Mind the music and the step,
> And with the girls be handy.

Description: On the verse, the dancers march around the circle with knees up high like prancing ponies. Arms are swung back and forth.

On the first two lines of the chorus, the center dancer of each set takes the dancer on his right by the right hand and they walk (or skip) around each other. On the next two lines, he does the same with the left hand dancer but using the left hand. When the center dancer (boy) comes back to his place in the line of threes, he moves forward to the set ahead of him and the dance repeats.

THREE BLIND MICE

Record: None

Formation: Children are in a hollow square formation facing the inside of the square with six to eight on each side of the square. Each of the sides performs independently in turn as one part of the four-part round.

Verse:

> Three blind mice,
> Three blind mice,
> See how they run,
> See how they run,
> They all ran after the farmer's wife
> Who cut off their tails with a carving knife
> Did you ever see such a sight in your life
>   as
> Three blind mice

Description: Sides of the square are numbered 1, 2, 3, and 4. Each acts as one part of the round and begins in turn. All perform the same movements when their turn comes up as part of the round.

Line 1. Clap hands three times
Line 2. Stamp the floor three times
Line 3. Four skips forward
Line 4. Four skips backwards to place
Line 5. Turn in place with four light steps
Line 6. Face the center, raising one hand above the other and make a cutting motion.
Line 7. Put both hands over the ears with a rocking motion sideways.
Line 8. Clap hands three times.

Sing through twice. Do not overlap the lines at the corners or there will be crowding when the children skip forward.

JUMP, JIM JOE

Record: Folkraft 1180

Formation: Double circle, partners facing. Boys are on the inside. Both hands are joined.

Verse:

> Jump, jump, and jump, Jim Joe,
> Take a little twirl and away we go,
> Slide, slide, and stamp just so--and
> Take another partner and jump Jim Joe

Desription:

Line 1. Two slow and then three fast jumps in place.
Line 2. Partners run around each other clockwise in a small circle in place and return to position.
Line 3. With hands on hips each person moves to his left with two draw steps (step left, close right, step left, close right), followed by three stamps. Each person has a new partner.
Line 4. Join hands with the new partner and run around each other back to place, finishing the turn with three light jumps on the words, "Jump Jim Joe."

CARROUSEL

Record: Victor 45-6179
           Folkraft 1183

Formation: Children are in a double circle, all facing inward. The inner circle, representing the merry-go-round, join hands. The outer players, representing the riders, place hands on the hips of the partner in front of them.

Verse:

Little children, sweet and gay, carrousel is running, It will run to evening, Little ones a nickel, big ones a dime, Hurry up, get a mate, or you'll surely be too late.

Chorus:

Ha, ha, ha, happy are we,
Anderson and Peterson and Henderson and me,
Ha, ha, ha, happy are we
Anderson and Peterson and Henderson and me.

Description: During the verse, the children take slow draw steps (step, close) to the left. This is done by taking a step to the side with the left foot and closing with the right on count two. This gets the merry-go-round underway slowly. Four slow stamps replace the draw steps when the words "Hurry <u>up</u>, get a <u>mate</u>, or you'll <u>surely</u> be too <u>late</u>". A stamp is made on each of the underlined words. The circle now has come to a halt.

During the chorus, the tempo is increased and the movement is changed to a fast slide. Be sure to have the children take short, light slides. When the chorus is repeated, the children reverse the direction of the merry-go-round.

All sing during the dance.

CHILDREN'S POLKA (KINDERPOLKA)

Record: Victor 45-6179
Russell 750 Folkraft 1187

Formation: Single circle, partners facing. Hands are joined and extended sideways.

Although this dance is called a polka, it does not use the polka step.

Measures:

1-2 Take two draw steps to the center --step, close, step, close. Finish with three light stamps.

3-4 Repeat, moving away from the center.

5-8 Repeat measures 1-4.

9-10 Clap thighs with the hands and then the hands together in slow tempo. Clap hands to partner's hands in three fast claps.

11-12 Repeat 9-10.

13 Extend the right foot forward on the heel, place the right elbow in left hand, and shake the forefinger three times at partner.

14 Repeat, extending the left foot and using the left forefinger.

15 Turn self around in place using four running steps.

16 Face partner and stamp lightly three times.

BLEKING

Record: Victor 45-6169

Formation: Single circle, partners facing with both hands joined. Boys are facing counter-clockwise and girls clockwise.

Part I. The Bleking Step

Measures:

1 Hop on the left foot and extend the right heel forward with the right leg straight. At the same time thrust the right hand forward. Hop on the right foot, reversing the arm action and extending the left foot to rest on the heel.

2 Repeat the action with three quick changes--left, right, left.

3-4 Beginning on the right foot, repeat the movements of measures 1 and 2.

5-8 Repeat measure 1-4.

Part II. The Windmills

Partners now extend their joined hands sideways shoulder high.

Measures:

9-16 Partners turn in place with a repeated step-hop. At the same time, the arms move up and down like a windmill. The turning is done clockwise with the boy starting on his right foot and the girl with her left. At the completion of the step-hops (16) the partners should be in the original places ready for Part I again.

Variation: Change original position to double circle, partners facing, with boys with backs to the center.

Part 1. As above
Part 2. All face counter-clockwise, partners

with inside hands joined. Partners do the basic schottische of "step, step, step, hop" throughout the Part 2.

CRESTED HEN

Records: Victor 45-6176
Methodist 108 Folkraft 1159

Formation: Children are in sets of three, two girls and one boy. Groups are scattered around the room.

Part I

Measures:
1-8 Dancers in each set form a circle. Starting with a stamp with the left foot, each set circles to the left using step-hops.
1-8 (repeated). Dancers reverse direction beginning again with a stamp with the left foot and following with step-hops. The change of direction should be vigorous and definite with the left foot crossing over the right in changing the direction.

Part II

During this part, the dancers use the step-hop continuously in making the pattern figures. The girls release their hands to break the circle and stand on each side of the boy.

Measures:
9-10 The girl on the right with four step-hops dances under the arch formed by the other girl and the boy.
11-12 The boy turns under his own left arm with four step hops forming again the line of threes.
13-16 The girl on the left now repeats the pattern going under the arch formed by the other two. The boy turns under his left arm to unravel the line.

As soon as the Part II is completed, dancers again join hands in a small circle. The entire dance is repeated.

HANSEL AND GRETEL

Record: Victor 45-6182

Formation: Double circle, partners facing with boys on the inside.

Part I

Measures:
1-2 Boys bow and girls curtsey.
3-4 Take partner's hands in crossed arm position, right hand to right hand and left to left.
5-6 Jump and extend the right heel forward. Repeat with the left heel.
7-8 Leaning away from partner, turn around in a small circle with seven light fast steps.

Part II
9-16 Take sixteen skips with partner around the circle with inside hands joined.

Part III

Measures:

17 Face partner, hands on hips
18 Stamp right, left, right
19 Stand still facing partner, hands on hips.
20 Clap hands three times.
21-22 Join hands, crossed hands position. Jump and extend the right heel then the left.
23-24 Turn with partner in a small circle using seven light steps

Part IV

This repeats Part III except that in measure 18 nod head three times instead of stamping. In measure 20, snap fingers three times instead of clapping. Hold hands about shoulder high when snapping.

Variation: The dance can be made a mixer by having the dancers, when they finish turning around in a small circle, move directly to the left to get a new partner. Thus there would be changes of partners at the finish of the partner turn for Parts I, III, and IV. The inside circle of boys would be moving counter-clockwise on the change while the outer circle would be moving clockwise.

GUSTAF'S SKOAL

Records: Methodist 108
Victor 45-6170
Folkraft 1175
Linden 701-A
RCA Victor EPA-4135

Formation: Similar to a square dance set of four couples, each facing the center. Boy is to the left of his partner. Couples join inside hands and outside hands are on the hips. Two of the couples facing each other are designated as the "head couples." The other two couples, also facing each other are the "side couples."

The dance is in two parts. During Part I, the music is slow and stately. The dancers perform with great dignity. Part II is light and represents fun and dancing.

Part I

Measures:

1-2	Head couples holding inside hands walk forward three steps and bow to the opposite couple.
3-4	Head couples take three steps backwards to place and bow to each other. During all of this the side couples hold their places.
5-8	Side couples perform the same movements while head couples hold places.
1-8	Dancers repeat entire figure.

Part II

9-12	Side couples raise joined hands forming an arch. Head couples skip to the center where they meet opposite partners. Each, after dropping his own partner's hand, takes the hand of the dancer facing him and skips under the nearest arch. After going under the arch, drop hands and head back to home spot to original partner.
13-16	Clap hands smartly on the first note of measure 13 while skipping. Skip toward partner, take both hands and skip once around in place.
9-16	(repeated). Head couples form the arches and the side couples repeat the pattern just finished by the head couples.

Variation: During the first part of Part I where the dancers take three steps and bow, a shout of "Skoal" at the same time raising the right fist about head high as a salute can be substituted for the bow. The word "Skoal" means a toast.

CSEBOGAR

Records: Victor 45-6182
                        Kismet 141

Formation: Single circle with partners. Girls are on the right, all are facing center with hands joined.

Part I

Measures:

1-4	Take seven slides to the left.
5-8	Seven slides to the right.
9-12	Take four skips to the center and four backwards to place.
13-16	Hook elbows with partner and turn around twice in place skipping.

Part II

Partners are now facing each other with hands joined in a single circle.

Measures:

17-20	Holding both hands of the partner take four draw steps (step, close) toward the center of the circle.
21-24	Four draw steps back to place
25-26	Toward the center of the circle with two draw steps
27-28	Two draw steps back to place
29-32	Hook elbows and repeat the elbow swing finishing up with a shout facing the center of the circle in the original formation.

Variation: Instead of the elbow turn, partners may use the Hungarian Turn. Partners stand side by side and put the right arm around the partner's waist. The left arm is held out to the side, elbow bent with the hand pointing up, and the palm facing the dancer.

Games Using Rhythmic Background

A number of interesting games can be played using music as a part of the game. These, in the main, are simple in principle and are based on the idea of movement changes when the music changes or stops. Some of these are similar to the old, old game of Musical Chairs.

Circle Stoop. Children are in a single circle facing counter-clockwise. A march or similar music can be used or the game can be played to the beat of a tom-tom. The children march in good posture until the music is stopped. As soon as the child no longer hears the music or beat of the tom-tom, he stoops and touches both hands to the ground without losing balance. The last child to touch both hands to the ground successfully pays a penalty by going into the mush-pot (center of the circle) or being eliminated. Children should march in good posture and anyone stooping, even partially, before the music is stopped should be penalized. The duration of the music should be varied, and the children should not be able to observe the stopping process if using a record player.

Variation: Employ different locomotor movements like skipping, hopping, or galloping using music suitable for the different locomotor movements.

Partner Stoop. The game follows the same basic principle of stooping as in Circle Stoop but is done with partners. The group forms a double circle with partners facing counter-clockwise, boys on the inside. When the music starts, all march in line of direction. After a short period of marching, a signal (whistle) is given, and the inside circle (boys) turns around and marches the other way--clockwise. Partners are now separated. When the music is stopped, the outer circle (girls) stands still, and the boys walk to rejoin their partners. As soon as a boy reaches his partner, they join inside hands and stoop without losing balance. The last couple to stoop goes to the center of the circle and waits out the next round.

Variation: The game can be played with groups of three instead of partners. The game begins by the groups of three marching abreast holding hands and facing counter-clockwise. On the signal, the outside players of the three continue marching in the same direction. The middle players of the three stop and stand still. The inside players reverse direction and march clockwise. When the music stops, the groups of three attempt to reunite at the spot of the middle player. The last three to join hands and stoop are put into the center for the next round.

Freeze. Children are scattered around the room. When the music is started, they move around the room guided by the character of the music. They walk, run, jump, or use other locomotor movements dependent upon the selected music or beat. When the music is stopped, they freeze and do not move. Any child caught moving after the cessation of the rhythm pays a penalty.

A tom-tom or piano provides a fine base for this game as the rhythmic beat can be varied easily and the rhythm can be stopped at any time. In the absence of a tom-tom or drum, two sticks or Indian clubs can be knocked together to provide the beat.

Variation: Instead of having the children freeze, they can fall to the ground.

Follow Me. The game has its basis in the phrasing of the music. The children are in circle formation facing in with a leader in the center. The leader performs a series of movements of his choice, either locomotor or non-locomotor, for the duration of one phrase of music (8 beats). The children imitate his movements during the next phrase. The leader takes over for another set of movements and the children imitate during the next phrase following. After a few changes, the leader picks another child to take his place.

Variation 1: A popular way to play this game is to have the children follow the leader as he performs. This means changing movement as the leader changes and performing as the leader does, with everyone keeping with the rhythm. A change is made as soon as the leader falters or loses his patterns or ideas.

Variation 2: The game can be done with partners. One partner performs during one phrase, and the other partner imitate his movements during the next phrase. The teacher can decide which couple is doing the most vivid and imaginative movements and is doing the best job of following the partner's movements.

Right Angle. A tom-tom can be used to provide the rhythm for this activity. Some of the basic rhythm records also have suitable music. The children change direction at right angles on each heavy beat or change of music. The object of the game is to make the right angle changes on signal and not bump into other children.

Arches. The game is similar to London Bridge. Arches are placed around the playing area. To form an arch, two players stand facing one another with hands joined. When the music starts, the players move in a circle, passing under the arch. Suddenly, the music stops and the arches come down by dropping the hands. All players caught in an arch immediately pair off together to form other arches, keeping in a general circle formation. If a "caught" player does not have a partner, he should wait in the center of the circle until one is available. The last players caught (or left) form arches for the next game.

The arches should be warned not to bring down their hands and arms too forcefully, so that the children passing under the arches will not be pummeled.

Also, children with glasses need consideration in the process of catching as the arches close, glasses can be knocked to the floor. Glasses should be removed or children with glasses can begin as part of the arches.

Variation: Different types of music can be used and the children can move according to the pattern of the music.

Whistle March. A record with a brisk march is needed. The children are scattered around the room individually walking in various directions, keeping time to the music. A whistle is blown a number of toots, at which signal lines are formed of that precise number, no more and no less. The lines are formed by having the children stand side by side with locked elbows. As soon as a line of the proper number is formed, it begins to march to the music counter-clockwise around the room. Any children left over go to the center of the room and remain until the next signal. On the next whistle signal (single blast) the lines break up and all walk individually around the room in various directions as before. Teaching hint: It may be well to make a rule that children may not lock elbows with any of the same children with whom they formed the previous line.

Chapter 11

Game-Type Activities for Primary Children

Practical Suggestions for Conducting Games
Exploration with Games
The Games Program for the First Grade
The Games Program for the Second Grade
The Games Program for the Third Grade

Every boy and girl in the public schools should have a chance to engage in a variety of games which are the collective heritage of centuries of children. The games have good recreational values, provide fitness values, and provide a necessary outlet for the natural exuberance of the children.

The greatest values for physical fitness in the games program are inherent in those activities in which many children are active at once, and in those where children strain and "put out" good physical effort. Some games are useful, however, in providing a period of lesser activity after a more strenuous activity. Games which make lesser demands on children are those in which there is a runner and a chaser while the remainder of the children have little part in the play.

The games for the first and second grade do not require a high degree of skill, and the lesser skilled children have good opportunity to excel. The third grade presents a little different picture. While many of the games are of the so-called low organized type, a number are introduced which present the first lead-up activities in the program. A lead-up game is defined as one which introduces a skill, strategy, or part of a sport. By the time the children finish the sixth grade, they should have played regular or modified versions of basketball, softball, soccer, volleyball, and flag football (boys). Leading up to these sport-type games are simplified activities which employ one or two skills or portions from the sport. Circle Kick Ball is a good example of the principle of a lead-up activity. The children form a circle, and the ball is kicked back and forth until it goes through or between one of the players. The players learn to kick, trap, and defend. The concentration is on these few skills.

Each game should be analyzed from the standpoint whether or not it requires a skill which the children should practice before playing the game. If practice is indicated, the teacher selects the appropriate drills and brings the children up to the point of necessary skill to play the game pleasurably. Drills and the acquisition of necessary skills become more meaningful when the children see the purpose for which they are needed.

Practical Suggestions for Conducting Games

1. Put the group in formation with all possible speed. Be careful of too formal methods of organization.
2. When explaining a game, talk briefly and to the point. Briefly tell what is to be done and what is to be avoided. Demonstrate or diagram when necessary. Students should be comfortable during explanations.
3. Correct outstanding faults but let details go in the beginning and get the game going. Avoid stopping the game too frequently to make corrections.
4. Ask for questions to clear up hazy points and reply so that all can hear.
5. Every unit or group should have a leader. Put someone in charge.
6. Where lines and limits are important, establish them definitely so there can be no mistake. Make the penalty clear for going out of bounds.
7. When playing a running game, do not allow the children to run to the wall. Use a line as a stopping or turning place.

8. Arrange for full participation. Use the "side line" players in officiating or helping with equipment.

9. Don't overdo competition. Too much emphasis makes the skilled resent being on the same team with those of lesser skill.

10. Where there is a mingling of players in team games and causes confusion, identify a team by crepe arm bands, hats, pinnies or similar devices.

11. Don't let a few more skilled players dominate a game. Arrange rotation of positions and put limitations on the times each player may complete certain acts.

12. Most games can be changed to suit conditions and facilities. Modify the game when needed, particularly when used indoors.

13. Be sure everyone has had a turn where this is practical. Have them raise their hands until selected or use a similar device.

14. The introduction of variation in the game awakens interest. Some of the following may be used to vary activities.
    (a) Change the distance to be run by either shortening or lengthening. For example, in Circle Chase, instead of having the runners go once around, double the distance.
    (b) Vary the route of the runner. This is particularly helpful in circle games.
    (c) Change the method of locomotion. Use hopping, walking, skipping, galloping, etc. instead of running.
    (d) Play the game with partners. Have them join inside hands and act as a single person.
    (e) Change the method of tagging. Limit where on the body a person may be tagged or with which hand he may be tagged.
    (f) Change the formation. For example, in Circle Soccer, make this a square. Make the formation larger or smaller.
    (g) Vary the boundaries.
    (h) Include penalties. A person who is caught a number of times (say, three) has to undergo a penalty.
    (i) Increase the number of key men or runners. This gets the game moving a little faster.
    (j) Use other helps or hindrances. In Cat and Rat, players may raise or lower hands, depending upon whether the cat or the rat is coming through.

(k) In tag or chase games, call out "Reverse". This means that the chaser now becomes the runner and the runner the chaser. Also, this can be used to change the direction of a ball around a circle.

15. Form several groups to keep participation and activity high.

16. Play occasionally with the class. They like to have you play with them.

17. Stress the social learnings involved in game experiences.

18. Carry on much of the explanation in the class room so that the youngsters have maximum activity on the playground.

19. Play outdoors whenever possible.

20. Give a definite signal for starting and stopping the game. Have a whistle, and use it when necessary. Demand instant attention when it blows--to get this, do not blow unnecessarily. Use a short, sharp and clear blast.

Safety Suggestions for Games

Slipping and falling. The need for care in running properly, and practice in turning and changing direction rapidly, should be stressed. The playing area should be kept free from hazardous objects. The teacher should make certain that all players are aware of hazardous conditions of the playing area, such as slickness, holes, or loose pebbles.

Collisions and tripping. The need for all players to be alert should be stressed. When playing goal games the group should be scattered to avoid collisions. If players are running in opposite directions, they should pass to the right. Children should be taught to tag properly by touching, not shoving, and the teacher should insist that it be done properly.

Hitting each other with Indian clubs, bean bags, or balls. Proper use of supplies should be taught.

Playing dodgeball games safely. Dodgeball games for children provide much enjoyment and competition. However, some controls are necessary. Glasses should be removed whenever possible. A soft slightly deflated volleyball or rubber playground ball should be used. Avoid a basketball or heavy ball which would punish the players. Hits should be made below the waist or at least below the shoulders. A penalty should be imposed on any throw that hits a child in the head. Restraining lines, if carefully marked or specified, will prevent the thrower from getting too close to the targets. Good direction will prevent vicious throwing and ganging up on certain individuals. A better game results when teams are balanced, and one or two players do not monopolize the throwing.

Exploration with Games

Children should have opportunity to make up or design games of their own origin. The teacher should set the problem by specifying what is available to them in the nature of space, equipment, and number of participants. For example, the space could be designated as a twenty-foot square or two parallel lines 30 feet apart. The game could be created without any equipment, or the children may be given a ball (any size) with which to work.

The teacher should divide the class into small enough groups so each child would be able to make a contribution. If a group is large, there is difficulty in resolving differences of opinion. Unless there is a specific reason, not more than three or four children should be assigned to a group. The groups can also be given different game problems to solve with respect to size of space, the equipment, and other details.

After a period of time, the groups should present the games they have originated. Discussion can be held with regard to value and possible changes that might make the game better. This is an excellent learning experience and prepares children for their own free time play.

The Games Program for the First Grade

The games for the first grade can be divided into two categories, namely, running and tag games and ball games. Few team activities are included as children are quite individualistic, and team play is beyond their capacities. The ball games require only the simples skills of throwing and catching.

The majority of the games keep many children active at one time. Some provide lesser activity. The character of the games is such that they need not be presented in any particular order. The list is presented alphabetically and the teacher can make choices depending upon the space, weather, and the interests of the children.

First Grade Games

Animal Tag
Back to Back
Cat and Rat
Charlie Over the Water
Circus Master
Gallop Tag
One, Two, Button My Shoe
Squirrel in the Trees
Tag Games--Simple
Where's My Partner?

Ball Passing
Ball Toss
Call Ball
Teacher Ball

ANIMAL TAG

Playing Area: Playground, gymnasium. Two parallel lines about 40 feet apart are drawn.

Players: Any number

Supplies: None

The children are divided into two groups, each of which takes position on one of the lines. The children of Group #1 get together with their leader and decide what animal they wish to imitate. Having selected the animal, they move over to within 5 feet or so of the other line. Here they imitate the animal and Group #2 tries to guess the animal correctly. If they guess correctly, they chase Group #1 back to its line, trying to tag as many as possible. Those caught must go over to the other team.

Group #2 now selects an animal and the roles are reversed. However, if the guessing team cannot guess the animal, the performing team gets another try.

To avoid confusion, have the children raise hands to take turns naming the animal. Otherwise, there will be many false chases.

If the children have trouble guessing, then have the leader of the performing team give the initial of the animal.

BACK TO BACK

Playing Area: Playground, gymnasium, classroom

Players: Entire class

Supplies: None

The number of children should be uneven. If the number is even, the teacher can play. On signal, each child stands back to back with another child. One child will be without a partner. This child can clap his hands for the next signal, and all children change partners with the extra player seeking a partner.

Variation: Considerably more activity can be secured by putting in an extra command. After the children are in partner formation back to back, the teacher can say, "Everybody -- run!" (or skip, hop, jump, slide, etc.) Other commands can be given such as, "Walk like an elephant." The children move around the room in the prescribed manner. When the whistle is blown, they immediately find a partner and stand back to back.

CAT AND RAT

Playing Area: Gymnasium, playground.

Players: 10 to 20

Supplies: None

All the children except two form a circle with hands joined. One of the extra players is the "Cat" and the other is the "Rat." The "Rat" is on the inside of the circle and the "Cat" is outside. The following dialogue takes place.

> "I am the Cat"
> "I am the Rat."
> "I can catch the Rat."
> "Oh no, you can't."

Whereupon the "Cat" chases the "Rat" in and out of the circle. The circle players raise the arms to help the "Rat", and lower again to hinder the "Cat". When the "Cat" catches the "Rat" or after a period of time if the "Rat" is not caught, the two children can select two others to take their places.

Variation: Instead of having the children raise and lower their hands to aid or hinder the runners, the teacher can call out, "High windows", or "Low windows". The circle players raise and lower their hands only on these signals.

CHARLIE OVER THE WATER

Playing Area: Playground, gymnasium, classroom

Players: 15 to 20

Supplies: None

The children are in circle formation with hands joined. One or more extra children are in the center, depending on the number of children in the circle. The one in the center is "Charlie." The circle children skip around the circle to the following chant:

> Charlie over the water, Charlie over the sea,
> Charlie caught a bluebird, but can't catch _me_!

On the word "me" all circle children drop hands, stoop, and touch the ground with both hands. The center players try to tag the circle players before they stoop. Any player tagged changes places with the center player. The game then continues.

Children should be held to retaining their balance while stooping. If they fall, they can be tagged.

The following can be used if a girl is in the center.

Sally over the river, Sally over the sea, etc.

Other positions can be stipulated instead of stooping. Stooping on one foot only, crab position, push-up position, and others can be used.

CIRCUS MASTER

Playing Area: Playground, gymnasium, classroom

Players: 10 to 40

Supplies: None

One child, the "Circus Master" is in the center of the circle formed by the other children. He stands in the center, pretends he has a whip, and gets ready to have the animals perform. He gives a direction like the following: "We are going to walk as elephants do, like this!" He then demonstrates in a small circle how he wishes the children to perform. He commands, "Elephants ready--WALK." The children imitate an elephant walking around the large circle while the "Circus Master" performs in a small circle in the center. When ready, the "Circus Master" calls "Halt". He takes a place in the circle, and another child comes forward to the center.

A prearranged order for "Circus Masters"

can be established which is excellent for young children as they can be prepared with a particular animal imitation. However, interest would die long before all the children could be in the center. Make arrangements to have other children be in the center for future times the game is played.

GALLOP TAG

Playing Area: Playground, gymnasium

Players: 12 to 20

Supplies: None

Children are in circle formation, facing in. One child walks around the outside and tags another child on the back. Immediately, he gallops around the circle in either direction with the child who was tagged chasing him but also galloping. If the player in the lead gets around to the vacated spot before being tagged, he joins the circle. If he is tagged, he must try again with another child.

Variation:
1. The children can run or skip.
2. Slap Jack
   Have the child tagged run in the opposite direction. The child which gets back to the vacant place first gets to keep the place. The other child tags again for another run.
3. Run for Your Supper
   The children stand with clasped hands. The runner goes in either direction, tags a pair of clasped hands, and says, "Run for your supper." The two children whose hands have been tagged run in opposite directions with the one getting back first keeping the place. The original runner after he tags the clasped hands merely steps into the circle, leaving only one space for which the two runners compete. Additional fun is to have the two runners, when they meet on the opposite side of the circle, bow to each other or shake hands, before continuing the run back to place.
4. Duck, Duck, Goose
   All children are seated cross-legged. The runner goes in either direction around the circle, tapping each child lightly on the head. As he does this he says, "Duck." When he wishes, he changes the word to "Goose," and that child then arises quickly and chases him around the circle back to the

vacant place. If the runner gets back safely, the chaser is the new runner. If the runner is tagged, then he must take another try as runner.

Cautions: These types of games should be played as resting activities and as such have a place in the curriculum. They are fun, but are low in developmental values. Also, there must be rapid action to keep things moving. Make a rule that the runners may travel only part way around a circle before choosing a chaser.

ONE, TWO, BUTTON MY SHOE

Playground Area: Playground, gymnasium. Two parallel lines are drawn about 50 feet apart

Players: Entire class

Supplies: None

One child is the leader and stands to one side. The remainder of the children are behind one of the lines. The leader says "Ready". The following dialogue takes place between the leader and the children.

Children	Leader's Response
One, two	Button my shoe
Three, four	Close the door
Five, six	Pick up sticks
Seven, eight	Run, or you'll be late!

The children are toeing the line ready to run and carry on the above conversation with the leader. When the word "late" is given by the leader, the children run to the other line and return. The first child across the original line is the winner and becomes the new leader.

The leader can give the last response in any timing he wishes by pausing or dragging out the saying. No child is to leave before the "late".

A variation is to have the children pantomime the leader's directions.

SQUIRREL IN THE TREES

Playing Area: Playground, gymnasium

Players: 15 to 35

Supplies: None

A tree is formed by two players facing each other with hands held or on each other's shoulders. A "Squirrel" is in the center of each tree and one or two extra "Squirrels" are outside. A signal to change is given. All "Squirrels" move out of their trees to another and the extra players try to find trees. Only one "Squirrel" is allowed in a tree.

To form a system of rotation, as each "Squirrel" moves into a tree, he changes places with one of the two forming the tree.

TAG GAMES--Simple

Playing Area: Playground with established boundaries, gymnasium

Players: Any number

Supplies: None

Tag is played in many different fashions. Children are scattered about the area. One child is "It" and chases others to tag one of them. When he does, he says, "You're IT." The new "It" chases other children. Different tag games are listed.

1. Being safe through touching a specified object or color. Touching wood, iron, the floor, or a specified color can make a runner safe.
2. Seeking safety by a particular action or pose. Some actions used to become safe are:

   Stoop--touch both hands to the ground
   Stork--stand on one foot (the other cannot touch)
   Turtle--be on your back
   Hindoo--make an obeisance with forehead to the ground
   Freeze--cannot move
   Nose and toe--nose must be touched by the toe
   Back to back--stand back to back with any other child

3. Locomotive tag--the person "It" specifies how the child should move. "It" also has to use the same kind of movement, i.e. skip, hop, jump, etc.

WHERE'S MY PARTNER?

Playing Area: Playground, gymnasium, classroom

Players: Any number can play

Supplies: None

Children are arranged in a double circle by couples, with partners facing. The inside circle has one more player than the outside. When the signal is given, the circles skip to the player's right. This means that they are skipping in opposite directions. When the command "Halt" is given, the circles face each other to find partners. The player left without a partner is in the "Mush Pot."

Children can gallop, walk, run, or hop instead of skipping.

Variation: The game can also be played with music. When the music stops, the players seek partners.

BALL PASSING

Playing Area: Playground, gymnasium classroom

Players: Entire class, divided into 2 or more teams

Supplies   5 to 6 different kinds of balls for each circle

The basis of this game is the child's love of handling objects. Not over 20 children should be in any one circle. Two or more teams combine to form a circle. The children need not necessarily be in any particular order.

The teacher starts a ball around the circle, which is passed from player to player in one direction. The teacher introduces more balls in the circle until 5 or 6 are moving around in the circle at the same time in the same direction. If a child drops a ball, he must retrieve it and a point is scored against his team. After a period of time, a whistle is blown and the points against each team are totaled. The team with the lowest score wins.

In the absence of sufficient balls for passing, bean bags, large blocks, and softballs can be substituted.

BALL TOSS

Playing Area: Playground, gymnasium, classroom

Players: Groups of 6 to 8

Supplies: A ball or bean bag for each group

The children form in a circle with one child in the center. The center player throws, the ball to each child in turn around the circle. The ball each time is returned to the center player. The object of the game is to make good throws and catches completely around the circle. After each child has had a turn in the center, the teacher can ask each circle to total the number of center players that were able to complete their throws without any errors.

Good form should be stressed.

CALL BALL

Playing Area: Playground, gymnasium, classroom

Players: 8 to 12 in each circle.

Supplies: A large playground ball or volley-ball.

The children form a circle with one in the center. The center child has a ball. He throws the ball into the air, at the same time calling out the name of one of the circle children. This child runs forward and tries to catch the ball <u>before</u> it bounces. If successful, he becomes the center player. If not, the center player throws again. If there are many in the circle, this moves quite slowly for the children. Other versions are:

1. Give the children numbers with more than one child with the same number. This makes the catching competitive.
2. Use colors or animals with more than one child so designated with the same color or animal.
3. Move the children back and have them catch the ball in first bounce.
4. <u>Catch the Cane.</u>
    Instead of tossing a ball into the air, balance a wand on one end on the floor. The child whose number is called, tries to catch the cane before it hits the ground. A little experimentation will determine how far back the circle should be from the cane.

TEACHER BALL (Leader Ball)

Playing Area: Playground, gymnasium

Players: 6 to 8

Supplies: Volleyball or rubber playground ball

One child is the teacher or leader and stands about 10 feet in front of the others who are lined up facing him. The object of the game is to move up to the teacher's spot by not making any bad throws or missing catches.

The leader, beginning with the child on his left, throws to each child in turn, who must catch and return the ball to him. Any child making a throwing or catching error goes to the foot of the line, on the leader's right. Those in the line move up, filling the vacated space.

If the teacher makes a mistake, he goes to the foot of the line, and the child at the head of the line becomes the new teacher.

The teacher scores a point for himself if he remains in position for three rounds (3 throws to each child). He takes his position at the foot of the line and another child becomes the leader.

This game should be used only after the children have practiced throwing and catching skills. It can be worked in as a part of the skill teaching program.

Variation: Provide specific methods of throwing and catching like, "Catch with the right hand only" or "Catch with one hand; don't let the ball touch your body."

The Games Program for the Second Grade

The games program is quite similar to that of the first grade. The second grade teacher should make use of any and all games presented in the first grade. Particularly, the simple ball games of the first grade have good values and should be included as a regular part of the second grade program.

Second Grade Games

Animal Chase
Caged Lion
Cat and Mice
Charlie Over the Water - Ball Version
Flowers and Wind
Hill Dill
Hound and Rabbit
Hunter
I Can Do What You Can!
Last Couple Out
Leaping the Brook
May I Chase You?
Midnight
Mouse Trap
Old Man (Old Lady)
Red Light

Stop and Start
Two Deep

Circle Stride Ball
Exchange Dodge Ball
Roll Dodge Ball
Stride Bowling
Repeat the ball games from the first
   grade

ANIMAL CHASE

Playing Area: Playground. Two goals
   are marked out 50 feet apart. Half way between the lines and off to one side, a ten-
   foot square represents the zoo.

Players: Entire class

Supplies: None

One child is the animal hunter and stands
in the center of the area. All children are stationed on one of the two goal lines. Each player is secretly given the name of an animal. If
the number is large, several players may have
the same animal.

This hunter calls out the name of an animal. If no one has this name, he continues different names until he hits upon one that a player has. This player runs to the opposite goal
line and returns. As soon as the runner starts,
the hunter must run to his zoo (to get his gun),
returns to the center area, and tries to tag the
runner. Generally, the runner can get to the
other goal line without difficulty. On the return
trip, he needs to dodge the hunter to return to
the other animals.

Any animals caught are taken to the zoo
and sit until all have run. If there are quite a
number of children playing the game, it might
be well to limit the number of times the hunter
can chase before getting a replacement. If two
children are named after the same animal, the
game is more exciting and moves faster.

CAGED LION

Playing Area: Classroom or gymnasium.
   A ten foot square is drawn.

Players: 10 to 20

Supplies: None

One child is selected to be the "Lion"
and takes a position on his hands and knees

inside the ten-foot square. Other players tan-
talize the "Lion" by standing in the cage area
or running through it. The "Lion" tries to tag
any of the children. Any child who is tagged
by the "Lion" trades places him him.

Variation:
1. The King's Land.
       The forbidden area, consisting of a 20-
   foot square, is known as the King's Land.
   A warden is appointed who tries to catch
   (tag) anyone who is on the King's Land.
   If so, the warden is released, and the
   tagged player becomes the new warden.
2. Tommy Tucker's Land.
   This is similar to the King's Land except
   that Tommy Tucker is guarding his land to
   prevent people from picking up gold and silver. The players stand on his land and pretend to pick up gold and silver while saying,
   "I'm on Tommy Tucker's land picking up
   gold and silver." Anyone tagged changes
   places with Tommy.

CAT AND MICE

Playing Area: Playground, gymnasium,
   classroom

Players: 15 to 20

Supplies: None

The children form a large circle. One
child is chosen to be the cat and three others
are the mice. The mice cannot leave the circle.
On signal, the cat chases the mice inside the
circle. As they are caught, they join the circle.
The last mouse caught becomes the cat for the
next round. The teacher should start at one
point in the circle and go round the circle selecting mice so that each child gets a chance
to be in the center.

CHARLIE OVER THE WATER - Ball Version

Playing Area: Playground, gymnasium

Players: 10 - 20

Supplies: One volleyball or playground ball

The children are in circle formation with
hands joined. One child, "Charlie," is in the
center of the circle holding a ball in his hands.
The children skip around the circle to the following chant:

Charlie over the water, Charlie over the sea,
Charlie caught a bluebird, but can't catch
<u>me</u>!

On the word "me" the children drop hands and scatter. On the same signal, "Charlie" tosses the ball into the air. He then catches it and shouts "Stop!" All children stop immediately and must not move their feet. "Charlie" rolls the ball in an attempt to hit one of the children. If he hits a child, that child becomes "Charlie." If he misses, he must remain as "Charlie," and the game is repeated. However, if he misses twice, he should pick another child.

If a girl is in the center, the chant should go:

Sally over the river, Sally over the sea, etc.

FLOWERS AND WIND

Playing Area: Two parallel lines are drawn long enough to accommodate the children. The lines are about thirty feet apart.

Players: 10 to 50

Supplies: None

The children are divided into two equal groups, one of whom is the "Wind" and the other the "Flowers." Each of the teams takes a position on one of the lines facing the other. The "Flowers" secretly select the name of a common flower. When ready, they walk over to the other line and stand about three feet away from the "Wind." The players on the "Wind" begin to call out different flowers trying to guess the flower chosen. When the chosen flower has been guessed, the "Flowers" take off and run to their goal line, chased by the players of the other team.

Any player caught must join the other side. The roles are reversed, and the other team chooses a flower to be guessed.

If one side has trouble guessing, then give the first letter, the color, or the size of the flower.

HILL DILL

Playing Area: Playground. Two parallel lines are drawn about 50 feet apart.

Players: 10 to 50

Supplies: None

One player is chosen to be "It" and stands in the center. The other children stand on one of the parallel lines. The center player calls, "Hill Dill! Come over the hill!" The children run across the open space to the other line while the one in the center tries to tag them. Anyone caught helps "It" in the center. The last man caught is in the center for the next game.

Once the children cross over to the other line they must await the next call.

Variation: There are many variations of this game pattern. An interesting version is called "Black Tom." The child in the center calls out, "Black Tom." The children run across to the other line. They must leave the line at once and not delay. To fool the players, the center child can call out, "Blue Tom," or "Red Tom." No child must cross his starting line unless "Black Tom" is called. Any child moving on a false signal is considered caught and joins the center group.

HOUND AND RABBIT

Playing Area: Playground, gymnasium

Players: 15 to 30

Players are scattered around the area by groups of threes. Two of the three make a tree by facing each other and putting hands on each other's shoulders. The third child, who takes the part of a rabbit, stands between them. An extra "Rabbit" is outside and is chased by a "Hound." The "Hound" chases the odd "Rabbit" who takes refuge in any tree. Two rabbits may not be in any tree so the other child must leave and look for another tree. When the "Hound" catches the "Rabbit", they exchange places and the game continues.

A rotation system should be used whenever a "Rabbit" enters a tree. The three in any one group should rotate so that the entering "Rabbit" becomes a part of the tree, and one of the children making up the tree becomes the "Rabbit."

THE HUNTER

Playing Area: Playground, gymnasium, classroom

Players: Entire class

Supplies: Markers are needed for the children if outdoors or in the gymnasium. In the classroom, the seats can be used for home.

A leader, the "Hunter," walks around the room in any manner he wishes. He begins the game with the question, "Who wants to hunt ducks?" (bears, lions, rabbits). The players chosen fall in line behind him and start on the hunt. The leader can go through various creeping and hunting motions. When he is ready, the leader shouts, "Bang!" All run for a marker or a seat, including the leader. The first one back to a marker or seat is chosen as leader for the next game.

To make the game interesting, the leader should take quite a few children on the hunt. Be sure that all get a chance to go at one time or another.

Variation: A novel method of making leader changes is to have one place (seat or marker) designated as the leader for the next time. This is picked only after the hunter takes the child out. The teacher can make this pick, the location of which is unknown to the runners.

I CAN DO WHAT YOU CAN!

Playing Area: Playground, gymnasium classroom

Players: Not more than 6 or 7 in a group. Any number of groups can play.

Supplies: Usually, none. The game can be played with each child with the same piece of equipment like a ball, wand, bean bag, etc.

This is primarily a "follow-the-leader" type of game. Each group works independently of the others. Each group forms a semicircle with the leader in front. The leader starts any type of activity he wishes and the other children attempt to perform the same moves along with him. After a brief period, the teacher blows the whistle, and another leader takes his place in front of the group.

This works well with different pieces of equipment provided each child in the group has the same type of equipment. Tossing, throwing, catching, bouncing, wand stunts, and bean bag tricks are some activities which are easily adapted to the game. Caution children not to demand outlandish or silly performances from the group.

LAST COUPLE OUT

Playing Area: Playground, gymnasium

Players: 10 to 15

Players are lined up by couples in a column formation with an "It" standing at the head of the column. He has his back to the column. He calls, "Last couple out!" The object of the game is to have the last couple separate and rejoin beyond the place where "It" is standing without being tagged by him. If "It" tags either of the two, that person becomes "It". The old "It" joins the remaining player as his partner, and the pair go to the head of the line.

If the couple is able to join hands without being tagged, they take places at the head of the column, and "It" takes a try at the next couple.

"It" is not permitted to look back and cannot start his chase until the separated couple comes up even with him on both sides.

Variation: The game can be played by partners who have inside hands joined.

LEAPING THE BROOK

Playing Area: Gymnasium or other flat surface

Players: Entire class

Supplies: None

A brook is marked off on the floor for a distance of about 30 feet. For the first 10 feet it is 3 feet wide, for the second 10 feet 4 feet wide, and for the last 10 feet the width becomes 5 feet.

The children form a single file and jump over the narrowest part of the brook. They should be encouraged to do this several times using different styles of both jumping and leaping.

Have the children do the jumping, hopping, and leaping using different turns and make different body shapes in the air.

Stress landing as light as possible on the balls of the feet in a bent knee position.

After they have satisfactorily negotiated the narrow part, they move up to the next width, and so on.

Teachers should remember that fitness values are only in repeated effort. Good form should be stressed throughout the game.

The selection of the distances is arbitrary, and if they seem unsuitable for any particular group of children, they can be changed.

MAY I CHASE YOU?

Playing Area: Playground

Players: 10 to 30

Supplies: None

The class stands behind a line long enough to accommodate all. The runner stands about five feet in front of the line. One child in the line asks, "May I chase you?" The runner replies, "Yes, if you are wearing - - - ." He can name a color, an article of clothing, or a combination of the two. All who qualify immediately chase the runner until one tags him. This person becomes "It."

The children will think of other ways to identify those who can run.

MIDNIGHT

Playing Area: Playground

Players: 6 to 15

Supplies: None

A safety line is established about forty feet from a den in which one player is standing as the "Fox." The others stand behind the safety line and move forward slowly asking, "Mr. Fox, what time is it?" The "Fox" answered in various fashions like "Bed time," "Pretty late," "Three-thirty," and similarly. He continues to draw the players toward him. At some point, he answers the question of time with "Midnight," and chases the others back to the safety line. Any player caught joins the "Fox" in his den and helps him catch others. However, no player in the den can leave until the "Fox" calls out "Midnight."

MOUSE TRAP

Playing Area: Playground, gymnasium, classroom

Players: 20 to 40

Supplies   None

One-half the children form a circle with hands joined, facing the center. The other children are on the outside of the circle. Three signals are given for the game. These can be given by word cues, or a whistle can be used.

The circle players represent the mouse trap, and the outer players are the mice.

Signal 1. The "Mice" skip around the circle, playing happily.

Signal 2. The trap is opened, that is, the circle players raise their joined hands to form arches. The "Mice" run in and out of the trap.

Signal 3. The trap snaps shut (the arms come down). All "Mice" caught join the circle.

The game is repeated until all or most of the "Mice" are caught. The players exchange places, and the game begins anew. Do not allow the children to run in and out using adjacent openings.

OLD MAN (OLD LADY)

Playing Area: Playground, gymnasium, classroom

Players: Entire class

Supplies: None

A line is drawn through the middle of the area. Any convenient line can be used. Half the children are on one side and half on the other. The children hold hands with a partner across the center line. There needs to be an odd person, who can be the teacher or another child. The teacher gives a signal for the children to move as directed in their side of the line. The children can be directed to run, hop, skip, etc. At a whistle, the children run to the center line and reach across to join hands with a child from the opposite group. The one left out is the "Old Man" (if a boy) or the "Old Lady" (if a girl). Children may reach over, but not cross the line. The odd person should alternate sides so that the "Old man" can be on the other side at times.

The game can also be done to music with the players rushing to the center line to find partners when the rhythm stops.

RED LIGHT

Playing Area: An area 60 to 100 feet across with goal toward which the players move.

Players: Entire class

Supplies: None

The object of the game is to be able to move across the area successfully without getting caught. One player is the leader and stands on the goal line. He counts very rapidly from one to ten while he has his back to the players. He quickly adds the words "Red Light" to the counting and turns around. In the meantime, the players have been moving across the area during the counting and must freeze on the words "Red Light." Any player caught moving after "Red Light" must return to the starting position. The first player across the area wins and is the leader for the next game.

After the leader has sent all back who were caught, he turns his back again to begin his count. The players may move when his back is turned. However, he can turn around quickly and catch any movement. Once he starts his counting he cannot turn around until he has called "Red Light."

Variation:
1. Instead of counting, the leader (with his back turned) can clap his hands five times, turning around to catch movement on the fifth clap.
2. Another excellent variation of the game is to have the leader face the oncoming players. He calls out "Green Light" for them to move and "Red Light" for them to stop. He can call other colors and the players should not move.
3. Different types of locomotion can be worked in. The leader would give the type of movement (i.e. hop, crawl, etc.) before turning his back to the group.

STOP AND START

Playing Area: Playground

Players: Any number can play

Supplies: None

The children are in the center of the playground, scattered enough so each has room to maneuver. The teacher or leader stands a little to one side and gives directions. He points in a direction and calls, "Gallop." Any other locomotor movement could be used. Suddenly, he calls, "Stop." All children must stop immediately without further movement. Any one moving can be sent over to the side to another group. These try to work their way back to the original group.

TWO DEEP

Playing Area: Playground, gymnasium

Players: 15 to 20

Supplies: None

All children except two form a circle standing about finger tip distance away and facing the center. A runner and chaser stand on the outside. The chaser tries to catch the runner who can save himself by stopping in front of any player. This player now becomes the runner and must avoid being caught. When the chaser tags the runner, the positions change immediately and the runner becomes the chaser.

Encourage the children to make changes often. If there seems to be too much running, make a rule that a child can travel only half way around the circle before he must make a change.

Since this game is a lead-up to Three Deep, it should be learned reasonably well.

CIRCLE STRIDE BALL

Playing Area: Playground, gymnasium, classroom

Players: 10 to 15

Supplies: 2 Volleyballs or rubber playground balls

Children are in circle formation, facing in. Each is in wide stride step with the side of the foot against the neighbors. The hands are on the knees.

The object of the game is to throw a ball between the legs of any player before he can get his hands down and stop it. Each time the ball goes between the legs of an individual, a point is scored against that individual. The players having the least points against them are the winners.

Be sure the children catch and roll the

ball rather than batting it. Another ball can be added to make more activity.

Children must keep their hands on their knees until the ball is thrown or rolled.

After a period of practice, the following variation should be played.

Variation: One child is in the center with a ball and is "It." The other children are in the same formation as above. The center player tries to roll the ball through the legs of any child he chooses. He should mask his intent, using feints and changes of direction. Any child that allows the ball to go through his legs becomes "It." All players start with hands on knees until the ball is thrown.

EXCHANGE DODGE BALL

Playing Area: Playground, gymnasium

Players: 12 to 20

Supplies: Volleyball or rubber playground ball

Children form a circle with one child, "It," in the center. The children are numbered off by fours or fives in such a fashion that there are 3 or 4 children who have the same number. The center player also has a number which he uses when he is not "It."

The center player has a ball which he lays at his feet. He calls a number, picks up the ball, and tries to hit one of the children who are exchanging places. When a number is called, all children with that number exchange places. The center player remains "It" until he can hit one of the children below the waist.

Variation: Use animal names instead of numbers.

ROLL DODGE BALL

Playing Area: Playground, gymnasium

Players: 20 to 40, divided into two teams

Supplies: Volleyball or rubber playground ball

One-half the children form a circle and the other half are in the center. The circle players roll the ball at the feet and shoes of the center players trying to hit them. The center players move around to dodge the ball.

When a center player is hit, he leaves the circle.

After a period of time or when all the children have been hit, the teams trade places.

Variation: Try the game using two balls at the same time.

STRIDE BOWLING

Playing Area: Playground, gymnasium

Players: 4 to 8

Supplies: Volleyball or rubber playground ball

Children may compete within a group or teams can compete against each other. One child is the bowling target and stands at stride position with his feet wide enough so the ball can pass through easily. Another child is the ball chaser and stands behind him.

A foul line is drawn 15 to 25 feet away from the target, depending upon the ability of the children. The bowlers line up behind this line for turns.

Children can get one chance or can be given a number of tries. The ball to score a point must go between the legs of the target. When the children on the throwing line have bowled, two of them relieve the target and chaser.

Variations:
1. Scoring can be changed to allow 2 points if the ball goes through the legs and 1 point if it hits a leg.
2. Other targets can be used. A box lying on its side with the opening pointed toward the bowler forms a good target. Two or three Indian clubs at each station make excellent targets. Scoring could be varied to suit the target.
3. Bowling One Step. For groups of squad size or smaller, the players each in turn get a chance to roll at an Indian club or bowling pin. A minimum distance is set up which should be short enough so most bowlers can hit the pin (10 to 15 feet). The player keeps rolling until he misses. The object is to take a step backward each time the pin is knocked down. The winner is the one who has moved the farthest back.

Children should be cautioned that accuracy not speed, is the goal. Also, the players could experiment with different spin effects to curve the ball.

The Games Program for the Third Grade

Compared with the two first grades, the games program undergoes a definite change in the third grade. The chase and tag games become more complex and demand more maneuvering. Introductory lead-up games make an appearance. The interests of the children are turning toward games which have a sports slant. Kicking, throwing, catching, batting, and other sports skills are beginning to mature. Outside sports influences like the Little League program add force to the sports interests.

Third Grade Games

Busy Bee
Broncho Tag (Hook On)
Couple Tag
Cross Over
Crows and Cranes
Eagle and the Sparrows
Flying Dutchman
Fly Trap
Frog in the Sea
Follow Me
Galloping Lizzie
Jump the Shot
Poison Circle
Right Face, Left Face (Maze Tag)
Steal the Treasure
Three Deep
Through the Tunnel Race
Triple Change
Weathervane

Bean Bag Target Toss
Bat Ball
Bounce Ball
Circle Team Dodge Ball
Club Guard
Competitive Circle Contests
One Step
Newcomb* (page 313)
Circle Kick Ball* (page 287)
End Ball* (page 266)

BUSY BEE

Playing Area: Playground, gymnasium, classroom

Players: Entire class

Supplies: None

* These are lead-up games and descriptions are found on the pages indicated among the sports outlines.

One-half the children form a large circle facing in and are designated as the stationary players. The other children seek partners from this group and each stands in front of one of the stationary players. An extra child is in the center and is the "Busy Bee."

The "Bee" calls out directions which are followed by the children.

"Back to back."
"Face to face."
"Shake hands."
"Kneel on one knee." (or both)
"Hop on one foot."

The center child then calls out "Busy Bee." Stationary players stand still, and all inner circle players seek another partner while the center player also tries to get a partner. The child without a partner becomes the "Busy Bee."

Children should be thinking of the different movements they might have the class do if they should become the "Busy Bee." In changing partners, children should be required to select partner other than the stationary player next to him.

After a period of time, rotate the active and stationary players. Also, vary by using different methods of locomotion.

Variation:
1. Select a definite number of changes--10 for example. All children who have not repeated any partner during the ten exchanges and who have not been "caught" as the "Busy Bee" are declared the winners.
2. Instead of having the children stand back to back, have them lock elbows and sit down as in the Chinese Get-up. After they sit down and are declared "safe" they can get up and the game proceeds as described above.

BRONCHO TAG (Hook On)

Playing Area: Playground, gymnasium

Players: 15 to 30

Supplies: None

One child is a runner and another the chaser. The remainder of the children are divided into groups of threes. Each group of threes forms a broncho by standing one behind the other with the last two grasping the waist of the person in front of him. The front player is the head, and the player on the end is the tail. The runner tries to hook on to the tail of any broncho. The head of that broncho now becomes the runner.

The chaser pursues the runner who tries to avoid being caught by hooking to a broncho. The chaser now has to pursue the new runner. If tagged, the roles are reversed and the runner becomes the chaser.

The game is more interesting if the children change rapidly.

COUPLE TAG

Playing Area: Playground, gymnasium. Two goal lines are established about 50 feet apart.

Players: Any number

Supplies: None

Children run by pairs with inside hands joined. All pairs except one line up on one of the goal lines. A pair is in the center and is "It."

The pair in the center calls "Come," and the children run to the other goal line, keeping hands joined. The pair in the center tries to tag any pair using only the joined hands. As soon as a couple is caught, it helps the center couple. The game continues until all are caught. The last couple caught is "It" for the next game.

CROSS OVER

Playing Area: Playground with two parallel goal lines about 40 feet apart.

Players: 15 to 40

Supplies: None

Divide the players in two groups, each of which stands on one of the goal lines. A catcher is in the center between the two lines. He faces one of the lines and calls out the name of one of the players. This player immediately calls out the name of a player in the other line. These two players try to change goal lines while the catcher tries to tag one of them. Any player tagged becomes the catcher for the next call.

If there are more than twenty children, it is best to divide the group into two games.

Since only two children run at a time, the game can drag with a large group as chances to run will not occur too frequently.

Variation: With a larger group, this game can be played by partners. In calling out names, it would be necessary to call only one of the partners. Tagging would be done by the free hands with the inside hands kept joined. No tagging would count if the catchers separated, and a pair running across the area would be counted as caught if they were unable to keep together. Watch out for favoritism among the children.

CROWS AND CRANES

Playing Areas: Playground, gymnasium. Two goals are drawn about 50 feet apart.

Players: Any number

Children are divided into two groups, the "Crows" and the "Cranes." The groups face each other at the center of the area about five feet apart. The leader calls out either "Crows" or "Cranes" using a "Kr-r-r-r-r-r" sound at the start of either word to mask the result.

If "Crows" is the call, the "Crows" chase the "Cranes" to the goal. If "Cranes" is given, then the "Cranes" chase. Any child caught goes over to the other side. The team which has the most players when the game ends is the winner.

Variation:
1. Have the children stand back to back in the center about a foot apart.
2. The game can be played with the two sides designated as "Black" and "White." A piece of plywood painted black on one side and white on the other can be thrown into the air between the teams instead of having anyone give calls. If black comes up, the "Blacks" run, and vice versa.
3. The game can also be played as Blue, Black and Baloney. On the commands "Blue" and "Black, the game proceeds as described above. On the command "Baloney" no one is to move. The caller should be sure to sound the "Bl-l-l-l" before ending with one of the three commands.
4. Another variation of the game is to have a leader tell a story using as many words beginning with "cr" as possible. The players run only when the words "Crows" or "Cranes" are spoken. Words which can be incorporated into a story are crazy, crunch, crust,

crown, crude, crowd, crouch, cross, croak, critter, etc. Each time one of these words is spoken the beginning of the word is lengthened with the cr-r-r-r sound. No one may move on any of the words except "Crows" or "Cranes."

EAGLE AND THE SPARROWS

Playing Area: Playground with two parallel lines drawn about fifty feet apart. A circle representing the eagle's nest is drawn in the center.

Players: Entire class

Supplies: None

One player is the "Eagle" and sits in his nest. The other players circle around him flying like sparrows until the "Eagle" suddenly gets up and chases the "Sparrows" to either line. Any "Sparrow" caught joins the "Eagle" and helps him catch others. However, no center player can chase until the "Eagle" starts first.

If the group is large, begin with two or three "Eagles" in the center.

Variation: All "Sparrows" must take three hops before they can start running.

FLYING DUTCHMAN

Playing Area: Playground or gymnasium

Players: 15 to 30

Supplies: None

The children are in a circle with hands joined. Two children with hands joined are the runners. The runners go around the outside of the circle and tag a pair of joined hands. Immediately, the runners continue around the circle while the tagged pair runs around in the other direction. The first pair back to the vacated spot gets to keep the spot and the other pair becomes the runners. Be sure to establish rules for passing when the couples go by each other on the way around. Couples should keep to the right in passing.

Variations:
1. The runners reverse their direction immediately when tagging.
2. The game can be played by groups of threes instead of couples. The tag is made on the back of any one person, who with the persons on each side of him form the groups of threes. Groups should retain clasped hands or be disqualified.

√ FLY TRAP

Playing Area: Playground, gymnasium

Players: Entire class

Supplies: None

One-half the class is scattered around the playing area sitting on the floor in tailor (cross-legged) fashion. These children form the trap. The other children are the "Flies" and buzz in and round the seated children. When a whistle is blown, the "Flies" must freeze at the spot. If any of the trappers can reach the "Flies," that fly is seated at his location and becomes a trapper.

The game continues until all the flies have been caught. Some realism is given to the game if the "Flies" make buzzing sounds and move with their arms out as wings.

A little experience with the game will enable the teacher to determine how far apart to place the seated children.

After all the "Flies" have been caught, the children trade places.

Change the method of locomotion occasionally.

FROG IN THE SEA

Playing Area: Any small area indoors or outdoors.

Players: 6 to 8 in each game.

Supplies: None

One player is the "Frog" and sits down tailor fashion (crossed legs). The others mill about him trying to touch him but at the same time keeping out of the reach of the "Frog." They can call, "Frog in the sea, can't catch me." The "Frog" must stay in his sitting position and try to tag those tantalizing him. Anyone tagged exchanges places with the "Frog."

Care should be taken so that the children do not punish the "Frog" unnecessarily.

Variations:
1. The "Frog" may not tag anyone until the teacher says, "Jump Frog."

2. The game proceeds as originally described. When the teacher says, "Jump Frog," the "Frog" can project himself in any direction with a jump. He is permitted to tag both during the original part of the game and at the jump.

FOLLOW ME

Playing Area: Playground, gymnasium

Players: 8 to 30

Supplies: A marker for each child. Squares of cardboard or plywood can be used.

Children are arranged roughly in a circle each standing with one foot on his marker. An extra player is the "Guide." He moves about the circle pointing at different players and asking them to "follow me." Each player as chosen falls in behind the "Guide." The "Guide" now takes his group on a tour performing just as "Guide" does. As the "Guide" skips and hops, so do his followers. The followers must move or stunt just as the "Guide" does. At the signal "Home" all run for places at the markers. One child will be without a marker. This child chooses another "Guide."

It is not a good idea to make the last child the new leader as this will cause some children to lag and try to be last. In our version, he gets to choose a new leader. One way to overcome the tendency to lag would be to make the first one back the leader or have a special leader marker. The first one to this marker becomes the new leader.

A penalty can be imposed on the one who doesn't find a marker.

GALLOPING LIZZIE

Playing Area: Playground

Players: 10 to 15

Supplies: Bean bag

This is a version of the game of Tag. One player is "It" and has a bean bag. The other players are scattered on the playground. The player with the bean bag runs after the others and attempts to hit one with the bean bag below the shoulders. This person becomes "It" and the game continues. Be sure that "It" must throw the bag and not merely touch another person with it.

Variation:
The game can be played by children in pairs. In this case, a pair of children come "It" with one of the players handling the bean gag. A specific kind of a toss can be specified--overhand, underhand, left hand.

JUMP THE SHOT

Playing Area: Playground, gymnasium.

Players: 10 to 20

Supplies: A jump-the-shot rope

The players stand in circle formation. One player with a long rope stands in the center. On the free end of the rope, a soft object is tied to give the end some weight. An old deflated ball makes a good weight.

The center player turns the rope under the feet of the circle players who must jump over it. Anyone who touches the rope with his feet is eliminated and must stand back from the circle. The object is to see who can stay in the circle the longest and become the rope turner for the next game.

The center player should be cautioned to keep the rope along the ground. The speed can be varied. A good way to turn the rope is to sit cross-legged and turn the rope over the head.

POISON CIRCLE

Playing Area: Playground, gymnasium

Players: 8 to 12 in each circle

Supplies: Volleyball or rubber playground ball

Players form a circle with hands joined. The hands should be joined with good solid grips. Inside the circle of players, another circle is drawn on the floor with chalk. This should be a foot or two smaller than the circle of children. The ball is placed in the center of this area.

At a signal, the circle pulls and pushes trying to force a child to step into the inner circle. When this occurs, everyone yells "Poison," and the children scatter. The one who stepped in the circle picks up the ball quickly and tries to hit one of the other children below the waist. He must throw from within the circle. If he hits a child, it is a "dud" against the child. If he misses, it is a "dud" against the thrower. Anyone with three "duds" can pay a penalty.

RIGHT FACE, LEFT FACE (Maze Tag)

Playing Area: Playground, gymnasium

Players: 20 to 35

Supplies   None

Children stand in straight rows both from front to rear and side to side. A runner and a chaser are picked. The children all face the same way and join hands with the players on each side. The chaser tries to tag the runner going up and down the rows, but not breaking through or under the arms. The teacher can help the runner by calling "right face" or "left face" at the proper time. At this command, the children drop hands, face the new direction, and again grasp hands with those who are now on each side. New passages are now available to the runner and chaser. When the runner is caught or the children become tired, a new runner and chaser are chosen.

Variation:

1. Directions can be used instead of the facing commands. The teacher can call out "North, South, East, or West."
2. The original game from which the game above was taken is called "Streets and Alleys." In this version, the teacher calls out "Streets" and the children face in one direction. The call "Alleys" causes them to face at right angles.
3. The command "Air Raid" can be given which means that the children drop to their knees and make themselves into a small ball tucking their heads and seat down.

STEAL THE TREASURE

Playing Area: Playground, gymnasium, classroom

Players: 8 to 12

Supplies   One Indian Club

A playing area of 20 feet square is outlined with a small circle in the center. The treasure is an Indian club and is placed in the circle. A "Guard" is set to protect the treasure. Players now enter the square and try to steal the treasure without getting caught. The "Guard" tries to tag them. Anyone tagged must retire from the circle and wait for the next game. The player who gets the treasure is the next "Guard."

If getting the treasure seems too easy, make a rule requiring the child to carry the treasure to the boundaries of the square.

Bear and Keeper. This game is similar in action. Instead of a treasure a "Bear" is seated cross-legged on the ground and is protecting by his "Keeper." Anyone who touches the "Bear" without being tagged becomes the new "Keeper," with the present "Keeper" becoming the "Bear." A rougher version of this game is played by boys in that the "Bear" stands crouched over and the boys try to swat him on the seat without getting tagged.

THREE DEEP

Playing Area: Playground, gymnasium

Players: 20 to 40

Supplies: None

A runner and chaser are chosen. One-half of the remaining children form a circle, facing in. Each of the other children stands behind one of the circle players, forming a double circle formation with all facing in.

The chaser tries to tag the runner who can escape by taking a position in front of any pair of players. This forms a three-deep combination from which the game gets its name. The outer player of the three now is the runner. When the chaser tags the runner, the positions are reversed.

The game becomes more interesting if frequent changes are made. It may be well to limit running to half way round the circle. In no case should the runner leave the immediate circle area.

Variation: The teacher can call out "Reverse," which means that the positions of the runner and chaser are reversed.

THROUGH THE TUNNEL RACE

Playing Area: Playground, gymnasium, classroom

Players: 6 to 8 on each team. Many teams can compete

Supplies: None

Teams compete against each other and are lined up in relay (lane) formation. The players spread their legs, and the last man of each line crawls through the legs. The other players follow in turn until the team is back in original order. As soon as a player has crawled through the tunnel, he stands up so the player coming through next can go through his legs. The team that gets back in original order first wins.

TRIPLE CHANGE

Playing Area: Playground, gymnasium

Players: 15 to 30

Supplies: None

Players form a large circle, facing in. Three children stand in the center. Those forming the circle and those in the center are numbered off by threes. The players in the center take turns, each calling out his own number. When a number is called, all those with that number change places. The one in the center with this number tries to find a place. The child without a place goes to the center and awaits until the other center men have had their turns.

Variation: The teacher could call out the numbers, not necessarily in order, to add an element of suspense to the game.

WEATHERVANE

Playing Area: Playground, gymnasium, classroom

Players: Entire class

Supplies: None

Children stand alongside their desks or are scattered throughout the area. A leader stands at the front of the class and gives the directions. He calls out the four main compass directions--North, South, East, and West. The children jump in place making the necessary turn in the air to face the called direction. This could involve a quarter, half, or three-quarter turn. If the direction is called which the children are facing, then each child jumps in the air with no turn. All turns should be in the same direction for a period of time to avoid confusion.

A child should be eliminated after a stipulated number of errors. An alternate method would be for each child to keep track of the number of errors he made.

After the children become skillful in turning, a number of variations could be used.

1. A full turn could be required when a direction is repeated.
2. Right and left turning could be alternated.

BEAN BAG TARGET TOSS

Playing Area: Classroom, gymnasium. Three concentric circles are drawn on the floor with radii of 10, 20, and 30 inches

Players: 2 to 6 for each target.

Supplies: Five bean bags, blocks of wood, or round smooth stones.

Players, in turn, toss the five bean bags in sequence toward the target. A throwing line should be established 10 to 15 feet from the target, the distance depending upon the skill of the children.

Scoring:
    Center area - 15 points
    Middle area - 10 points
    Outer area - 5 points
    Any bag touching a line - 3 points

A bag to score in an area must be completely in the area and not touching a line. If the bag touches a line, it scores 3 points.

Each child is given 5 throws and the score is determined from the final position of the 5 bags.

Variation:
1. Two children can compete against each other alternating single throws until each has taken the allotted five. The score of each is noted. For a second turn, the child scoring the highest from the previous effort throws first.
2. Outside, players can use flat stones on a hard surface.

BAT BALL

Playing Area: A serving line is drawn across one end of a field which is approximately 70 by 70 feet. A 3 by 3 foot base is drawn in the center of the playing field about 50 feet from the serving line.

Players: Two teams, 8 to 15 on each team.

Supplies: Volley or similar ball.

One team is scattered out in the playing area. The other team is behind the serving line with one player up at bat. The batter puts the ball in play by batting it with his hand into the playing area. The ball must land in the playing area or be touched by a member of the fielding team to be counted as a fair ball. As soon as the ball is hit, the batter runs to the base and back across the serving line. In the meantime, the fielding team fields the ball and attempts to hit the runner below the shoulders.

Scoring: The batter scores a run each time a fair ball is hit and he touches the base and gets across the serving line before being hit by the ball. He also scores a run if the fielding team commits a foul.

Out: The batter is out if the ball is caught on a fly. Two consecutive foul balls also put the batter out. The batter is out if hit by a thrown ball in the field of play.

Fouls: Fielders, in recovering the ball and attempting to hit the batter, may not run with the ball. The ball must be passed from fielder to fielder until thrown at the batter. A pass may not be returned to the fielder from whom it was received.

BOUNCE BALL

Playing Area: A rectangular court 40 by 60 feet divided into two halves by a center line. Each half is 30 by 40 feet.

Players: Two teams, 8 to 15 players on each.

Supplies: Two volleyballs or rubber playground balls of about the same size.

Each team occupies one of the halves and is given a volleyball. One or two players from each team should be assigned as ball chasers to retrieve balls behind their own end lines.

The object of the game is to bounce or roll the ball over the opponent's end line. A ball thrown across the line on a fly does not count.

Two scorers are needed, one at each end line. Players can move wherever they wish in their own areas but cannot cross the center line. After the starting signal, the balls are thrown back and forth at will.

CIRCLE TEAM DODGE BALL

Playing Area: Playground, gymnasium

Players: 20 to 40

Supplies: Volleyball or rubber playground ball

The children are divided into two teams, one of which forms a large circle. The other team is in the center of the circle, grouped together. One of the circle players has the ball.

When the starting signal is given, the circle players try to hit the center players with the ball. Any center player hit below the shoulders is eliminated and leaves the circle. Scoring can be done in several ways.

1. Establish a throwing time of one minute. Count the number of center players remaining.
2. Play until all center players have been eliminated. Score is determined by the number of seconds it takes to eliminate the players.
3. Allow a throwing time of one minute. Do not eliminate any center players but give one point to the circle players for each successful hit.
4. Limit the number of throws a team can take: After the specified number of throws, count the remaining center players.

The teams trade places and the scores are compared to determine the winner.

CLUB GUARD

Playing Area: Gymnasium, outdoor smooth surface.

Players: 8 to 10 in each game.

Supplies: Indian club, volleyball.

A circle about fifteen feet in diameter is drawn. Inside this circle at the center, an 18 inch circle is drawn. The Indian club is put in the center of the small circle. One child guards the club. The other children are back of the larger circle which is the restraining line for them. This circle should be definite.

The outer circle players throw the ball at the club and try to knock it down. The guard tries to block the throws with his legs or body.

He must, however, stay out of the smaller inner circle.

The outer circle players pass the ball around rapidly so one of the players can get an opening to throw as the guard needs to maneuver to protect the club. Whoever knocks down the club becomes the new guard.

If the guard steps in the inner circle, he loses his place to whomever has the ball at that time.

A small circle cut from plywood or similar material makes a definite circle so that it is known when the guard steps inside.

Variation: Set up more than one club to be guarded.

COMPETITIVE CIRCLE CONTESTS

Playing Area:　Playground, gymnasium

Players:　Two teams, 10 to 15 on each

Supplies:　2 volleyballs or rubber playground balls, 2 Indian clubs

Two teams can compete against each other in the form of independent circles. The circles should be of the same size, and lines can be drawn on the floor to assure this. The players of each team are numbered consecutively so that there is a player in each circle with corresponding numbers.

These numbered players go to the center of the opponent's circle in turn and compete for their teams against the circle of opponents.

To begin, the #1 players go to the opponent's circle. Three different contests are suggested, using the above arrangement as the basis.

1. Individual Dodge Ball. The circle players throw at the center players, who represent the other team. The circle which hits the center player first wins a point.
2. Club Guard. In this contest, the center player guards an Indian club similarly to the game Club Guard. Whichever circle knocks down the club first wins a point.
3. Touch Ball. The circle players pass the ball from one to another while the center player tries to touch it. Whichever center player touches the ball first wins a point for his team.

After the #1 players have competed, they return to their own team circle and the #2's go to the opponent's circles. This is continued until all players have competed. The team with the most points wins.

ONE STEP

Playing Area:　Playground

Players:　2. Any number of pairs can compete against each other depending upon the space available.

Supplies:　Ball or bean bag

The game is excellent for practicing throwing and catching skills. Two children stand facing each other about three feet apart. One has a ball or bean bag. The object of the game is to throw or toss the ball in the stipulated manner so that the partner can catch it without moving his feet from their position on the floor. When the throw is completed successfully, the thrower takes one step backward. He awaits the throw from his partner. Limits can be established back to which the partners step, or the two children who can move to the greatest distance apart as compared to other couples are the winners. Variables to provide interest and challenge are (1) the type of throw, (2) the type of catching, and (3) the kind of a step. Throwing can be underhand, overhand, two-handed, under one leg, around the back, etc. Catching can be two-handed, left hand, right hand, to the side, etc. The step can be a giant step, a tiny step, a hop, a jump, or some similar designation.

When either child misses, moves his feet, or fails to follow the directions, the partners move forward and start over. A line of children facing each other makes a satisfactory formation for having a number of pairs compete at the same time.

Stunts, Tumbling and Apparatus Primary Grades

Among children, particularly in the primary grades, stunts and tumbling activities play an important part in their daily activity. Apparatus play, too, is important in those schools which have the equipment. Children love to hang, climb, fall, balance, roll, and imitate various characters and objects. Utilizing these desires and interests for a program of these activities provides an excellent learning situation and makes available an excellent developmental medium for fitness values.

The lesson plan for a class in stunts and tumbling should consider the following:

1. Arrange the children in suitable formation for teaching.
2. Provide warm-up activity and review. Stunts previously learned which are similar in nature and can be classed as preliminary to the stunts in the lesson should be reviewed.
3. Describe and demonstrate the stunt.
4. Practice and perfect the stunt.
5. Evaluate the progress, and, if necessary, repeat the directions and continue the practice.

Each of the above steps will be discussed in turn.

Formations for Teaching Stunts and Tumbling

A number of different formations are available for organizing a class in the stunts and tumbling program. The arrangement of the children will depend upon the stunts selected and, in turn, whether or not mats are required. The following formations are the most useful in class work in the area.

Mass Formation. In this formation, the children are scattered throughout the area or floor. This formation is useful when the type of stunt is such that all the children can be active at the same time. The stunt the child is doing should not require too much space for him to perform.

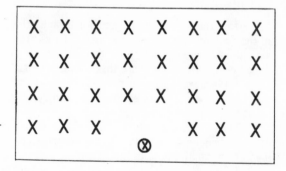

Line Formation. A number of lines are formed, one behind the other. Line formation is useful for stunts requiring forward motion. The class could be divided, for example, into four lines. The first line would perform for a stipulated distance and then retire around the others to reform at the rear. The next line then steps up for activity. Each line should await the instructor's signal to start.

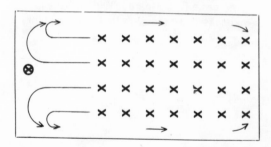

Squad Line Formation. Mats are placed in a line with the squads lined up behind the mats. Each child takes a turn and goes to the end of his line with the others moving up. An alternate method is for the child to perform and then return to his position. If the children are seated, this is the better method.

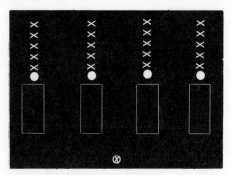

Squad File Formation. By positioning the mats so the children will approach the mats from the ends, a file formation can be arranged. The teacher is in front, and the children perform toward him. As soon as a child has completed his turn, he goes to the end of his line.

Hollow Square. Each group or squad performs on one side of a hollow square. The advantage of this formation is that the children can watch each other. It has the disadvantage that if the teacher is in the center, some portion of the children will be behind his back.

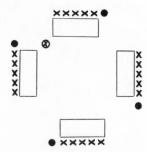

U Shaped Formation. The mats are formed in the shape of a U. The formation has good visual control possibilities for the teacher, and the children are able to see what their classmates are doing.

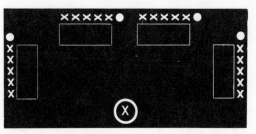

Warm-up Activity

The need for warm-up activity in a program of stunts and tumbling would depend upon the nature of the day's program. In many instances, a simple, previously learned stunt provides a satisfactory warm-up activity. In other cases, the teacher may wish to use movement exploration or exercises for this purpose. The exercises or activity should provide stretching of the body parts to be used later in the stunts.

Primary grades, generally, need only to use a simple type of stunt for warm-up. Warm-up activity could be completed before the children are put into the teaching formation.

Description and Demonstration

The teacher can describe and demonstrate simultaneously. While the teacher may wish to demonstrate some stunts, the children love to help the teacher and can provide effective demonstration. In presenting a stunt, the following pattern should prove helpful.

1. The significance of the name.
   Most of the stunts have a characteristic name and this should be a consideration in the teaching. If the stunt is of an imitative type, the animal or character represented should be described and discussed.

2. The stunt description.
   Most stunts can be approached from the following analysis and taught in steps.

   The starting position. Most stunts have a definite position to assume at the start. To perform properly, the student should be clear on the position he is to assume.

   The execution. Based on the starting position, the key movements for good performance in the stunt should be stressed. Such other factors as how far to travel, how long to balance, and how many times a movement should be done should be clarified to the student.

The finishing position. In some stunts a definite finishing position or act is a part of the stunt. In balancing stunts, for example, it is important that the child return to standing or other position without falling.

Safety considerations. Each child is entitled to know the inherent dangers of any stunt or tumbling activity. The safety factors to be followed and the duties of the spotters or helpers should be a part of the instruction.

3. The demonstration.

As the teacher describes the stunt, a student can demonstrate under the teacher's direction. If the stunt is one that is similar or based upon a previously learned stunt, the description should be brief as possible. In such cases, there may be little need for a demonstration. For primary children the stunts are varied and can take many forms. The teacher should look for children to demonstrate unique and interesting variations of the stunt.

The Performance

The character of each stunt would determine the amount of practice needed and the number of times the stunt should be performed. The teacher should analyze a stunt to the point where he can verbalize the various small points necessary for good performance. Such directions like "Point your toes forward," "Tuck your chin down," and "Fingers spread wide" are examples of cues for successful performance.

Movement exploration principles can be brought in. The children can experiment with different ways to do the stunts, and which variations add interest and challenge. In stunt descriptions, variations are suggested and should be utilized.

A reasonable standard of performance should be a part of the teaching. The teacher must answer the question of the child, "Did I do it?" Some stunts are on a pass-fail basis while others can be evaluated in quality terms. A child needs standards that are both a challenge and attainable.

Evaluation

Evaluation of a stunt performance can be in terms of what things were important to observe, and how well did children perform. Questions and comments over key points are important in evaluation.

Evaluation can also be in terms of the number of children who met the standards of the different stunts. Squad cards with a list of the children and the stunts covered provide an excellent device for evaluation. Not only is this excellent motivation, but the system enables the teacher to make checks of the progress of the children.

The teacher's own evaluation could be in terms of observations of the lesson and the children. Enjoyment, activity, reasonable success, good concentration on the tasks, and observance of social and safety rules are indications of the success of the lesson.

Program for the Primary Grades

The primary program relies on simple stunts with good developmental possibilities. Many of these can be classed as lead-up stunts because the principle or skill involved is used later in a stunt of a more complex nature. Stunts requiring exceptional body control, critical balancing, or the need for great strength should be avoided. Good principles of movement should be applied to stunt, tumbling, and apparatus skills. Standards of performance should be high enough to demand reasonable performance commensurate with the age level of the children. Stunts need to be repeated not only for the development of skills but also for the attainment of good muscular power, agility, and balance.

Methodology

1. Few spotters are needed in the primary program. Assistance in certain stunts like the forward and backward rolls should be given if needed.
2. The instructor should emphasize the character of the stunt. Take a little time to discuss the kind of an animal or object the children are imitating.
3. Form is not an important goal in the primary grades. Hold to reasonable standards within the capacity of the children.
4. Guard against over-fatigue and strain in young children.
5. Goals for the children of cooperating with a partner, a small group, the entire class, and the teacher should be

stressed. Showing consideration in taking turns is important.

6. While only a minority of the stunts require mats, children like to perform on mats, and every class in stunts should have mats in an appropriate arrangement.

7. Select different children to demonstrate stunts, but be sure the demonstration is correct.

8. Rubber soled gym shoes should be worn for tumbling and stunts.

9. If the second or third grade comes to you without previous experience in stunts and tumbling, start with the first grade material and work up to the present grade level.

10. Pockets should be emptied and glasses removed.

11. Proper clothing should be worn for the stunt program. On days for stunts, the girls can change to pedal pushers, play suits, jumpers, or shorts.

12. There is little need for a formalized warm-up period for the primary stunt program. Start the children with a simple known stunt to get the activity underway.

13. Children should be encouraged but not forced to try the stunts. In the primary program, there are few stunts so demanding that all children at least can make a try at them.

14. Horseplay and ridicule have no part in any program of stunts and tumbling. See that the children have fun but respect the efforts of their classmates in trying the stunts.

15. Many couple stunts work well only if the partners are of about the same size.

16. Stimulate many variations with ideas and directions. Repetition is also important.

First Grade — Stunts and Tumbling

The first grade program consists primarily of simple imitative walks and movements. The front roll is introduced but its refinement is left to later grades. Only a few simple balance stunts are included here, all using an upright position. The teacher should be concerned with the creative aspects of the activities as well as the performance standards. Children will tend to do the first grade stunts in many different ways because of different interpretations. Good terminology should be used in describing the different movements. Jumping, hopping, and leaping have different meanings in physical edu-

cation, and the terms should be used properly.

Activities for the First Grade

> Puppy Dog Run
> Bear Walk
> Rabbit Jump
> Elephant Walk
> Head Balance
> Tight Rope Walk
> Bouncing Ball
> Gorilla Walk
> Lame Dog Walk
> Cricket Walk
> Rising Sun
> Front Roll
> Balance Touch
> Heel Click
> Seal Crawl
> Crab Walk
> Rolling Log
> Lowering the Boom
> Turn Over

PUPPY DOG RUN

Place hands on the floor, bending the arms and legs slightly. Walk and run like a happy puppy. The teacher should see that the youngsters look ahead. By keeping the head up in good position, the neck muscles are strengthened.

Variation:

1. Children may also use the same position to imitate a cat. Walk softly, stretching at times like a cat.

2. Monkey Run. Turn the hands so the fingers point in (at each other).

BEAR WALK

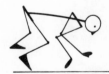

Bend forward and touch the ground with both hands. Travel slowly forward by moving the hand and foot on the same side together, that is, the right hand and foot are moved together and then the left side.

Variation: Have them lift the free foot and hand high while the support is on the other side.

RABBIT JUMP

Crouch to a deep knee bend position and place the hands on the floor in front of the feet with the knees pointed out. Move forward first with the hands and then bring the feet up to the hands.

Emphasize to the children that this is called a jump rather than a hop because both feet move at once.

Variation: Try with the knees kept together and arms on the outside. Also, try taking a great deal of the weight on the hands before the feet are placed.

ELEPHANT WALK

Bend forward, clasping hands together forming a trunk. Walk forward in a slow dignified manner with big steps, keeping the legs straight and swinging the trunk from side to side. He can also stop and throw water over his back with the trunk.

HEAD BALANCE

Place a bean bag, clock, or book on the head of the child. Have him walk, stoop, turn around, sit down, get up, etc.

The object should be placed so that the upper body is in good posture. Use hands out to the side for balance.

TIGHT ROPE WALK

Select a line, board, or chalked line for the stunt. Arms are held sidewards for balance. Children pretend to be on a high wire, losing and regaining balance, and making slow progress. Different stunts done on a high wire can be tried on the line.

BOUNCING BALL

Keeping the body straight, jump up and down from a bent knee position. Start with a high "bounce" and gradually lower the height of the jump to similate the ball coming to a rest. Avoid a full deep knee bend.

Variation: Do this as a partner stunt with one partner serving as the bouncer and the other as the ball. Reverse positions. Have children watch how a ball really bounces and then try to imitate.

GORILLA WALK

Bend knees slightly and carry the trunk forward. Arms hang at the side. As the child walks forward, he should touch his fingers to the ground at each step.

Variation: Let the children stop and beat on their chests like a gorilla. Also, bounce up and down with hands and feet touching the floor.

LAME DOG WALK

Walk on both hands and one foot. The other foot is held in the air as if injured. Walk a distance and change feet. Eyes should be forward. Also move backwards.

CRICKET WALK

The child squats and spreads his knees. He puts his arms between his knees and grasps the outside of his ankles with his hands. In this position, he walks forward or backward. He can chirp like a cricket. Turn around right and left.

RISING SUN

Lie on back. With using the arms only for balance, rise to a standing position.

Variation: Have the children fold arms over the chest.

FRONT ROLL

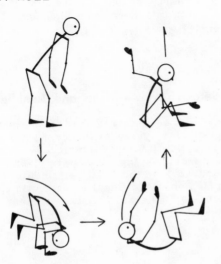

Stand with the feet apart facing forward. Squat and place the hands on the mat, shoulder width apart with the elbows against the inside of the thighs. Tuck the chin to the chest and make a rounded back. A push-off with the hands and feet provides the force for the roll. The child should carry the weight on his hands with the elbows bearing the weight of the thighs. By keeping the elbows against the thighs and assuming weight there, the force of the roll is easily transferred to the rounded back. The child should try to roll forward to his feet. Later, try with the knees together and no weight on the elbows.

Kneeling alongside the child, the instructor can help by placing one hand on the back of the child's head and the other under the thigh for a push.

BALANCE TOUCH

An object (eraser, block, or rolled up paper) is placed a yard away from a line. Balancing on one foot, the child reaches out with the other foot, touches the object, and recovers to the starting position. See that he does not place weight on the object but merely touches it.

Variation: Try at various distances. On a gymnasium floor, count the number of boards to get the distance of the touch.

HEEL CLICK

Stand with feet slightly apart. Jump up and click heels coming down with feet in original position.

Variation:
1. Have the child clap hands overhead as he clicks his heels.
2. Another variation is to have the child join hands with one or more children. A signal is needed. The children can count, "One, Two, THREE," jumping on the third count.

SEAL CRAWL

The child is in a front leaning (push-up) position, the weight supported on straightened arms and toes. Keeping the body straight, the child walks forward using his hands for propelling force and dragging his feet.

Watch to see the body is straight and the head is up.

Variation: Let the child walk forward a short distance and then roll over on his back clapping his hands like a seal.

CRAB WALK

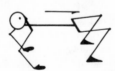

The child squats down and reaches back putting both hands on the floor without sitting down. With head, neck and body level and in a straight line, walk forward, backward, and sideward.

Children have a tendency to lower the hips. See that the body is kept in a straight line.

Variation:
1. As each step is taken with a hand, the other hand can slap the chest.
2. Move the hand and foot together on the same side.
3. Try balancing on one leg and opposite hand.

ROLLING LOG

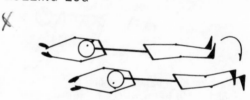

Lie on back with arms stretched overhead. Roll sideways the length of the mat. The next time roll with the hands pointed toward the other side of the mat. To roll in a straight line, keep the feet slightly apart.

LOWERING THE BOOM

From front leaning rest position (push-up position) lower the body completely to the ground by use of the arms only. The body remains straight. This is a preliminary to the push-up.

Variation: Come down inch by inch in stages.

TURN OVER

From a front leaning rest position (as in Lowering the Boom), turn over so that the back is to the floor. The body should not touch the floor. Continue the turn until the original position is assumed. Reverse the direction. Turn back and forth several times.

Second Grade — Stunts and Tumbling

The second grade program should begin with a review of the first grade stunts. As in the previous grade, a stunt using front leaning position is given. Continued work on the front roll should be carried on. Additional stunts build on the basis of the work in the previous grade.

Activities for the Second Grade

- Front Roll
- Frog Jump
- Walrus Walk
- Heel Slap
- Pogo Stick
- Wicket Walk
- Top
- Back Roller
- Measuring Worm
- Leg Balance
- Backward Curl
- Turk Stand
- Three Point Tip-Up
- Push-up

FRONT ROLL

There should be continued practice of the front roll. Children love to roll and some type of rolling should be a part of each lesson.

FROG JUMP

From a squatting position, with the hands placed on the floor slightly in front of the feet, jump forward a few feet lighting on the hands and feet simultaneously. Note the difference between this stunt and the Rabbit Jump (Grade One).

WALRUS WALK

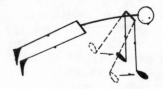

Similar to the Seal Walk (Grade One). Begin with a front leaning rest position with fingers pointed outward. Make progress by moving both hands forward at the same time. Some children may be able to clap hands as they each step.

Before giving this stunt, review the Seal Walk.

HEEL SLAP

From an erect position with hands at the sides, jump up into the air and slap both heels with the hands.

Variation: Use a one, two, three rhythm with small preliminary jumps on one and two.

POGO STICK

Pretend to be a Pogo Stick by keeping a stiff body and jumping on the toes. Hold the hands in front as if grasping the stick. Progress in various directions.

WICKET WALK

Pupils bend over and touch the floor with their weight evenly distributed on hands and feet. By keeping the knees straight, a wicket can be formed. Walk the wicket forward, backward, and sideward.

Be sure the knees are kept reasonably straight as the stunt loses much of its flexibility values if the knees are bent too much.

The stunt gets its name from the position of the child who resembles a wicket in a croquet game.

TOP

From a standing position with arms at the sides, have children try jumping and twisting to face the opposite direction, twisting three-quarters of the way around, and making a full twist facing the original direction. Number concepts can be stressed in having the children do half, three-quarter, and full turns.

Successful execution of the stunt should call for the child to land in good balance with hands near the sides.

Children should turn right and left.

BACK ROLLER

This stunt is a lead-up to the backward roll.

Form a human ball by bringing the knees up to the chest and clasping them with the arms. Roll back and forth. Try to roll forward to a stand. Begin with the feet crossed first and then progress next with the feet together.

MEASURING WORM

From a front leaning position, keeping the knees stiff, bring up the feet as close as possible to the hands by inching forward with the feet. Regain position by inching the hands forward.

Stress good form keeping the body straight when supported on the hands and feet. Part of the value is in the flexibility possibilities which is lost if the knees are not kept straight.

LEG BALANCE

Forward. With the knee straight, extend one leg forward with the toe pointed so that it is level to the floor. Balance on the other leg for 5 seconds. Use arms out to the side for balance.

Backward. Extend the leg backward until it is parallel to the floor. Keep eyes forward and arms out to the side while balancing on the other leg. Hold for 5 seconds without moving.

BACKWARD CURL

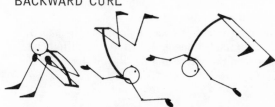

Begin in sitting position with the knees drawn up to the chest and the chin tucked down. Roll backwards until the weight is on the shoulders. Hands are placed alongside the head on the mat as the child rolls back. The hands should support much of the weight. Feet and legs come back over the head so that the toes can touch the mat. Roll back to starting position.

The teacher needs to recognize that this like the back roller is a lead-up to the backward roll. The hand pressure is an important item to be stressed. Teach the children to push hard against the floor to take the pressure from the back of the neck.

TURK STAND

Stand with feet apart and arms folded in front. Pivot on the balls of <u>both</u> feet and face the opposite direction. The legs are now crossed. Sit down in this position. Reverse the process. Get up without using the hands for aid and uncross the legs with a pivot to face original direction.

THREE POINT TIP-UP

Squat down on the mat, placing the hands flat, fingers pointing forward, with the elbows inside and pressed against the inner part of the knees. Lean forward, slowly transferring the weight of the body onto the bent elbows and hands until the forehead touches the mat. Return to position.

This stunt provides a background for the headstand given in a later grade.

Variation: Put the head down first and climb the knees on top the elbows.

PUSH-UP

From a front leaning rest position, lower the body and push-up back to original position. Be sure that the only movement is in the arms with the body kept rigid and straight. Girls should use the knee push-up

Variation: Stop half-way down and half-way up.

Third Grade — Stunts and Tumbling

In the third grade, more emphasis on form is applied to the stunts, particularly to the forward roll. This stunt and its companion, the backward roll, provide the basis for the child's tumbling experience through his school years and should be mastered as well as possible. Introduced also in the third grade is a number of couple and group stunts. Be sure to match youngsters in size when the couple stunt indicates this.

Activities for the Third Grade

    Forward Roll
    Forward Roll Variation
    Backward Roll
    Frog Handstand (Tip-Up)
    Russian Dance
    Leap Frog
    Coffee Grinder
    Mule Kick
    Squat Thrust
    Sit-Up
    Double Lame Dog
    Partner Pull-up (Couple Stunt)
    Partner Hopping (Couple Stunt)
    Wring the Dish Rag (Couple Stunt)
    Churn the Butter (Couple Stunt)
    Twister (Couple Stunt)
    Chinese Get-Up (Couple or Group Stunt)

FORWARD ROLL

Hands are on the mat, shoulder width apart, with the fingers pointed forward. The knees are between the arms. From this position, push off with the feet and rock forward on the hands. Just as you feel yourself falling off balance, tuck the head down between the arms with chin on chest. The back of the head touches the mat and the weight is then born by the rounded back. Grasp the shins and pull yourself onto your feet. For those who have trouble, put the hands between the knees and the elbows against the thighs.

FORWARD ROLL VARIATION

During the roll the child can cross his legs and come to his feet in this position. The legs can be uncrossed with a pivot which will face the performer in the direction from which he came. He can then roll back to position.

BACKWARD ROLL

Start with the back to the direction of the roll in the same squat position as in the forward roll. Push off with the hands quickly, sit down, and start rolling over on the back. At the same time bring the hands up over the shoulders, palms up, fingers pointed backward. Continue rolling backward with the knees close to the chest. The hands will now touch the mat at about the same time as the head. It is vitally important at this point to push hard with the hands. Continue to roll over the top of the head and push off the mat until ready to stand.

Variation: Some teachers have had good success with this stunt by having the child clasp his hands in back of his neck. He sits down rapidly and throws his knees over his head to provide the momentum. By keeping his hands in back of his neck the neck is protected and the elbows take the pressure.

Spotting

Care must be taken never to push a child from the hip, forcing him to roll over. This puts undue pressure on the back of the neck.

The proper method of aiding the child who has difficulty with the stunt is as follows. The spotter stands in a straddle position with his near foot alongside at about the spot where the performer's hands and head will make contact with the mat. His other foot is one stride in the direction of the roll. The critical point is for the spotter to lift the hips just as the head and hands of the performer make contact with the mat. This is accomplished by taking the back hand and reaching across to the far hip of the performer and getting under the near hip with the near hand. The lift is applied on the front of the hips just below the belt line. The object of this assist is to relieve the pressure on the neck.

FROG HANDSTAND (Tip-Up)

This follows the same directions as the three-point tip-up (second grade). Squat down on the mat, placing the hands flat, fingers pointing forward, with the elbows inside and pressed against the inner part of the knees. Lean forward using the leverage of the elbows against the knees and balance on the hands. Hold for five seconds. Return to position.

RUSSIAN DANCE

Squat down on one heel with the other foot extended forward with the weight on its heel. With the back straight and the arms extended forward, rapidly change the position of the feet.

Variation:
1. Try with the arms folded high in front.
2. Try with one foot out to the side and change to the side each time.

LEAP FROG

A back is formed by one student who bends over resting his hands either on the floor (low back) or on his knees (high back). The jumper, with a running start, must lay his hands flat on the "back" at the shoulders and vault over him. Stress the legs to be spread while clearing the "back" and emphasize good landing form.

Variation:
1. Have more than one back for a series of jumps.
2. Combine with a forward roll following the leap frog.
3. Vault from the side rather than from the rear.

COFFEE GRINDER

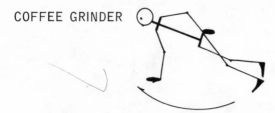

Put one hand on the floor and extend the body with that side to the floor in a side leaning position. The child walks around his hand making a complete circle while keeping his body straight. Repeat with the other hand.

MULE KICK

Stoop down and place the hands on the floor in front of the feet. The arms are the front legs of the mule. Kick out with the hind legs while the weight is entirely supported by the "front legs." The arms should be straight when the kick is made.

Variation: See if the children can make two kicks before the feet touch the ground.

SQUAT THRUST

While the squat thrust later is used as an exercise, the act of completing the cycle successfully is classified as a stunt. The stunt is done in four definite movements. Starting from the position of attention, on count one the child squats down on the floor placing the hands flat (shoulder width) on the floor with the elbows inside the knees. On count two, the feet and legs are thrust back so that the body is perfectly straight from head to toe in push-up position.

On count three, the child returns to squat position, and on the last count returns to the position of attention.

Girls should do 3 in 10 seconds and boys 4 in the same amount of time.

SIT-UP

Two children work together with one child holding the other's feet. The pupil lies on his back with the legs extended and feet 1 foot apart. The hands, with the fingers interlaced, are behind the lower part of the head.

The child sits up, alternating touching the right and left elbows to the opposite knees on sit-ups. One touch is made on each sit-up.

Boys should be able to complete 15 sit-ups while girls should be able to do at least 10.

Be sure the child returns the head completely to the floor each time. No rest should be allowed as the sit-ups must be continuous. The child may move at his own pace, however.

Variation: Curl-up. Take the same position except that the knees are up so an angle of 90 degrees is formed at the knee joint. The feet are flat (soles down) on the floor.

DOUBLE LAME DOG

Support the body on one hand and one leg (same side). Move forward in this position maintaining balance. The distance should be short (5'-10') as this is strenuous.

Variation: Keep the free hand on the hip.

PARTNER PULL-
'P (Couple Stunt)

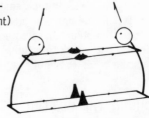

Partners sit down facing each other with soles of the feet against each other. Partners reach forward and grasp hands. By pulling cooperatively, both come up to a stand. Try to return to sitting position.

PARTNER HOPPING
(Couple Stunt)

Children can hop together a short distance. No hopping should be too far. Three combinations are suggested.

1. Stand facing each other. Hop on the right leg and extend the left leg forward to be grasped at the ankle by the partner.
2. The same can be done back to back with the knee bent and the leg grasped by the partner.
3. Side by side. Partners stand side by side with inside arms around each other's waist. Hop forward on the outside foot.
4. Using #1 or #2, turn a complete circle right and left. This is called a windlass.

If either partner starts to fall, the other should release the leg immediately.

WRING THE DISH RAG
(Couple Stunt)

Two children face each other and join hands. Raise one pair arms (right for one and left for the other) and turn under that arm continuing until back to original position. Care must be taken to avoid bumping head.

CHURN THE BUTTER
(Couple Stunt)

Partners should be approximately the same size in this stunt. Partners are back to back with elbows locked. One partner bends forward from the hips while the other partner springs from the floor, lifting his feet up. Alternate this movement between partners.

Children should not bring partner too high or too far back. A third child should act as a spotter. Knees should be lifted.

TWISTER
(Couple Stunt)

Partners face and grasp right hands like shaking hands. #1 swings his right leg over the head of #2 and turns around taking a straddle position over his own arm. #2 swings his left leg over #1 who has bent over, and the partners are now back to back. #1 now continues with his left leg and faces in the original direction. #2 swings his right leg over back to the original face to face position.

Partners need to duck to avoid being kicked by the other's foot as the leg is swung over.

CHINESE GET-UP (Couple or Group Stunt)

Two children sit back to back and lock arms. From this position both try to stand by pushing against each other's back. Sit down again.

Variation:

1. Try the stunt with three or four children.
2. From a half-way down position, move like a spider.

Apparatus Play

Hanging apparatus play has important physical fitness values for children. Climbing structures, horizontal ladders, exercise bars (horizontal bars), and climbing ropes provide development activity for the arm and shoulder girdle regions, an area which receives little development in running type activities. Apparatus that provides opportunity for hanging, swinging by the hands, traveling by the hands, chinning, climbing, and body control while suspended in the air makes good muscular demands on the arms and shoulder girdle. In addition, excellent values in flexibility are present. In contrast, the "sit and ride" types of apparatus have little value for physical fitness, and yield poor returns in strength and flexibility development.

The following pieces of apparatus will be discussed: climbing structures, horizontal ladder, exercise bars, climbing ropes, the balance beam, parallel ropes, and climbing sets.

Climbing Structures

Climbing structures commercially are on the market under many names and designs. Climbing apparatus is challenging to children and develops all the large muscles of the body. The necessary rules for the children and the types of stunts that can be done depend a great deal upon the design of the climbing structure.

RULES FOR CLIMBING

1. Bars are slippery on rainy days. Children should use the structures only when the bars are dry.
2. Children should not crowd.
3. The opposed thumb grip should be used. The child should face the bars either ascending or descending.
4. Children should keep hands to themselves.

STUNTS

1. Climb up the outside and down the inside.
2. Climb up the inside and down the outside.
3. Climb up going in and out of the rungs. Climb down
4. Climb sideways in and out.
5. Using arms and legs (without crossing), circle to the left and right.
6. Follow the leader.

The design of the structure will suggest many other feasible stunts.

Horizontal Ladder

The horizontal ladder is considered a valuable piece of apparatus because of the excellent body development possibilities which can result from its use. It provides for hanging, swinging, chinning, and many other forms of exercise. It is not a climb-

ing structure and should be used primarily for hanging or traveling by the hands.

RULES FOR THE HORIZONTAL LADDER

1. All children should travel in the same direction.
2. When one child is already on the ladder, the second should wait until the first is halfway across before starting.
3. The opposed thumb grip is important and the back of the hands should be toward the child.
4. Metal ladders are slippery when wet and the use should be avoided during rainy weather.
5. Dismount should be made in a bent-leg position, landing on the balls of the feet lightly.
6. Whenever the child is inverted so the head and shoulders are hanging down, there must be spotters.
7. Stunts should not be hurried as value comes from controlled hanging.

STUNTS ON THE HORIZONTAL LADDER

Stunts are divided into hanging activities (stationary), swinging hangs, and traveling activities.

HANGING STUNTS

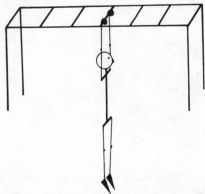

1. Pencil--child hangs from a rung with feet pointed to ground.

2. Knee Lift--A hang with the knees up so the thighs are parallel to the ground.

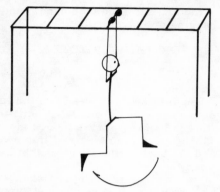

3. Bicycle--Same as #2 except that the feet move as if pedaling a bicycle.

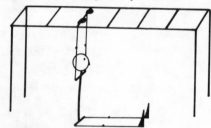

4. Half Lever--Legs are brought up parallel to the ground with the knees straight and the toes pointed.

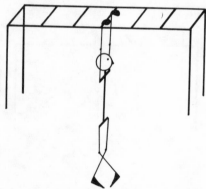

5. Scissors--Hang with the feet pointed and moving back and forth like a scissors. Move legs from side, crossing each time.

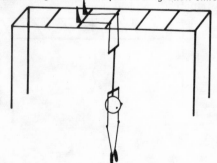

6. Leg Hang--Hanging to one run, bring the feet up and over the next rung until the feet

can hook under a rung. The back of the knees are now over the near rung and the feet with additional support under the next rung. Release the hand position and hang inverted.

7. Chin yourself once.

Swinging Stunts

1. Pendulum--Hang from a rung with the body straight and the feet pointed down. Swing back and forth like a pendulum. Swing from side to side.
2. Rocking Chair--From the knee hang position (#2 from previous list) swing back and forth like a rocking chair.
3. Leg Hang Swing--From the position of leg hand (#6 from previous list) fold arms across the chest and swing back and forth.

Traveling Stunts

1. Travel using the rungs.
   a. One rung at a time
   b. Every other rung
2. On the side rail using one rail only.
   a. Sliding along with the hands bringing one hand to the other.
   b. Sliding along with the hands crossing each time (hand over hand).
3. Using both side rails at the same time.
   a. Travel forward and backward

Exercise Bar (Horizontal Bar) for Primary Grades

Horizontal bars should be installed on the playground in series of at least three, at different heights. The primary program should be limited to simple hangs and climbs. To perform many of the more complicated stunts on the bar, it is necessary to have sufficient arm strength to pull the body up to and over the bar. Youngsters in the third grade will begin to have this capacity among some of the children, but the emphasis in the primary grades should be on a more limited program.

RULES FOR THE EXERCISE BAR

1. Only one child on a bar at a time.
2. Do not use the bar when it is wet.
3. Grip firmly with the hands in opposed thumb grip.

STUNTS ON THE EXERCISE BAR

1. Hangs: feet pointed, one or both knees up, half lever.
2. Swing back and forth. Jump forward.

3. Move hand to hand along the bar. Hand over hand.
4. Arm and Leg Hang--hang with one arm and one leg.
5. Arm Hang and Leg pull-up--bring the legs up and hook over the bar.
6. Sloth Travel--hang by hands and feet and travel along the bar like a sloth.
7. Chin--done with back of the hands to the performer.

Activities on Climbing Ropes for Primary Grades

Few of the activities used on climbing ropes for primary grades can be classed as actual climbing. Becoming used to the rope and gaining in confidence are important goals in this preliminary work to rope climbing. The emphasis of activity is on those types where the body is suspended in the air by a grasp on the rope. However, third graders can begin a little climbing but the majority of the children gain more from the simple pull-ups and hangs.

RULES FOR THE ACTIVITIES ON ROPES

1. Never go higher than your strength will allow. Always have enough strength left to get down.
2. In coming down, do not let the rope slide between the hands or thighs. Bad skin burns and blisters can be formed from the friction of the hands sliding down the ropes.
3. Use the hand over hand change of grip when climbing and when coming down.
4. Work hard on the simpler stunts to develop good grip and control.
5. When swinging on a rope, be sure the other children are out of the way.

STUNTS ON THE ROPES

1. Pull-ups and return--use hand over hand grips.
   a. Pull up from lying position to sitting.
   b. Pull up from sitting to standing.
   c. Pull up from lying to standing keeping the body straight.
2. Hang from standing--reach up as high as possible, come to a bent arm position and hang with feet in various positions.
   a. One or both knees up
   b. Bicycling movement
   c. Half lever
      Try on either side of the rope and also with the rope between the legs.

d. Full lever--bring the feet up to the face with the knees kept straight.
3. Jump Hang Position--jump as high as possible and hang.
   Repeat all the different leg positions from the previous stunt
4. Pull-up--jump up and grab rope. Pull the body up and lower several times.
5. Inverted Hang--jump to bent arm position. Swing the feet up over the head and grasp the rope between the legs holding the inverted position with both the hands and feet. While learning, the teacher should spot for the youngster to prevent injury in case of a fall.
6. Swing and Jump--holding the rope at an angle and standing on a low stool, jump up and grasp the rope, swinging over to the other end of the arc. At the height of the swing, the child lets go of the rope and drops to a mat. The children should land with a bent knee position on the balls of the feet.
7. Modified Climbing--some of the stronger and more skilled children can be allowed to climb 8 to 10 feet. Put a mark with adhesive tape on the rope to limit the climb.

Balance Beam Exercises for Primary Children

Activities on the balance beam are excellent to develop poise, confidence, and a sense of balance. The stunts should be done correctly and with good body control.

Gym shoes work much more successfully than street shoes. Children should be taught to toe directly forward on all steps.

RULES FOR THE BALANCE BEAM

1. Children should step, not jump, off the beam.
2. If falling, the student should step off quickly rather than teeter and finally dismount in awkward, rough fashion.
3. Success in a stunt is determined if the child can pause for a moment with good balance at the end of the beam and then step off.
4. Beginning activities should be done with two parallel beams about two feet apart.

EXERCISES ON THE BALANCE BEAMS

1. Partners on two parallel beams.
   a. Walk forward, inside hands joined. Walk backward.
   b. Walk sideward with both hands

joined.

  c. Walk sideward with both hands joined using grapevine step. Alternate crossing feet behind and in front while stepping.

2. Walking on a single beam

  a. Walking forward and backward with arms at different positions: held forward, sideward, overhead, behind back, on head, etc.

  b. Side step with hands in various positions. Use for closing steps, crossing front and rear, alternating crossing.

  c. Walk forward, backward, using follow steps.

  d. Move forward with one step for halfway; complete the trip with another step.

3. Stunt type beam activities

  a. Use various walks balancing an object on the head.

  b. Walk to the center, perform a stunt and continue. Stunts to be used include kneeling (one or both), touching the floor, walk under a wand, step over a wand.

  c. Hop on one foot moving across.

  d. Cat walk across.

  e. Wheelbarrow walk with feet of pusher on floor and on beam.

  f. Walk to center, do a side leaning rest (support on one arm and the feet). Try on the other side. Use only balancing acts like balancing on one foot.

4. Throwing, catching, bouncing.

  a. Roll a volleyball or playground ball across the beam.

  b. Bounce the ball across.

  c. Dribble the ball across. Bend low for short dribbles.

  d. Pass and receive from a partner at the head of the beam.

  e. Bat the ball back to a partner (like in volleyball).

Parallel Ropes

Two horizontal ropes parallel to each other are suspended across the room or across a corner of the room. The ropes need to be fastened securely for up to five children may be on them at one time. Some pulley or turnbuckle arrangement should be present to provide proper tension. The ropes can be from five to six and one-half feet in height from the floor, depending upon the age of the children.

Ropes lend themselves efficiently to good movement exploration possibilities.

Four or five children should be able to work on the ropes at one time, each of whom uses his own space carefully.

Teachers need to stimulate the children with simple directions so that they will experiment with a variety of movements. Try to get them to:

1. Hang a variety of ways from the ropes. Change from one position to another.
2. Move along the ropes using different hanging holds and body shapes.
3. See what they can do between, over, under, and around the ropes.

Bench Stunts

Bench stunts can be done with the bench in ordinary position on the ground and as an inclined bench, one end of which is supported by a small wooden horse. The teacher should make use of the movement exploration possibilities of this piece of apparatus as the variety of movements that can be done is endless. Some suggestions are:

1. Move along the bench using different means of locomotion. Touch heels or toes to the floor in combination with the movements.
2. Work with a ball--bounce, dribble, toss and catch, pick up from ground, handle ball under bench without touching the floor, roll ball, etc.
3. Work with a partner. Do balance stunts. Step over kneeling partner. Pass partner by side by side.
4. Use both hands and feet to move along the bench as in the following.

  a. Seat scooter. Lead with the heels, sit and scoot the seat along the bench. Go backwards.

  b. Use cat walk, seal crawl, lame dog, double lame dog, etc.

  c. Move along the length of bench in a front leaning rest position with the hands on the floor and feet on bench. Try with the same position, but instead of moving sidewards, turn the body over.

  d. The bouncer. Using the hands on top of the bench as support, see how high you can bounce from the floor.

  e. Crouch jumper. Move with crouch jumps with hands on the bench and both feet placed alternately on opposite sides of the bench. Make forward progress by moving the hands a little each time.

  f. Crawl under the bench or around

the end of the bench without touching the floor.

5. Run, hop, skip, or jump along the bench finishing with a jump for height from the the end of the bench. Try straddle jumps to the top of the bench and back to the floor.
   a. Jump from end and go into a front roll.
6. Use the inclined bench for many of the previous stunts. Finish with a jump for height from the end of the bench.

Combination Sets

Combination Sets like the following are available in a variety of equipment combinations. Somewhat the same effect can be secured from sturdy horses and appropriate benches, especially those which have the bench-balance beam combination. These are useful for 3 or 4 children at a time and should not be considered the basis for a program for the entire class.

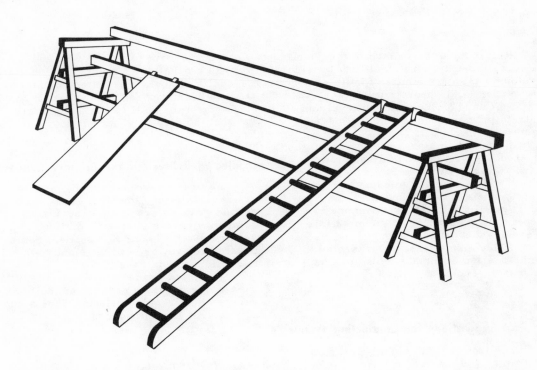

Chapter 13
Relays for Primary Children

Practical Suggestions for Conducting Relays
Selected Relays for the Primary Grades

Relays have their place in the physical education program in that they provide developmental opportunities for fitness, competition, and opportunity to exercise skills. Relays on the primary level concentrate primarily on locomotor movements and simple ball skills.

Relays in this presentation begin in the second grade as the individualistic characteristics of the first grade children do not lend themselves to organized team efforts. Relays can follow skills but caution is needed because performance can become sloppy because of the emphasis on speed and winning.

Relay formations are presented in the discussion under movement in Chapter 6 at the end of the chapter.

Practical Suggestions for Conducting Relays

1. Place from four to eight players on a team. Too many on a team drag out the race and the children lose interest.
2. If the teams have uneven numbers, either some players on the lesser teams should run twice, or a rotation system should be set up by which the extra players lay out in turn.
3. Be definite in the starting point, the turning point, and the finishing act. In some races, crossing the line would be the finishing act. In others, the captain may be required to hold up the ball while the rest of the players are in good formation. A definite finishing act eliminates arguments with regard to the determination of the winner.
4. Infractions should be penalized. It is good social learning for the children to experience the situation where they

must conform to rules or be assessed with a penalty. A team could be disqualified, points deducted, or other penalties imposed. Impartiality should be the rule. All teams and players should be on an equal basis.

Selected Relays for the Primary Grades

As previously mentioned, no relays are designated for the first grade. The second graders are given experiences in relays which use simple formations and require mostly locomotor skills. Some passing relays for bean bags and balls of the volleyball size are included.

The third grade relays expand on the base of the previous grade. In addition, relays which require rotation when a runner returns are introduced.

Second Grade Relays

Lane Relays

With one player at a time running to a turning point and back, many different relays using the basic locomotor skills can be scheduled. Running, walking (forward and backwards), hopping, skipping, galloping, sliding, and jumping are movements that can be used in relays.

BEAN BAG PASS OR BALL PASS RELAY

Supplies: Bean Bag or Ball for each team

Formation: Lane with players facing to the side

The player on the right starts the bean bag or ball. When it gets to the end of the line, the race is over. Be sure each player handles the bag or ball.

CIRCLE PASS RELAY

Supplies: Ball for each team

Formation: Each team forms a separate circle of the same size. At first the circle should be small enough so that the players can hand the ball to each other. Later, as skill increases, the circles can be enlarged.

Leader of each group starts the ball around the circle by handing. As soon as the ball gets back to the leader, the entire team sits down. The first team to be seated in good formation wins.

BOUNCE BALL RELAY

Supplies: Ball that will bounce for each team

Formation: Lane

A circle is drawn 10 to 15 feet in front of each team. The first player runs to the circle, bounces the ball once, runs back to his team, and gives the ball to the second player who repeats the same routine. Each player has a turn, and the team having the last man carry his ball back over the finish line wins. To vary, have the players bounce the ball more than once.

BOWL RELAY

Supplies: Ball for each team

Formation: Lane

The player at the head of each team has a ball. A line is drawn 15 to 20 feet in front of each team. The first player runs to the line, turns, and rolls the ball back to the second player. The second player must wait behind the starting line to catch the ball and then repeats the pattern of the first player. The race is over when the last player has received the ball and carried it over the forward line.

Third Grade Relays

Lane Relays

Using lane formation and a turning point, lane relays employing running, walking, and other locomotor movements should be run. In addition, relays can use the animal imitations explained in the stunts and tumbling program. The following are excellent for lane relays:

> Puppy Dog
> Bear Walk
> Rabbit Jump
> Lame Dog Walk
> Crab Walk
> Seal Crawl
> Pogo Stick
> Measuring Worm

PARTNER RELAYS

Supplies: None

Formation: Lane formation of partners

Children run with partners (inside hands joined) just the same as a single runner. Use running, walking, skipping, hopping, and galloping. Sliding can be used to make an interesting relay. Children face each other with both hands joined (as partners) and slide one way to a turning point, sliding back to starting point leading with the other side.

CROSS OVER RELAY

Supplies: Ball for each team

Formation: Lane

Review Bowl Relay from the Second Grade. This relay is similar. Two lines are drawn about 15 feet apart. The teams are in lane formation behind one of the lines. The player in front has a ball. On signal, each player with the ball runs to the next line and throws the ball back to the one at the head of the line, who runs forward and repeats the throw. The race is over when the last player in line catches the ball and runs forward across the forward line.

SNOWBALL RELAY

Supplies: None

Formation: Lane

Teams are in lane formation but the lanes must be from 10 to 15 feet apart. The first player runs forward, around the turning point, and back to his team where he takes the next player by the hand. He repeats the trip with the second player in tow. When the two reach the team again, the second player takes the hand of the third one in line. The trip is repeated and so on until on the last trip, the entire team will run around the turning point and finish over the starting line.

Variation: There is a variation of this race called Locomotive. The second player would hook on the engine (first player) and in turn each of the players would hook on until the entire team forms a train.

PASS THE BUCK RELAY

Supplies: None

Formation: Lane with teams facing sideways

Players are facing sideways with lanes about 5 feet apart. All players of a team are linked by joining hands. The leader is on the right of each team. On signal, the leader "passes the buck" to the next player (by squeezing his hand), who in turn passes it to the next and so on down the line. The end player, when he receives the "buck", runs across the front of his team, and becomes the new leader. He starts the squeeze which is passed down the line. Each player, in turn, comes around to the end of the line with the original leader finally returning to his original position.

Variation: Instead of "passing the buck," teams could pass a bean bag, Indian club, or ball.

STOOP AND STRETCH RELAY

Supplies: Bean Bag for each team

Formation: Lane

The players stand in lane formation about 2 feet apart. The player in front has a bean bag, which he reaches over his head and drops it. Using both hands, the second player picks it up, reaches over his head, and drops the bag behind him. The bag continues down the line until the last player picks it up. He comes to the front of the line and starts the bag back down the line. Each player in turn comes to the front, and the relay is over when the team has returned to its original position.

Chapter 14

Story Games and Dramatic Play

Stories
Dramatic Play with Poems
Other Experiences as a Basis for Dramatic Play

Story games and dramatic play have a part in the program of physical education for the primary grades, particularly in the first and second grades. The children love to interpret stories with gross body movements and dramatic movement patterns.

Story plays provide experiences similar to creative rhythms except that the children interpret the unfolding of the story in movement rather than taking cues from the rhythm. Story plays, however, can be conducted with the aid of rhythm.

A story play should provide a variety of creative opportunities, be a satisfying experience, allow freedom of response, and encourage all to participate at a level of ability, regardless of the quality of performance. The activity should be conducted in such a way informally which will allow children to investigate the range of body movement and give way to free response within the limits of the story. Story plays can give opportunity for each child to achieve status and find his place among his classmates.

Story games are so labeled because the children regard them as a game to match the words of the story with movement patterns. However, there should be no competition, nor should there be any elimination of children who do not achieve a certain standard or routine.

A skillful leader can do an effective piece of work in story games with comparatively simple materials. The old, familiar stories offer excellent material for stories. Then, too, the many poems can be utilized as a basis for movement experiences. The leader should be able to draw out ideas from the world of childhood and the adult world.

Formations should be informal with the children scattered or in a loose circle formation. All should be able to see and hear the leader. It is important that a good story basis be set for the stories so probably the teacher would need to do the relating. However, if children are capable, they can be utilized.

Stories

The children love to act out and dramatize many of the old, familiar stories. No doubt, both the children and the teacher have favorites. Some may be in the following list.

The Three Bears
The Three Pigs
Black Beauty
Cinderella
Rumpelstilskin
The Shoemaker and the Elves
The Pied Piper
Mother Goose Stories
Henny Penny
The Sleeping Beauty
The Town Musicians
Peter Pan

The list is only a starting point, but is given to illustrate the kinds of stories that have possibilities.

Stories may need to be adapted and rewritten, using only the main points of the story to direct the movement.

As an illustration, the story, "Jack the Giant Killer" is given with the story in the left hand column and the suggested actions on right. It should be emphasized that the actions grow out of the discussions with the children with respect to the best way they feel the story should be interpreted.

JACK THE GIANT KILLER

Once upon a time a giant called Carmaran lived on top of a mountain in a cave. He was a very wicked giant so the king of the country offered a large reward to the person who would kill the giant. So Jack, a country boy, decided he would try his luck.

1. One morning Jack took a shovel and pick and started toward the mountain. He hurried as he wished to climb the mountain before dark.

1. Picking up axe and shovel and running around in a circle.

2. Jack finally reached the foot of the mountain and started to climb up.

2. Walking around circle with high knee upward bending.

3. He came to a place where he had to use his hands to help him climb.

3. Climbing with opposite arm raising upward bending.

4. Just as it grew dark, Jack reached the top of the mountain. When he was sure the giant was asleep in his bed he took his pick and began to dig a hole outside the cave entrance.

4. Vigorous digging movement with trunk twisting, standing with feet apart.

5. After he had loosened the dirt with his pick, Jack took the shovel and threw the dirt up on all sides of the hole.

5. Vigorous shoveling movement, first right then left, throwing the dirt in various directions.

6. Then Jack covered up the hole with some long straws and sticks he picked up.

6. Forward downward bending, picking up straws, twisting alternately left and right.

7. After this was done, Jack waited until morning when he called loudly and wakened the giant who strode angrily out of the cave. As he was very tall, he took big steps.

7. Arms overhead, stretching up tall walking around circle on tiptoes.

8. The giant was so very angry he didn't look where he was going and walked right into the hole Jack had made. Down he fell and was killed.

8. Stooping quickly as if falling.

9. Then Jack filled up the hole with the dirt he had taken out.

9. Forward downward pushing dirt into hole, moving around in a circle and doing the same thing over again.

10. Jack went into the cave, got the giant treasure, and ran home to tell his mother about it.

10. Running around circle in the opposite direction.

11. When he got home he was so excited and tired he was all out of breath. Ever after this Jack was called the Giant Killer.

11. Deep breathing.

Dramatic Play with Poems

The field of poetry can be exploited to its fullest for source material for dramatic play. Mother Goose Rhymes are particularly suited for activity, and there are many others. Poetry has some advantages over stories because of the use of catchy phrasing, rhyming, and the "feeling" that is in much of it. An old familiar poem, "The Wind," is given as an illustration.

THE WIND

"I saw you toss the kites on high
And blow the birds about the sky:
And all around I heard you pass,
Like ladies skirts across the grass
    Oh Wind a-blowing all day long
    Oh Wind that sings so loud a song.

I saw the different things you did
But always you yourself you hid,
I felt you push, I heard you call,
I could not see yourself at all--
    Oh wind, a-blowing all day long
    Oh wind, that sings so loud a song.

Oh you that are so strong and cold,
Oh blower, are you young or old?
Are you a beast of field and tree
Or just a stronger child than me?
    Oh wind, a-blowing all day long
    Oh wind, that sings so loud a song.

First Verse:

1. Wind blowing very hard

   1. a. Tossing up kites, holding the string and skipping around the circle while the kites are in flight.
      b. Pulling the kites in hand over hand.

2. Birds being buffeted around in air.

   2. Little running steps with arms stretched sideways and swaying movements side to side in imitation of birds.

Second Verse:

3. "I saw the different things you did." Blowing poplar trees.

   3. With arms stretched overhead the children imitate tall poplar trees, then vigorous side bending alternating with forward downward bending.

4. Blowing a paper sack around

   4. Representation of empty paper sack, crouching on floor, then jumping up as high as possible, moving into the center of the circle.

5. "I heard you call."

   5. Long drawn out calls in imitation of the wind.

Third Verse:

6. The wind is so strong and cold that the children have to stop play and get warm.

   6. a. Jumping on toes with foot placing sideways and clapping of hands overhead and on thighs.
      b. Clapping arms around body.

7. Still the wind blows on.

   7. Deep breathing.

Another tale about giants that the children enjoy is the following:

THE GIANT

The Words	Action
1. Once a giant came a wandering	Children wander around the room in a swaggering giant type of step and movement.
2. Late at night when the world was still	Children become quiet and put a finger up to the lip to indicate silence.

3. Seeking a stool to sit on	Giant swaggers around looking for a place to sit.
4. He climbed on a little green hill	All children perform climbing movements to get to the top of the hill.
5. "Giant, Giant! I am under you,"	Children crouch down and pretend that they are stepped upon.
6. "Move or this is the last of me."	Children try to push the giant away.
7. But the giant answered, "Thank you,"	Children walk around surveying the country side.
8. "I like it here, don't you see."	Swaggers around with thumbs under arm pits.

Other Experiences as a Basis for Dramatic Play

Many everyday experiences both from the childhood and adult world can form the basis for much dramatic play. The children can help the teacher plan the story to guide the play. A simple idea like the Railroad Train can be a good basis. It could be developed in the following fashion.

RAILROAD TRAIN

Each child is given the name of a part of a freight train. Several trains may be formed. A story is told by the teacher, in which the various parts of the train are mentioned in the telling. Several children are the engines, and the story usually begins with this portion of the train. After the story unfolds, the children form in line one behind the other in the order named. After the trains have been assembled and all "cars" are on the train, the story continues by describing a train trip. The route is described in detail with the train going slow, up and down grades, around curves, stopping at stations, and finishing up with a wreck. It is also possible to assemble the trains by having each of the parts of the train on "side tracks" and the train backing up to hook on the "cars."

Some attention should be given to the story as the imagination of the teller is very important. Also, children can make suggestions for the train ride.

It is apparent that there is no dearth of material or ideas. Imagination plays a big part in widening out the scope of dramatic play.

For another illustration of how an idea can be expanded, let us take the children on an imaginary hike.

THE HIKE

1. Today, we are going on a hike. What are some of the things we need to take?	1. Children will suggest various articles which should be included.
2. We are going to roll our packs into a nice, neat bundle. Put down your tarp first, next arrange your blankets, and put the rest of your things in. Now let's roll the pack and tie it up.	2. Children lay out packs, roll, and tie.
3. Off we go	3. Children march two by two around the room carrying packs.
4. Time to rest.	4. All remove packs and sit down.
5. Off again.	5. Resume marching.
6. Make blazes so we can find our way back. Make trail markers.	6. Children make blazes in various manners. Arrange stones for markers.
7. Here we are. Pick out a good spot for the tent and put it up.	7. Cut stakes and poles. Drive stakes and put up tents. Arrange beds.

8. We need lots of wood for the campfire. Will you see what you can find?
9. Build the fire and broil the steaks.
10. Bugle call for "turning in."

8. Children go out and drag in logs and wood. Some cutting may be needed.
9. As directed.
10. Children go to one side, brush their teeth, wash up, and then turn in. They crawl in tent, cover themselves carefully, and go to sleep.

It should be noted that integration with other subject fields is possible. Conservation practices can be stressed. Safety in the woods can be emphasized.

Some suggestions of how other ideas can be used follow.

Playing
    In the leaves
    In the snow, making a snow man,
        sledding
    Riding a bicycle, wagon, tricycle,
        kiddie car, or other vehicle
    On the playground
    Flying a kite

Going To
    A circus
    A zoo
    A toy shop
    The farm

Doing Common Things Like
    Washing clothes and hanging up
    Washing dishes
    Trimming a Christmas tree
    Pitching hay
    Sowing grain
    Making a garden
    Shaking and beating rugs
    Cutting grain

Pretending to Be
    An Animal--bear, deer, squirrel,
        giraffe, elephant, pony, etc.
    An Imaginary Creature--giant, witch,
        dwarf, troll, etc.
    An official or worker--conductor,
        policeman, engineer, etc.

Having Fun at
    Paddling a canoe, rowing a boat
    Playing baseball, football, track,
        basketball, etc.
    Skiing, ice skating, roller skating,
        water skiing
    Swimming using different strokes

Celebrating
    Holidays--Christmas, Halloween,
        Thanksgiving, 4th of July
    Seasons--Fall, winter, spring, summer

Industries, Professions like
    Lumbering
    Fishing
    Construction
    Road Building

Chapter 15

Classroom and Limited Area Activities

At times, the teacher will be faced with the problem of conducting physical education activities in the classroom or in limited spaces like the hall or cafeteria. Because of the shortage of regular facilities, sometimes the stage of the auditorium is made available for instructional work.

In a classroom, movable furniture can be pushed back, or to the center, depending upon the activity. Where there are fixed seats, the aisles can be used to good advantage.

The noise problem must be solved. Several suggestions are offered. The children need to recognize that the activity is a privilege and their cooperation is essential. They need to keep their exuberance under control to the point that the class activity does not interfere with other classes. Another solution would be for the same section of the school to have physical periods at the same time. If the classes in the same part of the building are all playing at the same time, there is little disturbance of each other. This would also be true if one class were directly above the other. The noise, particularly from shuffling and moving feet, would seriously interfere with a recitation, lecture, or study period. If both were holding physical education at the same time, the upper group probably would have little effect on the play of the class below them.

Halls can be used for classes in stunts and tumbling. Movement exploration is another type of activity which lends itself to such an area. If the noise can be tolerated by the other classrooms, relays can be adapted to the space.

Suggestions for Classroom and Limited Space Activities

1. Many regular program activities can be adapted for classroom or limited spaces. In addition, there are many other activities available which supplement the regular program. Many of these are designated as special classroom activities.

2. Fitness values accrue in relationship to the amount of movement by each child. Select activities which demand movement among the children. If the space does not permit all the children to be active, work out some form of rotation so that all get an opportunity to participate. Use as many as you can at a time.

3. Only supplies that will not damage should be used. Small sacks stuffed with excelsior or other light material make good throwing and catching objects. Fleece balls, bean bags, sewn rolled up sox, balloons, and similar articles can be used with little danger of damage.

4. Watch for overheating. Excess clothing should be removed, and, depending upon the activity, the temperature should be lowered.

5. Do not put too much emphasis on running. In relays, children can walk, hop, or jump.

6. For relays and other activities requiring movement, have the children keep feet under the desks. At times, use alternate rows for activity.

7. In relays, have competition by rows with each row having the exclusive use

of one aisle. In some cases, have one child from each row active. This works well with a game like Red Light.

8. Players should be cautioned about colliding with the chairs and desks. Alertness should be stressed.

9. Some space limitations make it wise to organize small group play in different corners of the room or available space. All players should understand the necessity for cooperation and know the limitations of indoor play.

Activities for the Primary Children in the Classroom and Limited Spaces

Too many teachers look for special classroom activities when the necessity to use the room for physical education occurs. Some end up with a program of trivial games which only provide entertainment and relief from tensions.

It needs to be stressed that if the regular types of activity--stunts and tumbling, movement exploration, story plays, creative rhythms, and folk dances--have values for children, these values can be enhanced through classroom use. Many of the mentioned activities are individual in nature and demand for each child only a small area, making them suitable with possibly some adaptation to classroom instruction. This would be particularly true in situations where there was movable furniture. These activities provide not only developmental features, but also give relief from tension.

Balance beams provide a basis for desirable classroom activity. At least two beams, and preferably more, should be present. Balance beams can be constructed from ordinary materials available at a builder's supply company and last indefinitely with a minimum of care.

If fixed desks are present, the rows can be used for target games involving rolling (bowling), bouncing, or tossing. Targets can be placed at the heads of the aisles and the aisles used as pathways for the balls or bean bags.

Games Suitable for Classroom Activity-- Primary Grades

In addition to the games presented in this section, many of the games in the section for playground and gymnasium can be used for the classroom or limited space. Some will, of course, need to be modified and adapted for use in the space available.

BEAN BAG PITCH

Playing Area: Classroom

Players: Two to 6 for each target.

Supplies: Bean bags and a small box for target for each team.

A target box is placed at the head of each row. A pitch line is drawn 10 to 15 feet back of the target. Each player takes a specified number of pitches at the box. Scores are taken for each player and the team with the highest score wins.

BICYCLE RACE

Playing Area: Classroom

Players: One-half the class

Supplies: The desks are needed

Alternate rows perform at a time. The children stand in the aisle between two rows of desks. Each child places one hand on his own desk and one on the desk next to him. Upon the signal, "Go," each child imitates riding a bicycle with his legs, while supported by his hands. The child who rides the longest without touching the floor with his feet is the winner for his row. Winners can complete later for the champion bicycle rider of the room.

BOILER BURST

Playing Area: Classroom, playground

Players: Entire class

Supplies: None

The seats are arranged so that there will be one less seat than players. The extra player stands at the front of the class and begins a story. At a dramatic moment, he says, "And the boiler burst!" The children exchange seats and the narrator tries to secure a seat. If successful, another child replaces. The new narrator may develop his own story or continue that begun by his predecessor.

The game can be adapted to an outdoor situation by having markers for each child. To make the game more vigorous, the children could be required to run to a turning point and back. The child who does not secure a marker is the new story teller.

CAT AND MICE (Classroom Game)

Playing Area: Classroom, playground

Players: 5-20

Supplies: None

This is an excellent activity in the classroom. One player is designated as the "Cat" and sits at the front desk (teachers) and puts his head down on his hands on the desk so he cannot see. The remainder of the children are the "Mice." One "Mouse" from each row comes to the front stealthily, approaches the desk, and scratches on the desk. When he is ready, the "Cat" gets up from his chair and chases the "Mice" back to their seats. Any child caught joins the "Cat" at the desk and helps catch the others. The game is over when each of the children have had a chance to approach the desk.

CHANGE SEATS

Playing Area: Classroom

Players: Entire class

Supplies: None

All seats should be occupied, removed, or books put on them to indicate that they are not to be used. The teacher gives the commands "Change Left, Change right, Change front, or Change Back." One or more children are "It" and do not have seats.

At each command, the children move <u>one seat</u> in the direction of the call. The children who are "It" try to move into any seat they can. When the command "Change front," is given, the child in the front seat must turn and move to the rear seat of his row. Similarly, those on the outside rows on "Change left," or "Change right," must move around to the other side of the room to get his proper seat.

It needs to be emphasized that on command each child is to move to the designated seat in keeping with the command. If he is in error, one of the players who is "It" takes his seat.

If the game seems to become too boisterous, the children should be made to walk.

DO THIS, DO THAT

Playing Area: Playground, gymnasium, classroom

Players: Entire class

Supplies: None

One child is the leader and performs various movements, which are accompanied by either "do this," or "do that." All players must execute the movements which are accompanied by "do this." If the directions are "do that," no one is to move. Those who move at the wrong time are eliminated and sit down in place. The game continues until all are eliminated. The last player is the winner and becomes the leader for the next game.

LOST CHILDREN

Playing Area: Classroom

Player: Entire class

Supplies: None

One child is chosen to be the policeman (or policewoman) and leaves the room. The other children walk around the room. The teacher or leader calls the policeman in and says, "The children are lost. Will you please take them home safely?"

The policeman then takes each child to his seat. The players stay where they are until the policeman seats them. Success for the policeman is determined by the number of children he can seat correctly. He is not permitted to look in the desks or in books for clues to correct seating.

OVERHEAD RELAY

Playing Area: Classroom

Players: Each row in a classroom forms a team

Supplies: Bean bag, eraser, or similar object for each team

The first person in each row has the object to be passed on his desk in front of him. At the signal to pass, he claps his hands, picks up the object, and passes it overhead to the child behind him. This child places the object on the desk, claps his hands, and passes overhead. When the last child in the row receives the object, he runs forward to the head of the row, using the aisle to his right. <u>After</u> he has passed by, each child, using the <u>same</u> aisle, moves back one seat. The child who has come to the front now sits down in the first seat, places the object on the desk, claps his hands, and passes overhead.

This continues until the children are back in their original seats and the object is on the front desk. The first row done wins.

TEN, TEN, DOUBLE TEN

Playing Area: Classroom

Players: Entire class

Supplies: Small object

All the children except one leave the classroom. The child left in the room places the object in some place visible but not too easily found. The children come back into the room. As soon as a child sees the object, he continues searching for another moment so not to give away the position. He calls out, "Ten, ten, double ten, forty-five, fifteen, buckskin six" and sits down in his seat. The child who found the object first gets to place it for the next game. The child who was last finding it or any who did not must remain in their seats for the next turn.

SIMONS SAYS

Playing Area: Classroom

Players: Entire Class

Supplies: None

One player is selected to be "Simon" and stands in front of the class. He gives a variety of commands like, "Stand up," "Clap your hands," "Turn around," and others. He may or may not precede a command by the words, "Simon says." No one is to move unless the command is preceded by these words. Those who move at the wrong time are eliminated and must sit out the game.

The leader gives commands rapidly, changing to different movements. He tries to confuse the class by doing all movements himself.

Variation: Birds Fly. In this game, the children hold their hands and arms out as if ready to fly. The leader calls out commands like "Dogs fly," "Birds fly," and "Horses fly." Each time he makes a flying motion as he calls out. The

children should move their arms only when the creature is one that can fly. Otherwise, they are eliminated.

WHERE, OH WHERE

Playing Area: Classroom

Players: Entire class

Supplies: Spool or other small object which can be hidden in a closed hand.

The children are seated in regular seats or can be in a circle formation seated on the floor. One child is chosen to be it and turns his back to the group while hiding his eyes.

The object is passed among the children from hand to hand until a signal is given. "It" turns around and attempts to guess who has the object. He gets three guesses. All children, including the one who has the object, do various movements and stunts to confuse the guesser. The object must be held in the hand, however. If the guess is correct, the child with the object becomes the new guesser. If not, "It" tries again. If a child misses on three turns in a row, he should choose another child to be "It."

If the number is large, two children can be "It," thus doubling the chances of guessing as each should be allowed three guesses.

ZOO

Playing Area: Classroom

Players: Entire class

Supplies: None

Six children are chosen to stand in front of the class. Each of the children chooses the name of his favorite animal, and a leader places the children in line in any order he wishes, saying the name of the animal.

On signal #1, the six children imitate the animal they have chosen but in so doing, remain in the selected order. Ten to fifteen seconds should be allowed for this.

On signal #2, the children not chosen as animals stand, wave their arms, jump or hop in place, turning around if they wish, and sit down with their heads on the desks. The eyes are closed and covered with the hands.

The leader rearranges the children in a different order and when this is completed the seated children raise to sitting position. Another signal is given and the animals perform once more for a short period.

After this is completed, any child can volunteer to place the children in the original position and name the animal in each case. If this child can place the animals in their original stand position and call them by their chosen names, he may become an animal in the zoo and choose a name for himself. He takes his place among the animals. The game continues until twelve or some designated number are in the zoo.

Other categories such as flowers, Mother Goose, play characters, and objects can be used.

Chapter 16
The Physical Education Program for the Intermediate Level

Fourth Grade Program
Fifth Grade Program
Sixth Grade Program
Skills for Intermediate Grade Children

Guides for planning and the general features of the physical education program were discussed in Chapter 4. In the present chapter, a more detailed review of the program for each of the intermediate grades will be made available. The percentage allotments suggested for each activity type and the recommended activities under each of the major divisions will be presented.

Note that Swimming and Water Safety is included in each of the intermediate grade programs without a definite percentage allotment of time. If swimming is to be included where facilities and instruction are available, probably 10 per cent of the year's program should be allotted to the activity. The other areas of the program should be reduced proportionately.

It is recommended that the certified program of either the Red Cross or the YMCA be the basis of the instruction. For this reason, no program of instruction of aquatics is included in this guide.

Fourth Grade Program

The fourth grade program consists of seven different activity types. New to the program is an allotment for special fitness activities. This, together with the percentage suggested for movement exploration, provides time for special developmental movements.

There is increased emphasis on the teaching of skills, which are outlined in the sports units. Relays are continued with good emphasis, along with the tumbling and apparatus work. The rhythmic program is centered primarily on folk dances. The following chart lists the suggested activities together with the number of whole class periods which are based on a 180 day school year.

Activity Type		Recommended Percentages	Class Periods*
Movement Exploration and Body Mechanics		5%	9
Rhythmic Activities - Folk Dances, Mixers		15%	27
Stunts, Tumbling, Apparatus		15%	27
Special Fitness Activities and Testing		10%	18
Relays		10%	18
Game-Type Activities		15%	27
Running, Tag, Circle Games	7%		
Simple Ball Games, Dodge Ball	8%		
Athletic Skills and Games		30%	54
Skills, Skill Drills	10%		
Lead-up Games	10%		
Athletic Team Games	5%		
Individual and Dual Activities	5%		
Swimming and Water Safety		**	**
Total		100%	180

* Based on a 180 day school year.
** If available, allot 10%.

- 149 -

An analysis of the chart will reveal several features of the fourth grade program. The largest proportion of time is devoted to the sports areas. This, however, does not mean an over-emphasis on the sports program. A breakdown of the area shows that lead-up games and the teaching of skills are stressed. Individual and dual activities also form a part of the area.

The fourth grade program in rhythms can be labeled an "in-between" program. Singing games and creative rhythms are not included, although creativity should be a part of all dance programs. In couple dances, there is much opportunity for individual creativity. The second part of the schottische pattern, for example, offers the dancers a variety of movements. There is creativity, but within the limits of the folk dance.

While 19 whole periods are allotted to fitness activities, in practice, this is seldom done. Special fitness activities can be scheduled for short periods of time over many class periods, the total time allotment to make up about 10%.

Fifth Grade Program

The activities for the fifth grade show similarity to those suggested for the fourth grade, except for some shifts of emphasis.

Activity Type	Recommended Percentages	Class Periods*
Movement Exploration and Body Mechanics	3%	5.4
Rhythmic Activities Folk Dance, Mixers	15%	27
Stunts, Tumbling, Apparatus	15%	27
Fitness Activities and Testing	10%	18
Relays	5%	9
Game-Type Activities	15%	27
Running, Tag, Circle Games	7%	
Simple Ball Games, Dodge Ball	8%	

* Based on a 180 day school year.
** If available, allot 10%

Activity Type (Cont.)	Recommended Percentage	Class Periods*
Athletic Skills and Games	37%	66.6
Skill, Skill Drills	15%	
Lead-up Games	10%	
Athletic Team Games	10%	
Individual and Dual Activities	2%	
Swimming and Water Safety	**	**
Total	100%	180 days

From the chart, certain aspects of the fifth grade program can be emphasized Increased emphasis on athletic skills and games is made, with a major portion of this devoted to the teaching of skills. Lead-up games continue to be stressed, and more athletic games of a modified nature are scheduled.

Compared to the fourth grade, a decreased allotment to relays can be noted. The decrease, however, may not be actual as the skills teaching probably will include relays to practice the various sports skills. The majority of the rhythmic emphasis is still on folk dances and mixers.

Games, because of their contribution to fitness qualities, continue to have an important place in the program. The games included are the active, vigorous types where many children are active at a time.

Special fitness activities and testing, stunts, tumbling, and apparatus carry the same recommended percentage designated for the fourth grade program.

Sixth Grade Program

When a child has finished his elementary school physical education program, he should have had experiences in regular or modified versions of the sports of basketball, softball, soccer, volleyball, flag football (boys), speedball, and track and field. This is reflected in the chart of activities for the sixth grade.

Activity Type	Recommended Percentages	Class Periods*
Movement Exploration and Body Mechanics	3%	5.4
Rhythmic Activities	15%	27
Folk Dances, Mixers, Couple Dances	12%	
Square Dances	3%	
Stunts, Tumbling, Apparatus	15%	27
Fitness Activities and Testing	10%	18
Relays	5%	9
Game-Type Activities	10%	18
Running, Tag, Circle Games	5%	
Simple Ball Games, Dodge Ball	5%	
Athletic Skills and Games	42%	75.6
Skills, Skill Drills	15%	
Lead-up Games	5%	
Athletic Team Games	20%	
Individual and Dual Activities	2%	
Swimming and Water Safety	**	**
Total	100%	180 days

The shift to more emphasis on athletic games is apparent from the chart. The teaching of skills is also considerably stressed. Since regular and modified versions of the sports are played, there is less need for lead-up games. Square dance receives some emphasis in the program of dance activities. When compared to the percentage allotments of the fifth grade, there is little change in the other areas with the exception of the simple games program, which is decreased.

The sixth grade program also can be viewed as a transitional curriculum to a junior high school program.

Skills for Intermediate Grade Children

In the presentation of recommended skills for primary children, it was feasible to include the skills in one comprehensive list. This was possible primarily because the skills were of the fundamental type, applicable to a wide range of activities.

In the intermediate grades, the skills are more closely related to different activities. For this reason, the progression of skills for any one activity is included in the discussion within that topic.

---

* Based on a 180 day school year.
** If available, allot 10%.

Chapter 17

The Program for Physical Fitness in the Intermediate Grades

The emphasis in the intermediate grades differs from that in the primary level in that more formal fitness activities and fitness testing are introduced. In addition, activities for the intermediate grades should be selected so that physical fitness values are possible, and conducted so that these values can be attained. Values are inherent both in the selection and the method of presentation. This is an important concept. Simply to assume that because we have fitness activities, we will automicaly develop fitness is erroneous. The program for the physically undeveloped must be emphasized. The development and maintenance of good posture habits is also an important consideration in physical fitness.

Americans, by and large, are not likely to become good physical specimens simply because of the directed programs which are carried on in the public schools. Rather, if we are to reach desirable levels of physical fitness, the school program and other opportunities for youth should be regarded only as the springboard for good fitness. The teacher needs to stimulate the individual to take upon himself the responsibility for making and keeping himself a good physical specimen. Only then can permanent and lasting fitness be attained. The physical education program is a step in this direction, but only a step.

A program for attaining desirable fitness levels for the intermediate grades involves consideration for the following areas.

1. The Low Fitness Program
2. Exercises for Fitness
3. Isometric Conditioning Activities
4. Circuit Training
5. The Obstacle Course
6. Postural Fitness
7. Miscellaneous Fitness Activities
8. Testing for Fitness

The Low Fitness Group-Screening

Students who are underdeveloped physically should be identified by a screening test as part of a health appraisal. A feasible screening test* is recommended by the President's Council and is designed to measure strength, flexibility, and agility. The test consists of three items.

1. Pullups (arm and shoulder strength).
2. Situps (flexibility and abdominal strength).
3. Squat thrusts (agility).

Instructions for the Test

1. Divide the class into pairs. One pupil acts as scorer for his partner while the other pupil performs the test.
2. After each test, the results are recorded by the teacher on a record form.
3. The only equipment needed is a chinning bar, a stop watch (or watch with a sweep hand), and record forms.

PULL-UP (Boys)

Equipment: A chinning or exercise bar that can be gripped.

Starting Position: Grasp the bar with palms facing forward; hang with arms and legs fully

* Youth Physical Fitness pp. 19-26.

extended, with feet clearing the floor. Partner stands slightly to one side to count and keep the body from swinging.

Action: Pull up the body until the chin is <u>over</u> the bar and lower the body back to a <u>fully</u> extended arm position. One count is given for each completed pull-up.

To Pass: Boys must complete at least one pull-up.

Rules: The body must not swing. Neither can the knees be raised or the legs kicked as in climbing. The pull-up must be a pull and not a snap. Since only one pull-up is required, it should be done in reasonable form.

MODIFIED PULL-UP (Girls)

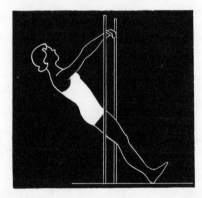

Equipment: Any bar adjustable in height and comfortable to grip. A piece of pipe placed between two ladders and held securely may be used.

Starting Position: Adjust height of bar to chest level. Grasp bar with palms facing out. Extend the legs under the bar, keeping the body and knees straight. The heels are on the floor. Fully extend the arms so they form an angle of 90 degress with the body line. The partner braces the pupil's heels to prevent slipping.

Action: Pull body up with the arms until the <u>chest</u> touches the bar. Lower the body until the elbows are fully extended.

To Pass: Girls must complete at least 8 modified pull-ups.

Rules: The body must be kept straight. The chest must touch the bar and the arms must be <u>fully</u> extended on each return. No resting is permitted.

SIT-UPS (Boys and Girls)

Starting Position: Pupil lies on his back with his legs extended and his feet about 1 foot apart. The hands, with fingers interlaced, are grasped behind the neck. Another pupil holds his partner's ankles and keeps his heels in contact with the floor while counting each successful sit-up.

Action: Sit up and turn the trunk to the left, touching the right knee with the left elbow. Return to starting position. Sit up and touch right elbow to left knee. Return. Each time the body is returned to the floor, one sit-up is counted.

To Pass: Boys are to do 14 sit-ups and girls 10.

Rules: Knees must be kept on the floor, and the sit-up must bring the elbow down to the knee rather than meeting with the uplifted knee. A <u>full</u> return to lying position must be made.

SQUAT THRUSTS (Boys and Girls)

Equipment: Stopwatch or sweep-second hand watch

Starting Position: Pupils stand at attention. The test is a four-count movement.

1. Bend knees and place hands on the floor in front of the feet. Hands may be outside, inside, or in front of the knees. Note that the best support is made when the hands are placed at shoulder width apart.
2. Thrust the legs back far enough so that the body is perfectly straight from the shoulders to the feet (the push-up position).
3. Return to squat position.
4. Return to erect position.

To Pass: A ten-second time limit is made during which boys must complete 4 and the girls 3 complete squat thrusts.

Rules: The pupil must return to the position of attention each time. The pupils should have had enough practice to be familiar with the movements so that the test is one of agility and not one of motor educability. Since the time period is short, it is important that it be established accurately.

After the low fitness pupils have been identified, a plan of action for them needs to be established. Any plan should consider three approaches to the problem. The first is a determination of the cause of the low fitness level.

A professional approach to the diagnosis is needed. An examination of the health status of the child is a first consideration. Available health records should be consulted and, if needed, an examination by a physician should be scheduled. Next, through consultation with the parents and the child, the health habits of the child should be evaluated. After all the information has been sifted and checked, the measures to be taken for each child can be established.

Corrective steps for possible health conditions amenable to correction should be made. If health habits need adjustment, changes here should also be made. Beyond this, it becomes a matter of a program of developmental exercises and activities designed to raise the physical performance to desirable levels. The students should be tested periodically to determine progress.

An excellent procedure to handle low fitness problems is on a committee basis. Each case can be reviewed and remedial procedures prescribed. Such a committee can be composed of the school nurse, a physician, the school principal, the physical education supervisor or teacher, and teachers from the elementary school.

Cooperation with the home is essential. Corrective and developmental measures will succeed only if there is cooperation from the parents. It is advantageous to assign homework in the form of physical activities which the student is able to do at home. Both the parent and the child should understand why the child is in the low fitness group and what direction their efforts should take to have the child reach a desirable level of fitness. Some schools find it helpful to have printed material with appropriate activities to be done. The particular activities to be stressed by the child can be checked, providing a more scientific approach than a word of mouth method. The directive should include not only the activities to be done, but also directions and illustrations for better execution.

As the child works toward better fitness, periodic re-testing is important. As well as providing an indication of progress, the testing is motivation in itself.

Exercises for Fitness

Exercises in the physical education program have specific purposes and are not to be regarded as a substitute for the other activities in the program. Exercises can make the following contributions to the program:

1. Warm-up activity. Before taking part in any strenuous activity, youngsters should warm up first. Bending, stretching, and jumping exercises are most commonly used for this purpose.
2. Developing and maintaining specific muscle groups. Emphasis should be on those muscle groups which give support to the body in the matter of posture. The important muscle groups include those of the feet, the abdominal wall, the back muscles, and the muscle groups holding the shoulders and head in normal position of good posture.
3. General over-all physical activity. Vigorous exercises involving most or many of the large muscle groups in the body are used for this purpose.
4. Carry-over activity. By providing exercises in the program, the youngster can learn their use and lay the basis for desirable activity in later life when the more vigorous games and activities are not recommended.

Cautions in Giving Exercises

Certain cautions in giving exercises should be observed. These also have application to other physical education activities in addition to the exercises.

1. Good postural alignment should be maintained. In exercises where the arms are held in front, to the side, or overhead, the abdominal wall needs to be tensed and flattened to maintain proper position of the pelvis. The feet in most activities should be pointed reasonably straight ahead. The chest should be up, and the head and shoulders kept in good position.
2. Some care needs to be taken in using

exercises requiring a straight leg position with no bending at the knee joint such as in doing forward bending exercises. These activities tend to force the knee back in a hyperextended position which contributes to posture faults. Some stretching of the leg muscles is excellent for flexibility, but the knee joint should be relaxed <u>slightly</u> rather than forced back to a back-kneed position.

3. Repeated deep knee bending exercises can be injurious to the knee joint. While an exercise or activity which demands an occasional deep knee bend causes little harm, an activity which calls for repeated full knee joint bending should not be done.

4. The activity known as the "Bicycle Ride" or the "Bicycle" should be used only if there is no over stretching of the muscles in the back of the neck. In the "Bicycle" the child is on the back of his neck and shoulders with his feet going in circles like riding a bicycle. The exercise should be done with the weight mostly on the back of the shoulders, not high on the back of the neck.

5. In each set of exercises, there should be an exercise for the arm-shoulder girdle and one for the abdominal wall.

6. There is need to isolate the abdominal muscles from the psoas muscle group in doing activities designed to strengthen the abdominal wall. This is particularly true in the sit-ups. Sit-ups have better abdominal value if the soles of the feet are flat on the floor with the heels close to the seat. This is the bent knee position. In addition, when the upper part of the body comes up (as in the sit-up), the movement should be a roll-up with the chin and upper part of the chest leading the movement. The psoas muscle group by being strengthened unnecessarily can increase the curve in the lower back, which is opposite to the desired effect of strong abdominal muscles. By lifting the knees to a bent knee position in the sit-up, the tension is taken from the psoas muscle group, and the sit-up becomes primarily abdominal muscle work. The same is accomplished by the roll-up of the upper body.

7. In exercises using leg raising, such as marching in place or running in place, the knees should be lifted to the point where the thigh is parallel to the floor. By lifting the knees high, more and different muscles are brought in play, which ordinarily would not be true with a moderate knee lift.

Setting Formation

In giving exercises to a class, the first problem is to get the students into an appropriate formation quickly. This can be done a number of ways:

1. In an early session of the class, set up a formation for the exercise program. Upon a signal, the students take their places in this prearranged formation.
2. Have the students scatter, taking sufficient room for the activity.
3. Using a line formation, have the students count off by fours, and then have each student double his number and take that many steps forward.
4. Use squad formation and extend the formation to fingertip length.

Giving Exercises

Once the students are in formation, the instructor then proceeds with a description of the exercise. For example, he can follow the procedure outlined below:

1. "The first exercise we are going to do is the Side Straddle Hop."
2. "Starting Position is the position of attention. It is a two-count exercise."
3. "On count one, jump to a side straddle position with arms overhead." Illustrate.
4. "On count two, recover to starting position." Illustrate.

The instructor now has the class go through the exercise slowly (by the numbers) with him until he is satisfied that he can put them through the activity in cadence. Exercises are usually performed in rhythm, four to eight counts. The number of repetitions will vary according to the group.

After the instructor has given his description and has the group go through the exercises slowly, he is ready for class activity. Generally, this routine is satisfactory for most exercises.

Put the group in Starting Position

1. This is done by describing the starting position and then giving the command for the students to assume this position.
2. The command can be "Starting position--TAKE." The emphasis is on

the last word with a hesitation between the preliminary part and the command word.

3. The next command gets the group off together in rhythmic execution. The starting command can be "Ready-- exercise" or "In time--exercise." This should be given at approximately the same cadence as the exercise rhythm.

4. The count now proceeds and the exercise should be done in unison. The count goes (for example) "1-2-3-4, 1-2-3-4." To halt the group together, slow down the count, change the tone of the voice, and use "1-2-and-halt."

5. The exercise should be followed by a brief period of relaxation. Give the group "At ease" or "In place--rest."

6. To start the next exercise, call the class to attention before beginning the explanation.

Combinations of Exercise

An interesting fitness activity can be fashioned by combining exercises in the following manner. Make a rule that after an exercise is given (in the normal fashion) the child immediately does a prescribed floor exercise like push-ups or sit-ups. A teacher's directions could go like this: "We are going to do a series of exercises. Just as soon as you finish an exercise, you immediately do five push-ups without waiting for any direction from me." This system works better if the directed exercises are given from a standing position, so that either the push-ups or sit-ups make a definite change. After the child has completed his floor exercise (on his own), he immediately stands and awaits the next directed exercise from the teacher.

Combinations can also be done with running in place or around the area. Jumping, hopping, and other movements can be combined with the exercises.

Selected Exercises

The number of repetitions for an exercise will depend upon the exercise and the capacity of the children. The number should be built up gradually in increasing dosages. The exercises are divided into categories according to the developmental possibilities.

ARM-SHOULDER GIRDLE EXERCISES

1. PUSH-UPS

Starting Position: front leaning rest. The body is straight from head to heels.

Cadence: moderate or at will.

Movement:
(a) Bend elbows and touch chest to ground, keeping body straight.
(b) Straighten elbows, raising body in straight line.
Modification: If student is unable to perform the activity as mentioned above, have him start with knees or hips in contact with the floor. Girls use the knee support position.

The purpose of this exercise is to strengthen the arm and shoulder extensor muscles.

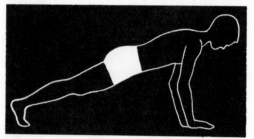

2. RECLINING PULL-UPS
Starting Position: one pupil lies on back. His partner stands astride of him, looking face to face, with his feet alongside the reclining child's chest. Partners grasp hands with fingers interlocked.

Cadence: moderate to slow

Movement:
(a) Pupil on floor pulls up with arms until his chest touches partner's thighs. His body remains straight, with the weight resting on the heels.
(b) Return to position

3. ARM CIRCLING

Starting Position: Erect, feet together, arms to the side with palms up.

Cadence: Moderate

Movement:
(a) Five forward 12-inch circles with both arms simultaneously

(b) Five backward 12-inch circles with both arms simultaneously

Good posture position should be maintained with the abdominal wall flat and the head and shoulders in good position.

4. CRAB KICKING

Starting Position: Crab position – the body is supported on hands and feet with the back to the floor. The knees are at right angles.

Cadence: Moderate

Movement:
(a) Kick as high as possible toward the ceiling, alternating the feet.
(b) Thrust both feet forward so the legs are straight and the weight is on the heels. Recover.
(c) Have the children move forward, backward, sideward, and in a small circle (in place) while maintaining the crab position.

5. WING STRETCHER

Starting Position: Stand erect; raise elbows to shoulder height, fists clenched, palms down in front of the chest.

Cadence: moderate

Movement:
(a) Thrust elbows backward vigorously and return. Be sure to keep the abdominal wall flat and the head erect. Keep elbows at shoulder height.
(b) Return to position

In addition to the preceding five exercises, an additional three are included on page 49 with the discussion of posture development. These are

6. THE SWAN

7. HOOK LYING

8. TAILOR EXERCISE

ABDOMINAL EXERCISES

1. KNEE RAISE (Single and Double)

Starting Position: On back with knees slightly flexed, legs extended flat on the floor, and arms at the side.

Cadence: moderate

Movement:
a. Raise one knee as close to the chest as possible.
b. Return.
c. Raise the other knee.
d. Return.

The exercise should be done later with both knees coming up at once and returning.

2. LEG SIT

Starting Position: Pupil sits on floor with legs extended and hands on hips.

Cadence: moderate

Movement:

a. With a quick, vigorous action, raise the knees and bring both heels as close to the seat as possible. The movement is a drag with the toes touching lightly.
b. Return to position

The head and shoulders should be held high in good postural position during the exercise. Exercises under the discussion of posture on page 50 should also be included here.

3. SIT-UP

4. ROWING

5. CURL-UP

AGILITY EXERCISES

1. RUNNING IN PLACE

Starting Position: standing with arms in loose thrust position.

Cadence: slow, fast, slow

Movement: stationary run. Begin slowly (counting only on left foot). Speed up somewhat, raising knees to height of hips, then run at full speed, raising knees hard, then slow down.

Running in Place is essentially a warm-up exercise, but has good values for agility.

Variation: March in place lifting knees high and swinging the arms well up.

2. SIDE STRADDLE HOP

Starting Position: at attention.

Cadence: moderate.

Movement:
(a) On count one, jump to a straddle position with arms overhead.
(b) On count two, recover to starting position.
Side Straddle Hop is a coordinating exercise.

3. THE SQUAT THRUST

Starting Position: attention.

Cadence: moderate.

(a) Bend slightly at the knees and sharply at the hips; place hands on the ground in front of the feet in a squat position with the elbows inside the knees.
(b) Thrust feet and legs backward to a front leaning rest position with body straight from shoulders to feet, weight supported on hands and toes.
(c) Return to the squat position.
(d) Resume standing position.
The Squat Thrust is one of the best exercises to develop agility. It reaches and strengthens primarily the muscles of the trunk, thighs and hips. It also serves as an additional warm-up exercise.

4. THE TREADMILL

Starting Position: Pupil assumes push-up position except that one leg is brought forward so that the knee is under the chest.

Cadence: moderate

Movement:
(a) Reverse position of the feet, bringing the other leg forward.
(b) Change back with original foot forward.
The exercise is continued rhythmically with feet alternating. The Treadmill is one of the test items in the New York State Physical Fitness Test.

FLEXIBILITY EXERCISES

1. THE BEAR HUG

Starting Position: The pupil stands, feet comfortably spread, with hands on hips.

Cadence: slow.

Movement:
(a) Take a long step diagonally right, keeping the left foot anchored in place;

tackle the right leg around the thigh by encircling the thigh with both arms. Squeeze and stretch.
(b) Return to position.
(c) Tackle the left leg.
(d) Return to position
The value in flexibility comes from forcing a good stretch.

2. SIDE FLEX

Starting Position: Lie on side, arms extended overhead. The head rests on the lower arm. Legs are extended fully, one on top of the other.

Cadence: moderate

Movement:
(a) With a brisk action, raise the topmost arm and leg vertically. Attempt to make contact with hand and foot, without bending elbow or knee.
(b) Repeat for several counts and change to the other side.

3. KNEE HUG

Starting Position: Standing erect, hands at the side.

Cadence: slow.

Movement:
(a) Raise the left knee up to the chest, at the same time pulling in to the chest with the left hand on the knee and the right hand just above the ankle.
(b) Return to starting position.
(c) Raise the right knee, pulling it in with the right hand on the knee and the left hand just above the ankle.
(d) Return to starting position.
When lifting the legs alternately to the chest, be sure to maintain the erect position of the chest, shoulders, and the head. The knee and leg should be brought up to the chest, and not the chest down to the knee.

4. BEND AND STRETCH

Starting Position: Standing erect, hands on hips, feet shoulder width apart with feet pointing forward.

Cadence: slow.

Movement:
(a) Bend forward, touch the knuckles to the floor twice

(b) Return to position.

The knees should be relaxed slightly if needed to prevent a back-knee position.

5. TOE TOUCHER

Starting Position: flat on back, feet apart sideward about two feet, arms extended overhead.

Cadence: slow.

Movement:

(a) Roll up, thrust arms forward and touch toes, knees straight.

(b) Roll back to original position.

(c) Raise legs, swinging them over head, keep knees straight, touch toes to ground behind head.

(d) Lower legs to starting position, slowly

This exercise strengthens the muscles of the abdomen, thighs and hips. It also stretches the hamstring muscles which aid in the development of suppleness and flexibility. The massaging effect on the abdominal viscera is very beneficial.

6. TRUNK TWISTER

Starting Position: standing with feet about two feet apart sideward, with hands clasped behind head, elbows held backward, chin in.

Cadence: slow.

Movement:

(a) Bend and bounce downward, knees straight. Recover slightly. Do this vigorously.

(b) Bounce downward, but simultaneously rotate trunk sharply to left.

(c) Same to the right.

(d) Return to original position, pulling head back and chin in strongly.

The Trunk Twister reaches and strengthens all muscles of the trunk. It has excellent postural benefits. It results in greater flexibility of the lower back region.

Isometric Conditioning Activities

An isometric exercise is characterized by having virtually no movement of the body part, but a high degree of muscular tension. In this type of activity, the muscles should undergo a holding contraction of ten slow counts. To prevent movement, the pulling, pushing, or twisting

action is braced against some external stabilizing force. This can be against a wall, the floor, the sides of a door frame, or a special isometric apparatus. Or, an individual could work one set of muscles against another so that there is no movement. In addition, isometric exercise can be done with partners, with one partner providing the stabilizing action.

In the regular classroom, where the narrow confines and furniture limit activity, an isometric program has value because of the "no movement" feature. Furthermore, many of the activities can be done by children seated at desks, with the desks themselves used as braces to prevent movement.

Isometric exercises are useful for building strength, but only strength. Other activities where movement occurs, particularly endurance type activities which contribute to the development of the cardio-respiratory system, are needed to round out the program. Isometrics have value in the posture program in strengthening the anti-gravity muscles, thus contributing to better postural habits.

The exercises are simple, and there is little, if any, danger of injury. Children can use these activities as "home work," particularly in the program for the low fitness group. The exercises have good carryover value as they can be used on any age level.

It needs to be stressed that maximum or near maximum tension of the muscle group to be developed must be made, and this tension be held for approximately ten seconds, hence the ten slow counts. At any one session, there is no need for repetition of an exercise as maximum strength development is gained from one contraction at an exercise session. Contractions should be repeated three or four times per week.

Individual Isometric Exercises

1. Arms. Standing or seated.

   With the left palm up and the right palm down, clasp the arms in front of the body, chest high. Press down with the right hand, resisting with the left. Reverse.

2. Fingers and Grip. Seated.

   Two ordinary books are needed so that together the thickness is over one inch. Grasp the books in an opposed thumb grip. Squeeze hard with the fingers of both hands.

3. Arm and Shoulders. Standing or seated.
  Clasp the fingers together in front of the chest with the forearms held level to the floor (elbows out). Pull against the fingers to force the elbows out. Be sure to keep the chest up, shoulders back, and the head erect.

4. Arm and Shoulders. Standing or seated.
  Using a grip with the palms together, the fingers interlocked (knuckles upward), push the palms together. Be sure the elbows are up and out.

5. Legs. Seated.
  With the right foot on the floor, move the left foot on top of it, with the heel about half way to the ankle. Lift the right foot, resist with the left. Reverse. The same exercise can be done by crossing the feet so the pressure is ankle against ankle.

6. Legs, Arms, Abdominals. Seated.
  Place hands, palms down with fingers extended, on the lower portion of the top of the thighs. Press down with the hands and up with the legs.

7. Arms and Shoulders. Seated.
  Drop the hands to the sides so that they are straight down. Curl the fingers under the seat. Pull up with the shoulders, keeping the body erect.

8. Neck and Arms. Standing or seated.
  Clasp the arms behind the back of the head. Keeping the elbows well out, force the head back against the pressure of the hands.

9. Back, Arms, Thighs. Seated.
  Sitting as erect as possible, place both hands under the thighs close to the knees. Pull up with the hands against downward pressure of the thighs.

10. Legs. Against a wall.
  This is called the Skier's Sit. With the heels about 12 inches away from the wall, go into a sitting position (no chair or bench) so that back is against the wall, the thighs are parallel to the floor. A right angle is formed by the thighs and the body, and again at the knee joint. Hold for 30 seconds. The arms are folded across the chest. The head and shoulders are up and maintain contact against the wall.

11. Abdominals. Hook Lying Position.
  Hook the feet under a mat or have a partner hold. With the hands clasped behind the neck, knees bent, come up to a half way position of the sit-up. Hold for 30 seconds. In this position, try to keep the back straight and the abdominal wall flat.

12. Back and Shoulders. Lying on the Back.
  The hands are placed alongside the buttocks, palms down. Lift the body from the floor so that only the heels, hands, and head touch. If the hands are placed out to the sides, a more demanding exercise can be given.

13. Arms, Abdominals, General Body.
  The child stands about three feet behind a chair. He bends forward at the waist until he can put his hands on the back of the chair (elbows are straight). With a strong downward pull from the abdominal wall and the arms, he pulls down against the chair.

14. Flexed Arm Hang.
  A chinning bar is needed. This can be done also with a horizontal ladder or climbing rope. The child hangs from a bar so that his mouth is just even with his hands (palms away grip). Hang for 30 seconds or more.

Partner Isometric Exercises

  The exercises which can be done by partners are innumerable. Most of the exercises described in the previous section as individual isometrics can be adapted as partner activities. A partner can keep arms or legs from being lifted or forced down, moved together or apart, raised or lowered, etc. A few partner exercises will serve as illustrations.

1. Push-up Position.
  One partner in push-up position with arms bent so that the body is about half way up from the floor. The other partner straddles his head and puts pressure on top of his shoulders, forcing down. The amount of pressure takes judgment by the partner as too much will simply cause the bottom man to collapse. This can also be done as a resistive exercise where the push-up is actually done with the top man supplying resistance.

2. Neck. On hands and knees.
  One partner is down on hands and bent knees. The other is immediately in front of the head. Pressure is down against the back of the head. A second exercise is to apply pressure by a lift with the clasped

hands, which are positioned under the forehead.

3. Legs. Prone position.

The child is face down with his hands overhead, palms down. His legs are lifted so that the soles of the feet are toward the ceiling, with a right angle bend at the knee joint. Partner kneels near the feet and pulls back on one heel. The child tries to flex his leg against the resistance. Change to the other leg. Both legs can be done at once, but it is a little awkward to hold both legs at the same time.

Circuit Training

Circuit training is an exercise program consisting of a number of stations arranged in the form of a circuit. Each of the stations demands an exercise task from the child and he moves from station to station in sequential order.

Basic Theory

The exercise tasks composing the circuit should contribute to the development of all parts of the body. In addition, the activities should contribute to the various components of physical fitness, i. e., strength, power, endurance, agility, flexibility and others. Thus, circuit training can be a valuable tool in the development of physical fitness.

Methodology

Each station should provide an exercise task which is within the capacity of the children. The type of activity at each station should be one that the child can learn and do without the aid of another child. As the child moves from one station to the next, the exercises which directly follow each other should make demands on different parts of the body so that the performance at any one station does not cause local fatigue which could effect the ability to perform the next task.

It is important that sufficient instruction in the activities be given so that the children can perform correctly at each station. Also, the children should be taught to count the number of repetitions correctly.

For any one class, the children can be divided so that some start at each station. From the standpoint of supplying necessary equipment at each station, this method keeps the demands low. For example, if there are thirty children for a circuit of six stations, five children would start at each spot. The maximum equipment at each station in this case would be that necessary for five children.

Timing and Dosage

In general, a fixed time limit at each station seems to offer the best plan for circuit training on the elementary level. Each child attempts to complete as many repetitions as he can during the time limit at each station. Increased work load can be accomplished by increased number of repetitions (by the child) and increasing the amount of time at each station. A suggested progressive time schedule to be used as a guide for timing the circuit is as follows:

Introduction	15 seconds at each station
1st two weeks	20 seconds at each station
2nd two weeks	25 seconds at each station
After four weeks	30 seconds at each station

Keeping in mind that the children need to be challenged, the above schedule should be modified according to how well the children are challenged. Children need to be "pushed" and the time limit is adjusted to accomplish this. A circuit that is too easy will contribute little to the development of fitness.

A 15-second interval should be established to allow children to move from one station to the next. Later, this can be lowered to 10 seconds. Students may start at any station as designated, but must follow the established order of stations.

A second method of timing is to sound only one signal for the change to the next station. Under this plan, the child ceases his activity at one station, moves to the next, and immediately begins the task at that station without awaiting another signal.

Another means of increasing the activity demands of the circuit is to change the individual activities to more demanding types. For example, a station could specify knee or bench push-ups and later change these to regular push-ups, a more demanding exercise.

Some teachers find it helpful to

record the number of repetitions each child does in the time limit. This means that each child must have an individual form and a pencil, both of which he takes with him as he moves from station to station. Immediately after finishing an exercise task at a station, he records the number of repetitions on the form provided. Some planning is necessary so that the distribution of the forms and pencils will not consume too much class time. A monitor can issue the cards and pencils to each of the stations where the children are to start.

The Stations

The manner in which a circuit is organized can vary according to what is to be accomplished. Equipment needed is also a consideration, and it is recommended that exercise tasks at the different stations be selected from those requiring a minimum of equipment. Exercise programs can include weight lifting activities, but this is hardly feasible for the average elementary school.

The number of stations can vary, but probably should be not less than six and not more than eight. Activities should be selected so that consecutive stations do not make demands on the same section of the body. The exercise activities for circuit training designated at any station will be either for general body conditioning or for a particular section of the body.

A circuit should always include activities for exercising the arm and shoulder girdle and for strengthening the abdominal wall. A wide variety of activities are available for the circuit. The following are suggested. These are put into classifications from which one may be selected.

1. General Body Activity
   Rope Jumping
      Use single-time speed.
   Side Straddle Hop
      This two-count exercise is also called the Jumping Jack (p. 157).
   Jump and Reach
      This is the same as Jump and Reach Test, except that the child touches as high as he can with his right hand for five times, and then works with the left hand for five.
2. Push-up Types - Arm and Shoulder Girdle
   Push-ups - knee or regular (p. 156).
   Squat Thrusts - four count exercise (p. 157).

3. Agility Runs - Legs
   Agility Run - Touch With the Toes
      Two lines are established 15 feet apart. The child moves between the two lines as rapidly as possible touching one line with the right foot, and the other with the left.
   Agility Run - Touch With the Hand
      The same as above except that the lines are touched with the respective hand instead of the foot.
4. Arm Circles - Arm and Shoulders
   Standing Arm Circles (p. 156)
   Lying Arm Circles
      The child lies face down, with the arms out to the side. Alternate circles five times forward and five times backward should be made. The head and shoulders are lifted from the ground during the exercise.
5. Abdominal Exercises
   Rowing (p. 50)
   Sit-ups (p. 50)
   Curl-ups (p. 50)
   Alternate Toe Touching
      Child begins flat on his back with hands extended overhead. He alternates by touching the right toe with the left hand and vice versa. He should bring both the foot and the arm up at the same time and return to the flat position each time.
      For the sit-ups and curl-ups, some means of anchoring the feet may be desirable. Mats can be used so that the child can hook his feet under the edge to provide support which ordinarily is given by another person holding his feet.
6. Crab Position - Arm and Shoulder Girdle
   Crab Walk (see page 157 for description)
      Two parallel lines are drawn 6 to 8 feet apart. The child starts with his hands on one line and his feet in the direction of the other. He moves back and forth between the lines in crab position, touching one line with his heels and the other with his hands.
   Crab Kick (p. 157)
      The child is in crab position and alternates with right and left foot kicking toward the ceiling.
7. Leg Exercises
   Step-ups
      A bench is needed for each three children who are at this station. The child begins in front of the bench stepping up on the bench with the left, then up with the right. The next step is up with

the right, then up with the left. Thus, the series of step-ups alternate in beginning with the right and the left. This is not a natural movement and must be practiced.

Running in Place

Be sure the knees are lifted to a point on each step where the thighs are up parallel to the floor.

Treadmill (p. 158)

Straddle Bench Jumps

The child straddles a bench. The child alternates jumping to the top of the bench and back to the floor. The activity is quite strenuous. Since the degree of effort is dependent upon the height of the bench, benches of shorter height should be considered. These can be constructed in the form of small elongated boxes 4 feet long, 10 inches wide, and different heights of 8, 10, 12, and 15 inches. A 4-foot box will accommodate two children at one time.

Squat Jumps

The child crouches to about a three-quarter bend with his hands on the floor, slightly to the front and side of his feet. One foot is slightly in front of the other. He springs into the air about 4 inches, changing the position of his feet. Each time he uses his hands to absorb some of the shock of the returning position. The full-knee bend should be avoided.

8. Bend and Stretch - Flexibility and Back

Bend and Stretch (p. 158)

Alternate Toe Touching

The position is similar to the previous exercise except the hands and arms are out to the side with palms facing forward. The child bends over, touching the left toe with the right hand, returns to erect position.

Trunk Twister (p. 159)

9. Others

Many other exercises, stunts, or movements can be used. Some can be used in combination. In leg exercises, for example, the task can be designated as 25 steps running in place and then 5 pogo jumps into the air. This is repeated.

If chinning bars, horizontal ladders, and climbing ropes are present, circuits can make use of these. Chinning, climbing, and traveling activities may be prescribed for tasks at a station.

Sample Circuit Training Courses

SIX STATION COURSE

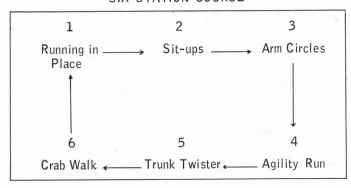

Supplies and Equipment: Mats for sit-ups (to hook toes)
Time Needed: 4 minutes--based on 30 second activity limit, 10 seconds to move between stations.

EIGHT STATION COURSE

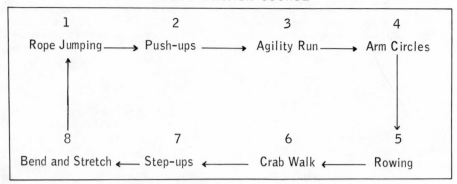

Supplies and Equipment: Jumping ropes, mats for knee push-ups (if used), benches or first row of portable bleachers.

Time Needed: 6 minutes--based on 30 second activity limit, 15 seconds to move between stations.

Red, White, and Blue Circuits

This method of operating the circuit employs definite dosages at each of the stations. The repetitions at each of the stations are established under this kind of a formula:

Red: Modest challenge. Most children can do these.
White: Moderate challenge
Blue: Considerable challenge

Under this system, for example, the following could be established for the push-ups.

Red: 10 White: 15 Blue: 20

Naturally, the number of repetitions and the progression would depend on the capacity of the children and their fitness level. Some experimentation is needed to set the repetition progressions at each of the stations.

Since the children progress at individual rates from station to station, the problem of sufficient equipment and space at each station is an important consideration. Signs are valuable at each station to designate the number of repetitions for each of the colors.

Another suggestion found valuable is to have super circuits labeled silver and gold. These could be award type of circuits combining the repetitions and a time to do them. Thus, to qualify, the student would do the specified dosages at each station and complete the circuit within a designated time. The silver and gold circuits would be special events and not part of the regular program of activi-

ties. Specially designed emblems could be awarded. It should be emphasized that awards of this type should be enough of a challenge to make them respected. The gold award, especially, should be difficult enough so to be within the range of only the top fitness students. Standards should be set for different grade levels and be different for boys and girls.

Target Time Method

There is a third method of operating the circuit, a method which is complicated and not generally suitable for the elementary school. This is the original method employed when circuit training was first established in England. The method employs the concept of target time.

The first step is to determine the specific work load for each student at each of the stations. First, the number of repetitions which a student can do at a station in one minute is counted. A good method to use here is to have one-half the students do the activity and the remainder act as counters. Some record form is necessary so each student's performance at each station may be recorded. Since this activity of one minute duration is strenuous, it is best to check not more than three of the stations in any one day.

After the number of repetitions each student can do at a station in one minute has been determined, the work load at a station for any one student is set by taking one-half of this figure. For example, if a student can turn a rope in the rope jump 120 times in one minute, then his work load at that station is 60.

To set target time, each child runs the circuit doing the number of repetitions as set for him. He is timed for one complete circuit. His target time becomes three-fourths of this time. This means that he shoots to meet the target time as soon as he can. Improvement is judged by lowering the circuit time and trying to meet the target time. When a student meets the target time, new work loads and a new target time should be set.

It is also possible to use target time for two or three continuous circuits. However, there can be jamming up at various stations with this system if equipment and space is a problem.

The teacher or a student can stand in the center of the room and count out aloud the seconds passed so that each child may note his performance time as he finishes. This is recorded on an appropriate form.

The Obstacle Course

The obstacle course, so familiar to men in the Service during World War II, is becoming increasingly popular as a tool for fitness development in the elementary school. Obstacle courses can roughly be divided into two types; the outdoor (generally permanent) and the indoor (portable).

The courses can be run against a time standard or can be done just for the exercise values alone. A course should be designed to exercise all parts of the body through a variety of activities. By including running, vaulting, agility, climbing, hanging, crawling, and other activities, good fitness demands are present when the child moves through the course as rapidly as he can.

Such physical education equipment as mats, parallel bars, horizontal ladder, high jump standards, benches, and vaulting boxes can make effective obstacle courses. A great variety of courses can be designed dependent upon the length and the different tasks to be included. Indoors, the space available would be an important factor. Some schools, fortunate enough to have a suitable wooded area, have established permanent courses.

An illustration of an indoor course is given based on the assumption that a horizontal ladder is present. The list of items needed are:

3 benches (16 to 18 inches)
3 tumbling mats (4 by 8 feet)
1 folding card table
1 set of high jump standards (2) with cross bar
1 Horizontal ladder
1 36" vaulting box or wooden horse
5 chairs

COURSE CONTINUITY

Start: Lying face down with hands, palms down, near the chest ready to get up.

1. Run forward, around the first chair and back around the second.
2. Three benches are placed about 5 feet apart. Child hurdles or jumps over them.
3. This station consists of a mat with a card table placed on it to form a tunnel for the runner. The runner goes under the card table on hands and knees.
4. The bar on this station is placed between the two high jump standards. The bar is 30 inches above the ground. Runner does a scissors jump.
5. The task here is a crab walk across the length of the mat. He should begin with his feet pointed in the direction he is to go. He finishes when his feet are off the mat at the far end.
6. The run is made in a figure eight fashion in and around the chairs. He goes in figure eight fashion down to the end of the three chairs, back to the first chair, and down to the end once more.
7. Station 7 is a hand walk on the horizontal ladder. The child should use the side rails to hand walk the length of the ladder.
8. The runner does a log roll the length of the mat.
9. A vault over a vaulting box or wooden horse 36 inches high is made.
10. Cross finish line where time can be checked.

The starting and finish lines are close enough together to be convenient for the timers. Timing can be systematized in having runners leave the starting line at ten second intervals. The faster children should run first to avoid conflict at any one station, as the course is such that only one child can be at any one station at a time. However, timing for elementary children is not an important aspect of the activity. The run can be made just for the values of the activity.

The course can be shortened or lengthened and the stations changed with respect to order. Also, children can run the course more than one circuit around at a time.

166

OBSTACLE COURSE - INDOOR

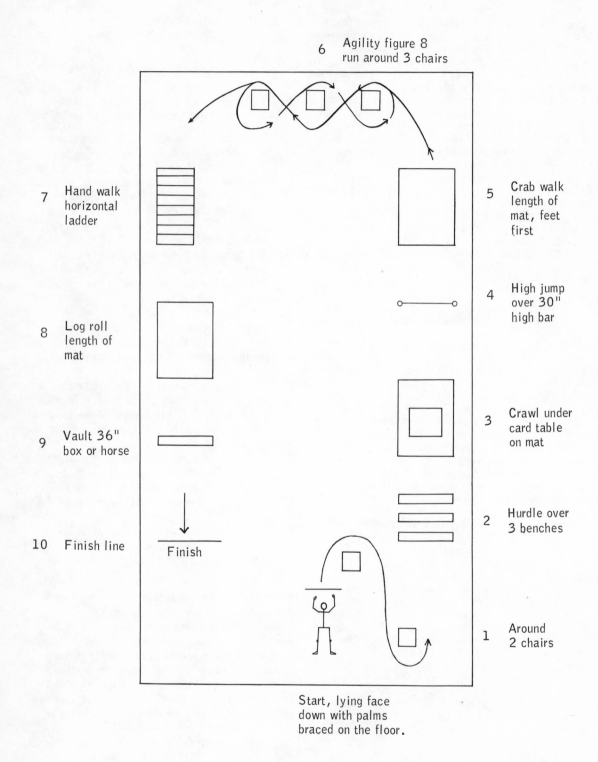

6   Agility figure 8
run around 3 chairs

7   Hand walk horizontal ladder

8   Log roll length of mat

9   Vault 36" box or horse

10   Finish line

Finish

5   Crab walk length of mat, feet first

4   High jump over 30" high bar

3   Crawl under card table on mat

2   Hurdle over 3 benches

1   Around 2 chairs

Start, lying face down with palms braced on the floor.

Postural Fitness

The problems of posture for elementary children already have been given considerable treatment in Chapter 6. Only a short discussion of the methods of implementation of postural emphasis will be made here.

When pupils who have poor posture do not improve, they should be given special instruction, including posture exercises. The teacher should seek the advice and aid of the physical education specialist or teacher in this area.

Acute structural and functional defects should be subject to referral to proper medical authorities, as there are limitations to how much the teacher can be of help in posture. However, the teacher should see that good posture is practiced in the activities where it is a part. Dance activities, for example, lend themselves well to postural instruction.

Proper foot position while standing and walking should be given strict attention. The feet are the basis for weight carrying, and early attention to good foot posture will pay dividends later. A slight toe-in is preferable to toeing out. However, any marked toeing in or out marks the case for referral.

Apparatus work involving hanging is particularly excellent for upper arm and shoulder girdle development and flexibility, so necessary for good upper torso posture. Inclusion of these activities is a "must" in the program.

In the groups of exercises, there should be at least one for the development of the upper back muscles and one for the strengthening of the abdominal wall.

Miscellaneous Fitness Activities

While all activities in physical education should make contributions to the fitness of youngsters, at times, the teacher can use special activities particularly suited for this objective in physical education. A variety of these are available based upon changes in movement upon command. Some involve combinations of running and other movements, while others use slower movement patterns.

1. Walk, Trot, Sprint

Students are scattered around the circumference of the room, all facing counter clockwise. The signals are given with a whistle. On the first whistle, the students begin to walk around the room in good posture. The next whistle signals a change to a trotting run. On the next whistle, the students run as rapidly as they can. Another whistle signals for them to walk again. The cycle is repeated as many times as the need indicates.

2. The Basketball Slide Drill

The students are scattered on the floor or playground, with each assuming a guarding stance as in basketball. One foot is ahead of the other, and the hands are out as if guarding. The movements forward and backward should be made using a shuffle step with the feet retaining their approximate position. Movements to the side should be a slide.

The leader stands in front with a whistle. He points in a direction and immediately the players move that way (forward, backward, or to either side). When the whistle is blown again, all stop. Other signals, such as "GO" or "Stop" could be used in lieu of a whistle.

Another method to move the students is to station a player in front of the group with a basketball. He dribbles rapidly in any direction, and the players move in relative position with him.

3. Movement Experiences

The patterns are based upon the principles of Movement Exploration, which were discussed in the primary grade program.

Basically, two elements are necessary. The first is to put the students in some kind of a position. The second requires imagination and inventiveness by the teacher or leader to provide a number of movement experiences having fitness values. Many of the starting positions taken from exercises can be the basis for movement. As an illustration, five suggested starting positions are listed. Many others are possible.

a. Lying flat on the back with legs extended and together, hands overhead.
b. Push-up position.
c. Sitting tailor fashion.
d. Sitting with feet spread and hands supporting on the floor slightly behind hips.
e. Standing (feet together, apart, at stride position, etc.)

Let us assume you have selected the position #1 for your movement experiences. Have the children scatter around the room so each has sufficient room. They should be suitably dressed for the activity, or the boys can be located forward (facing the teacher) and the girls occupying the back half of the room.

What movement can be done from a lying position? While the directions are better phrased in the forms of questions to the students, the following tasks suggest the procedures which can be followed. "Can you ------------"

Sit up and touch both toes with your hands?

Sit up and touch the right toe with the left hand? The other way?

Bring up your toes to touch behind your head?

With hands to the side, bring our feet up straight and then touch them by the right hand? By the left hand?

Lift your feet up slowly an inch at a time? Without bending your knees?

Pick up your heels about 6 inches from the floor and swing them back and forth? Cross them and twist them?

Many other big-muscle movements can be suggested to and experienced by the students in varied degrees. Another illustration using a familiar exercise position should help clarify the possibilities of development through movement experiences. Ask the children to assume the push-up position.

PUSH—UP POSITION

From this position we ask the children if they can--

Lift one foot high. Now the other foot.

Bounce both feet up and down. Move the feet out from each other while bouncing.

Inch the feet up to the hands and go back again. Inch the feet up to the hands and then inch the hands

out to return to the push-up position.

Reach up with one hand and touch the other shoulder behind the back.

Lift both hands from the floor. Try clapping the hands.

Bounce from the floor with both hands and feet off the floor at the same time.

Turn over so the back is to the floor. Complete the turn to push-up position.

Lower the body an inch at a time until the chest touches the floor. Return.

Inch the hands (one at a time at first) out to the sides. Return.

There is value in maintaining the push-up position for a length of time. The various tasks to be done provide interest and challenge to the youngsters. The informal and individual approach stimulates the child to good effort in muscular work.

4. Grass Drills*

Grass drills have been with us a long time, having been used for many decades in the development of football teams. They are strenuous since they are performed in quick succession and at top speeds. Progression is gained by gradually increasing the length of the work periods. The drills are executed in place.

Grass drills involve moving rapidly from one to the other of three basic positions:

a. "Go"--running in place at top speed on the toes and balls of the feet, knees raised high, arms pumping, body bent forward slightly at the waist.

b. "Front" --prone position, palms flat on the ground directly under the shoulders, legs together and extended.

c. "Back" --supine position (flat on the back), arms extended alongside the body with palms down, legs together and straight.

The drill is conducted by giving the commands, "Go," "Front," and "Back" in a varied sequence. Sufficient time should be allowed for the children to make each change.

5. Guerilla Exercises

The President's Council calls these "Astronaut Drills.**" The chil-

---

* Youth Physical Fitness, p. 79.
** Ibid., p. 79-80.

dren are in a large circle formation spaced about 6 feet apart. Form a double circle if necessary. The children walk around at a slow pace, but not necessarily in step. The teacher gives various commands designating the activity to be performed while moving in circle formation. After performing the exercise, the children again resume the slow walk.

A leader can be put in the center from whom the children can take the cues to change activity as he changes his own movements. The activity becomes a kind of a "Follow the Leader" game.

The following activities are suitable for this drill:

a. On all fours. Walk forward, backward, sideward (in line of direction).
b. Perform stunt movements like the Crab, Seal Walk, Lame Dog Walk, Gorilla Walk, and others.
c. Move to fundamental locomotor movements like running (various ways), hopping, sliding, leaping, jumping, etc.
d. Do various movements in place like push-ups, sit-ups, and other exercises.

The author used the drills with football teams for many years and found them to be excellent conditioners. However, he combined the Grass Drills with the Guerilla Exercises.

6. Free Running
There should be time for simply running. When the signal is given, the children run around the gym or playground in any direction they wish with the stipulation of not colliding with other children.

Free running can also be combined with abrupt changes of movement signaled by a whistle. The teacher can specify the following changes which are to be made when the whistle signal is given.

a. Abrupt change of direction with the stipulation of not bumping into other children.
b. Touch the floor (specify one or both hands).
c. Jump high into the air.
d. Turn around quickly, continuing in the original direction. Combinations of other movements can be used.

7. Fast Stepping
Each child does very fast stepping in place just as rapidly as he can. This is kept up for ten seconds and then ten seconds of rest. The cycle is repeated. This is quite strenuous and the children should be checked carefully to determine dosage.

8. Timed Activities
Children are stimulated to good effort if they know that they are being timed and are competing against other children. Timing can be done for 30, 45, 60 seconds, or some other interval. The following should be considered.

a. Rope jumping for time. The object is to turn the rope as fast as possible during the time limit. The number of successful jumps are counted.
b. Agility run between lines. Two lines are selected, any convenient distance between 10 to 20 feet, just so all children are faced with the same distance. The child touches the lines alternately with the hands. He should touch one line with the left hand and the other with the right.
c. Potato relays for time. A potato type relay can be organized in the following fashion.

Start   Box

(all distances between the start, box, and blocks -- 10 ft.)

A box is placed ten feet in front of the starting line, with four blocks in individual circles the same distance apart. The runner begins behind the starting line. He puts the blocks one at a time in the box and finishes across the original line. He can bring the blocks back one at a time to the box in any order he wishes. All blocks must be put inside the box. The box should be 12" by 12" with a depth of 3" to 6". Blocks must be placed, not thrown, into the box.

Testing for Physical Fitness

Testing for physical fitness can serve four purposes. The first is to make a diagnosis of the fitness condition of the individual. Secondly, the test can provide a measure of evaluation of the physical education program with respect to the attainment of one of its objectives. A third purpose would be the motivation for the individual child. A fourth purpose is the aid that the fitness testing can provide to the counseling program for the child.

Testing is always a problem for the individual teacher without help. It is difficult for children to supervise each other and secure reliable measurements.

This source would like to recommend a plan where the school secure the help of the P. T. A. in the testing program. Interested parents make excellent testers. A team of parents for testing can be established on a school, group of schools, or school district basis, depending upon the situation. Where such a plan is in operation, school districts report enthusiastic support of the testing and of the entire physical education program.

The testers must first undergo orientation and training in the testing procedures. A trial run with one class or a small group will help iron out most difficulties. The testing program should be organized efficiently with good testing procedures. Each tester should have detailed instructions for each station.

If enough parents are available, it is well to have two testers at each station. One has a clip board and does the recording, while the other does the measuring.

Two systems of recording the information can be used. One is to have class lists at each station for recording. The second is for each child to have an individual record card, which he carries with him from station to station. The first method is speedier, but care must be taken to match the correct name with the performance. The class lists will need to be transferred to the individual cards after the testing is over.

Some school districts are having good success in using IBM cards on which to record the data. This provides a ready and easy means of analyzing the data. Laborious hand tabulation of the results is eliminated.

Throughout the school year, testing should be scheduled at least three times. Testing should be done at the beginning of the school year to select the low fitness children and to point out directions the program should take. Testing at a point near the middle (January or February) can give an indication of the progress made. The testing at the end of the school year can provide information with respect to what has been accomplished.

The test results, or at least the interpretation thereof, should be a part of the child's health records and should be included in the periodic progress report to the parent. The school report card should contain a section devoted to the physical side of the child.

The results of a class and for the school should be interpreted in light of national norms and comparison with local achievement. Testing is meaningless unless the real concern is for upgrading the physical education program and raising physical levels of the children to desirable standards.

The test selected for the program is the one that has been adopted by the American Association for Health, Physical Education, and Recreation. It affords an opportunity for each child to be compared with national norms and interpret each individual test item in qualitative terms of poor, satisfactory, good, and excellent.

Careful attention to the manner each test item is given is important. The test can be given easily in three class periods. However, it is better to take more time than to try to rush through procedures.

The overall test consists of seven different test items.

1. Pull-ups (Modified for girls)
2. Sit-ups
3. Shuttle Run
4. Standing Broad Jump
5. Fifty-yard Dash
6. Softball Throw for Distance
7. 600 Yard Run-Walk

A program for the test items could follow this plan:

1st day
    Pull-ups, Sit-ups, Shuttle Run
2nd day
    Standing Broad Jump, Fifty-yard Dash, Softball Throw for Distance.
3rd day
    600 Yard Run-walk

The children for the first two days testing can be divided into three groups, each of which would take positions at one of the test stations. At the conclusion of the testing for the station, the groups rotate to the next station.

Three groups can be used for the final day's testing for the 600 yard run-walk. However, there is necessity for only two groups in the administration of this test.

PULL-UPS (Boys)

The technique for the pull-up is described in the screening test, presented in this chapter on page 152.

Standards for Pull-ups (Boys)

Age	10	11	12	13
Excellent	6	6	7	8
Good	3	4	4	5
Satisfactory	2	2	2	3
Poor	1	1	1	2

MODIFIED PULL-UPS (Girls)

The technique for this test is described on page 153 of this chapter. Top limit is 45.

Standards for Pull-ups (Girls)

Age	10	11	12	13
Excellent	45	45	45	45
Good	40	40	40	40
Satisfactory	30	30	29	30
Poor	17	20	20	20

SIT-UPS

Like the pull-ups, the sit-up is a part of the screening test and is described under that topic on page 153. Top limit is 50 for girls.

Standards for the Sit-ups

	Boys			
Age	10	11	12	13
Excellent	60	67	78	73
Good	47	50	51	54
Satisfactory	30	31	37	40
Poor	22	23	28	30
	Girls			
Excellent	50	50	50	50
Good	33	34	30	30
Satisfactory	22	25	22	21
Poor	15	18	17	17

SHUTTLE RUN

Equipment: Two blocks of wood, 2 by 2 by 4 inches (blackboard erasers can be used) and stopwatch. Mark two parallel lines 30 feet apart. Place the blocks of wood behind one of the lines.

Starting Position: Pupil stands behind the line opposite the blocks, ready to run.

Action: On the signal, "Ready!--Go!" the pupil runs to the blocks, picks up one and places it behind the starting line. He does not throw or drop it. He then runs and picks up the second block and carries it back across the starting line.

Rules: Two time trials are allowed, with the better recorded to the nearest tenth of a second. Disqualify if the blocks are dropped or thrown.

Standards for the Shuttle Run
In seconds to the nearest tenth

	Boys			
Age	10	11	12	13
Excellent	10.3	10.2	10.0	9.7
Good	11.2	11.0	10.5	10.3
Satisfactory	11.9	11.6	11.1	10.8
Poor	12.3	12.0	11.7	11.5
	Girls			
Excellent	11.2	10.9	10.4	10.7
Good	11.8	11.6	11.3	11.3
Satisfactory	12.4	12.2	12.0	12.0
Poor	13.1	12.9	12.6	12.4

STANDING BROAD JUMP

Equipment: Any level surface and tape measure

Starting Position: Pupil stands ready to jump just behind the take-off line. Preparatory to jumping, the pupil should have knees flexed and should swing the arms backward and forward in a rhythmical motion.

Action: The jump is made with the arms swung forcefully forward and upward, taking off with the balls of the feet.

Rules: Three trials are allowed with the best scored in feet and the nearest inch. Measure from the take-off line to the heel or the part of the body that touches nearest to the take-off line.

Standards for the Standing Broad Jump
In feet and inches

	Boys			
Age	10	11	12	13
Excellent	5-6	5-10	6-2	6-8
Good	5-0	5-4	5-8	6-0
Satisfactory	4-8	5-0	5-4	5-8
Poor	4-4	4-7	4-11	5-2

	Girls			
Age	10	11	12	13
Excellent	5-4	5-7	5-8	5-9
Good	4-10	5-0	5-2	5-4
Satisfactory	4-5	4-8	4-9	4-11
Poor	4-1	4-3	4-5	4-6

FIFTY YARD DASH

Equipment: Stopwatch

Starting Position: Pupil stands behind the starting line. The starter takes a position at the finish line with a stopwatch. He raises one hand preparatory to giving the starting signal.

Action: When the starter brings down his hand quickly and hits his thigh, the pupil leaves his mark. The time is noted and recorded.

Rules: One trial is allowed except if it is obvious that the child did not have a fair trial. Time is recorded to the nearest tenth of a second.

Standards for Fifty-Yard Dash
In seconds to the nearest tenth

	Boys			
Age	10	11	12	13
Excellent	7.6	7.3	7.0	6.5
Good	8.1	7.9	7.5	7.2
Satisfactory	8.6	8.3	8.0	7.6
Poor	9.0	8.7	8.3	8.0
	Girls			
Excellent	8.0	7.5	7.2	7.4
Good	8.5	8.2	8.0	7.9
Satisfactory	8.9	8.6	8.4	8.2
Poor	9.5	9.0	9.0	8.8

SOFTBALL THROW FOR DISTANCE

Equipment: Softballs (3), tape measure, small metal or wooden markers.

The Field: Marked off at 5 yard intervals up to a restraining line. A football field marked in conventional fashion makes an ideal area for the test.

Starting Position: Pupil stands several feet behind the restraining line, ready to throw. The throw must not be from a run.

Action: The pupil throws the ball overhand as far as he can from behind the restraining line.

Rules: Three trials are allowed with the best trial measured to the nearest foot. The first is marked, and the mark is moved if a longer throw is made. Only an overhand throw is permitted, and the thrower cannot cross the restraining line during the throw.

Standards for the Softball Throw
In feet

	Boys			
Age	10	11	12	13
Excellent	122	130	151	171
Good	103	115	132	148
Satisfactory	92	103	118	129
Poor	82	94	102	115
	Girls			
Excellent	69	88	94	106
Good	56	68	78	88
Satisfactory	45	56	65	75
Poor	38	48	55	63

600-YARD RUN-WALK

Equipment: Stopwatch, running area with starting and finish lines to cover 600 yards. (see note)

Starting Positions: Pupils are divided into pairs. While one runs, the other stands near the timer listens for the time for finishing. The timer calls out the number indicating the time on a continuous basis, until all the runners have crossed the finish line.

Action: On the signal to start, the pupil starts running the 600 yard distance. Students should be cautioned to pace themselves.

Rules: The time is recorded in minutes and seconds. Walking is permitted but the object is to cover the distance in the shortest time.

Standards for the 600-Yard Run-Walk
In minutes and seconds

	Boys			
Age	10	11	12	13
Excellent	2:15	2:10	2:05	2:0
Good	2:30	2:24	2:19	2:13
Satisfactory	2:45	2:37	2:32	2:25
Poor	2:58	2:50	2:46	2:36

Age	Girls 10	11	12	13
Excellent	2:30	2:25	2:22	2:24
Good	2:49	2:44	2:41	2:43
Satisfactory	3:06	3:01	3:03	3:0
Poor	3:21	3:16	3:21	3:20

Note: A quarter-mile track makes a satisfactory running area. However, on a playground a small track can be laid out so the runners take two laps around it to cover the distance. If a square is laid out 75 yards on a side, two laps by each child would cover the 600 yards. A rectangle could be used with 50 yards on the shorter sides, and 100 on the longer sides.

State of Oregon Motor Fitness Test

A second test included in this guide is found in the Appendix on page 325. This test has the advantage over the national test in having fewer test items, and consequently, less of a time demand in the program. The test is composed of only three items and can given to a class of thirty or so in one class period. The test is included by permission of the Oregon State Department of Education, under whose sponsorship directions and individual record forms are made available to schools in the State of Oregon. A sample copy of the test directions and forms may be secured by writing to the Director of Physical Education, State Department of Education, Salem, Oregon.

Motivation in Physical Fitness

Motivation in the development of physical fitness is of major importance. Motivation can be provided in a number of ways.

1. Extrinsic awards can be given in the shape of emblems, certificates, badges, and similar items. These should be given for high levels of fitness and for commendable progress. Special badges for fitness are available from the American Association for Health, Physical Education, and Recreation. Standards for awards can be set locally.
2. The bulletin board in the gymnasium and in the classroom can be utilized for items of interest and stimulation with regard to fitness. The material should be appropriate, up-to-date, and changed periodically.
3. Although a fallacy exists in trying to get "everyone over the average," the publication of school norms and records gives the students a goal at which to strive.
4. The use of visual aids should be exploited. There are a number of good films available with respect to fitness.
5. An excellent motivation for fitness is an understanding by each child concerning the values of physical fitness and how, physiologically, fitness can be developed and maintained.
6. As previously mentioned, cooperation by the home is essential. Children are more likely to be fit if their parents are concerned about this area.
7. School demonstration for parents and physical education exhibitions can feature the topic of fitness.
8. The level of fitness should be an item of report on the periodic progress report of the child to the parent.

Folk and Square Dancing Intermediate Grades

The emphasis of the rhythmic program on the intermediate grade level is on fundamental skills of dancing, which if mastered will lead to a lifetime of enjoyment in dancing. As differed from the emphasis on the primary level on fundamental movements to rhythm and their application to simple rhythmic activities, the intermediate program introduces dance steps and incorporates them into many dances. Providing a door to new and varied rhythmic experiences, dance steps like the two-step, polka, waltz, varsouvienne, and schottische give the program of dance activities new and exciting breadth.

Not to be overlooked, however, are the immediate values to children. Folk and square dancing provide vigorous activity for both boys and girls and require a minimum of equipment and space. Soon the children will be taking part in social functions sponsored by the school in which the ability to participate successfully in rhythmic activities is important.

Due to differences between sexes in growth, development, and capacity, it becomes necessary to separate boys and girls for certain vigorous activities. It is vitally important that boys and girls play together in some portion of the physical education program on all grade levels. The rhythmic program offers ideal activity to meet in part this objective.

Important attitudes and social learnings can be promoted through a well conducted program of dance activities. To be at ease with the opposite sex, to learn social graces, and to make common elements of courtesy a practice are important goals of rhythmic program. Almost all dances on the intermediate level are couple dances and offer excellent opportunity to achieve these goals.

At the intermediate level, instruction in rope skipping to music should be emphasized. This material is presented as a sequence for the three grades rather than according to separate grade levels. The teacher in any one grade should start with the students at the particular point of achievement and work up from that point.

Program Suggestions

1. Start the class with a familiar dance they know and enjoy. A good suggestion is to have a child assigned to set up, warm up, and have the music going when the children arrive. With a known dance, there is little need other than to get them into the proper formation.
2. Provide a balance of activity and rest. Mix in and alternate active and more restful dances.
3. Vary the program with different types of dances rather than having all one type, unless the period is quite short.
4. At times have a choice dance.
5. Finish the dance program with one that they enjoy and will leave a good taste in their mouths.

Introducing New Steps or Skills

The level of ability of the group and the degree of difficulty of the basic step will influence the manner in which a step is presented for learning. The sequence in the presentation and the starting point will vary. Several approaches may be necessary for everyone to learn the step. The following considerations are important:

1. Analysis of the Basic Step
   Explain and discuss accents, the characteristics of the rhythm, and the foot pattern in relation to the rhythm.
   a. Listen to the music
   b. Clap hands to the rhythm
   c. Write out on the blackboard the relation of the rhythm to the movement
   d. Demonstrate the step
2. Method of Presentation
   a. Walk through with analysis and demonstration
   b. Practice
   c. Apply basic step in a simple sequence
   d. Use the basic step in a dance
3. Factors to be Considered in Presenting a Dance Step
   a. What formation should be used for teaching
      Scatter
      Line
      Single Circle
      Double Circle
   b. Position of the dancers
      Alone
      With partner
      In teaching couple dancing use the open position before the closed position. With the partners side by side, concentration on the steps can be made better if there is little worry about proper position.
   c. The use of accompaniment and cues needs to be considered. If the step is taught first by cues (verbal directions), the cues should build up to the tempo of the record.
   d. Movement direction should be controlled. Movement sequence can follow this pattern.
      In place
      Forward and backward
      Sideward and diagonal
      Turning

Suggestions for Teaching Dance Activities

While the application of the following suggestions will depend upon the nature of the dance to be presented, the suggestions have enough of a widespread application to warrant inclusion of a general list.

1. Material should be selected to interest and challenge the children. It should be part of an overall curriculum which shows progression from grade to grade.
2. Specific dance steps, in most cases, need to be taught carefully. Special attention to progressing from the simple to the more complex, slow to fast, alone to with a partner, and from the familiar to the unfamiliar is important in the learning process.
3. Dances should be repeated often enough so that there is reasonable mastery. Too much repetition, however, can kill interest.
4. Conduct activities as informally as possible but retain control of the group.
5. Change partners often and make frequent use of mixers. This makes for better sociability, adds interest, and gives all an equal opportunity to have good dancing partners.
6. Do not hold the class to the pace of the slow learner. Assign some of the more able as partners.
7. Get the group into formation as soon as possible. Children are able to grasp an understanding of the dance or step if they are in the formation used for the activity.
8. Stress enjoyment which comes from knowing a dance and being able to do it well. As an instructor, know the dance, have the lesson prepared and the music ready.
9. Occasionally, a class can invite another class to share the rhythmic program. This motivates the children to good educational goals.

Getting Groups in Position

While it is a goal to have the boys secure partners from the girls, there are times the teacher may wish to use other means to pair off the boys and girls. Suggested methods of getting the class in position are:

1. Down the center by two's. The boys are one side of the room and the girls on the other, both facing the same direction towards the one end of the room. All march forward to the end of the room, turn toward each other, come down the center by two's, and around in a circle formation.
2. Boys join hands in a circle and each girl steps behind a boy.
3. Boys stand in a circle facing counter clockwise while the girls form a circle around them facing clockwise. Both circles move in the direction they are facing and on signal stop. The boys takes the girl nearest him as his partner.
4. For square dances, take the first four couples from any of the previous formations to form a set. Continue until all sets are formed.

Introduction of a New Dance

1. Put the children in formation and let them sit down.
2. Tell something about the dance, its characteristics.
3. Listen to and analyze the piece for accents, phrases, changes.
4. Determine if a step should be taught. Use any appropriate method to teach the step.
5. Walk through the dance at least twice to instructions.
6. Dance with a decreased tempo.
7. Repeat difficult steps if necessary and walk through the dance again.
8. Gradually increase the tempo to normal.

Changing Partners

Change partners often by having the boy walk forward one or more partners ahead in a circle dance. Have the boy move one couple to the right in square dances.

Courtesy

Impress on the youngsters the importance and value of courtesy. The boy should escort the girl to and from the floor. Both should accept all partners gracefully and the boy should thank the girl for the dance.

Getting Underway

The teacher should arrange to have the record player set up previous to class. A child should be appointed as monitor to turn on the record player and get it warmed up before the children enter the room. It is an excellent practice to have the record playing when the children enter the room.

Sample Daily Program

While the day's lesson plan will vary according to the material to be presented, the following outline for the daily lesson may be helpful.

Minutes

5	Introductory Dance
	Generally, a dance the children know and enjoy
5-10	Review of material from previous class
	Time would vary according to how much review is needed.
10-15	Presentation of new material
5-10	Older dances already mastered with emphasis on enjoyment.
	A musical game or other type of game could be played.

Dance Positions

Closed Position. This is the social dance position. The boy faces the girl, holding her right hand in his left hand out to the side about shoulder level with the elbows bent. His right hand is on the girl's back just below her left shoulder blade. Her left arm rests lightly on the top of his right arm with her left hand on his shoulder.

Open Position. From the closed position, the boy turns to his left and the girl to her right, with the arms remaining about the same. Both are now facing in the same directions and are side by side.

Varsouvienne Position. Boy and girl stand side by side, facing the same direction. The boy holds the girl's left hand with his left hand in front. She brings her right hand directly back over her right shoulder and the boy reaches behind her back at shoulder height and grasps this hand with his right.

Peasant Position. Also called the waist-shoulder position. Partners face each other, and the boy places his hands on the girl's waist. The girl places her hands on the boy's shoulders.

Skaters Position. This is the crossed-hands position where the dancers stand side by side, facing the same direction, with the right hand held by the right, and the left by the left.

Dance Steps

1. Step-hop (even 2-4 or 4-4 time)
   The dancer takes a step with his left foot and then hops on it. He takes a step with his right and hops on it.
2. Polka (uneven 2-4 time)
   Step left, close right, step left, hop left; step right, close left, step right, hop right.
3. Schottische (even 4-4 time)
   The stepping is actually a light run. Step left, step right, step left, hop left; step right, step left, step right, hop right. The second part of the schottische pattern is four step-hops beginning (for the boy) on the left foot.
4. Two-Step (even 2-4 time)
   Step left, close right, step left; step right, close left, step right.
5. Waltz (even 3-4 time)
   Step left, step right, close left; step right, step left, close right.
6. Waltz Balance (even 3-4 time)
   Step forward with the left (count 1),

close right but put no weight on it (count 2), and hold (count 3); step back with the right (count 1), close with the left without weight on it (count 2), and hold (count 3).

7. Varsouvienne (3-4 time)
   The dance is too lengthy to describe here and is found on page 199.

Creative Rhythms in the Intermediate Grades

In the intermediate grades, rhythms involving basic movements have a definite place in providing creative activity. The teacher needs to challenge the boys and girls to improve their motor movements to rhythm. Consideration should be given to both locomotor and axial movements. Children should have experiences in being able to handle themselves effectively in the use of various floor patterns and space. The children at this level have generally outgrown those creative activities in which they imitate animals and objects. They can, however, be given problem solving activities involving the use of various locomotor movements, changes in direction, changes to other types of activity, and the like. In particular, the movements should be vigorous and challenging so that there is good acceptance by the more skilled, particularly the boys.

An example of activity of this kind is the change of movement on alternate phases of a piece of music. For the first phrase (8 counts) the child moves in a straight line either walking (slow rhythm) or running (rapid rhythm). During the second phrase (8 counts), he changes his movement according to the type of the problem set up. The directions could limit him to any kind of movement so long as he stays in his own space. The directions might call for a movement where the hands are placed on the floor. Thus, he alternates between the locomotor movement and a movement within the limitation of the problem.

The use of the tom-tom is recommended. A skillful teacher can vary the tempo, signal movement changes, and provide a variety of interesting activity. The teacher can pound out a beat, with the boys and girls moving according to the rhythm provided. Some variety can be added by the following devices: (1) upon a single loud beat, each student abruptly changes direction, or turns around, or jumps into the air, or leaps into the air; (2) a very quick heavy double

beat is given, signaling the children to stop in place without any movement, or fall to the floor; (3) various changes in beat patterns and accents can be given, with the children following the pattern with movement.

Axial movements are a little more difficult because of the limitation on locomotor movement. The student remains in one place and moves various parts of the body to music. It is suggested that the teacher may wish to use some of the fitness exercises which involve axial movements and base the rhythmic problem on this.

Some teachers have had good success having the children handle chairs to the accompaniment of a swinging type of a waltz music. These are used to provide resistive type of activities for arm and shoulder girdle development by setting up the challenge so that the children use these in much the same manner as weight training apparatus. A swinging type of waltz music or a "dreamy" fox trot makes suitable accompaniment for these activities.

Ball bouncing skills should be continued, particularly dribbling with various challenges set. Rope jumping to music is also very popular and should be developed through regular practice.

Fourth Grade Program

Basic Dance Steps
   Step-hop, two-step.

Suggested Dances
   American Indian Dances
   Glow Worm Mixer
   Grand March
   Tunnel Under
   Shoemaker's Dance - Two-step Version
   Tantoli
   Little Brown Jug
   Norwegian Mountain March
   Oh Susanna
   Pop Goes the Weasel
   Crested Hen
   Virginia Reel
   Green Sleeves

Rope Skipping (see page 202)

Learning the Two-Step. The forward two-step can be taught simply by moving forward on the cue "step, close, step" starting on the left foot and alternating thereafter.

Form couples in a circle formation, all facing counter clockwise with the boys on the inside. Both start with the outside foot. Later, have the partners face to face when the boy is leading with his left foot and back to back when leading with his right foot.

Learning the Step Hop. Place the children in a single circle with all facing counter clockwise. Teach the step hop in this formation beginning slowly with the cue "step hop, step hop, etc." Later increase the tempo to the speed of the music and add the music.

AMERICAN INDIAN DANCES

Most savage tribes included dance as an important part of their living. This is especially true of the American Indian. Dances were done as preparation for war, harvest and other kinds of celebrations, animal pantomimes like the buffalo and eagle dances, and religious ceremonies. In many cases the dance routines were quite precise, while in other cases there was little conformity. There are many different types of steps used in the many American Indian tribal dances. To introduce the dance of the American Indian, only four of these steps are presented. Body positions in the dances should be exaggerated with much bending, twisting, turning, and grotesque movements.

1. The Shuffle. This is a light one-count movement where the pressure is on the balls of the feet with the feet dragging or just barely clearing the floor. The dancers shuffle forward, backward, turn around, move in various directions.
2. The Toe-heel Step. This is a two-count movement which is done from a crouched position at moderate rhythm. On the first part of the step the foot comes down on the toes with the heel kept high in the air. On the second count, the heel is dropped to the ground.
3. The Three-in-one Step. Four counts are needed to complete one step. With the weight completely on the left foot, the right toe is touched to front (count one), to the side (count two), and to the rear (count three). On the fourth count a step to the front is taken with the right foot. The weight is now on the right foot and the step is repeated using the left foot to tap. The cue is, "Tap, tap, tap, step."
4. The War Dance. The War Dance is done to a fast beat and can be either a fast step-hop or a double bounce. The latter is in the nature of two flat footed bounces on each foot alternating. It is fast and vigorous and accompanied with exaggerated body movements. Extreme facial contortions are a part of the war dance.

No attempt is made to put the steps together in a sequence. This could be a movement problem for children, using these steps as well as others. Decide on the type of dance and let the children establish the routines together with the basic beats.

GLOW WORM MIXER

Record: Imperial 1044, MacGregor 310

Formation: Double circle by partners, all facing counter clockwise. Partners have joined inside hands and boys are on the left.

The dance is done in 16 steps and is best described in terms of four patterns of 4 steps each.

Steps: *Action:*

4	1. Four walking steps forward
4	2. Face partner and back away 4 steps. Steps should be short.
4	3. Boys change partners by walking 4 steps to the girl of the couple ahead of him. The girl of that couple moves forward to meet him.
4	4. Join right elbows with the girl and make a four step turn. At the end of the turn, release elbows immediately, join inside hands, and get ready to repeat the dance.

Variation: This can be made a get-acquainted activity. Change #4 of the above to the following:

    4. Meet the girl, stop, shake hands, and say "How do you do."

GRAND MARCH

Record: Any good march or square dance record with about the same tempo.

Formation: Girls on one side of the room, facing the end. Boys on the other side, facing the same direction (end). This is the foot of the hall. The teacher or caller stands at the other end of the room, the head of the hall.

Call:	*Action:*
1. Down the center by two's	1. Lines march forward, turn the corner, meet at the center of the foot of hall, and march in couples toward the caller. The girls' line should be on the proper side so that when the couples come down the center, the boy is on the girl's left. Join hands coming down the center. Odd couples are #1, 3, 5, etc. Even couples are #2, 4, 6, etc.
2. Two's left and right	2. Odd couples go left and even couples right around the room and meet at the foot of the hall.
3. Down the center by four's	3. Couples walk down the center four abreast. When they approach the caller--
4. Separate by two's	4. Odd couples go left, and even couples right. They meet again at the foot.
5. Form arches	5. Instead of coming down the center, the odd couples form arches and the even couples tunnel under. Each continues around the sides of the hall to meet at the head.
6. Other couples arch	6. The even couples arch and the odd couples tunnel under. Each continues around the sides of the room to the foot.
7. Over and under	7. The first odd couple arches over the first even couple and they duck under the second even couple's arch. Each couple goes over the first couple and under the next. Continue around to the head of the hall.
8. Pass right through	8. As the lines come toward each other, they mesh and pass through each other in the following fashion. The girls pass between the opposite couples. Continue to the foot of the hall.
9. Down the center by four's	9. Down the center four abreast.
10. Four's left and right	10. The first four go left around the room and the second four right. Fours meet at the foot.
11. Down the center by eight's	11. Eight abreast down the center
12. Grapevine	12. All persons join hands in each line and keep them joined. The leader takes either end of the first line and starts around the room with the line trailing. The other lines hook on and form one large line.
13. Wind it up	13. The leader winds up the group in a spiral formation like a clock spring. The leader makes the circles smaller and smaller until he is in the center.

14. Reverse (unwind)	14. The leader turns and faces in the opposite direction and walks between the lines of the winding dancers. He unwinds the line and leads it around the room.
15. Everybody swing	15. After the line is unwound, everybody swings.

TUNNEL UNDER

Record: Any good march or square dance record.

This is an informal fun activity which is thoroughly enjoyed by the children. It can be used for entering or leaving the room at the beginning or finish of a rhythmic lesson. The children are in a column of partners with the girl on the right of the boy and inside hands joined. To begin--the boy and girl in the lead couple face each other and form an arch by both hands joined overhead. The next couple goes under the arch and immediately forms a second arch. The remainder of the couples in turn go through the tunnel and form arches. Just as soon as the last couple passes under, the original lead couple follows through the tunnel. The teacher should direct the tunnel so that it forms turns and corners, ending at the selected point. If the children are leaving the room, the tunnel can head eventually in the direction of the door. As the couples reach the door, they pass directly out without forming any more arches.

The tunnel can be unraveled at any time by having the lead couple, after passing under the tunnel, walk into circular formation with the other couples following.

SHOEMAKER'S DANCE (Two-step Version)

Record: Victor 45-6171 or 20450

Formation: Double circle, partners facing, boys on the inside.

Measure: *Action:*

1-2	Arms, shoulder high and with fists clenched, quickly rotate the fists around each other three times and then reverse direction.
3	Cut the thread with scissors. "Snip, snap."
4	With hands in a fist, tap one on top the other 3 times.
5-8	Repeat measures 1-4.
9-16	Partners join inside hands, face counter clockwise, and two-step around the circle, beginning with the outside foot.

TANTOLI

Record: Victor 45-6183

Formation: Double circle, girl on right of partner in open social dance position. Boy puts his right arm around the girl's waist, and the girl's left hand is on the boy's right shoulder. Outside hands are on hips.

Part I:

Measures:	*Directions:*	*Action:*
1-2	Heel and toe. Step, close, step	Tilt body backward and place left heel (right for girls) forward on floor with toe pointing up. Tilt body forward and place the left toe (right for girls) backward on the floor. Do a two-step (step, close, step).

3-4	Heel and toe.	Repeat starting with the other foot.
	Step, close, step	
5-8	Repeat measures 1-4	

Part II:

| 9-12 | Step-hop | With inside hands joined, partners take 8 step-hops forward, swinging arms back and forth. |
| 13-16 | Turn away | The boys turn to the inside making a small circle with 8 step-hops to the girl behind them for a new partner. The girls turn to the outside (right) and step-hop one turn in place, awaiting a new partner. |

Part II can be done with a polka step or two-step.

LITTLE BROWN JUG

Record: Columbia 52007

Formation: Double circle, partners facing with boys on the inside. Partners join hands shoulder high.

Directions are given for the boys; girls use the opposite foot.

Measures: *Actions:*

1-4	Boys touch left toe to the side and then bring the foot back beside the right foot. Repeat. Three slides to the left and close.
5-8	Repeat to the opposite direction leading with the right foot. The three slides bring the dancers back to original position.
9-12	All clap hands to the side three times Clap partner's left hand three times Clap partner's right hand three times Partners clap both hands three times.
13-14	Partners hook right elbows and skip around until the boy faces the next girl, the one who <u>was</u> on his right in the original formation.
15-16	Boy hooks left elbow with this girl who is his new partner. He skips completely around her with a left elbow swing, back to the center of the circle and all get ready to repeat the dance.

Teaching suggestion: When the boy hooks right elbow, he has only to make about a three-quarter turn until he faces the girl who is to be his new partner.

NORWEGIAN MOUNTAIN MARCH

Record: Victor 45-6173

Formation: Sets of threes, one boy and two girls. The boy stands in front and the two girls behind him forming a triangle. The girls join inside hands and the boy reaches back to take the girls' outside hands. The dance portrays a guide leading two climbers up a mountain.

The basic step of the dance is a fast waltz run with the first beat of each measure accented and the bodies of the dancers should sway to the music. Throughout the dance the dancers retain the joined hands.

Measures:	Directions:	Action:
1-8	Waltz run	Run forward 24 steps, bending and accenting the first note of each measure.
9-16	Waltz run	Repeat action of measure 1-8
17-18	Boy under	The boy moves backward under the girls' raised arms for 6 steps.
19-20	Left girl under	The girl on the boy's left takes six steps to cross in front of the boy and go under his raised <u>right</u> arm.
21-22	Right girl turn	The girl on the right with six steps turns under the boy's right arm.
23-24	Boy turn	The boy turns under his own right arm. The dancers should be in the original triangle.
25-32		A repeat of measures 17 to 24 is made except that the right girl goes under the boy's left arm, followed by the left girl turning under the same left arm. The boy turns under this arm to unwind the group.

Teaching suggestion: Time must be taken to practice the turns. It may be a good plan to have a demonstration group.

OH SUSANNA

Record: Victor 45-6180

Formation: Couples in a single circle facing the center with the boy on the left of the girl. All hands are joined.

Measures:	Directions:	Action:
1-4	Slide right	All take 8 slides to the right.
5-8	Slide left	All take 8 slides to the left.
9-12	To the center and back	Four skips to the center and 4 skips back.
13-16	Grand right and left	Partners face, join right hands, walk past each other right shoulder to right shoulder and give a left to the next. Continue grand right and left until the music changes. Pick the next girl for partner.
17-24	Promenade	Promenade or two-step around the circle.

The dancers should promenade until the verse portion of the piece begins again for a repeat of the dance.

During the grand right and left, if a dancer does not secure a partner, he or she should come to the center of the circle. After finding a partner, the couple joins the promenade.

POP GOES THE WEASEL

Record: Victor 45-6180; RCA Victor LPM-1623; Folkraft 1329; Folk Dancer MH 1501

Formation: Double circle, couples facing. In each set of two couples, #1 couple is facing clockwise and #2 counter clockwise.

Measures:	Action:
1-4	Couples walk or skip 4 steps forward and then 4 backwards.
5-6	Each set of two couples joins hands and skips clockwise one full turn, returning to position.
7-8	#1 couple lifts joined hands and #2 couples skips under to move forward (counter clockwise) to meet the next #1 couple.

Repeat as long as desired.

Variation 1

Formation:　Dancers are in sets of threes, all facing counter clockwise. Each set forms a triangle with one child in front and the other two with joined hands forming the base of the triangle. The front dancer reaches back and holds the outside hands of the other two dancers. The groups of three are in a large circle formation.

Measures:	Action:
1-6	Dancers skip around the circle for the first six measures.
7-8	On the "Pop goes the weasel," the two back dancers raise their joined hands and the front dancer backs up underneath to the next set. This set, in the meantime, has "popped" its front dancer back to the set behind it.

CRESTED HEN

Records:　Victor 45-6176; Folkraft 1159

Formation:　Sets of three scattered around the room, composed of one boy and two girls, or one girl and two boys. The odd child (boy or girl) is in the middle.

Measures:	Action:
1-8	Each set forms a small circle. Beginning with the left foot and moving to the left, the dancers start with a stamp and circle using a fast step-hop.
9-16	Dancers jump high in the air, reverse direction, and circle to the right with the same fast step-hop.
17-18	Dancers are now in a line of three, the girls on the outside and joined to the boy in the center. The girl on the right step-hops under the arch formed by the boy and the girl on the left.
19-20	Boy turns under his left arm.
21-24	Repeat actions of measures 17-20 with the left girl leading.

Teaching Suggestions:　During the latter part of the dance all should continue the step-hop pattern.

VIRGINIA REEL

Record:　Any good reel. Methodist M 102 or M 103; Imperial 1092; Folkraft 1141

Formation:　6 to 8 couples in a longways set of two lines, facing each other, boys in one line and girls in the other. The boy on the left of his line and the girl across from him are the head couple.

During the first part of the dance, all perform the same movements.

Measures:	Calls:	Action:
1-4	All go forward and back	Three skips forward, curtsey or bow. Three skips back to place and close.
5-8	Right hands around	Move forward to partner, join right hands, turn once in place, and return to position.
9-12	Left hands around	Repeat the action with the left hands joined.
13-16	Both hands around	Partners join both hands and turn once in clockwise direction and back to place.
17-20	Dos-a-dos your partner	Partners pass each other right shoulder then back to back, and move backwards to place.
21-28	Head couple sashay down, sashay back	Head couple with hands joined slide 8 slides down to the foot of the set and 8 slides back to position.
29-64	Head couple reel	The head couple begins the reel with linked right elbows and turns 1-1/2 times. The boy is now facing the next girl and his partner is facing the next boy. The head couple now each link left elbows with the person facing them and turn once in place. Head couple meets again in the center and turns once with a right elbow swing. The next dancers down the line are turned with a left elbow swing and then back to the center for another right elbow turn. Thus, the head couple progresses down the line, turning each dancer in order. After the head couple has turned the last dancers, they meet with a right elbow swing but turn only half way round and sashay back to the head of the set.
65-96	Everybody march	All couples face toward the head of the set, with the head couple in front. The head girl turns to her right and the head boy to his left, and each goes behind the line of dancers to the foot of the set, each followed by a line of dancers. When the head couple reaches the foot of the set, they join hands and make an arch, under which all other couples pass. The head couple is now at the foot of the set and the dance is repeated with a new head couple.

The dance can be repeated until each couple has had a chance to be the head couple.

CIRCLE VIRGINIA REEL

Variation: A simpler dance using some of the same principles can be done in a circle formation.

Formation: Double circle, boys on the inside with partners facing.

Action: The dancers follow the calls given, and after a series of patterns, change partners by having the boys move to the next girl to his left. The calls can come in any order and the change of partner is made with "On to the next." The following calls work effectively:

Forward and back	Dos-a-dos your partner
Right hand swing	Right elbow swing
Left hand swing	Left elbow swing
Both hands swing	Swing your partner

FIVE-FOOT-TWO MIXER

Record: Ed Durlacher Album, Series III, Record 301, Honor Your Partner Album.

Formation: Couples are in a double circle formation, facing counter clockwise, boys on the inside holding partner in a varsouvienne position.

Measures	*Directions:*	*Action:*
1-2	Two-Steps	Take 2 two-steps in line of direction, beginning on the left foot for both boy and girl.
3-4	Walk	4 walking steps.
5-6	Two-steps	2 two-steps in line of direction.
7-8	Walk and turn	The girl turns out with 4 walking steps, while the boy walks forward 4 steps. The left hand grip is dropped and the right and grip is retained. A single circle is now formed with the men facing out and the girls facing in.
9-10	Balance forward and balance back	Each does a two-step forward and a two-step balance back.
11-12	Walk around your partner	Drop neighbor's left hand, keep, continue with partner's right hand, walk four steps to make a half circle to face the opposite direction. A new single circle is now formed with the boy facing in and the girl facing out. This maneuver amounts simply to the partners exchanging places.
13-14	Balance forward and balance back	All do a two-step forward and a two-step balance back.
15-16	Walk with a new partner	Drop right hand grip (with partner), keep hold of new partner with left hand and use the 4 steps to walk into varsouvienne position with the new partner. Everyone is now in the original formation, but with a new partner.

GREEN SLEEVES

Record: Victor 45-6175

Formation: Couples are in circle formation, all facing counter clockwise. Boys are on the inside and inside hands are joined at shoulder height. Couples are #1 and #2. Two couples form a set.

Measures:	*Directions:*	*Action:*
1-8	Walk	Walk forward for 16 steps
9-12	Right hand star	Couple #1 turns to face the couple behind them. All join right hands and circle clockwise (star) for 8 steps.
13-16	Left hand star	Reverse and form a left hand star. Circle counter clockwise. This should bring couple #1 back to place and they face in original position (counter clockwise).
17-20	Over and under	Couple #2 arches and couple #1 backs under 4 steps while couple #2 moves forward 4 steps. Couple #1 now arches and couple #2 backs under--4 steps for each.
21-24	Over and under	Repeat measures 17-20.

Fifth Grade Program

Basic Dance Steps

Schottische, Step Swing, Polka,
Two-Step Pivot

Suggested Dances

Schottische
Schottische Mixer
Horse and Buggy Schottische
Horse and Buggy Schottische Mixer
Ace of Diamonds
Heel and Toe Polka
Klappdans
Come Let Us Be Joyful
Seven Jumps
Sicilian Circle
La Raspa
Narcissus

Rope Skipping (see page 202)

Learning the Two-step Turn. Begin with the students in a number of lines with enough space between to maneuver. Begin by teaching a quarter turn first. To help the students, have them watch the wall they are facing. They should face in turn the north, east, south, and west walls. The cue is a "left, close, pivot," and a "right, close, pivot." Next, do this with partners, first with both hands joined in front, and later in social dance position.

Another method is to use the slide as the basis of instruction. The following steps comprise this method. Every one is in a single circle, facing the center with hands joined.

1. Moving to the right, take four slides right and then four left. Repeat, emphasizing that the last slide is not a full slide, but getting ready to stop and change direction.
2. Repeat the above, taking only two slides right and two left. Repeat several times.
3. Moving in the line of direction (right), take four slides, pivoting to the right on the last slide to face out. Now, facing out, take four slides with the left foot still moving in the line of direction. Pivot clockwise on the last slide to face the center. Repeat.
4. Moving in the line of direction, take two slides pivoting clockwise to face out, then two more slides in the line of direction, pivoting clockwise to face in. Repeat.
5. Next, boys take a partner in closed dance position forming a circle of couples with the boy's back to the to the center of the circle. Steps 1 through 5 are repeated with a partner.

Learning the Schottische. The schottische can be taught in a single circle, all facing counter clockwise. Later, the step should be practiced by couples in a double circle, all facing counter clockwise. Children can experiment with steps and turning until there is a reasonable mastery of skill. The cue is "step, step, step, hop; step, step, step, hop; step, hop, step, hop, step, hop, step, hop."

Learning the Polka
Several methods can be used to learn the polka.

1. Step by Step Rhythm Approach
   Analyzing the step very slowly, have class walk through the steps together in even rhythm. Cue is "hop, step, close, step." Gradually adapt the rhythm until there is a quick hop and a slower step close step. Accelerate the tempo to normal polka time and add the music.
2. Two-step Approach
   Beginning with the left foot, two-step with the music, moving forward in line of direction in a single circle. Gradually accelerate the tempo to a fast two-step and take smaller steps. Without stopping change to a polka rhythm by preceding each two-step with a hop. Use a polka record for the two-step but slow it down considerably to start.
3. The Gallop Approach
   Form the students in lines of 6 to 8 on one end of the room. Have them cross the floor by taking 8 gallops to the left and then 8 to the right. Repeat several times. Emphasize that in order to change from a left gallop to a right (and vice versa), a hop is needed. Repeat the gallops across the room alternating 4 at a time. Repeat later alternating 2 on each side. This is the polka step.
4. The polka movement can be also taught based on skipping. If children skip twice on the same side and alternate these movements, they are doing the polka.
5. By partners
   After the polka step has been learned by one of the four methods, the step should be practiced by partners in a double circle formation, boys on the inside and all facing counter clockwise with inside hands joined. Practice should also be made with the varsouvienne and the skater's position.

SCHOTTISCHE

Record: Victor 26-0017 or any good schottische

Formation: The dance is done by couples facing line of direction (counterclockwise). The boys are on the girls' left and inside hands are joined.

There are many variations of the schottische based upon the basic pattern of the schottische step. The pattern can be divided into Part I and Part II.

Measures:

Part I

1-2   Partners start with the outside feet and run forward three steps and hop on the outside foot.

3-4   Beginning with the inside foot, run forward three steps and hop with the inside foot.

Part II

5-8   Four step-hops are taken beginning with the outside feet. A number of different movement patterns may be done while the four step-hops are taken.

 1. Drop hands, turn away from each other on the four step-hops to rejoin hands again in original position.
 2. Turn in peasant position, clockwise direction.
 3. Join both hands and "dishrag" (turn under the joined hands).
 4. Boy kneels and girl takes the step-hops around him counter clockwise.

SCHOTTISCHE MIXER

Formation: Double circle by partners, all facing counter clockwise. Boys are on the left of the girls. Inside hands are joined.

Action: Two full patterns of the schottische step are done with each exchange of partners.

Part I - 4 measures
    All run forward 3 steps and hop. Repeat.

Part II - 4 measures
    All do 4 step-hops moving forward.

Part I - 4 measures
    All run forward 3 steps and hop. Repeat.

Part II - 4 measures
    Boys turn in a small circle to the inside on the 4 step-hops to circle to the girl immediately behind him. This is his new partner.

    Girls turn to the outside (right) in a small circle in place on the 4 step-hops and look for the boy circling to them from the couple ahead.

HORSE AND BUGGY SCHOTTISCHE

Record: Any good schottische. MacGregor 400; Imperial 1046

Formation: Couples are in sets of fours in a double circle, all facing counter clockwise. Couples join inside hands and give the outside hands to the other couple.

Action: Part I - All run forward step, step, step, hop; step, step, step, hop.

    Part II - During the four step-hops, one of two movement patterns can be done:

1. The lead couple drops inside hands and step-hops around the outside of the back couple, who moves forward during the step-hops. The lead couple now joins hands behind the other couple and the positions are reversed.
2. The lead couple continues to hold hands and move backward under the upraised hands of the back couple, who untwist by turning away from each other.
3. Alternate 1 and 2.

HORSE AND BUGGY SCHOTTISCHE MIXER

Formation: Same in previous dancè

Action: Two full patterns of the schottische step are needed to make the exchange for the mixer. This means that Part I and Part II will be repeated.

Part I - 4 measures
All run forward 3 steps and hop. Repeat.

Part II - 4 measures
The front couple of each set drops inside hands and step-hops around the other couple to reverse positions in the set.

Part I - 4 measures
All run forward 3 steps and hop. Repeat.

Part II - 4 measures
The front couple in each set, keeping inside hands joined, backs under the upraised hands of the back couple. The couples separate and continue in separate directions. The backing couple now joins hands with the couple from the set behind to form a new set. This means that the couple who had the upraised hands should go forward until they meet another couple (backing) for form a new set.

ACE OF DIAMONDS

Record: Victor 45-6169

Formation: Couples are in a double circle, partners facing with boys on the inside of the circle. Girls, with hands on hips, are facing the center.

Measures:	*Action:*
1-4	Clap hands once, hook right arms with partners, and walk around partner clockwise for 6 steps.
5-8	Clap hands once, hook left elbows, and walk around partner for 6 steps in counter clockwise direction. Partners should now be back to original place.
9-12	With arms folded high, all take 4 slow step-hops toward the center. The boy moves backward and begins with the left foot while the girl moves forward. The step is made on the first beat of the measure and the hop on the second.
13-16	Four step-hops back to place.
17-24	Join inside hands and polka counter clockwise around the circle.
Variation:	For measures 9-16. Bleking type step. Partners should hop on the left foot and thrust the right heel forward. Hop on the right and put the left heel forward. Four more changes are made rapidly. The rhythm is slow, slow, fast, fast, fast, fast. Repeat.

HEEL AND TOE POLKA

Record: Old Timer 8005, MacGregor 400

Formation: Double circle, all facing counter clockwise. Boys are on the inside, and partners have hands joined.

Directions are for the boy. Girl uses opposite foot.

Measures:	Directions:	Action:
1-2	Heel-toe, step-close-step	With weight on the inside foot, extend the outside heel forward on the floor. On "toe", bring the toe alongside the instep. Weight is still on the inside foot. Step left, right, left.
3-4	Heel-toe, step-close-step	With weight on the outside foot, repeat the measures 1-2 beginning with the inside heel and toe. Step right, left, right.
5-6	Heel-toe, step-close-step	Repeat measures 1-2
7-8	Heel-toe, step-close-step	Repeat measures 3-4

9-16   With inside hands joined and partners side by side, do 8 two-steps in line of direction.

Repeat as often as desired.

Variation: 1. The dance can be done as a couple dance in social dance position. During the 8 two-steps, the dancers can do two-step turns.
2. The polka step can be substitued for the two-step.
3. Heel and Toe Polka Mixer. A mixer can be made out of the dance in the following manner. The entire dance is done as illustrated above (Measures 1-16). During the next repetition of the dance, measures 1-8 are not changed. During measures 9-16, the dancers change partners by the boys turning in a small circle to the left to the girl behind them, while the girl turns to her right in a small circle returning to her position. She looks for the boy coming from the couple ahead of her.

KLAPPDANS

Record: Victor 45-6171; Folkraft 1175

Formation: Double circle, all facing counter clockwise. Boys on the inside. Inside hands are joined and the other hand is on the hip.

Measures:	Action:
1-8	Beginning with the outside foot, partners polka around the circle.
9-16	All do a heel and toe polka, leaning back on the "heel" and forward on the "toe."
17-20	Partners face each other and bow. Clap hands 3 times. Repeat.
21-22	Clap partner's right hand, own hands, partner's left hand, and own hands.
23	Each makes a complete turn in place to the left, striking right hand against right hand in turning.
24	Stamp 3 times
25-32	Repeat measures 17-24
Variation:	A mixer can be made out of the dance by having the dancers on measures 23 and 24 progress one partner to the left while whirling. There would be two changes of partners for each complete pattern of the dance.

COME LET US BE JOYFUL

Record: Victor 45-6177

Formation: A set is composed of two lines of three facing each other. Sets are in a circle formation. Each line of three has hands joined.

Measures:	*Action:*
1-2	All walk forward and bow--3 steps and a bow.
3-4	Walk backward 3 steps and close (bring feet together).
5-8	Repeat measures 1-4.
9-10	Center dancer in each set hooks right elbows with partner on the right hand and turns her in place.
11-12	Hooks left elbows with the other partner and turns her in place.
13-16	Repeats measures 9-12.
17-20	Walk forward 3 steps and bow, walk backward 3 steps and close.
21-24	Both lines advance again but instead of bowing and retiring, move through (right shoulders pass each other) to the oncoming group of three to form a new set.

The dance is repeated.

SEVEN JUMPS

Record: Methodist M-108; Victor 45-6172; Victor 21617

Formation: Single circle with hands joined.

There are seven jumps to the dance. Each jump is preceded by the following:

Measures:	*Action:*
1-8	The circle moves to the right with 7 step-hops, one to each measure. On the eighth measure, all jump high in the air and reverse direction.
9-16	Circle to the left with 7 step-hops. Stop on measure 16 and face the center.

First Jump

17	All drop hands, place on hips, and lift the right knee upward.
18	Stamp right foot to the ground on the first note and join hands on the second note.

Second Jump

1-18	Repeat measures 1-18, except do not join hands.
19	Lift left knee, stamp, and join hands.

Third Jump

1-19	Repeat measures 1-19. Do not join hands.
20	Put right toe backward and kneel on right knee. Stand, join hands.

Fourth Jump

1-20	Repeat measures 1-20. Do not join hands.
21	Kneel on left knee. Stand, join hands.

Fifth Jump

1-21	Repeat measures 1-21. Do not join hands.
22	Put right elbow to floor with cheek on fist. Stand, join hands.

Measures:	Action:

Sixth Jump

| 1-22 | Repeat measures 1-22. Do not join hands. |
| 23 | Put left elbow to floor with cheek on fist. Stand, join hands. |

Seventh Jump

| 24 | Repeat measures 1-23. Do not join hands. |
| | Forehead on floor. Stand, join hands. |

Finale

| 1-16 | Repeat measures 1-16. |

SICILIAN CIRCLE

Record: Methodist 104; Columbia 52007 (Little Brown Jug)
Folkraft 1115; Folkraft 1242 (with calls)

Formation: Couples are in sets of two couples, one of which is facing clockwise and the other counter clockwise.

Measures:	Directions:	Action:
1-4	Go forward and back	Couples with inside hands joined move forward (4 steps) toward the opposite couple and return.
5-8	Circle four hands round	Couples circle once around clockwise.
9-12	Right and left through	Couples give right hands to the person opposite and pass the person opposite. Couples join inside hands and turn in place to the left so that they face each other.
13-16	Right and left back	Couples repeat and return to original position.
17-20	Ladies Chain	Girls cross to opposite places by giving each other the right hand as they start and dropping hands as they pass each other. They give left hands to the opposite boy and the boys turn them in place.
21-24	Chain right back	Repeat, chaining back to original partner.
25-28	Go forward and back	Repeat measures 1-4.
29-32	Go forward and pass through	Couples walk forward toward opposite couple, drop hands, and pass through. The girl walks through between the two boys.

Each couple walks forward after passing through to meet an oncoming couple, forming a new set. The dance is repeated.

LA RASPA

Record: Imperial 1084

Formation: A partner dance, with couples scattered around the room.

Measures:	Action:
1-4	Partners face in opposite directions standing left shoulder to left shoulder. Boy clasps his hands behind his back, girl holds skirt. Do one bleking step, beginning with the right.

Measures:	Action:
5-8	Couples now face the other way, with right shoulder to right shoulder. Do one bleking step, beginning with the left.
9-16	Repeat measures 1-8.
17-20	Hook right elbows, turning with 8 running steps. Clap hands on the eighth step.
21-24	Hook left elbows and repeat in the reverse direction.
25-32	Repeat measures 17-24.

NARCISSUS

Record: Windsor 7601

Formation: Couples in a double circle. Boys have their backs to the center of the circle and have both hands joined with the girls, who are facing them.

Directions are for the boys; girls use the opposite foot.

Directions:

1. Step left, close right, step left, close right

   Two draw steps to the boy's left.

2. Slide, slide, slide, dip

   Continue in the same direction with three slides and a dip.

3. Step right, close left, step right, close left

   Repeat #1 beginning to the right.

4. Slide, slide, slide, dip.

   Continue to the right with three slides and a dip.

5. Step left, swing, step right, swing.

   Step left, swing right across, step right, swing left across.

6. Step left, swing, step right, swing

   Repeat #5 and immediately take girl in social dance position.

7. Four two-steps in social dance position turning twice (two full turns) clockwise while keeping relative position in the circle with the couple progressing in a counter clockwise direction.

Variation: For #7, have the dancers retain the two-handed grip and during the four two steps make one complete turn (a quarter turn for each two step).

Variation for Mixer

A change of partners can be made during the four two-steps (#7). The boy hooks right elbow with his partner and takes 2 two-steps around her clockwise. Instead of returning to his own place, he takes the remaining 2 two-steps to move in position in front of the girl who originally was on his right. This is his new partner and the dance is repeated.

Sixth Grade Program

Dance activities for the sixth grade introduce three important new elements. These are the waltz, varsouvienne, and square dancing. This, in turn, means that more emphasis is placed on individual couple dances. The teacher must be more concerned with the change of partners be-cause in some dances, the children are in a scattered formation, and the usual technique of having each partner move forward so many places may need to be modified. One simple solution is to have the nearest couples exchange partners with the stipulation that no one should dance a second time with the same partner.

Introductory material for square dance is found in many of the dances already presented. While not actually having the dancers in a square dance set, many of the basic square dance maneuvers are used in previous dances. In particular, a dance like the Sicilian Circle employs many of the skills needed in square dancing.

Dance Steps

Waltz, Square dancing, Varsouvienne

Suggested Dances

The Waltz
Rye Waltz
Little Man in a Fix
Spanish Circle
Badger Gavotte
Lili Marlene
Brown-Eyed Mary Mixer
Varsouvienne
Varsouvienne Mixer
Teton Mountain Stomp (Mixer)

Square Dances
Oh Johnny, Oh
My Little Girl
Hot Time

Rope Skipping (see page 202)

Learning the Waltz. The waltz consists of three walking steps to a measure, one long (on the first count) and two short. The first count should always be emphasized. This gives the waltz its characteristic "swing." The waltz is generally written with two measures coming together. One measure is heavy and the other light. The boys should start on the heavy beat with his left foot. The progression of teaching the waltz is:

The rhythm
The waltz balance
The waltz box
The waltz turn

1. The rhythm

Have the class clap hands accenting the first beat of each measure. Work out combinations where one-half the class claps the first beat and the other half the second and third beats of each measure. Let them tap with their feet.

Put in the class in circle formation with all facing in and holding hands. Have them step in place with an accent on the first beat of each measure. Start with the left. In the learning stages, both boys and girls follow the same directions. The cue is "Step, step, step; step, step, step."

2. The waltz balance

After the dancers have learned to identify the first beat and have gotten somewhat the feel of waltz music, the waltz balance can be introduced. Retain the circle formation for this instruction. The balance is performed forward and backward first.

Step forward (count 1) with the left foot, close with the right foot along side the left (count 2), and step in place (count 3) with the left foot. Step backward with the right foot (count 1), close with the left foot (count 2), and step in place with the right foot (count 3). Later the students will step very lightly on the third count or simply balance during this count.

The balance should be practiced to the side. The movement is step left (to the side), close right, step left in place. Step right (to the side), close left, and step right in place.

The patterns of the waltz balance should be done with partners. Both hands are joined, partners facing, and boys on the inside. The boy steps forward with his left while the girl steps backward right. The next progression is to perform the balance in social dance position. After some practice in the circle formation, the couples can be on their own around the room for practice.

3. The waltz box

First learn the box pattern individually. The pattern can be practiced in a line formation with a number of lines one behind the other, or a large single circle can be used. The boy steps backward on the left (the girl forward on the right in the normal waltz movement), steps directly to the side with the right, and brings the left foot to the right in a closing movement. To complete the box, the boy steps forward on the right, sideward on the left, and closes with the right. The cue is "step, side, close; step, side, close."

Next the box is practiced with a partner first in the double hand grasp and next in closed (social) dance position. Note that the boy must step forward or backward for the start of the box. At this time only the backward step is taught leading up to the clockwise turn. To turn counter clockwise, the boy would step forward with the left foot to start the sequence.

4. The waltz turn

When teaching the waltz turn, it is a pivot (left), step (right), close (left); pivot (right), step (left), close (right). To pivot the boy turns his leading foot inside if it moves backward, and to the outside, if the step is forward.

At first the children should make quarter turns. They can check this by facing each wall in turn in a clockwise direction. Later, a complete turn is made in six counts (two measures).

The turn should be practiced individually and then with a partner. Turning counter clockwise (to the boy's left) should also be added. This necessitates the boy leading forward with his left. However, it is important to master the clockwise turn since many of the dances call for this turn. The dancers should learn to make progression around the room in line of direction (counter clockwise) while the couples themselves are turning clockwise. This is accomplished more easily if the boy will take the initial backward step in the line of direction.

Square Dancing. Introductory square dancing is fun and a challenge for youngsters because of the adult slant of the activity. In many cases the children have come in contact with the activity because the parents belong to square dance clubs or have been square dancers.

The teacher is sometimes concerned over the prospect of not being able to call square dance figures. The skill of calling does take practice and study, but in some instances, the youngsters can call successfully. However, the fun of square dancing begins in a good, solid caller.

Singing calls, however, present a little different approach. Children can learn the music and the words together with the movements. The entire group could sing while dancing or one or more children could provide the singing call.

Innumerable square dance records with calls are on the market and the teacher should have a variety of simple dances. Some records duplicate the music on sides. One side presents the music with calls, and the other without the calls.

On an adult level, many square dance clubs have failed in their purposes of fun and entertainment because the caller is too ambitious in keeping up with all the latest fads, frills, and dances. The basic skills should be a challenge but not a chore to the children. It needs to be emphasized that square dancing is continued throughout the junior high school program, and that the sixth grade work is only an introduction.

Teaching Suggestions
1. Teach youngsters to listen to the call. It is equally important that they know what the call means. Youngsters are to have fun but must be quiet enough to hear the call.
2. Generally, the caller will explain the figures, have the children walk through the patterns, and then call the figure.
3. It is important to follow the directions of the caller and not to move too soon. Children should be ready for the call and move at the proper time.
4. The teacher should remember that there are many different ways or opinions how different turns, swings, hand positions, etc., should be done. Settle on good principles and stick with them.
5. If a set is confused, they should return to home positions (for each couple) and try to pick up from that point. Otherwise the choice is to wait until the dance is over or a new sequence has started.
6. Change partners at times through the dancing. Have each boy move one place to his right and take a new partner. Another way is to have the girls (or boys) keep positions, and the partners change to another set.
7. The shuffle step should be used rather than a skipping or running step beginners usually tend to use. The shuffle step makes a smoother and more graceful dance, has better carry-over values for dancing, and conserves energy. The shuffle step is a quick walk or about a half slide in time to the music. It is done by reaching out with the toes in a sliding motion. The body should be in good posture and not be bouncing up and down on each step.

The Square Dance Formation. Each couple is numbered around the set in a counter clockwise direction. It is important to have the couples know their positions. The couple with their backs to the music is generally couple #1 or the head couple. The couple to the right is #2, etc. While the head couple is the #1, the term "head couples" includes both #1 and #3. In some dances, couples #2 and #4 are the side couples.

With respect to any one boy (gent), the following terms are used:

Partner - the girl at his side

Corner Lady - the girl on the boy's left

Right Hand Lady - the girl in the couple to the boy's right

Opposite or Opposite Lady - the girl directly across the set

Other terms that are used are:

Home - the original or starting position

Active or leading couple - The couple leading or visiting the other couples for different figures.

Square Dance Figures

Honor your partner - partners bow to each other

Allemande left - face your corner, grasp left hands with your corner, walk around your corner, and return to your partner. Generally, the next figure is a right and left grand

Right and left grand - facing your partner, touch right hands with partner, walk past your partner, and touch left hands with the next person in the ring and so on down the line. This causes the boys to go in one direction around the circle and the girls in the other, alternately touching right and left hands until partners meet. The girl reverses direction by turning under uplifted joined right hands and the couple promenades home.

Promenade - walk side by side with your partner with the right hand joined to the right hand and left to left in a crossed hand (skaters') position. Walk around once to home position.

Swing your partner (or corner) - the boy and girl stand side by side with right hip against right hip. The dancers are in social dance position except that the boy's right arm is more around to the side than in back at the shoulder blade. The dancers walk around each other until they reach starting position.

Right and left through (and back) - two couples pass through each other, girls to the inside, touching right hands passing through. After passing through, the boy takes the girl's left hand in his left, puts his right hand around her waist, and turns

her in place so that the couples are again facing each other. On "right and left back" the figure is repeated, and the couples return back to place. Note that the term "pass right through" used in some of the previous dances is similar only that the couple does not turn around but continues on to the next couple.

Dos-a-dos your partner (or corner) - walk around your partner passing right shoulder to right shoulder. Return to place by partner.

Ladies Chain - from a position with two couples facing each other, the ladies cross over to the opposite gent, touching right hands as they pass each other. When they reach the opposite gent they join left hands with him, at the same time the gent places his right arm around the lady's waist, and turns her once around to face the other couple. On "chain right back" the ladies cross back to partners in a similar figure.

All around your left hand lady, seesaw your pretty little taw - boy does a dos-a-dos with his corner girl, and then meet partner, passing around left shoulder to left shoulder.

Do-pass-so - give left hand to your partner and walk around your partner. Release your partner and, with right hands joined, walk around your corner. Return to partner, take left hand in left hand, and turn her in place with the arm around the waist. The turning movement is similar to the figure used in "Right and left through," and "Ladies chain."

Circle right (or left) - all eight join hands and circle. You can add "Into the center with a great big yell." The circle generally broken with a swing at home base.

Other calls - there are many other calls which can be used. The figures presented are basic and provide enough material for sixth grade square dancing. However, there will be other sequences which are needed for special dances. These can be learned along with the dance.

RYE WALTZ

Record: MacGregor 298, Old Timer 8009

Formation: Couples in closed position forming a circle with the boys' backs to the center of the circle.

Directions are for the boys; girls use opposite foot.

Part I. The Slide

1. Point left toe to side (count 1) and return to the instep of the other foot (count 2). Repeat (counts 3 and 4).
2. Take three slides to the boy's left and dip (counts 5, 6, 7, and 8). The dip is made by placing the right toe behind the left foot.
3. Repeat #1 using the right foot for pointing.
4. Repeat #2 but sliding to the right.
    (some records repeat 1-4)

Part II. The Waltz

5. Starting with the boy stepping back on the left foot, waltz for 16 measures, turning clockwise.
6. At the end of the waltz, some records repeat II. This means that the couple waltzes until the music changes doing then three slides to the left and a dip (or lift the girl into the air with both hands).

LITTLE MAN IN A FIX

Record: Michael Herman 1053

Formation: Two couples form a set, scattered out on the floor. The two boys lock or hook left elbows, having right arms around the girl's waist. The girl places left hand on the boy's shoulder and the free hand is on the hip.

Measures:	*Action:*
1-8	Turn in place counter clockwise using 24 little running steps.
9-16	Without stopping, men grasp left hands, and take the left hands of the partners in their right hands. The object now is to form a "wheel." The boys raise joined hands, forming an arch under which the girls pass right shoulder to right shoulder. After they pass under, the girls turn left, face each other and join hands over the boys' joined left hands. The wheel continues to turn left to complete a total of 24 running steps.
17-20	Boys release joined left hands, girls release joined right hands, leaving partners holding own hands. Couples have backs to each other. Couples now do four Tyrolean Waltz steps, stepping on the outside foot while swinging the inside foot and joined hand forward. Then, step on the inside foot while swinging joined hands backward. On the third count of the measure, the outside foot is swung across.
21-24	In regular dance position, waltz 4 measures with partner.
25-32	Repeat Tyrolean Waltz and closed position waltz.

The music now begins over again and couples try to find other couples to form a set. There should be one extra couple whose boy is the "Little Man in a Fix." When the couples pair off to form a set, one couple will be left over and goes to the center of the room.

SPANISH CIRCLE (Waltz Mixer)

Record: MacGregor 633

Formation: Double circle, couples facing. A set is formed by two couples, one of which is facing counter clockwise, and the other clockwise.

The dance involves a new figure in the waltz. The girls turn under the lifted arms. Practice can be done in the regular formation.

Measures:	*Action:*
1-2	Couples are side by side with inside hands joined. Couples balance forward and back, swinging arms forward and back. Start with outside foot.
3-4	With two waltz steps, exchange partners. On the first waltz, which is forward, the inside hands are swung forward. Hands are released immediately, and the boy takes the opposite girl's left hand in his right, and she turns under the upraised arms to a new position alongside him. Couples are now facing inside and outside of the circle.
5-8	Repeat action of measures 1-4. Couples have now progressed one-half around the circle. Note that the boy progresses clockwise and the girl counter clockwise.
9-16	Repeat measures 1-8. Couples are back in home position.
17-24	All join right hands and do four waltz steps turning clockwise. Drop hands, form with the left hand, and turn back to place with four waltz steps back to position.
25-28	The boys do a side balance and back to place. Repeat. The girls join right hands and balance forward and back. They waltz past each other (right shoulder to right shoulder) to exchange places. This is done by dropping hands and turning around to the _left_ and backing into place. Each boy has a new partner.
29-32	Boys join inside hands with a new partner and balance forward and back. During the new two waltzes, couples pass through each other to form a set with the oncoming couple.
Variation:	
25-32	In closed dance position, with the boy taking his lead step in the direction he is originally, the two couples waltz around each and back to place, moving around to the right. Continue around the right and forward to meet the oncoming couple, forming a new set.

BADGER GAVOTTE

Record: MacGregor 610

Formation: The dance is by couples. Couples are arranged in a circle formation in open position, each with inside hands joined and facing counter clockwise.

Directions are for the boys. Girls use opposite foot.

Measures:	*Directions:*	*Action:*
1-4	Walk-2-3-4, slide, slide slide, dip	Beginning with the left foot, walk forward four steps, face and join hands, and take three slides and dip. Touch the right toe behind the left foot for the dip.
5-8	Walk-2-3-4, slide, slide, slide, dip	Change hands, walk in the reverse direction starting with the right foot. Repeat the four steps, the three slides, and dip to the clockwise direction.
9-12	Two-step	In closed dance position, do four two-steps, moving in line of direction but circling clockwise.

Measures:	Directions:	Action:
13-14	Pivot, pivot, pivot, pivot	Boy turns girl clockwise using four pivots, beginning with the left foot.
15-16	Turn your girl and bow	Boy stands in place for two counts and then steps back on his left and bows. In the meantime, he turns the girl under his right hand arched with the girl's left. She turns with right and left steps in place and then steps back with the right and curtseys.

Dance is repeated.

LILI MARLENE

Record: Western Jubilee 725, MacGregor 310

Formation: Couples in circle formation, facing counter clockwise. Inside hands are joined.

Directions are for the boys. Girls use opposite foot.

Measures:	Directions:	Action:
1-4	Walk-2-3-4, slide, slide, slide, close	Starting with the left foot, walk forward four steps, turn and face partner, join both hands, take three slides in line of direction and close.
5-8	Walk-2-3-4, slide, slide, slide, close	Repeat measures 1-4 but start with the right foot and travel in the opposite direction.
9-12	Step swing, step swing	Still with joined hands, step to the left and swing the right foot across the left. Step to the right and swing the left across. Repeat right and left.
13-16	1-2-3-turn, 1-2-3-turn	Facing counter clockwise with inside hands joined, take three steps in line of direction beginning with the left foot and pivot on the fourth count with the right foot pointed clockwise. Dancers change hands and are faced clockwise. Repeat beginning with the right foot and turning (pivot) on the right foot. Couples should now be facing line of direction with inside hands joined.
17-20	Two-step	With inside hands joined, take four two-steps forward.
21-24	Two-step away	Drop inside hands, and on four two-steps, circle away from partner. Boy makes a larger circle to the girl behind him. Girl circles back to place.

BROWN-EYED MARY MIXER

Record: Little Brown Jug. Columbia 52007; Old Timer 8051

Formation: Couples facing counter clockwise, boys on the inside. Right hands and left hands are joined in crossed hands position (promenade).

Measures:	Directions:	Action:
1-4	Two-step left and two-step right, walk-2-3-4	Do a two-step left and a two-step right and take four walking steps forward.
5-8	Repeat measures 1-4	

Measures:	Directions:	Action:
9-10	Turn your partner with the right	Boy takes girl's right hand with his right and walks around this girl to face the girl behind him.
11-12	Now your corner with your left	Turns girl behind him with the left.
13-14	Turn your partner all the way around	Turns own partner with the right going all the way around
15-16	And pick up the forward lady	Boy steps up one place to the girl ahead of him who is his new partner.

VARSOUVIENNE

Record: MacGregor 398; Old Timer 8077; Folkraft 1034

Formation: Couples in varsouvienne position.

Measures: *Action:*

1   Bend left knee and bring left foot in front of right leg on the up-beat. Step forward with the left and close with the right, taking the weight on the right foot.

2   Repeat measure 1.

3-4   Cross left foot over right instep, then swing the left foot behind the right foot taking a step. Step with the right foot to the right (behind partner), step forward with the left (alongside partner), and point right toe forward. The girl in the meantime does the same steps but almost in place moving slightly to her left. The girl is now on the left side of the boy still in varsouvienne position.

5-8   Repeat measures 1-4 beginning with the crossing of the right foot.

9-10   Cross left, step left, step right, step left, point right. Retaining only the left hand grip, the boy does the stepping in place while the girl rolls out to the left away from the boy.

11-12   Cross right, step right, step left, step right, point left. Still retaining the left hands, the girl turns under the boy's lifted left hand and walks back to the varsouvienne position.

13-16   Repeat measures 9-12.

VARSOUVIENNE MIXER

Record: Same as previous dance.

Formation: Couples are in circle formation all facing counter clockwise in varsouvienne position.

Measures: *Action:*

1-12   The first 12 measures are the same as the previous dance.

13-14   The girl rolls to the center with the cross, step, step, step, point. Left hands are still held.

15-16   The girl walks to the boy of the couple behind her, crossing in front of him to varsouvienne position. They both finish with the left foot pointed.

Teaching Suggestion: The girl should look behind her to see who her next partner will be.

TETON MOUNTAIN STOMP (Mixer)

Record: Windsor 7615; Western Jubilee 725

Formation: Double circle, partners facing with both hands joined. Boys are on the inside.
Directions are described for the boys. The girls use the opposite feet.

Measures:	Directions:	Action:
1-4	Left, right, left, stamp	Step left, close right, step left, stamp right.
	Right, left, right, stamp	Repeat the other way with the right.
5-6	Left, stamp, right, stamp	Step left, stamp right, step right, stamp left.
7-8	Walk - turn	Both face line of direction, join inside hands and walk 4 steps. On the last step, the boy turns around.
9-10	Walk - turn	The boy backs four steps while the girl moves forward four steps. Both are moving counter clockwise, the girl facing and the boy with his back to line of direction. Both turn around on the last step. The girl now has her back to line of direction.
11-12	Walk	Each takes 4 steps <u>forward</u>. The boy walks in line of direction but the girl is now walking clockwise. They each skip one person and meet the next for a new partner.
13-16	Two-step, two-step, walk	Both face counter clockwise with inside hands joined. They take 2 two-steps, beginning on the outside foot and then 4 steps in line of direction.

Variation: For measures 13-16.

When the boy meets his new partner, he swings her for 8 counts (twice around).

OH JOHNNY, OH

Record: Folkraft 1037

Formation: Square set of four couples

Call (All sing):

1. All join hands and you circle the ring
2. Stop where you are and you give her a swing
3. Now you swing that girl behind you
4. Now swing your own if you have time then you
5. Allemande left on your corners all
6. And dos-a-dos your own
7. And all promenade with the sweet corner maid, singing, "Oh Johnny, Oh Johnny, Oh!"

Action:

1. Circle of eight moving left
2. Swing your partner
3. Swing the corner lady (on man's left)
4. Swing your partner
5. Turn the corner lady with the left hand
6. Pass right shoulders and back to back with partner
7. Promenade with new (corner) lady

The dance is repeated three more times until original partners are together again.

Variation: The dance can be done in a circle formation with partners facing counter clockwise and girls on the right. The corner girl is the one from the couple immediately in back.

Teaching Suggestion: In the circle formation, couples should swing around only once.

MY LITTLE GIRL

Record: Folkraft 1036

Formation: Square set of four couples

Call (singing):

1. First couple promenade the outside
   around the outside of the ring

2. Head ladies chain right down the center
   and they chain right back again

3. The ladies chain the right hand couple
   and they chain right back again

4. The ladies chain the left hand couple
   and they chain right back again

5. Now it's all the way around your left hand
   lady - Oh Boy! What a baby

6. See saw your pretty little taw
   Prettiest girl I ever saw

7. Allemande with your left hand
   A right to your honey and a right and
   left grand

8. Deedle--l, Deedle--l, Deedle--l, Do
   You meet your gal and promenade

9. And listen while I roar
   You swing your honey till she feels funny
   She's the gal that you adore

Action:

1. The first couple promenades around the outside of the set while the other couples move into the center.

2. Ladies #1 and #3 chain and chain right back.

3. Ladies #1 and #3 chain and chain back with the right hand ladies.

4. Chain with the left hand ladies.

5. The four boys move around their corner girls returning to position.

6. Move around behind partners and return to position.

7. Self explanatory

8. Self explanatory

9. Promenade back to position and all swing.

        The dance is repeated three times with the 2nd, 3rd, and 4th couples promenading.
        For couples #2 and #4, the word "side" for "head" under line 2.

HOT TIME

Record: Folkraft 1037; Windsor 7115

Formation: Square set of four couples

        This is a singing call and everyone should sing. Much of the action is self explanatory.

Call:

Introduction

All join hands and circle left the ring
Stop where you are and everybody swing
Promenade that girl all around the ring
There'll be a hot time in the old town tonight.

Action:

Circle left
All swing
All promenade

The Figure

First couple out and circle four hands 'round
Pick up two and circle six hands 'round
Pick two more and circle eight hands 'round
There'll be a hot time in the old town tonight,
    my baby

First couple to the couple on the right and
    circle four
Pick up the third couple
Pick up the fourth couple and all circle.

Allemande left with the lady on the left
Allemande right with the lady on the right

Do a left allemande
After allemande left, pass partner by (right shoulders) without touching and go on to the next lady.
Allemande right is the opposite of the allemande left and is done with the right hand.
Again pass partner by without touching, to corner lady. Self explanatory.

Allemande left with the lady on the left
And a grand old right and left around the town.

When you meet your honey, it's dos-a-dos
around

At the end of the grand right and left, partners
go back to back.

Take her in your arms and swing her round and
    round

All swing

Promenade home, you promenade the town
There'll be a hot time in the old town tonight,
    my baby

All promenade

Repeat three more times with the 2nd, 3rd, and 4th couples leading out. Do not repeat the introduction.

Finale

All join hands and circle left the floor
Swing her 'round and 'round, just like you
    did before.

Circle left
All swing

Because that's all, there isn't any more
There'll be a hot time in the old town tonight

Continue swinging

Additional Square Dances

For additional dances to round out the program, the following are suggested:

Take a Little Peek
Birdie in the Cage - 7 Hands Round
Forward Six and Back
Duck for the Oyster
Red River Valley
Star by the Right
Divide that Ring

These and others are available from a number of sources in the form of single records or in albums. In addition, the square dance patterns and steps, previously described in this chapter, are on records in simple, "walk-through" instructions. Square dance records may be secured with or without calls.

The following sources, among others have excellent material in square dance records and albums suitable for the elementary school program:

Educational Record   David McKay Co.
   Albums   119 West 40th Street
                         New York 18, N. Y.

Honor Your Partner   Square Dance Asso-
   Records   ciates
                        Freeport, N. Y.

Square Dance   Teaching Aids
   Records   Service
                        31 Union Square W.
                        New York 3, N. Y.

Rope Jumping to Music*

Rope jumping is an excellent complete body activity. It increases coordination, rhythm, and timing. It tones up the circulo-respiratory system and increases both speed and endurance. It makes a contribution to weight control and total physical condition. It can contribute to good posture habits. It has good carry-over values.

* The material on rope skipping is used by permission of the
    Seattle Public Schools, William Haroldson, Director of
    Physical Education. The Seattle Public School Bulletin
    on Rope Skipping was based originally on terminology and
    steps excerpted in part from the pamphlet, Rope Skipping
    Fundamentals by Paul Smith, Physical Education Super-
    visor, Shoreline Public Schools, Seattle, Washington.

From an educational standpoint, it has value in the school program. It allows for a maximum amount of student activity within a minimum amount of time and space. The activities are in good progression. The teacher can begin at the level of the student and develop from that point. It is inexpensive and easily taught.

For the children it provides a creative activity that has unlimited possibilities for new material. The further the youngsters progress the more they tend to invent steps and routines of their own. It is not seasonal in character.

For the teacher and administrator, it provides excellent program material for P. T. A. meetings and other demonstrations.

Because it is a learned activity, the material is not allocated to grades. Teachers should begin the year with a complete review of all fundamentals and such other material that the children have mastered.

Some people prefer to refer to the activity as rope skipping. In the material which follows, the terms are used interchangeably.

Records for Rope Jumping

Any record with a steady tempo of 120 to 150 beats per minute will suffice to begin. Some records that have been found to work well are:

1. PR 980 Ball Bouncing and Rope Skipping, Album #12--Durlacher
2. Marches, Album #1--Durlacher
3. Waiting for the Robert E. Lee-- 45 RPM, Jack Barbour--Accent Sunny Hills AC 102-S.
4. Wheels and Orange Blossom Special --45 RPM, Billy Vaughn, Dot, 45-161774.
5. Yankee Doodle--El Molino--Shoo Fly, all on Windsor School Series Record-- Happy Hour Records--A-7S1, Windsor.
6. Pop Goes the Weasel is another record which is good for rope jumping. The fact that there is a verse and a chorus arrangement means that one type of jumping (half-time) could be done to the verse and another (single-time) could be done to the chorus. Folk Dancer MH 1501 and Victor 45-6180) are good records.

The teacher will discover countless other records and albums that will work well as you progress and become more familiar with the various rope skipping activities.

The Rope

To determine the proper length of rope for a particular individual, stand on the center of the rope. The ends, when drawn up each side of the body, should terminate at approximately armpit height. For elementary schools all ropes may be cut in 9 foot lengths. Any adjusting for smaller children may be done by wrapping the rope around the hands.

The best rope available is a yellow plastic (not nylon) tight weave (not loose weave) 3/8 inch diameter rope. It wears extremely well and the ends can be melted permanently with an alcohol burner (or match) in seconds. (This type of rope can be purchased at sporting goods or hardware stores.)

These ropes work well without handles, but excellent handles can be made if a drill press is available in the following manner. Obtain wooden dowels 1 to $1\frac{1}{4}$ in. in diameter. Cut in lengths of 4 inches. Drill out a 3/8 inch center. Ream out one end slightly so that the larger melted "blob" at the rope's end will fit down into the dowel.

Explanation of Terminology
1. Rebound

This is simply a hop in place as the rope passes over the head. Better jumpers will only bend the knees slightly without actually leaving the floor. It is used only in half time jumping (explained below) and its object is to carry the rhythm between steps.

All steps can be done in three different rhythms--half time, single time and double time.

2. Half time

In half time rhythm the performer jumps over the rope, rebounds (hop in place) as the rope passes over the head, then executes the second step, or repeats the original step a second time, on the second jump.

The performer actually jumps over the rope to every other beat of the music in half time rhythm. The odd beat occurs as the rope passes over the head. The rhythm is carried by the rebound.

The rope is rotating slowly (passes under the feet on every other beat) and the feet also move slowly since there is a rebound between each jump.

Half time rhythm--slow rope, slow feet.

3. **Single time**
In single time rhythm we have the opposite of half time. The rope rotates
in time with the music which means
twice the number of rope turns for the
same tune as in half time. The rope
will be turning fast (120 to 180 turns
per minute depending upon the tune's
tempo) and the performer executes a
step only when the rope is passing
under the feet.
  Single time rhythm--fast rope,
fast feet.

4. **Double time**
In double time rhythm the rope is
turned at the same speed as half time
(slow) but rather than taking the rebound the performer actually executes
another step while the rope is passing
over the head, as in single time. A
slow rope with fast feet.
  Double time is the most difficult
to master. When the feet are speeded
up there is a tendency to speed the
rope up also (which is wrong).
  Double time rhythm--slow rope,
fast feet.

Progression of rope-jumping
  All explanations are given and should
usually be learned first in half-time
rhythm. After the students master all
the steps in the different rhythms, routines may be devised combining the different steps and rhythms.
  If a student has difficulty with a step,
have him go through the foot motions without the rope first.
  Placing offset marks on the gym
floor with a marking pen helps students
keep their stations.
  Begin using music almost immediately. The music tells the performer
when to do the step and also helps him
to keep a steady rhythm.
  Place your best jumpers together
in one line. They tend to help one another
keep the proper rhythm.
  To use rope skipping as a conditioner for other sports, use the single time
rhythm and turn the rope at high speed
for designated periods of time. 180 turns
of the rope per minute (try the Can-Can)
is a very fast time and excellent for varsity sports type of conditioning.
  Continually watch for different steps
and tunes that will lend themselves to new
routines.

1. **2 foot basic step**
With feet together, jump over the rope
as it passes under the feet and take a
preparatory rebound while the rope is
over the head.

2. **Alternate foot basic step**
As the rope passes under the feet,
the weight is shifted alternately from
one foot to the other, raising the un-
weighted foot in a running position.

3. **Swing step forward**
Same as alternate foot basic step except that the free leg swings forward.
Keep knee loose and let foot swing
naturally.

4. **Swing step sideward**
Same as swing step forward except
free leg is swung to the side. Knee
should be kept stiff.

5. **Rocker step**
One leg is always forward in a walking stride position in executing the
rocker step. As the rope passes under the feet the weight is shifted from
the back foot to the forward foot. The
rebound is taken on the forward foot
while the rope is above the head. On
the next turn of the rope the weight is
shifted from the forward foot to the
back foot repeating the rebound on
the back foot.

6. **Spread legs, forward and backward**
Start in a stride position as in the
rocker, with weight equally distributed
on both feet. As rope passes under
feet, jump into the air and reverse
feet position.

Remember, all steps can be done in three
different rhythms--half time, single time
and double time. After the youngsters
have mastered these first six steps in
half time you may wish to introduce single and double time. The alternate foot
basic step and spread legs, forward and
backward are two steps that seem to
work well in introducing double time
jumping.

7. **Cross legs sideward**
As the rope passes under the feet,
spread legs in a straddle position
sideward. Take rebound in this position. As the rope passes under the
feet on the next turn, jump into the
air and cross feet with right foot forward. Repeat with left foot forward.
Continue to alternate forward foot.

8. **Toe touch forward**
As rope passes under feet, swing
right foot forward. Land with weight
on left foot touching right toe forward.
Alternate, landing on right foot and
touching left toe forward.

9. **Toe touch backward**
Same as swing step sideward (4) except toe of free foot touches to the
side at the end of the swing.

10. **Shuffle step**
As rope passes under feet, push off

with right foot, side stepping to the left, Land with weight on left foot and touch right toe beside left heel. Repeat in opposite direction.

11. Heel toe

As rope passes under feet, jump with weight landing on right foot touching left heel forward. On next turn of the rope, jump, landing on the same foot and touch left toe beside right heel. Repeat, using opposite foot.

12. Heel click

Do two or three swing steps sideward in preparation for the heel click. When the right foot swings sideward instead of a hop or rebound when the rope is above the head, raise the left foot to click the heal of the right foot. Repeat on the left side.

13. 3 step tap

As rope passes under feet, push off with right foot and land on left. While the rope is turning above the head, brush the sole of the right foot forward, then backward. As the rope passes under the feet for the second turn, push off with the left foot, landing on the right and repeat.

14. Crossing arms forward

When the rope is above the head starting the downward swing, bring the right arm over the left and the left arm under the right until the left hand is under the right arm pit and the right hand is against the upper left arm. Jumping can be continued in this condition or the arms can be crossed and uncrossed on alternate turns of the rope.

15. Double turn of the rope

Do a few basic steps in preparation for the double turn. As the rope approaches the feet, give an extremely hard flip of the rope from the wrists. Jump from 6-8 inches into the air and continue practicing until the rope passes under the feet twice before landing.

Everything explained above can be done to single and double time rhythms as explained earlier. The steps explained can also be done to the three rhythms while turning the rope backwards.

Going from forward to backward skipping without stopping the rope

1. As the rope starts downward in forward skipping, rather than allowing it to pass under the feet, the performer swings both arms to the left or the right and makes 1/2 turn of his body in that direction (turn facing the rope.) On the next turn spread the arms and start skipping in the opposite direction. This method can be used from forward to backward skipping or vice versa.

2. When the rope is directly above the head, the performer may extend both arms, causing the rope to hesitate momentarily. At the same time as he extends both arms, the performer makes a 1/2 turn in either direction and continues skipping with the rope turning in an opposite direction from the start.

3. From a cross arm position as the rope is going above the performer's head, he may uncross the arms and turn simultaneously. This will start the rope turning and the performer skipping in the opposite direction.

ROPE JUMPING ROUTINES

It is in this area where the opportunities for creative activity are endless. The teacher can select a basic piece with suitable rope jumping rhythm, and the children can devise routines. An example is given for the piece Pop Goes the Weasel. The music is in two parts, a verse part and the chorus. In this, the first four basic steps of the teaching routine are combined with half time and single time. Here is one way a routine can be organized to this music.

1st verse part	2 foot basic step	half time
Chorus	2 foot basic step	single time
2nd verse part	Alternate basic foot step	half time
Chorus	Alternate basic foot step	single time
3rd verse part	Swing step forward	half time
Chorus	Swing step forward	single time
4th verse part	Swing step sideward	half time
Chorus	Swing step sideward	single time.

This is a simple basic routine plan for a piece of music. There are many other possibilities for this one piece. Many other records lend themselves well to this activity.

Chapter 19
The Games Program for the Intermediate Grades

Games are important in the development of a good physical education program. Games represent the traditions of many children and many countries. Intermediate level games emphasize running, tagging, dodging, throwing, and catching skills. Games for the intermediate grades are included in two sections in this book. In this chapter are found those games of a tag and general nature which do not merit their inclusion under any of the sports type activities. The lead-up activities to basketball, football, volleyball, soccer, softball, and track are found with the discussions of the particular sport.

In planning, the intermediate grades should make good use of any and all of the primary games which are suitable or can be adapted to the intermediate program. Children in the intermediate grades enjoy and play many of the games which are introduced earlier, particularly in the third grade.

Practical Suggestions for Intermediate Games

1. Know the game well before attempting to teach it. This means identifying the safety hazards, anticipating the difficulties, and being able to adapt the game to the group and facilities.
2. Enforce the rule once they are established. Discuss with the children the reason for the rules.
3. For maximum participation, divide the class into a number of groups determined by the selection of the activity. Many games play best with 10 to 15 players.
4. Play occasionally with the class. They like to see you in action.
5. The principal ingredient of successful game leadership is a vigorous, snappy approach. A hustling attitude combined with the spirit of enthusiasm will do much toward producing the desired results.
6. Watch the game carefully for a decrease of interest. Bring in variations or changes which could serve to stimulate interest. Otherwise, change to another activity.
7. Minor faults can be corrected during the course of the game. Do not attempt to cover all rule infractions previous to any participation. Cover enough to get the game underway and fill in with additional rules as needed.
8. Complete all preparations before starting to introduce the game. Draw boundaries, starting and finishing lines, and have supplies handy and ready for distribution.
9. Most games can be modified to meet the equipment and supplies available. Some games are best played with the equipment and supplies designated for them. Boundaries can be widened, lengthened, or shortened as needed.
10. In team games where it is a factor, be sure the teams are balanced in both numbers and capacity. Nothing destroys a game more than to have one team annihilate the other.
11. Help and encourage the losing side. We want our children to be good losers but not "easy" losers.
12. Watch for fatigue, particularly by a chaser who is unable to catch a runner. The teacher may call "Reverse," which makes the runner the chaser, or stop the game and have another child take the part of the chaser.
13. Suggestions and coaching hints should be a part of the conduct of games. "Lean forward a little for a faster

start," or "Handle the ball with the pads of the fingers" are examples of the application of good principles in executing skills.

14. For demonstrations and explanation, be sure the children are reasonably comfortable. During an explanation which interrupts a game, seat the children if the explanation is long enough. The children can sit down on the floor or field right where they are.

15. Be careful of the poor citizenship situation where some child is made the "goat" or butt of jokes. Psychological hurt or trauma may be deep and permanent. The possibility of physical hurt or punishment must not be ruled out. The slow, heavy child, who cannot move readily, is at a disadvantage in dodgeball games and other activities demanding mobility.

16. While games which eliminate children in the course of the play have a place in the program, these should be used with caution. Elimination should not be carried down to the "bitter end." It is better to play the game so a portion of the children are eliminated and then declare the remainder the winners.

17. In number calling type games, where children compete against each other in some specified task, if possible, all teams should be given points for performance so that any disqualification results in loss of the possible place points, even for last place.

Safety Considerations

The intermediate games offer more movement, more maneuvering, and more strategy than the primary games. In addition, the dodgeball games need some special safety considerations.

1. The participants should be coached to stop immediately when the whistle blows. A child may be down, or some other safety hazard needs attention.

2. Unnecessary roughness must be controlled. Pushing, tripping, and similar unsportsmanlike acts have little place in a games program.

3. In dodgeball type games the following should be observed:
   a. Children should remove glasses.
   b. Throwing should be below the shoulders or waist.
   c. A soft missile should be used.
   d. Restraining lines for the thrower should be observed. Line restric-

tions are there for a purpose.
   e. Vicious and punishing throwing must be controlled.

4. Sufficient room for the games should be maintained. Colliding with fences and walls during running and chase games is an ever present danger. Lines should be drawn far enough from these and other obstacles to preserve safety.

5. Fingernails should be kept trimmed or filed.

6. All injuries, abrasions, cuts, or bruises should be reported.

Selected Games for Intermediate Children

It should be recognized that the allocation of games to any grade level is dependent upon a number of factors. These include the capacity of the children with respect to fitness qualities and skills. Modifications of the game with respect to boundaries and rules allow games to be used on many levels. Then, there are the games which children can play on many age levels with little change. An example of a popular game which can be played throughout the elementary, junior high, and senior high school physical education classes is team dodgeball. In the progression of activities proposed by the author, team dodgeball is introduced in the third grade. The game should be used throughout all grade levels. The point to be stressed is that the teacher, in planning, should examine the games listed under previous grades for any and all that can be used. However, the teacher should avoid the inclusion of games which are to be introduced in future grades. The allocation of games to grade levels assures the children of new experiences for each grade level. It is vitally important that a school or school system make some decisions with regard to this allocation. The proposed list which follows offers a good starting point.

The games presented in this chapter are only a portion of the games program. The lead-up games are found in the following sections:

Basketball, pages 266 to 271
Flag Football, pages 277 to 281
Soccer, pages 287 to 292
Softball, pages 302 to 308
Volleyball, pages 313 to 315

Other activities are found in the section on individual and dual activities, pages 320 to 324.

Fourth Grade Games

ALASKA BASEBALL

Playing Area: Playground

Players: Entire class

Supplies: Volleyball or soccer

The players are organized into two teams, one of which is at bat and the other in the field. A straight line provides the only out-of-bounds, and the team at bat is behind this line at about the middle. The other team is scattered in the fair territory.

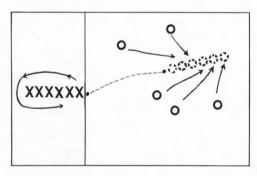

One player propels the ball by either batting (as in volleyball) or kicking a stationary soccer ball. His teammates are in a close file just behind him. As soon as he sends the ball into the playing area, he starts to run around his own team. Each time the runner passes the head of the file, the team gives a loud count.

There are no outs. The first fielder to get to the ball stands still and starts to pass the ball back over his head to the nearest teammate who moves directly behind him to recieve the ball. The remainder of the team in the field

must run to the ball and form a file behind the ball. The ball is passed back overhead with each player handling the ball until the last player in line has a firm grip on it. He shouts "Stop." At this signal, a count is made of the number of times the batter ran around his own team. In order to score a little more sharply, a half count should be made. Allow 5 batters to bat and then change the teams. This is better than allowing one entire team to bat before changing to the field as the players in the field get quite tired from too many consecutive runs.

BOX BALL

Playing Area: Playground, gymnasium

Players: Four teams, 6 to 10 on each team.

Supplies: A sturdy box, 2 by 2 feet and about 12 inches in depth. One volleyball or similar type for each team.

Any number of teams can play the game, but four makes a convenient number. Each team occupies one side of a hollow square at an equal distance from the center. Each team is facing inward and numbers off consecutively from right to left. The teams should be of even numbers.

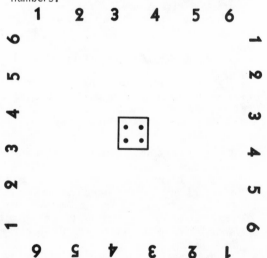

A box is put in the center containing as many balls as there are teams. The instructor calls a number, and the player from each team who has this number runs forward to the box and takes a ball. He now runs to the head of his line and takes the place of #1. In the meantime, the players in his line have moved to the left just enough to fill in the space left by the runner. Upon reaching the head of the line, the runner passes the ball to #1 and so on down the line to the end man. The last man runs forward and returns the ball to the box. The first team to return the ball to the box scores 1 point.

The runner must not pass the ball down the line until he takes his place at the head. The ball must be caught and passed by each man. Failure to conform to each of these rules results in disqualification.

The runner now stays at the head of the line. He retains his number but it is not important to maintain the line in consecutive number sequence.

CAGEBALL KICK-OVER

Playing Area: Playground (grassy area), gymnasium

Players: Two teams, 7 to 10 on each team

Supplies: A cageball--18, 24, or 30 inch size

The two teams sit facing each other with their legs outstretched and the soles of the feet about 2 feet apart. Each player supports his weight on his hands which are placed slightly back of him while maintaining the sitting position.

The teacher rolls the cageball between the two teams. The object of the game is to kick the ball over the other team. After a point is scored, the teacher rolls the ball into play again.

If the ball is kicked out at either end, no score results and the ball is put into play again by the roll.

Variation: Allow the children to use their hands to stop the ball from going over them. Also, a system of rotation can be used whereby, when a point is scored, the player on the left side of the line takes a place on the right side, moving all the other players to the left for one position.

CIRCLE CHASE

Playing Area: Playground, gymnasium

Players: 20 to 40

Supplies: None

The group is arranged in the circle, standing elbow distance apart, and facing the center. Depending upon the size of the group, count off by 3's, 4's, or 5's around the circle. The teacher calls out a number. All the players with this number start running around the circle. Players try to catch and tag the player ahead. Those tagged drop out of the game, while those not tagged make one lap around the circle and back to place. Players should try both to tag and keep from being tagged.

After each number has been called, the remaining players reform the circle and count off to get new numbers. The game is then repeated until a designated number remains.

The game is interesting and competitive, but has the basic weakness that those who are eliminated, the slower children, probably need the running the most. It is best to get them back into the game as soon as practical.

Variation: Instead of having each player run once around, let them run 2 or 3 times around before stopping at their positions.

CIRCLE ONE STEP
Playing Area: Playground

Players: Not more than 5 or 6 in a group

Supplies: 2 - 3 balls for each group.

The teacher should review and play One Step, a game for the Third Grade. The game is for a small group of 3 to 6. The children form a circle facing in so that with arms outstretched to the side, the hands can touch. One child is designated as the leader. The leader throws the ball around the circle either right or left consecutively. After each person in order handles the ball successfully (throwing and catching), the ball is back to the leader. Each child now takes a step back, enlarging the circle. This action is repeated until one of the children makes an error. Errors are made by dropping the ball, not throwing properly, or moving the feet more than a half step in any direction while catching.

Different kinds of throws can be designated or each child must throw in the fashion of the leader. The kind of a step back can be specified as a "giant step," "a tiny step," or something similar.

Teachers should recognize that the circles could become quite large and may need a limitation. If the group would reach the maximum size specified for the circle, then they would score one point and start over. The groups should be scattered widely over the available playground space so the circles will not interfere with each other.

DOUBLE TAG

Playing Area: Playground, gymnasium.
  Two parallel lines 40 feet apart

Players: 15 to 40

Supplies: None

The game is played by pairs. Each pair join inside hands. One pair is "It" and is in the center of the area. The other children are on one of the two lines.

The object of each pair is to run across the area to the other line without being tagged by the couple in the middle. Tagging can be done only with the joined inside hands of the "It" pair. Any pair tagged joins the center pair and aid in tagging the others. The last couple to remain without being tagged is "It" for the next game.

FOUR SQUARE

Playing Area: Usually outside on a hard surface, according to the following diagram.

Players: 4 players play the game, but others. are in line for a turn.

Supplies: Playground ball or volleyball.

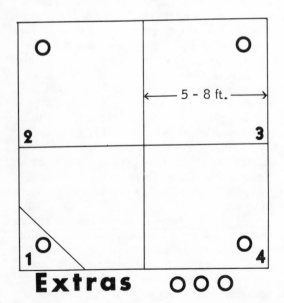

The squares are numbered 1, 2, 3, and 4. A service line is drawn diagonally across the far corner of square #1. The player in the #1 square must stay behind this line when he serves. The serve always starts from the #1 square.

The ball is served by dropping it and serving it underhanded from the bounce. If the serve hits a line, the server is out. The server can hit the ball to any of the other three courts. The player receiving the ball must keep it in play by striking the ball after it has bounced once in his square. He directs it to any other square with an underhand hit. Play continues until one player fails to return the ball or commits a fault.

The following are faults:

1. Hitting the ball side arm or overhand.
2. Ball landing on a line between the squares. Ball landing on an outer boundary is considered good.
3. Stepping in another square to play the ball.
4. Catching or carrying a return volley.
5. Allowing ball to touch any part of the body except the hands.

When a player misses or commits a fault, he goes to the end of the waiting line and all players move up. The player at the head of the waiting line move into square #4.

Variation: A two-foot circle can be drawn at the center of the area in which the ball must not be hit or an error is scored.

HAND HOCKEY

Playing Area: Field, about 100 by 100 feet

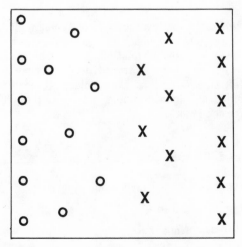

Players: Two teams composed of 12 to 15 each

Supplies: Soccer or volleyball

One-half the players of each team are guards and are stationed on the goal line they are defending. The other half of the players on each team are active players and are scattered throughout the playing area.

The object of the game is to bat or push the ball with either hand so that it crosses the goal line the other team is defending. Players may move as in hockey, but may not throw, hoist, or kick the ball. The defensive goal line players are limited to one step into the playing field when playing the ball.

The ball is put in play by rolling it into the field of players at about the center. After a goal has been scored or after a definite time period, guards become active players, and vice versa.

Out of bounds goes to the opposite team and the ball is put in play by rolling it from the sidelines into the playing area. If the ball becomes entrapped among players, play should be stopped and the ball is put into play again by a roll from the referee.

Players must play the ball and not resort to rough tactics. A player who is called for unnecessary roughness or illegally handling the ball must go to the sidelines (as in hockey) and remain in the penalty area until the players change positions.

Players should scatter and attempt to pass to each other rather than bunch around the ball.

HOOK ON

Playing Area: Playground, gymnasium

Players: 15 to 30

Supplies: None

One child is a chaser and another a runner. The remainder of the children are scattered by pairs around the area. They stand with inside hands joined and outside hands on hips, making a loop on which the runner can hook on.

Whenever the tagger catches the runner, the positions are reversed. The runner to get away hooks on with his arm to any pair. This makes three in a line, and the child on the other end of the line becomes the runner.

Teaching Suggestion: Do not let the run-

ner go too far without hooking to one of the pairs. The fun comes from a constant change of partners.

ISLANDS

Playing Area: Gymnasium, hard top surface outside

Players: Entire class

Supplies: None

With chalk, a number of patterns of "Islands" are laid out on the floor in the following fashion.

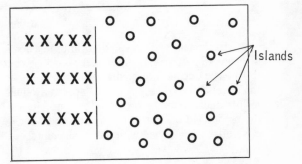

The object of the game is for the children to step, jump, or hop from "Island" to "Island" without error. Errors occur by stepping on a line or outside of an "Island." "Islands" can be of different sizes and in different arrangements, depending upon the ability of the children. Courses can be laid out under two plans. The first would be to establish courses in order of increasing difficulty. The children would move to a more difficult course when completing one successfully. The other plan would be to make each course reasonably easy at the start and increase the difficulty as the course progresses. Children can leap, jump, or hop from "Island" to "Island."

It would be well for the teacher to review and play Leap the Brook, a game in the Second Grade list, before introducing "Islands."

JUMP THE SHOT VARIATIONS

Playing Area: Playground, gymnasium, classroom

Players: 10 - 30

Supplies: A jump-the-shot rope

Review the jump the shot as described in the Fourth Grade Games (p. 113).

Variation 1.   Squads line up in the following fashion in spoke formation.

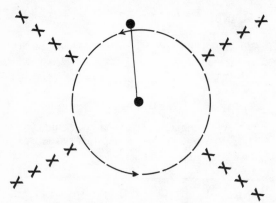

Each member is given a definite number of jumps (3, 4, or 5). The next squad member in line must come in immediately without missing a turn of the rope. A player scores a point for his squad when he comes in <u>on time</u>, jumps the prescribed number of turns, and exits successfully. The squad with the most points wins.

Variation 2.   Try with couples as in Variation 1. Couples must join inside hands and stand side by side when jumping.

LOOP TOUCH

Playing Area: Playground, gymnasium.
    Three parallel lines are drawn 15 feet apart.

Players: 2 players work together. As many pairs can play as there is room to run.

Supplies: None

The activity is played on an area which has three parallel lines across the length, forming two outside lines and a center line. Partners form a team and compete against other pairs.

The partners are divided, each standing on an outside line, facing each other ready to run. On the starting signal, the partners run to the center line, grasp right hands, run around each other (right hand loop), and run back and touch the outside line. Without stopping, they run back to the center, meet and make a left hand loop, and run back for another touch. Continuing--they meet again in the center,

make a two-hand loop, and back to the outside line for a touch. Once again, they run to the center, join hands, raising the joined hands above the head for a finishing act.

The first pair to finish wins. The children need to be reminded that each time they return to the outside line, they must touch it with a foot. Failure to do so results in disqualification.

Variation: Other stunts could be done in the center such as:

1. Leap frog.
2. Crawl through the other's legs.
3. Do a specified number of sit-ups with partner holding the legs.

LOOSE CABOOSE

Playing Area: Playground, gymnasium

Players: 12 to 30

Supplies: None

One child is designated as the "Loose Caboose" and tries to hook on to a train. Trains are formed by 3 or 4 children standing in a column formation with each child placing his hands on the waist of the child immediately in front of him. The trains by twisting and turning endeavor to keep the "Caboose" from hooking on to the back. Should this happen, the front child in the train becomes the new "Caboose." Each train should attempt to keep together and not break apart. If the number of children is 20 or more, or there seems to be difficulty in hooking the "Caboose" to the end of a train, there should be two "Cabooses."

MARCH ATTACK

Playing Area: Playground, gymnasium.
    Two parallel lines are drawn about 400 feet apart.

Players: 15 to 40, divided between two teams.

Supplies: None

One team takes a position on one of the lines with their backs to the area. These are the chasers. The other team is on the other line facing the area. This is the marching team.

The marching team moves forward on signal, marching in good order toward the chasers.

When they get reasonably close, a whistle or other signal is given and the marchers turn and run back to their line, chased by the other team. If any of the marchers are caught before reaching their line, they change to the other team. The game is repeated with the roles of marcher and chaser exchanged.

O'GRADY SAYS

Playing Area: Playground, gymnasium, classroom

Players: Entire class

Supplies: None

This game is borrowed from the U. S. Army. Different facing directions are given like "right face", "left face", and "about face". Also, calling to attention and standing at ease can be used. A leader stands in front and calls out the various commands. The players are to follow only if the command is preceded by "O'Grady says". Any one moving at the wrong time is eliminated.

Additional commands involving other movements can be used. To be effective, the commands must be given rapidly.

RUNNING DODGE BALL

Playing Area: Playground, gymnasium. Two parallel lines are drawn about 40 feet apart to form a gauntlet. The gauntlet is about 60 feet in length.

Players: Two teams, 10 to 20 on each team.

Supplies: 4 volley or rubber balls suitable for dodge ball.

Team A does the throwing and Team B runs the gauntlet. Team A's players are divided with half on one side of the gauntlet and half on the other. Four volleyballs are split between them.

Team B's players line up at one end of the gauntlet. They are to run through the gauntlet between members of Team A without getting hit. In moving through, they can run separately or all together.

The throwing team may recover the volleyballs lying in the running area, but must return to the sides before throwing. After a count is made of the successful runners, the teams trade

places and the game is repeated.

Variation:
1. Instead of having the team run once across, designate that the players are to run across and immediately start back. They score a point only if they make the round trip without being hit.
2. A good active game can be played by having the ball rolled instead of thrown. This causes the players to jump high into the air to avoid being hit.

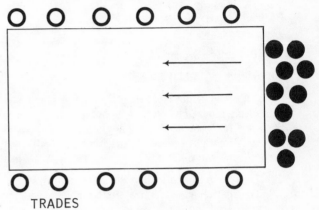

TRADES

Playing Area: Playground, gymnasium, classroom

Players: Entire class

Supplies: None

The class is divided into two teams of equal numbers, each of which has a goal line. Team B, the chasers, remains behind its goal line. Team A approaches from its goal line marching to the following dialogue:

Team A	"Here we come."
Team B	"Where from?"
Team A	"New Orleans."
Team B	"What's your trade?"
Team A	"Lemonade."
Team B	"Show us some."

Team A moves up close to Team B's goal line and proceeds to act out the motions of an activity, occupation, or specific task, which they have chosen previously. The members of team B make as many guesses as necessary to guess what the pantomime represents. Team A gives the initials of the activity to help. A correct guess means that Team A must run back to its goal line chased by Team B. Any member caught must join Team B. The game is repeated with the roles reversed. The team ending with the greater number of players is the winner.

Teaching Hint. If one team has trouble guessing, the other players should provide hints. Also, teams should be encouraged to have a number of activities chosen so that not too much time is consumed in the huddle choosing the next activity to be guessed.

WHISTLE BALL

Playing Area: Playground, gymnasium, classroom

Players: Groups of 6 to 8

Supplies: A ball for each group

A group of not more than 8 children stand in a circle formation. A ball is passed rapidly back and forth among them in any order. The object is to stay in the game the longest. Children sit down in place if:

1. They have the ball when the whistle blows. The teacher should set a predetermined time period, at the end of which a whistle is blown. This can be anywhere from 5 to 20 seconds, with the time periods varied.
2. If a child makes a bad throw or fails to catch a good throw.
3. If a player returns the ball directly to the person from whom he received it.

When the game gets down to two or three players, the time limits should be short.

WHISTLE MIXER

Playing Area: Playground, gymnasium, classroom

Players: Any number

Supplies: Whistle

Children are scattered throughout the area. To begin, they walk around in any direction they wish. The teacher blows a whistle a number of times in succession with short, sharp blasts. Whatever the number of blasts, the children form small circles with the number in the circle to equal the number established by the whistle signal. Thus, if there are four blasts, the children form circles of four--no more, no less. Any children left out are eliminated. Also, if a circle is formed with more than the specified

number, the entire circle is eliminated.

After the circles have been formed and the eliminated children have been moved to the sidelines, the teacher calls "Walk" and the game continues. In walking, the children should move in different directions.

Variation: A fine version of this game can be done with the aid of a tom-tom. Different beats of the tom-tom would indicate various locomotor movements--skipping, galloping, slow walk, normal walk, running. The whistle would still be used to set the number to be in each circle.

Fifth Grade Games

Battle Dodge Ball
Black Tom
Bombardment
Circle Hook On
Circle Tug-of-War
Four Team Grab Ball
In the Creek
Jolly Ball
Mickey Mouse
Number Tug-of-War
Touchdown
Two Square
Wiggle Worm Race

BATTLE DODGE BALL

Playing Area: Playground, gymnasium

Players: Two teams, 10 to 15 on each team

Supplies: Two volleyballs or rubber playground balls

The teams form one circle, each occupying one-half the circle. Players on each team are numbered consecutively. For any one number, there is a player on each team. Two volleyballs are placed about 5 feet apart in the center of the circle, one on each side of a center line which separates the teams for each other.

The teacher calls out the number she chooses. The two players with the number run forward, secure a ball, and try to hit the other. Players on the sides of the circle may retrieve balls and throw them to their teammate in the center. However, each competing player must stay in his half of the circle.

The winning player scores a point for his team. Play for a certain number of points or or play until each has had a turn to compete.

Teaching Suggestion: It is helpful if the teacher jots the numbers down on a card to keep the order of competition clear.

Variation: Call two numbers which means that two compete against two in the center.

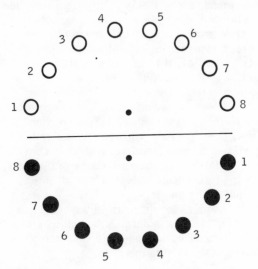

BLACK TOM

Playing Area: Two parallel lines are drawn about 50 feet apart.

Players: Entire class. 20-40

Supplies: None

One player is "It" and is in the center between the lines. All other children are on one of the two lines. The object is to cross to the other line without being tagged by "It."

All players must run across immediately when "It" calls "Black Tom." Anyone who doesn't come immediately is considered caught. Also, no player may run if a signal other than "Black Tom" is given. If he does, he is considered caught. The center player calls out "Green Tom" or "Red Tom" to confuse the runners.

Any player tagged by "It" or who makes a mistake joins "It" in the center and helps him catch the others. The last caught is "It" for the next game.

BOMBARDMENT--(Indian Clubs)

Playing Area: Gymnasium

Players: Two teams, 10 to 15 on each team.

Supplies: 12 Indian Clubs for each team. Four volley or rubber playground balls.

A line is drawn across the center of the floor from wall to wall. This divides the floor into two courts, each of which is occupied by one team. Twenty-five feet from the center line in each court, another line is drawn. This is the club line. Each team sets their Indian clubs on this line. These should be spaced. Each team is given two of the balls.

The object of the game is to knock over the other team's clubs. Players throw the balls back and forth but cannot move over the center line. Whenever a club is knocked over by a ball or accidently by a player, the club is removed. The team with the most clubs standing is declared the winner.

Out-of-bounds balls can be recovered but must be thrown from the court.

Variation: Instead of removing the clubs, they can be reset. Two scorers, one for each club line, are needed for this version.

CIRCLE HOOK ON

Playing Area: Playground, gymnasium, classroom

Players: 4

Supplies: None

This is a game of one against three. The three have hands joined. By dodging and swinging around, the object is to prevent the fourth child from tagging the child opposite on the back.

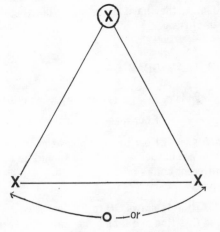

Variation:
1. Use a piece of cloth, handkerchief, or "flag" tucked in the belt in back of the child opposite. The fourth child tries to pull the "flag" from the belt.
2. Instead of tagging, the chaser tries to hook on the child being protected.

Teaching Hints: Watch for roughness by the two in the circle protecting the third. The game works better if the children are about of equal ability physically. Allow a period of time and rotate if the chaser is not successful. In any case, the children should rotate so that each has a chance to be the tagger.

CIRCLE TUG-OF-WAR

Playing Area: Playground, gymnasium

Players: 10 to 15 in each circle

Supplies: 12 to 15 Indian clubs

The object of the tug-of-war is to have the other players break a grip or knock over a club. A circle is formed by the players who join hands with good grips. In the center of the circle, the Indian clubs are placed in a scattered formation. After the starting signal, the players pull or push to eliminate other players. Both players are eliminated who break a grip or any player who knocks over a club in the struggle is out. After about half are eliminated, re-form the circle and start anew. After the players have left the circle, the ring of players is re-formed, and the game is repeated until only three or four players are left. These are the winners.

Variation: The game can also be played with the players facing out. With their back to the center, they have more trouble dodging the Indian clubs.

FOUR TEAM GRAB BALL

Playing Area: Playground, gymnasium

Players: Four teams, 6 to 8 on each.

Supplies: Four balls of approximately the size are needed. The balls should be of different colors or marked so they can be told apart.

A line is drawn 30 to 50 feet from a wall. Behind this line and facing the wall, the teams are in file formation. A wall or fence is neces-

sary to limit the length of the throws.

The player at the head of each file has a ball. At a signal, each player throws or rolls the ball in the direction of the wall. The object of the game is to recover a ball (not your own) and return first to the line. The first child back with another ball scores 2 points for his team. The second scores 1 point. No points are given for third and fourth place. If it so happens that the child brings back the ball which he threw, his team loses one point. After the children run back to the line, they take places at the end of the line and the game is repeated with four new players.

There is less confusion if the teams are permanently assigned a ball. To start each throw, then, the balls must be returned to the respective teams. However, if there is considerable difference in the performance of the balls, then the team should throw the ball which was returned by its player.

The children will learn very quickly that the advantage lies in keeping the ball as close to the fence or wall as possible since the other players have to run farther.

IN THE CREEK

Playing Area: Playground, gymnasium, classroom

Players: Entire class

Supplies: None

A creek is formed by drawing 2 parallel lines 2 to 3 feet apart, depending upon the ability of the children. The lines should be long enough to accommodate the children comfortably with enough room for each to jump. If necessary, two or three sets of lines can be drawn.

The children line up on one of the banks all facing the creek and facing the same direction. The object of the game is to make the children commit an error in the jumping.

The teacher or leader gives one of two directions:
              "In the creek."
              "On the bank."
Children now on the bank, jump into the creek or over to the other bank depending upon the command. When they jump on the bank, they immediately turn around and get ready for the next command.

If children are in the creek and the command, "In the creek" is repeated, they must not move.

Errors are committed when a child steps on a line, makes a wrong jump, or moves when he should be still.

Children who make a mistake can be sent down to another game or eliminated. The first is the better suggestion as this keeps them in activity.

After a period of time, the original directions may not challenge the children. Different combinations can be set up. "In the creek" means to jump and land with both feet. "On the bank" one way would be a leap. "On the bank" other way would be a hop. Also, false commands can be given like "In the ocean," or "In the lake." No one is to move on these commands under penalty of elimination.

It is a good plan to keep things moving fast with crisp commands. Children should be charged with judging their own errors and drop out when they feel they have made a mistake.

JOLLY BALL

Playing Area: Playground, gymnasium

Players: 20 to 30

Supplies: Cageball 24" or larger: or a pushball.

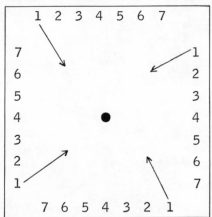

Four teams are organized each of whom forms one side of a hollow square. The children are sitting down facing in with hands braced behind them. On each team, the children are numbered consecutively from one to as far as needed. Each child waits until his number is called. When a number is called, the four active players (one from each team) move forward in crab position and try to kick the cageball over the heads of any one of the three opposing teams.

The players on the teams kick the ball inside. Ordinarily, the hands are not to be used, but this could be allowed among less skilled children and in the learning stages of the game.

A point is scored <u>against</u> a team that allows the ball to go over their heads. A ball that goes out at the corner between teams is dead and must be replayed. When a point is scored, the active children retire back to their teams and another number is called. This game is quite strenuous for the active players in the center, and time should be called after a reasonable length of time if no score develops.

Variation: The game can also be played by allowing two children from each team to be active at a time.

MICKEY MOUSE

Playing Area: Playground, gymnasium, classroom

Players: Entire class

Supplies: 4 Indian clubs

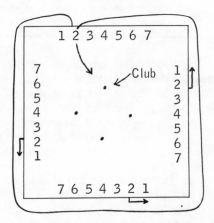

A hollow square, about 10 yards on a side, is formed by four teams, each of which occupies one side facing in. The teams should be even in numbers. Each team is numbered consecutively from right to left. This means that there is one person on each with the same number.

A number is called by the teacher. The four children with this number run to the right all the way around the square and through their <u>own</u> vacated space toward the center of the square. Near the center in front of each team stands an

Indian club. The first child to put the Indian Club down on the floor is the winner. The clubs should be of equal distance in front of the teams and far enough away from each other to avoid collisions in the center.

Scoring is kept by the word "Mickey Mouse." The player who puts the club down first gets to write two letters of the name. The player who is second, gets to put down one letter. The lettering can be done in a space in front of each team where the name would be reasonably protected from the runners. The first team to complete the name is the winner.

In number games of this type, the numbers are not called in order. The teacher should keep some kind of a tally to assure that each number is called.

NUMBER TUG-OF-WAR

Playing Area: Playground, gymnasium, classroom

Players: 10 - 16

Supplies: Individual tug-of-war rope

The Rope

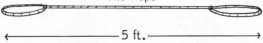

←———————— 5 ft. ————————→

Two parallel lines are drawn about 20 feet apart. The game is between teams, each of whom lines up behind one of the lines. The players on each team are numbered consecutively. There is a player on each team designated by the same number. In the center between the two lines lying crosswise is an individual tug-of-war rope.

The teacher calls out any number, and the two players with that number rush out to the rope. If either can get back to his side without the other getting a hold on the rope, he wins. Otherwise, if both can secure holds on the rope, then a tug-of-war contest ensues. The winner is the player who is able to touch his base line with his foot.

Variation: Call out two numbers or set up the original game so that two children on each side have the same number. The tug-of-war then is two against two. This will accommodate more children in the game.

TOUCHDOWN

Playing Area: Playground, gymnasium. Two parallel lines are needed about 60 feet apart.

Players: Two teams, 10 to 15 on each team.

Supplies: Small object which can be concealed in the hand.

Two teams face each other, each standing on one of the parallel lines. One team goes into a huddle and the members decide which player is to carry an object to the opponents goal line. The team moves out of the huddle and takes a position like a football team. On the charge signal, "Hike," the players run toward the opponents goal line, each player holding his hands as if he were carrying the object. On the charge signal, the opponents also run forward and tag the players. When a player is tagged, he must immediately stop and open both hands to show whether or not he has the object.

If the player carrying the object can reach the goal line without being tagged, he calls "Touchdown," and scores a point for his team. The team scoring the point retains possession of the object and gets another try. If the player carrying the object is tagged in the center area, the object is given to the other team. They go into a huddle and try to run it across the field and score.

TWO SQUARE

Playing Area: Generally outside on a hard surface according to the Four Square diagram:

Players: 2 players, but others may be in line for a turn.

Supplies: Playground or volleyball

The basic rules are the same as for Four-Square except that only two players are involved and two squares are used. If there are players waiting for a turn, the active player who misses or fouls can be eliminated as in Four-Square. If two players wish to play, a score can be kept.

In Two Square, the ball must be served from behind the base line.

WIGGLE WORM RACE

Playing Area: Playground, gymnasium, classroom

Players: 5 to 10 players form a team. The amount of room would determine the number of teams.

Supplies: None

Arrange the team in parallel files behind a starting line. The finish line is 20 to 30 feet in front. Have each player reach back between his legs with his right hand and grasp the left hand of the player just back of him. At the signal, the teams move forward, keeping files unbroken, and cross the finish line. The first team completely across the finish line with the line unbroken wins.

Variation: The race can be run around a turning point and back to the starting line. A chair, base, or other marker should be used to assure a definite turning point.

Sixth Grade Games

Beater Goes Round
Cageball Target Throw
Chain Tag
Fox and Geese
Jump the Shot
Low Bridge
Odd and Even
One Base Dodge Ball
Over the Wall
Pin Dodge Ball
Prisoner's Base
Scatter Dodge Ball

BEATER GOES ROUND

Playing Area: Playground, gymnasium

Players: 10 to 15

Supplies: Knotted towel

All players except one stand in a circle facing counterclockwise with their hands behind them. The extra player walks around the circle in line of direction and puts the knotted towel into a player's hands. This player immediately starts hitting the player in front of him, who runs around the circle with the striker after him. The player who gave the towel steps into the circle at one of the empty places. The new player with the towel now continues the game.

Some control is necessary in this game. Children should be hit across the seat and not over the head and shoulders. Also, see that no child is repeatedly punished. No beater should be permitted to give the towel back to the player from whom he received it.

CAGEBALL TARGET THROW

Playing Area: Gymnasium with a space about the size of a small basketball court.

Players: 2 teams, 10 to 20 on each team.

Supplies: One cageball (18, 24, or 30 inches), 12 to 15 balls of various sizes.

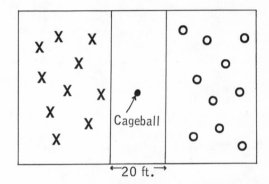

An area about 20 feet wide is across the center of the playing area, with a cageball in the center. The object of the game is to throw the smaller balls against the cageball forcing it across the line in front of the other team. Players may come up to the line to throw, but may not throw while inside the cageball area. However, a player may enter the area to recover a ball. No one is to touch the cageball at any time, nor may the cageball be pushed by a ball in the hands of a player.

If the cageball seems to move too easily, it can be deflated slightly. The throwing balls can be of most any size--soccers, volleyballs, playground balls, etc.

Variation: Have two rovers in the center area, one from each team, to retrieve balls. These players cannot block throws or prevent a ball from hitting the target, but are there merely to retrieve balls for their teams.

CHAIN TAG

Playing Area: Playground with two parallel lines about 50 feet apart.

Players: 20 to 40

This game is essentially like other goal exchange games except in the manner that players can be caught. In this case, the center is occupied by three players who form a chain with joined hands. The free hands on either side of the chain are the only ones that can do the tagging.

The players in the center call "Come" and the other children cross from one line to another. The "Chain" tries to tag any of the runners. Any one caught joins the "Chain." When the "Chain" becomes too large, it should be divided into several smaller "Chains."

Variation: Catch of Fish.

In this game, "Chain" catches the children by surrounding them like a fish net. The runners cannot run under or through the links of the "Net."

FOX AND GEESE

Playing Area: Playground, gymnasium

Players: 15 to 30

Supplies: A handkerchief, strip of cloth, or other flag; one for each file.

One player is the "Fox," and the remainder of the players are divided into groups of 4 or 5. At the head of each group is a "Gander," and the rest of the group are "Geese." The "Geese" line up in file behind the "Gander" and firmly grasp the waist of the player in front. The last player in the file has a handkerchief tucked in his belt at the back.

The "Fox" attempts to get the handkerchief while the "Gander" tries to protect his "Geese." If the "Fox" gets the handkerchief, the "Gander" of that file becomes the new "Fox." The old "Fox" joins the group as rear player and puts the handkerchief in his belt at the back.

If the file breaks in moving around, this is considered the same as if the handkerchief were pulled.

JUMP THE SHOT VARIATIONS

The sixth grade teacher should emphasize the Jump the Shot routines and variations as listed in the Fourth Grade Program. The emphasis in the sixth grade should be more on squad rather than individual competition. The following should be added to the activity routines.

Two squads are in file formation and face the rope turner.

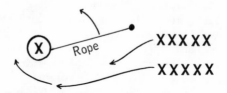

1. Each player runs clockwise (against the turn of the rope) jumping the rope as often as necessary to return to the squad.
2. Each player runs counterclockwise in the same direction as the rope is turning and tries to run around the circle before the rope can catch up with him. If this happens, he must jump to allow the rope to go under him. The best time for a player to start is just after the rope has passed him.
3. Try some of the stunts where the hands and feet are on the ground and see if the players can have the rope pass under them. The rabbit jump, push-up position, lame-dog and others offer possibilities.

LOW BRIDGE

Playing Area: Gymnasium, classroom

Players: 5 - 10

Supplies: Wand, low standards.

This game is popular in many lands and some players develop a fine degree of skill in the task required. The object of the game is to move under a bar supported like a high jump bar without dislodging the bar nor touching the ground with the hands or body. The bar should be started high enough so all children can go under it successfully. Each child is to get three tries to go under the bar. If he fails, he is eliminated and acts as an official for the event.

Blocks could be used together with different sized boxes to support the wand. Some kind of a system is needed so that the wand can be lowered a little for each repetition of the event. The wand is lowered after all children have gone under or have had three misses. Two miniature standards similar to the type used for the high jump make the event precise and easy to administer.

Variations:
1. Try going under the bar with the use of the feet <u>and</u> hands only. It is ruled a miss if the body touches the ground or the wand is dislodged.
2. Go under with a partner.

ODD AND EVEN

Playing Area: Playground, gymnasium. Two parallel lines about 40 feet apart.

Players: 10 to 40 with the players divided into two groups (teams).

Supplies: A cubical box numbered like a dice. A box 6 by 6 inches with large numbers painted on the sides, the numbers running 1 through 6.

The two groups face each other about five feet apart in the center between the two parallel lines. One group is the "Odd's" and the other is the "Even's". The box is rolled between the two lines of players. If an odd number comes up (1,3,5) then the even team chases the "Odd's" to the line back of the odd team. If an even number (2,4,6) comes up, the chase is the other way.

Those caught before reaching their home line can be handled in one of two ways:

1. Any player caught joins the other side. This has a tendency in some cases to make the players careless. The team with the most players at the end of the time period wins.
2. They are eliminated and stand back of their line until the game is declared over. The team with the most players left wins.

Variation: The game can also be played as Black and White. A card with black on one side and white on another is substituted for the large dice. One team is designated as the white team and the other the blacks.

ONE BASE DODGE BALL

Playing Area: Playground, gymnasium. A home line is drawn at one end of the playing space. A base or standard is placed about 50 feet in front of the home line.

Players: Two teams, 8 to 15 on each team.

Supplies: Base, volleyball or playground ball.

One team is scattered out in the fielding area. The boundaries of this area are determined by the number of children. The other team is lined up in single file behind the home line. Two children are running at a time.

The object of the game for the fielding team is to hit the players with the ball as they round the base and head back for the home line. The game is continuous, meaning that as soon as a running team player is hit or crosses the home line, another player immediately starts.

The fielding team may not run with the ball but must pass it from player to player trying to hit one of the runners.

The running team scores a point for each player who successfully runs around the base and back to the home line.

To start the game, the running team has two players ready at the right side of the home line. The others on the team are in line waiting for a turn. The teacher throws the ball anywhere in the field and the first two runners start toward the base. They must run around the base from the right side. After all have run, the teams exchange places. The team scoring the most runs wins.

Teaching Suggestions: Players on the fielding team should make short passes to a person close to a runner so that the runner can be hit. They must be alert because two children are running at a time.

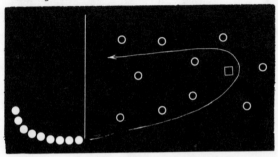

The next player on the running team must watch carefully so that he can start the instant that one of the two preceding runners is back safe or has been hit.

OVER THE WALL

Playing Area: Playground

Players: Entire class

Supplies: None

Two parallel goal lines are drawn about 60 feet apart. Two additional parallel lines about 3 feet apart are laid out parallel to the goal lines in the middle of the game area. This is the "Wall." Side limits need to be established.

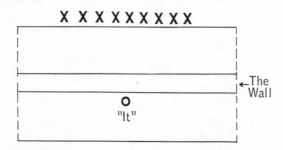

One player is "It" and stands on or behind the "Wall." All other players are behind one of the goal lines. "It" calls, "Over the Wall." All players must then run across the "Wall" to the other goal line. "It" tries to tag any player he can, who, if caught, helps him catch the others. Players are also considered caught if they step on the "Wall." They must clear it with a leap or jump and cannot step on the "Wall" including the lines. Players after crossing over to the other side safely must wait for the next call, "Over the Wall."

The game can be made more difficult by increasing the width of the "Wall." "It" can step on or run through the "Wall" at will.

PIN DODGE BALL

Playing Area: Gymnasium

Players: Entire class

Supplies: 2 volleyballs, 6 Indian clubs

Two teams of equal numbers play the game. Each team is given 1 volleyball and 3 Indian

clubs. A court 30' x 60' or larger with a center line is needed. The size of the court would be dependent upon the number of children in the game. The object of the game is to eliminate all players on the opposite team or knock down the opposing team's Indian clubs. The volleyballs are used to throw at the opposing team members or knock down the clubs. Each team stays in its half of the court.

A player is eliminated if:

1. He is hit <u>on the fly</u> by a ball he does not catch.
2. Steps over the center line to throw or retrieve a ball. Any opposing team member hit under these circumstances is not eliminated.
3. He attempts to block a thrown ball with a ball in his hand and the thrown ball touches him in any manner. A player can legally block a thrown ball with a ball held in his hand.

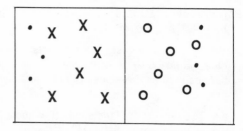

A foul is called if a player holds a ball longer than 15 seconds without throwing at the opposing team. The ball is immediately given to the opposing team.

Players who are eliminated should move to the sidelines and sit down so that it can be clearly determined who is still active.

The Indian clubs are put any place in the team area as desired. Players may guard the clubs, but must not touch them. When a club is knocked down, it is removed immediately from the game. If a club is knocked down unintentionally by a member of the defending team, the club is counted as "down."

A player can be "saved" if the ball hits him and is caught by a teammate before it touches the ground.

A referee should take his position at the side of the court near the center line. When a foul is called for holding the ball over 15 seconds, play stops and the ball is rolled to the offended team.

The game is won whenever all the players from one team have been eliminated or all three clubs on one side have been knocked down.

PRISONER'S BASE

Playing Area: A rectangular area marked off as in the diagram. The size of the area would depend somewhat upon the number playing.

Players: Two teams with 5 to 15 on each side. Each team has a captain.

Supplies: None

To win the game, a team must have one of its players enter the opponent's goal area without being tagged, or one team must capture all players from the opposing team. The basic rule of the game is that any player may be tagged only by an opponent who has left his own goal area <u>after</u> the player who is tagged. The game is started by players moving into the neutral area to entice the other team to chase them. Other players await their chances to tag an opponent who has left his goal line earlier. Each player tries to tag an opponent to make him a prisoner, and, in turn, tries to avoid being tagged.

Players may return to their own goal line as often as they wish in order to become eligible to tag an opponent. Prisoner and tagger return without penalty to the tagger's prison.

A prisoner must keep one foot in the prison and can stretch forward as far as he is able to make rescue easier. To be rescued, a prisoner must be tagged by his own teammate who has been able to reach him without being tagged. The rescued and the rescuer return to their own goal line without the penalty of being tagged. Both are now active players.

If more than one prisoner is captured, they form a chain by holding hands with last prisoner caught acting as anchor and keeping one foot in the prison. Only the first prisoner at the end of the chain can be released.

The captain directs his team strategy as some players need to guard the goal, others the prisoners, and another group to act as taggers.

Any player who crosses a side line to avoid being tagged is considered a prisoner.

Variation: A popular version of this game is called "Stealing Sticks." The game is played in the same manner except ten sticks or Indian clubs are added. These are divided with five to each team. Any player crossing the opponent's goal line without being tagged is eligible to take home one stick. The game continues until one side has lost its sticks. If the play is ended before either side has possession of all the sticks, the team with the most sticks wins.

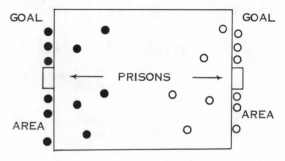

SCATTER DODGE BALL

Playing Area: Playground or gymnasium. If outside, definite boundaries should be set.

Players: Any number can play.

Supplies: Two volleyballs or rubber balls suitable for dodge ball.

The children are scattered throughout the area. The teacher rolls the two balls into the playing area. Anyone may pick up a ball and throw it at anyone else. If a person is hit or the ball in his hand is struck with a ball, he goes to the sideline. Should he have a ball in his hand, he should drop it immediately and not attempt to throw. If two children throw at each other and both are hit, then both are eliminated.

No player may have possession of both volleyballs. The ball must be actually thrown as touching another player while the ball is held in the hand does not put the player out.

Children should be cautioned not to punish others unnecessarily with hard hits. Throws should be below the waist whenever possible, and a throw hitting the head puts the thrower out of the game.

Chapter 20
Stunts, Tumbling, Apparatus and Combative Activities Intermediate Grades

Before proceeding with the program of activities of stunts, tumbling, apparatus, and combatives, the teacher should review both the procedures and the activities suggested for the primary grades. The progression for the intermediate grades proceeds from this base. This is particularly true for classes which lack experience in these activities.

The review of the simplified materials builds confidence, improves techniques, and also provides good fitness values. It will also aid the teacher in making an evaluation of the individual differences in the capacity to perform in these areas. The formations, in particular, presented in the primary grade discussions are equally adaptable to the intermediate program.

A program using a variety of activities is certainly big-muscle in nature and has excellent potential for physical fitness development. Strength, agility, balance, flexibility, and body control can be developed through a diverse and varied program. Particularly, the horizontal ladder, the exercise bar, and the climbing ropes give opportunity for arm and shoulder girdle development.

Although the many activities in the stunt program differ greatly in difficulty and in the safety precautions which should be observed, it is possible to establish some general guides for good teaching and proper regard for safety.

Teaching Suggestions and Safety Precautions

1. Safety is a foremost consideration. Each stunt should be analyzed from a safety aspect and trained spotters should be assigned and made routine for those stunts in which there is danger from falling. Where the body is inverted, as in the head stand, spotters should be required, particularly in the learning phases.

2. Emphasis on how to fall should be made. Children should be taught either to roll out or bridge out of a stunt when balance is lost.

3. It is important to relate new activities to those previously learned. This is the soul of progression. In many cases, it is good practice to review the stunt from the previous grade which leads up to the new activity.

4. Children in the intermediate grades should begin to emphasize form in doing stunts. This, however, should be within the capacity of the children.

5. Warm-up activity should be considered. Warm-up can be in the nature of a relatively less-demanding stunt or it could be an exercise or special activity for that purpose.

6. Permit no horse play. Nip this early at its first appearance.

7. Proper clothing for mixed groups is important. On days that stunts are scheduled, girls can change from skirts to pedal pushers, slacks, jumpers, or play suits.

8. Be sure the performer understands the correct method of performing a stunt before starting. Particularly so, should he be aware of the critical points of a particular stunt.

9. Encourage, but do not insist a child do a stunt, Patience is needed if a mental block or other problem is present.

10. Mats are needed in sufficient numbers (at least four) for a stunt and tumbling program. The newer type synthetic mats have the advantage of being transportable and easily cleaned. A 4 by 6 or 5 by 8 foot size makes a satisfactory mat.

11. The teacher should take enough time to describe each activity emphasizing the techniques, the critical points, and the safety considerations. Pupils should be used for demonstrations whenever possible.

12. Gymnasium shoes should be worn for the stunts and tumbling program. Children should be permitted to tumble in stocking feet if they do not have the proper shoes.

13. No practice periods should be permitted without the presence of the teacher.

14. Should the class be without previous experience in a stunt and tumbling program, the teacher should go back at least one grade and go through all the activities. It might be well to select certain stunts even farther back than one grade. These stunts would be of the type which are basic and are lead-up to those in the present grade.

15. Pockets should be emptied and lockets, glasses, watches, and other articles of this nature removed. Have a special place for these things or, better yet, leave them in the classroom.

16. Seek pride in accomplishment with the principle that only through proper practice can one reach a high degree of perfection.

17. Some stunts are performed by pairs or groups. If the stunt so indicates, match individuals in size and strength. Where one child bears the weight of the other, be sure the support child knows precisely how this is to be done.

18. Where the stunt calls for it to be held a number of counts, use a standard counting system like, "A thousand and one, a thousand and two, etc."

19. Children should have fun with their friends in these types of activities, but do not allow them to laugh at an inept child.

20. Good motivation is provided if a check-off system is established for the children when stunts are completed. Two systems are suggested. The first would simply check those stunts which the student has completed. The second system would differ between a stunt done well and one that meets minimum requirements. In the latter system, the teacher could make a diagonal line (/) for a stunt meeting minimum requirements and cross that line with another making an "X" for a stunt well done. The lists of the stunts with the children's names by squads can be put on the bulletin board or kept on squad cards for convenient use in the stunt lesson.

A glance at the stunt cards will enable the teacher to know what stunts need to be reviewed and practiced. An analysis of this type makes a better educational experience for the children. However, care must be taken that the "check out" system does not take too much teaching-learning time.

21. Teachers should allow opportunity for creative movement. Variations in stunts can be in direction, speed, shape, and parts of the body. At times the teacher should structure movement problems by use of basic directions within which children can move with some choice. For example, the directions may call for the children to put together a series of three stunts including one locomotor, one rolling, and one jumping. Other challenges can be posed for the children. The children might be told to try the stunt with the hands and feet as far apart (or close together) as possible. Or, they can hold the hands and feet in various positions.

Stunts and Tumbling

Fourth Grade Program

The fourth grade program continues emphasis on the forward and backward rolls with the addition of variations and combinations. The side roll and the head stand are introduced on this grade level. The following activities are allocated to the fourth grade.

Forward Roll Combinations
Backward Roll Combinations
Leg Dip
The Head Stand
Stoop and Stretch
Knee Dip
Squat Jumps
Tanglefoot
Egg Roll
Toe Touch Nose
Seat Balance
Finger Touch
Side Roll
Toe Tug Walk
Wand or Stick Stunts
   Wand Catch
     Thread the Needle - V Seat
     Thread the Needle - Standing

Grapevine
Back Scratcher
Face to Knee Touch
Balance Jump
Toe Toucher (Partner Stunt)
Wheelbarrow (Couple Stunt)
Centipede (Couple or Group Stunt)
Partner Support Stunts
Double Bear
Table
Lighthouse
Hip-Shoulder Stand
Movement Exploration Support
Stunts

Forward Roll Combinations.   The forward roll should be reviewed with increased emphasis on proper form.   Combinations that can be introduced are:

1.   Forward roll to standing position.
2.   Forward roll preceded by a short run.
3.   Two forward rolls in succession.
4.   Leap frog and forward roll.
5.   Forward roll to a jump in the air vertically and repeat.
6.   Rabbit Hop and forward roll.

Backward Roll Combinations.   The backward roll technique should be reviewed. Continued emphasis on the push off by the hands needs to be made.   Combinations to be taught are:

1.   Back roll to standing position.   Correct use of the hands must be emphasized.   A strong push by the hands is necessary to provide enough momentum to land on the feet.
2.   Two back rolls in succession.
3.   Crab Walk into a back roll.
4.   Children can add a jump into the air at the completion of the roll combination.

LEG DIP

Extend both hands and one leg forward, balancing on the other leg. Lower body to heel seat and return without losing the balance or touching the floor with any part of the body. Try with the other foot.

THE HEAD STAND

Starting from a squat position, with hands pointed forward, fingers spread and slightly cupped, about shoulder width apart, put the head on the mat about 10 inches from the hands. Keeping the weight on the forward part of the head (near the hairline), walk the feet forward until the hips are high over the body. Keep one foot on the mat and kick the other up, quickly following with a push by the mat foot to bring that leg up to the one already in upright position.

Feet should be together with legs straight and toes pointed, and the back is arched with weight evenly distributed among the hands and head.

Children should be taught how to come down. The safest way is to return to the mat in the direction that was used going up. If the child overbalances and falls forward, he can either arch his back and make contact with his feet first or he can tuck the head under and come down with a forward roll.

The triangle formed by the hands and the head is important, as well as the weight on the forward part of the head. The majority of the troubles which occur while doing the head stand come from incorrect head-hand relationship. The correct placement can be insured by making sure the head is placed the length of the performer's forearm from knees, and the hands placed at the knees.

When learning, children should work in units of three students. One child attempts the stunt with a spotter on either side. Positions are rotated.

Do not let students stay in the inverted position too long nor should there be contests to see who can stand on his head the longest.

STOOP AND STRETCH

Hold a piece of chalk with <u>both</u> hands. Place the heels against a line with feet about shoulder width apart. Reach between the legs with the knees straight and make a mark as far back as you can. Try writing a number, drawing a small circle, or other figure.

Variation: Allow the knees to be bent and a squatting position assumed.

KNEE DIP

Grasp the right instep behind the back with the left hand, balancing on the left foot. With the other arm out for balance, lower and touch the floor with the bent knee. Regain balance. During the learning stages, the teacher can place a book under the knee being lowered making an easier stunt. Try with the other leg.

Variation: Hold the right leg with the right hand.

SQUAT JUMPS

Take a deep squat position with the trunk erect and one foot slightly ahead of the other so that the heel of the front foot is even with the toe of the back. Hands are placed palms down on top of the head. Spring into the air and change the relative position of the feet. Make 5, 10, and 15 changes, clearing the floor by 4 inches.

Variation: A more difficult stunt occurs when the knees are completely straightened on each jump.

TANGLEFOOT

Stand with the heels together and the toes pointed out. Bend the trunk forward, extend both arms down between the knees and behind the ankles. Bring the hands around the outside of the ankles from behind and clasp the hands in front of the ankles. Hold this position in good balance for 5 seconds, without releasing the handclasp.

EGG ROLL

Hold the same position with the hands and feet as in Tanglefoot, except that the individual lies on his back. Roll back over each shoulder in turn to make a full circle back to place. This is accomplished by four rolling shoulder turns, two right and two left. If mats are used, two should be placed side by side to cover the extent of the roll.

TOE TOUCH NOSE

From a sitting position on the floor, using the aid of both hands, try to touch the toe of either foot to the nose. More flexible youngsters will even be able to bring the foot on top of the head or behind the neck. While this is a flexibility exercise, caution should be used in forcing the leg too far. Do first with one foot and then the other.

Variation: Perform from a standing position without losing balance.

SEAT BALANCE

Sit on the floor holding the ankles in front with the elbows inside the knees. The feet are flat on the floor, and the knees are bent approximately at a right angle. Raise the legs so that the knees are straight with the toes pointed and balance on the seat for 5 seconds.

Variation: Make a quarter turn of the body using the seat as the pivot point. Try other turns of farther distances.

FINGER TOUCH

Put the right hand behind you with the index finger straight and pointed down. Grasp the right wrist with the left hand. From an erect position with the feet about 6 inches apart, squat down and touch the floor with the index finger. Regain erect position without losing balance. In learning the stunt, the teacher can use a book to decrease the distance making the touch easier.

SIDE ROLL

The child is on hands and knees with the side selected for the roll toward the direction of the roll. By dropping the shoulder and tucking both the elbow and knee under, roll over completely on the shoulders and hips, coming again to the hands and knees position. Momentum is needed to return to the original position. Children should practice rolling back and forth from one hands-and-knee position to another.

Variation: Spring up in the air from the

hands and knee position to start the roll.

TOE TUG WALK

Bend over and grasp the toes with the thumb on top. Knees are bent slightly and the eyes are forward. The child should walk forward without losing the grip on the toes. Walk backward and sideward to provide more challenge. Also, the child can walk in various geometric patterns like a circle, triangle, or square.

Variation: Try doing the walk with the right hand grasping the left foot and vice versa.

WAND OR STICK STUNTS

1. Wand Catch. Stand a wand on one end and hold it in place with the index finger on top. Bring the foot quickly over the stick, letting it go and catching the stick with the finger before it falls. Do this right and left, inward and outward for a completed set.
2. Thread the Needle - V Seat. Maintaining a V seat position, with the wand held in front of the body with both hands, bend the knees between the arms and pass the wand over them and return, without touching the wand to the legs.
3. Thread the Needle- Standing. Holding wand in both hands, step through stick one leg at a time and return without touching stick. Try from side to side with the stick held front and back.
4. Grapevine. Holding wand near ends, step with right foot around right arm and over wand inward towards body. Pass the wand backwards over head and right shoulder until you are standing erect with wand between legs. Reverse back to original position. Try with the left foot first.
5. Back Scratcher. Hold wand with under grip (palms up) with arms crossed in front of the body. Bend the elbows so that the wand can go over and behind the head. Attempt to pass the wand down the length of the body from the back of the shoulders to the heels. Do not release grip on wand.

FACE TO
KNEE TOUCH

CENTIPEDE
(Couple or Group
Stunt)

With the hands on hips, balance on one foot with the other leg extended backward. Bend the trunk forward and touch the knee of the leg that is supporting the body with the forehead. Watch for taking hands off hips, losing balance, or not returning to original position.

BALANCE
JUMP

With the hands and arms out to the front and the body parallel to the ground, one leg is extended behind and the weight is balanced on the other leg. Quickly change balance to the other foot, resuming the initial position with the feet exchanged. Be sure that the body is maintained parallel to the ground.

TOE TOUCHER
(Partner Stunt)

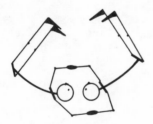

Partners lie on back with heads touching and feet in opposite directions. Partners grasp each other's hands and bring up legs (both partners) so that the toes touch.

WHEELBARROW (Couple Stunt)

One partner gets down on his hands with his feet extended to the rear. The other partner grasps his legs halfway between the ankles and the knees. The wheelbarrow walks forward on his hands supported by the pusher.

Children have a tendency to grasp the feet too low. Also, the pusher must not push too fast.

The under person should be the stronger and larger individual. He gets down on his hands and knees. The top person faces the same direction, placing his hands about 2 feet in front of those of the under person. Now he places his legs and body on top of the under person. The feet are on top and not hooked under. The centipede walks with the top person using hands alone, and the bottom player using both hands and feet. While walking, the support child does not use his knees for support on the floor.

Variation: More than two can do this stunt. After getting in position, the players should keep step by calling right and left out loud.

PARTNER
SUPPORT STUNTS

1. Double Bear

Bottom man is down on his hands and knees. Top man assumes the same position directly above with hands on shoulders and knees on the hips of the bottom man.

2. Table

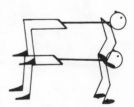

Base is in crab position. Top man assumes the same position directly above him. Hands are on the shoulders with fingers pointing backwards and the feet are on top of the knees of the bottom performer.

229

3. The Lighthouse

Support is down on hands and knees. Top man completes the figure by standing on the shoulders of the support facing the same direction. He stands erect with hands out to the sides.

4. Hip-Shoulder Stand

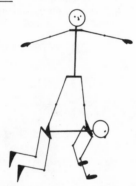

Support is on hands and knees. Top man faces to the side and stands on the support with one foot on the hips and the other on the shoulders. Care must be taken not to step on the small of the back.

Variation: Have the support turn around in a small circle with the partner keeping his standing balance.

5. Movement Exploration

There are many different ways that children can support each other. It is suggested that a portion of the time be given to having the children devise different ways of supporting a partner.

Fifth Grade Program

The fifth grade teacher should review all stunts from the previous grade. The repetition is valuable because many of the fifth grade activities have their basis in the simpler stunts on the fourth grade.

The children at this stage should be quite skillful in doing both the forward and backward rolls. Additional routines are added. The shoulder roll, cartwheel, and Eskimo roll continue the mat type activities. Improvement in the head stand should be expected. The following stunts make up the suggested fifth grade program:

Forward and Backward Roll
    Combinations
Head Stand Variations
The Cartwheel
Turn-Over
Wand Stunts
    Wand Whirl
    Twist Under
    Jump Stick
    Wand Juggle
Shoulder Roll
Fish Hawk Dive
Sit-up (Modified)
Skier's Sit
Crazy Walk
Seal Slap
Rocking Horse
Heel Click - Side
Scooter
Double Scooter (Partner stunt)
Circular Rope Skip
Stiff Man Bend
Walk Through
Jump Through
Eskimo Roll (Double Roll)
Sitting Balance (Couple Stunt)
Tandem Bicycle (Couple or Group
        Stunt)

Forward and Backward Roll Combinations. Combinations from the fourth grade should be reviewed. The following routines can be added:

1. Alternating forward and backward rolls. Begin the combination with a forward roll, coming to the standing position with the feet crossed. By pivoting the body to uncross the feet, the back is now in the line of direction for a backward roll. By coming to a crossed feet position from the backward roll, another pivot can be made continuing the series.

2. <u>Back Extension</u>. Carry the backward roll to the point where the feet are above the head and slightly over. Push off with the hands vigorously and shoot the feet into the air, landing on the feet.

<u>Head Stand Variations</u>. The head stand should be reviewed. See if the children can clap the hands during the head stand. The weight needs to be shifted momentarily to the head and back to the hands after the clap.

Use different leg positions for the head stand. Legs can be split, forward and back, knees bent, etc.

CARTWHEEL

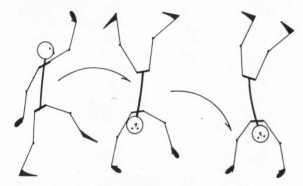

Begin with the legs and arms spread, with the left side toward the direction of wheeling. For a preliminary movement (wind-up), swing the left arm up and keep the right arm at the side. Now throw the weight smoothly to the left side, bringing the right arm up and the left arm down so that the hand takes a position about 2 feet from the left leg. The right arm now comes down to the mat, and the right leg follows upward.

Just before the right hand touches the floor, there is a push off with the left foot to give momentum to the roll. Swing both legs up and over the head. The right foot touches first, followed by the left. As the left foot approaches, a good push is given with the right hand to return the individual to standing position. It is important to keep the head up throughout the stunt.

The entire body in the stunt must be in the same plane, and feet need to pass directly overhead.

A spotter may assist in this stunt by standing behind the performer and grasping the performer's waist. He assists by giving a lift and a spin at the waist.

TURN-OVER

From a front leaning rest (push-up) position, the object is to turn completely around using only the arms and hands as the movement forces. The remainder of the body is kept straight. The feet, particularly, must be stiffened.

Lift one hand, depending upon the way the turn is made, and at the same time turn the body so the back is to the floor. The lifted hand returns quickly to the floor for support. The weight is now on the hands and heels. Continue with the other hand and complete the turn. Return by reversing the direction and making a complete turn back the other way.

Variation: Make a jump flip-flop by propelling the body into the air and reversing the body position as in the Turn-Over. Flip back.

WAND OR STICK STUNTS

1. <u>Wand Whirl</u>. Stand wand upright in front of you. Turn around quickly and grasp wand before it falls. Do it right and left. Try making two full turns and catch the wand.
2. <u>Twist Under</u>. Grasp upright standing wand with right hand. Twist around under the right arm without letting go of wand, taking it off the floor, or touching knee to floor. Repeat using left arm.
3. <u>Jump Stick</u>. Holding the wand in front with both hands, jump over the wand. Jump back. The wand passes under the body during the jumps. Hold the wand with the tips of the fingers. A rope or towel may be substituted for children having difficulty.
4. <u>Wand Juggle</u>. Balance wand with one hand or on one finger, keeping it upright. Walk forward and back. Sit down, lie down, or move into other positions keeping the wand balanced.

SHOULDER ROLL

The shoulder roll is a basic safety device to prevent injury from falling. By rolling and "taking the fall", the chances of injury are lessened.

For a shoulder roll to the left, the child should stand with his feet well apart, and the left arm extended at shoulder height. Start by throwing the left shoulder toward the mat in a rolling motion. With the left forearm and elbow touching the mat, the roll is made on the shoulder and upper part of the back. The finish is up on the knee and then back to the standing position.

The children probably have a preferred side on which to roll. However, both right and left rolls should be practiced.

FISH HAWK DIVE

Place a folded paper on the floor with the edge up so that it can be picked up with the teeth. Kneel on one leg with the other leg extended behind you and the arms out for balance. Lean forward and pick up the paper with the teeth and return to position without losing balance.

The stunt is easier if the paper is put on a book or pile of books for learning purposes. Try the stunt kneeling on the other leg.

SIT-UP (Modified)

This sit-up position differs from the straight leg sit-up in that the feet are apart and flat on the floor. The knees are bent at approximately a right angle. By bringing the knees up, the sit-up movement is done primarily by the abdominal muscles. Otherwise, as with the long leg position, there is considerable aid of the upper leg muscles (psoas group). The stunt can be done two ways.

1. With the arms folded in front of the chest.
2. The hands, with fingers interlaced, are grasped behind the lower part of the head. The left elbow touches the right knee on the first sit-up and the right elbow to the left knee on the next.

Boys should do from 10 to 15 while the girls should do 8 to 10. Gradually increase the number during the year. Done properly and regularly, this exercise has good values in the maintenance of proper posture.

SKIER'S SIT

The skier's sit is an isometric type of activity which is excellent for developing the thigh extensor muscles. The child assumes a sitting position against a wall so that his thighs are level to the floor and there is a right angle at the knee joint. His body position is the same as if he were sitting in a chair, but, of course, there is no chair. The arms are folded across the chest. The feet should be flat on the floor and the legs straight up and down. Children should try to sit for 30 seconds, 45 seconds, and one minute. This exercise is done by skiers to develop support muscles used in skiing.

CRAZY WALK

The child makes progress forward in an erect position by bringing one foot behind <u>and</u> around the other to gain a little ground each time. Set up a specified distance and see which children can cover this with the least number of steps.

SEAL SLAP

Review the Seal Walk and the Walrus Walk from previous grades. From the same position (front leaning rest), push the body up in the air by quick force of the arms, clap the hands together and recover to position.

Variation: Try clapping the hands more than once.

ROCKING HORSE

The child is face down on a mat with the arms extended overhead, palms down. With the back arched, rock back and forth. Some children may need to have someone start them rocking.

Variation: The stunt can be done by reaching back and grasping the insteps with the hands.

HEEL CLICK (Side)

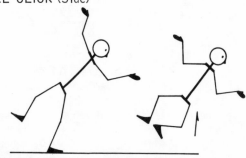

Balance on one foot with the other out to the side. Hop on the supporting foot, click heels, and return to balance. Try with the other foot.

Variation:

1. The stunt can also be done moving. Take a short lead step with the right foot. Follow with a cross step with the left and then a hop on the left foot. During the hop, click the heels together. To hop on the right foot, reverse the above directions.
2. See how high the children can jump into the air before clicking heels.

SCOOTER

This is an excellent abdominal developmental exercise. The child sits on the floor with his feet extended in front of him. His body is erect and the arms are held high, about the level of the chin. To scoot, the child must lift his seat and move it forward toward his heels. He then extends his legs again.

DOUBLE SCOOTER
(Partner Stunt)

This stunt should be done by two children of about the same size. The children sit facing each other, sitting on the other's feet. With arms joined, they scoot forward or backward by cooperating. When one child moves his seat, the other child should lift with his feet.

CIRCULAR ROPE SKIP

Crouch down in a three-quarter knee bend, holding a folded skipping rope in one hand. Swing the rope under the feet in circular fashion, jumping it each time. Reverse the direction of the rope. Work from both right and left sides with either a counterclockwise or clockwise turn of the rope.

STIFF MAN BEND

Place a small piece of folded paper 6 inches behind the left heel. With the lower legs completely extended, grasp the right toe with the right hand. Pick up the paper with the left hand without releasing the hold of the right hand or bending the knees. For a more challenging exercise, increase the distance of paper behind the heel.

WALK THROUGH

From a front leaning rest position, walk the feet through the hands using tiny steps until the body is fully extended with the back to the floor. Reverse the body to original position.

JUMP THROUGH

This is related to the previous stunt except instead of walking through, jump the feet through with one motion. Reverse with a jump and return to original position. The hands must push sharply off the floor so that the body is high enough from the floor to allow the legs to jump under.

ESKIMO ROLL
(Double Roll)

This is one of the older stunts and a favorite of many youngsters. The stunt is done with two children who are designated as #1 and #2. #1 lies on the mat with feet in the direction of the roll. #2 takes a position with his feet on either side of #1's head. #1 reaches back and grasps #2's ankles with the thumbs on the inside. #1 raises his feet so #2 can similarly grasp his ankles.

#2 propels his hunched body forward, while #1 sits up and takes the position originally held by #2. Positions are now reversed. The roll continues. Be sure that the top man hunches well and ducks his head to cushion the roll on the back of the neck and shoulders. Also, when the top man propels himself forward, his bent arms should momentarily take his weight. It is important that the underneath performer keep his knees in a bent knee position.

Variation: Try rolling backward after reaching the end of the mat. To begin a reverse roll, the top man sits backward and pulls vigorously on the legs of the bottom man.

SITTING BALANCE
(Couple Stunt)

The under or support person lies on his back with arms out to the side for support. He keeps his feet in a position as if pushing up the ceiling. He bends his knees and the partner sits on the soles. Partner is balanced in sitting position with arms out for balance and feet extended forward with toes pointed.

Be sure a spotter is stationed behind the pair so the top man does not go over backwards.

Variation: Top man instead of sitting, lie back level to the floor.

TANDEM BICYCLE

Like a tandem bicycle, the stunt can be done with 2 or more players. A bicycle is formed by the first player bending his knees. The second child backs up and sits down lightly on the knees. Other children may be added in the same fashion. The hands are on the hips of the person immediately in front for support. Forward progress is made by moving the feet on the same side together.

Sixth Grade Program

Continued practice on the roll stunts, the cartwheel, head stand, and other stunts which take time to perfect should be held. The sixth grade program adds the dive forward roll, hand stand, and forearm stand to the tumbling stunts. As suggested in the other programs, the stunts from the previous grade should be reviewed and mastered, providing a good basis for the stunts of the coming grade. In the case of certain stunts, the teacher should review the lead-up activities if they can make contributions to the stunt to be learned.

Recommended stunts for the sixth grade are:

The Pretzel
Front Seat Support
Elbow Balance
Long Reach
High Dive
The Bouncer
Knee Jump to Standing
Wrestler's Bridge
Toe Jump
V-Up

Dive Forward Roll
Hand Stand
Forearm Head Stand
Forearm Stand
Knee Walk
Jack Knife
Heel and Toe Spring
Three Man Roll (Stunt for 3)
Partner Support Stunts
    Knee and Shoulder Balance
    Press
    The Angel
    Side Stand

THE PRETZEL

    The child lies face down. The object is to touch the back of the head with the toes by raising the head and trunk and bringing the feet to the back of the head. Try one foot at a time and then both feet.

FRONT SEAT SUPPORT

    Sit on the floor with the legs straight out in front. The hands are placed flat on the floor halfway between the hips and the knees. Support the entire weight of the body on the hands, holding for three or five seconds.

ELBOW BALANCE

    The object of this stunt is to balance the body face down horizontally on the two hands with the elbows supporting the body in the hip area. To get into position, support the arched body with the toes and forehead. Work the forearms underneath body for support with the fingers spread and pointed to the back. Try to support the body completely on the hands for 3 seconds, with the elbows providing the leverage under the body.

LONG REACH

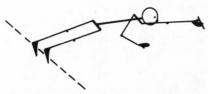

    With a piece of chalk and keeping the toes behind a line, reach out as far as you can, supporting the weight on one hand and the feet. Make a mark with the chalk and recover without touching the supporting hand a second time. The supporting hand should go out only as far as the child can recover in one movement.

Variation: Since the distance the child can reach is dependent upon his height, measure how far the child can reach beyond his height. Let the child lie on the floor and make a mark at his heels and at the top of his head. Now see how far he can reach beyond the mark made at his head and still keep his feet behind the heel line.

HIGH DIVE

    Fold a piece of paper that can be picked up by the teeth. Using the arms for balance and standing on one foot only, try to pick up the paper with the teeth. If this seems too difficult, shorten the distance to the paper by elevating it on a box or book.

THE BOUNCER

    Student is in push-up position. Bounce up and down with both the hands and the feet leaving the ground at the same time. Try clapping while doing this. Move in various directions.

KNEE JUMP TO STANDING

The starting position is kneeling with heels and seat touching and toes pointing backward (shoe laces against the floor). Jump to a standing position with a vigorous upward swing of the arms.

Variation: Jump to a standing, <u>at the same time</u> face the opposite direction by a half turn in the air. This is a jump and turn in the air in one quick motion.

WRESTLER'S BRIDGE

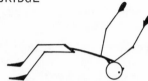

Lie on the mat bringing up the feet so that they are flat on the mat. Push up with the body and arch the neck so that the support is on the feet and head.

Variation:

1. Do a head stand and fall forward to a wrestler's bridge. During the fall, the knees are bent for landing on the soles of the feet. After falling into the bridge position, the hands can be removed from the support.
2. Do an easy front roll and land in a wrestler's bridge position. The knees are kept straight in a "piked" position. When the feet are overhead, whip them down by bending the knees, landing in the bridge position, supporting the body with the hands, head, and feet. The support of the hands can be then released.
3. Do a turn under and back by reversing the body position and still keeping the hands away from the floor.

TOE JUMP

Hold the left toe with the right hand. Jump the right foot through without losing the grip on the toe. Jump back again. Try with the other foot.

V-UP

The child is on his back with the arms overhead and extended. Keeping the knees straight and the feet pointed, the legs and upper body are brought up at the same time to form a "V". The entire weight is balanced on the seat and should be held for 5 counts.

This exercise, like the sit-up, is excellent for the development of the abdominal muscles.

DIVE FORWARD ROLL

The stunt is similar to the regular forward roll except that the roll is preceded by a run and short dive. The child should take a short run and take off with both feet so that he is partially turning already in the air as his hands come down to cushion the fall. The head should be tucked under and the roll is made on the back of the neck and shoulders.

The teacher should avoid contests to see how far a student can dive. The stunt described is actually only an elongated forward roll during which the player is off the ground for a short period of time.

Diving over objects or other students is dangerous and has no place in the <u>regular</u> class situation.

HAND STAND

Place hands on mat, shoulder width apart, fingers spread, slightly cupped and pointed straight ahead. Keeping one leg straight, walk up close with the other leg to elevate the hips. The arms are straight and the shoulders well forward of the hands. Kick up with the straight leg and push off with the bent leg. With the back arched, the shoulders are brought back to a point directly over the hands.

Spotters should be stationed on either side of the performer. The back should be arched and the head up. The feet are together and the toes pointed toward the ceiling. It is important that the spotter on each side have a firm grip beneath the shoulders of the performer. The other hand of each spotter can assist the lift by upward pressure on the thigh.

Variation: Do a hand stand to a partner standing in front of you to catch your feet. Another variation is to do a hand stand against a wall. In either case, the hands should be placed about one foot from the partner or wall. It is better to be too close than too far. By keeping the back properly arched during the stand, better balance is possible. The eyes should look forward which helps to retain the proper arch.

FOREARM HEAD STAND

The stunt is similar to a head stand except for the way the supporting base is formed. Take a kneeling position, with both elbows on the mat and the forepart of the head in the cupped hands. From this position, support the body in an inverted upright position. Spotters are needed on either side of the performer.

FOREARM STAND

Place the forearms down on the mat with the palms down and the elbows out, forming a triangle base. Do an elbow stand so that the forearms and hands support the weight of the inverted body.

KNEE WALK

Kneel at the end of the mat. Reach back and hold both feet up from the floor. Walk the mat on the knees. Walk forward, backward and sideward. Turn around at the center and continue.

JACK KNIFE

Stand erect with the hands out level to the front and a little to the side. Jump up and bring the feet up to touch the hands quickly. Vary by starting with a short run. Be sure that the feet come up to the hands and not the hands moving down to touch the feet. Do several in succession.

HEEL AND TOE SPRING

The heels are against a line. The object of the stunt is to jump backwards over the line while bent over and grasping the toes. Lean forward slightly to allow for impetus and then jump backward over the line. Try jumping back again. To be successful, the grasp on the toes must not be loosened.

To get started, the teacher could have the children hold to the ankles and make the jumps. This is more easily done than while holding to the toes.

THREE MAN ROLL

Practice and review the side roll (grade 4). Three children get down on their hands and knees on a mat with heads all in the same direction to one of the sides. The rollers are about 4 feet apart.

The performers are numbered 1, 2, and 3, with the #1 child in the center. The action always starts with the center child. #2 is on the right and #3 on the left. #1 starts rolling toward and under #2 who projects himself upward and over the player underneath him. #2 is now in the center and rolls toward #3 who projects himself upward and over #2. #3, in the center, rolls toward and under #1 who after clearing #3 is now back in the center. Thus, each player in the center, rolls toward and under the outside person. The children should be taught that just as soon as they roll to the outside, they must get ready immediately to go over the oncoming child from the center. There is little time for delay.

PARTNER SUPPORT STUNTS

1. Knee and Shoulder Balance

The support partner is on his back with the knees well up and the feet flat on the floor. He puts his hands out ready to support the shoulders of the top man. The top man takes a position in front of the knees and places his hands on the knees. He leans forward so his shoulders are supported by the hands of the bottom player and kicks up to a hand and shoulder stand.

Spotters are needed on either side of the pair. If the top man begins to fall, the support should maintain the support under the shoulders so the top player lights on his feet.

Key points for the top performer are to keep the arms straight, and the head up so he can look directly into the eyes of the support man.

2. Press

Bottom man lies on back with bent knees. Top man takes a straddle position over the bottom. Both performers now join hands with each other. The joined hands are then pressed into either side of the top man's hip while the top man lays his calves across the bottom man's knees. Hold for a specified time. Both elbows are straight for both performers.

3. The Angel

The Angel is formed by the top man standing erect on support's knees with his arms level out to the side. The bottom man takes hold of the top's waist and leans back to place the figure in balance. Hold for 5 seconds.

4. Side Stand

Support gets down on hands and knees to form a rigid base. Top performer stands to the side, hooks his hands, palms up, underneath the chest. He leans across, steadying with his hands, kicking up to an inverted stand. Spotters are needed on the far side.

Pyramids

Pyramids are pleasurable activities for children and provide a use for many of the skills and abilities learned in the stunts and tumbling program. The emphasis in this section is on smaller pyramid groups. A larger pyramid can be formed by utilizing three of the smaller groups. Generally, a pyramid is composed of a center group and two side groups, usually similar to give balance and symmetry to the entire figure. Pyramids provide good opportunity for movement exploration as the variety of figures that can be made are endless. While the figures presented are composed of three performers, four and five performers can be combined together into similar formations.

Should the teacher wish to use pyramids for demonstration purposes, whistle signals or spoken commands can use the following pattern. Children should be at attention along a line or at the edge of the mats (if used).

Signal 1. All base performers get in position and top performers move to place.

Signal 2. All top and balance performers mount and get into position.

Signal 3. Hands are out to the sides or up for the finishing touch. This signal is used to show the pyramid in all of its "glory."

Signal 4. Pyramid is disassembled and children move to line and stand at attention.

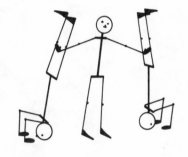

Children should not do pyramids unless the appropriate basic balance skills have been mastered. Stunts using only one performer or pairs should also be considered in pyramid building.

Selected Pyramids

Pyramid #1 is the basic pyramid and may be made as large as the capacity of the children will permit. Utilizing the basic pyramid, a larger arrangement can be made by flanking it symmetrically with any of the other pyramid groups. Whole classes may be involved in this manner.

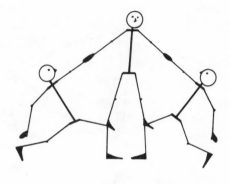

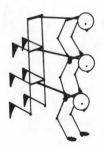

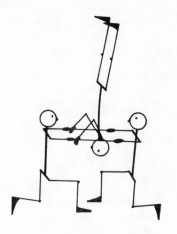

Horizontal Ladder Stunts for the Intermediate Grades

The intermediate grade stunts should be built upon the basis of the beginning stunts outlined in the primary program in Chapter 12. The teacher should review the stunts and the suggestions for the conduct of the ladder activity. Additional stunts with a greater degree of difficulty are listed.

Special Note: In any of the stunts involving an inverted position, assistance may be given by the spotter placing one hand at the back of the thigh and the other in the middle of the back. Help is given by lifting in this position.

1. Corkscrew Hang. Hang with one hand to a rung. Twist the body as far one way as it will go, and then twist it back the other way like a corkscrew.
2. Chin. Using the palms away grip, raise the chin above a rung.
3. Hip Pull-Over. With the hands on the rails and the body facing out, bring the feet up over the top of the ladder. Return to position.
4. Travels. Move forward using every other rung. Try using every third rung.
5. Jumping on the Side Rails. With the hands on the side rails, make progress forward by moving both hands at once. Also, move backwards.
6. Hand Jumping. Jump both hands at once from one rung to the next. Body swing is important.

7. Flexed Arm Hang. Using the palms away grip and the hands at shoulder width, hang without movement with the chin even with the hands. Hang for 30 seconds. Use any part of the ladder.

8. Jump and Chin. Begin on the first rung and raise the chin over the rung. Jump to the next rung with both hands at once and again chin. Repeat down the ladder.

9. Monkey Crawl. Travel underneath the bar with the hands and feet. Move forward and backward.

10. Bean Bag Carries. Using movement exploration, have a child carry a bean bag anyway he wishes as he moves along the ladder. Also, transfer the bean bag from one player to the other while each approaches from opposite sides of the ladder.

Rope Climbing

Rope climbing has high developmental possibilities of the upper trunk and arms, together with good training in coordination of the different parts of the body. Ropes are relatively inexpensive when compared to other pieces of apparatus and last indefinitely. In considering a program of rope climbing skills the following points should be considered.

1. Mats should be under all ropes.
2. The hand-over-hand method should be used for climbing and the hand-under-method for descending.
3. Children should be cautioned not to slide or there may be rope burns on the hands and skinned places on the legs.
4. If a climber becomes tired, he should stop and rest. Proper resting stops should be taught with the climbing.
5. Always leave enough margin to descend safely. No child should go higher than his strength will allow.
6. Spotters should be used where the body is inverted in stunts. Spotters may hold the rope steady while the child climbs.
7. Resin in powdered form and magnesium chalk are aids to better gripping. These should be used particularly when the rope becomes slippery after use.

While climbing the rope is the ultimate goal of the program, the children should realize that there are basic skills in hanging and resting which need to be mastered before the actual climbing can be done.

Simple hanging activities are in Chapter 12 of the primary program and should be reviewed.

In climbing, the crossed foot or scissors grip is the basic technique. Instruction should begin with this skill. The following activities or skills make up a program for rope climbing for the intermediate grades.

Rope Climbing Skills and Activities

1. Scissors Grip. Approach the rope and reach as high as possible, standing with the right leg forward of the left. Raise the back leg, bend at the knee, and place the rope inside of the knee and outside the foot. Cross the forward leg over the back leg and straighten the legs out with the toes pointed down. This should give a secure hold. The teacher should check this position.

2. Leg Around Rest. Using the right leg (or left) and keeping the rope between the thighs, wrap the right leg completely around the rope. The bottom of the rope now crosses over the instep of the right foot from the outside. The left foot stands on the rope as it crosses over the instep, providing pressure to prevent slippage. To provide additional pressure, release the hands and wrap the arms around the rope, leaning from the rope at the same time.

3. Climbing Using the Scissors Grip. From the scissors grip position (#1), raise the knees up close to the chest with the rope sliding between them while supporting the body with the hand grip. Now lock the rope between the legs and climb up with the hand-over-hand method as high as the hands can reach. Bring the knees up to the chest and repeat the process until the following goals are reached:
   a. Climb half way
   b. Climb three-fourths of the way
   c. Climb to the top mark

A top mark should be established beyond which the children should not be permitted to climb.

4. Descending. There are four methods of descending the rope. The differences are only in the use of the leg locks as the hand-under-hand is used for all descents.
   a. Reverse of the Scissors Climb. From an extended position, lock the legs and lower the body with hands until the knees are against

the chest. Hold with the hands and lower the legs to a new position. This is the reverse of the scissors climb.

b. Using the Leg Around Rest. From the leg around rest, lower hand-under-hand until the knees are against the chest. Lift the top foot and let the rope slide loosely to a lower position. Again secure with the top foot. Repeat until down.

c. Stirrup Descent. The rope is on the outside of the right foot and is carried under the instep of the foot and over the toe of the left foot. Pressure from the left foot holds the position. To get into position, let the rope trail along the right leg, reach under, and hook it with the left toe. By varying the force of the left leg, the rope can slide smoothly while the descent is made with the hands.

d. Instep squeeze. The rope is squeezed together by keeping the heels together and the rope between the insteps. The hand-under-hand movement lowers the body while the rope slides between the insteps.

5. Review the basic hangs, including inverted, single lever, double lever and others. Refer to page 133 for descriptions. Add the following:

a. Flexed arm hang. Jump to a flexed arm hang so that the mouth is level with upper hand. Hang in this position for 30 seconds or more.

b. Sitting Hang. From a sitting position on the floor with the feet out straight, reach as high as possible and grasp the rope with both hands. Pull up so that the body clears the floor completely. The performer should lean back somewhat to balance the body weight when he pulls up. Hold for 5 or more seconds.

c. Chinning. Jump to a hang and then chin a number of times. Be sure the arms are fully extended each time.

6. Climbing for Time. A stop watch is needed and a definite mark on the rope. The height of the mark will depend upon the skill and capacity of the children. Each child should have three trials (not in succession, however) and take the best time. The climber should start from a standing position with hands reaching as high as the climber wishes. Climbing without the use of the feet can also be timed, but the climber must start from a sitting position. The de-

scent should not be included in the timing as too much emphasis on speed in the descent causes children to drop from too much height or promotes rope burns on the hands and other parts of the body.

7. Climbing Without the Use of the Feet. This strenuous activity should be attempted only by the more skillful. The target of height should be low enough during early sessions. Start from a sitting position.

8. Swinging and Vaulting. A Swedish vaulting box can be used or the children can take off from a bench. High jump standards and a cross bar provide a good vaulting objective for height. Vaulting for distance makes and interesting contest.

9. Organize a Tarzan Club. Put a marker at the top limit of the rope and make each child who can climb and touch the marker a member of the Tarzan Club. Form a Super Tarzan Club for those who can climb to the marker without using the feet. Climber must start from a sitting position on the floor.

If two ropes hang close enough together, a number of stunts and climbs can be performed on a pair of ropes.

1. Preliminary Hangs
   a. Straight Arm Hang
      Jump up, grasp ropes with the hands, and hang with the arms straight.
   b. Bent Arm Hang
      Jump up to a bent arm hang.
   c. Add different leg positions to the straight and bent arm hangs.
      Single and double knee lifts
      Half lever - feet are brought up parallel to the floor, toes pointed.
      Full lever - bring feet up to the face.
      Bicycle - pedal like a bicycle.
   d. Pull-Up
      Jump to an extended arm position. Raise and lower the body several times.
   e. Inverted hangs from three positions
      With the feet wrapped about the rope.
      With the feet against the inside of the rope.
      With the feet balanced and pointed inside the ropes but not touching either rope.
   f. The Reverse (Skin the Cat)
      From a bent arm position, bring the feet over the head, continuing

the body roll until the feet touch the mat. Return to starting position.
Use spotters for this stunt.

2. Swinging. Many of the hangs can be done while the ropes are swinging. However, considerable caution is needed for the inverted hangs.
3. Climbing
   a. Climb up one rope and down the other, making a transfer about half-way up.
   b. Climb up one rope about half-way, transfer to the other rope, and continue the climb to the top. Reverse the procedure on the way down.

Combative Activities

Combative activities include contests between individuals or between groups based primarily on strength. Some include maneuvers and considerations involving strategy. Basically, these are contests of strength within the limitations of the defined body positions.

Combatives have excellent possibilities in fitness because the strength demands are high. In many of the activities, all-out performance is demanded and in some is continued over a period of struggle.

Conducting Combative Activities

1. Define what constitutes a win. This would establish the limits of the struggle beyond which means losing the contest. The number of trials should be designated.
2. Equate competition. By pairing contestants of equal stature, contests become more interesting because of the uncertainty of the outcome.
3. Work out a system of rotation so that a contestant will have a variety of opponents who are evenly matched.
4. Provide an equal start for the contest. Both contestants should start from an equal, neutral position so neither secures an advantage because of initial position.
5. Safety factors should be considered. In contests between individuals this is not critical, but in group contests the safety factors must be considered.
6. Sportsmanship should be stressed. Children should be encouraged to make the utmost effort to win, but only through fair means.

7. In group contests, good supervision and a quick whistle is needed. Children should learn to freeze when the whistle is blown so that the child in need of help can be aided to a better position.

Formations for Conducting Combative Activities

Different formations for conducting combatives add interest and provide good motivation in the contests. Some of the plans feature one team against another with a system of rotation of opponents. Others stress the individual and base a change of opponents on the outcome. The following plans have proven successful in working with combative activities.

1. Winner-loser eliminations by groups of fours. Four evenly matched contestants are grouped together. In each activity they are matched by pairs with the winners competing against each other and the losers for third place. To save time, in the next contest each individual should compete against the partner with whom he just finished. Winners again compete against winners and losers against losers.
2. Groups of threes. The children are divided into groups of threes. In any three, two players compete against each other, and the third child acts as the referee. Opponents are changed and another child referees. One more change completes a round.
3. Double line by teams. Two teams of four to five on each team compete against each other. The teams are in lines facing each other. Each child pairs off with an opponent facing him. After competing against an opponent, the children in one of the teams rotate in the following manner. The child on the left moves behind his team and takes a new position on the right side of his team's line. All other members of his team move down one place to the left to face a new opponent. The members of the other team maintain their positions.
4. Double circle by teams. One team forms a large circle with the members facing the center of the circle. The members of the other team pair off against this team on the inside, in effect forming another circle. After each bout, the contestants move to the next opponent on the left. One of the circles can remain stationary with

the other moving to the left to find new partners.

Individual Combative Activities

In each activity it is important to establish the starting or initial position, and then describe the action of the contest. A number of variations for different contests are presented. The activities are allocated to grade levels beginning with the fourth grade. The first activity presented is the age-old Hand Wrestle.

Fourth Grade

1. HAND WRESTLE

Starting Position: Contestants place right foot against right foot and grasp right hands in a handshake grip. The left foot is firmly implanted to the rear for support.

Action: Each contestant tries to upset the other by hand and arm pressure to make him move his back (left) foot.

Variation:
1. Stand left foot against left foot and contest with the left hands.
2. Lift the back foot from the floor. A player loses if the front foot is moved or the back foot touches.

2. TUG-OF-WAR (Individual)

The basic piece of equipment needed for the individual tug-of-war contests is a rope 5 feet in length including a loop on each end. To make the rope, cut a piece of rope 9 or 10 feet in length. Heavy sash cord is good. Use two pieces of garden hose each about 15 inches in length to line the loops. Thread the rope through the piece of hose and then tie the loop securely. The hose provides a reasonably good hand hold.

Starting Position: Two opponents face each other across a line.

Action: The first child to pull the other across the line wins.

Variation: Use various ways of pulling.
1. Right hand only, left hand only, both hands.
2. Grasp with the right hand with the body supported by the left hand and the feet. Change hands.
3. Pull with back to each other, with the rope between the legs.

Teaching Suggestion: If the distance to be pulled (over the line) seems to be not far enough, two parallel lines can be drawn from 5 to 10 feet apart. The contestants begin between the lines and attempt to pull the opponent out of the area between the lines.

3. TOUCH KNEES

Starting position: On feet facing each other.

Action: The object is to touch one of the opponent's knees without having your knees touched in turn. Allow 5 touches to determine victory.

Variation: See who can step on the other's toes first.

4. ROOSTER FIGHT

Starting Position: Players stoop over and clasp hands behind the knees.

Action: The object is to upset the other player or make him lose his hand hold.

Variation:
1. Squat down and hold the heels with the hands. Player loses if he is upset or his hands come loose from his heels.

5. ROOSTER FIGHT (Group Contest)

Starting Position: Rooster position as described in the previous contest. The children can be divided into two or more teams or the group can be on an individual basis to see which child can be the last one left.

Action: Place children around the edges of an area sufficient to contain the group. On signal, the children come forward and compete team against team or as individuals.

Fifth Grade

1. TUG-OF-WAR (Individual)

Repeat the tug-of-war stunts from the Fourth Grade. Add the following.

a. Opponents are face down on all fours with the feet toward each other. Hook the loops around one ankle of each opponent. The pull is made with both hands and the foot that is on the floor for each contestant.

b. Opponents in crab position. The rope is pulled by hooking a toe through the loop.

2. BREAKDOWN

Starting Position: Both opponents

are in front leaning rest position facing each other. This is the push-up position.

Action: The object is to break down the other's position with the use of a hand by pushing or dislodging the support, and still maintain your own position.

3. ELBOW WRESTLE

Starting Position: Lying on the floor or sitting at a table facing each other. Right hands are clasped with elbows held against each other.

Action: The object is to force the other's arm down while keeping elbows together.

Variation:

1. Change to a position using left arms.

4. INDIAN WRESTLE (Leg Wrestle)

Starting Position: Two opponents lie on their backs on the floor or mat with heads in opposite directions, trunks close, and near arms locked at the elbows.

Action: Three counts are given. On each count each player lifts the leg nearest the opponent to a vertical position. On the third count, he hooks his opponent's leg near the foot with his heel and attempts to roll him over backward.

Variation:

1. Use right and left legs in turn.

5. CATCH AND PULL TUG-OF-WAR
(Group Contest)

Starting Position: Two teams face each other across a line.

Action: The object is to pull any opponent across the line. When an opponent is pulled across the line, he waits back of the opponent's team until time is called. The team capturing the most players wins.

Variation:

1. Have those pulled across the line join the other team. This keeps the children in the game but sometimes makes the players careless.

Teaching Suggestions: Pulling by catching hold of clothing or hair is not permitted. Penalty is disqualification. Players may cross the line only if they are securely held by a teammate or chain of players.

Sixth Grade

1. INDIVIDUAL TUG-OF-WAR

Review and use the individual tug-of-war contests from the Fourth and Fifth Grade. Add the following.

a. Peg Pick-up. Instead of having opponents pull each other across a line, put a peg (Indian club) behind each opponent at a suitable distance. Each one then tries to pull the other toward his own peg so he can pick it up.

b. Four Corner Peg Pick-up. Tie two individual ropes together at the center of each so that four loops are now available for pulling. Put four pegs in the form of a square and let four children contest to see who can pick up his peg.

c. Doubles. Have two children pull against two. The loops should be big enough so that both can secure hand holds on them. Use right hands only, left hands only, etc.

d. Japanese Tug-of-War. Two children take hold of a rope, each with both hands on a loop. The children are positioned close enough together so that there is some slack in the rope. A third party grasps the rope to make a 6 inch bend at the center. The contestants pull the rope so that there is no slack. On the signal "go" the third party drops the loop and the opponents try to pull the other off balance. To move a foot is to lose.

Teaching Suggestion: The individual tug-of-war rope offers good possibilities in movement exploration. Let the children try to devise other ways than those mentioned by which they can pull against each other.

2. SHOULDER SHOVE

Starting Position: On one foot with the other foot held by the opposite hand.

Action: Each contestant tries to knock or bump the other off balance so that he will let go of the leg.

Variation:

1. Have each child stand on one foot and fold arms. The aim is to knock the the other person off balance so the uplifted foot will touch the ground.

2. Using a 6 or 8 foot circle, see which player can force the other out of the circle.

3. Use the kangaroo theme where each contestant must carry a volleyball between his legs at the knees. The object is to get him to lose control of the ball.

3. SHOULDER SHOVE (Group Contest)

Starting Position: Children may compete by teams or as individuals in a group contest. Have each take a position at the edges of the defined area.

Action: Any player losing his hand hold or touching the uplifted foot is eliminated. The team or individual lasting the longest wins.

Teaching Suggestions: Children may bump others from the front or side but not from the back on penalty of elimination.

Variation:

1. King of the Circle. Draw a circle large enough to accommodate the group. Using the shoulder shove position, the children try to shove each other out of the circle or make others lose their shoulder shove positions. A quick whistle is needed to stop the action in case any player is down on the ground. The fallen players should be removed before the game is continued. No player may contact another from behind.

4. KING OF THE MAT

Starting Position: All players are on hands and knees on the edge of a large mat.

Action: Each player is trying to make another player touch any part of his body to the floor outside the mat.

Cautions: The activity can become rough and needs good supervision. Watch for unfair tactics. Players should keep on hands and knees.

Variation:

1. The children can be divided into teams and compete team against team.

Teaching Suggestion: The game works best if the mat is a single one and not a combination of two or more mats. Smaller mats grouped together must be kept together if they are to be of use.

5. STICK WRESTLE

Starting Position: Two players face

each other grasping a broom stick between them. Be sure the grips are fair with each child having an outside hand.

Action: By twisting and applying pressure on the stick, either player tries to get the other to relinquish his grip.

Variation:

1. Basketball Wrestle. Use a basketball instead of a stick. Be sure each has the same grip advantage at the start.
2. Have both players squat down while holding onto the stick. The object is to take away the stick or upset the opponent.

6. CHINESE PULL-UP

Starting Position: Opponents sit on the floor facing each other with knees straight and the soles of the feet against the opponent's soles. Each bends forward until he can grasp a broom stick between them.

Action: By a straight pull only, the object is to pull the other player forward or make him release his grip on the stick.

7. BULLDOG OR NECK PULL

Starting Position: Opponents are on hands and knees facing each other. Two towels are knotted together to make a circular loop around the back of both necks.

Action: The object is to pull the other player across a line by backing with a neck pull. Player loses if he is pulled across a line between the contestants or if he loses the neck halter.

8. ROPE TUG-OF-WAR

Starting Position: Two equal teams face each other on opposite ends of a rope. A piece of tape marks the center of the rope. Two parallel lines are drawn about 10 feet apart. At the start, the center marker is midway between the lines.

Action: Each team tries to pull the center marker over its near line.

Teaching Suggestions: The rope should be long enough to accommodate the children without crowding. It should be at least three-quarters of an inch in diameter or larger. Never permit a child to wrap the rope around his hands, arms, or body in any manner.

Balance Beam Activities

1. Walk forward and backward to middle of beam, kneel on one knee (right or left), straighten leg forward until heel is on the beam and knee is straight. Rise and walk to end of beam.

2. Hop forward and backward on right or left foot, the full length of beam. Variations: Hop length of beam, then turn around and hop back. Hop to middle of beam, turn around on same foot and hop backward to end of beam.

3. Walk to middle of beam, balance on one foot, turn around on this foot and walk backward to end of beam.

4. Walk to middle of beam left sideward, turn around and walk to end right sideward.

5. With arms clasped about body in rear, walk forward to middle, turn around once, walk backward the remaining distance.

6. Place eraser at middle of beam, walk out on it, kneel on one knee, place eraser on top of head, rise, turn around and walk backward to the end of beam.
   Variation: Kneel on one knee, pick up eraser and place it on the beam behind pupil, rise and continue to the end. Walk beam left sideward, pick up eraser, place it on right side of beam, turn around the walk right sideward to end of beam.

7. Walk the beam backward with an eraser balanced on the back of each hand. At the center, turn around and walk backward to the end of beam.

8. Ball stunts. Roll a ball on the beam. Bounce to the side as you move. Dribble on the floor. Pass back and forth to a partner beyond the end of the beam.

Toss the ball to self moving along the beam.

9. Walk to middle of beam, do a balance stand on one foot, arms held sideward with trunk and free leg held horizontally.

10. Hold wand 15 inches above beam. Balance eraser on head, walk forward, backward, sideward right or sideward left, stepping over wand.

11. Have wand held at a height of three feet. Walk forward and backward, hands on hips, and pass under it.

12. Fold a piece of paper at right angle so it will stand on beam at the middle. Walk to paper, kneel, right-side or left-side support pick it up with teeth, rise and walk to end of beam.

13. Walk beam forward, backward, sideward, left or right, eyes closed.

14. Stand on beam (feet side by side, one foot in advance of the other, on right or left foot) eyes closed, and record number of seconds balance is maintained.

15. Partners start at opposite ends, walk to middle, pass each other, and continue to end of beam.

16. Place hands on beam; have partner hold legs (as in the wheelbarrow), and walk to the end of the beam.
    Variation: Both on beam.

17. "Cat Walk" forward and backward on beam. Walk on "all fours", hands and feet on beam.

18. Do various balance stunts such as foot and knee balance, hand and knee balance, head and knee balance, push-up position, rear support, side support, front balance, side balance, knee dip, side leg extension, and others.

Chapter 21

Relays for the Intermediate Grades

Physical Fitness Through Relays
Practical Suggestions
Selected Relays for the Intermediate Grades

Relays have an important place in the program of physical education for intermediate grade level children. Not only do they offer fun and enjoyment, but when properly conducted provide good values in fitness, skills, and social objectives. Children can learn to cooperate with others in the interest of winning, to conform to rules and regulations, and to use skills in situations of stress and competition. However, if rules are not enforced and the child finds that he can get by without obeying the rules, he is learning that he can win by cheating.

Relays can be combined with skills teaching. After skills have been taught with sufficient practice, they can be put into relays. Skills need to be sufficiently mastered before subject to relay competition or, in the haste to win, the child forgets to perform the skills correctly. In addition, correct performance may mean too much interference with the runner's progress, so technique is sacrificed to haste.

Ingenuity and inventiveness are needed to make the most of the relays. Slight variations of the skills required or of the manner of running the relays add interest and stimulate the children to vigorous activity.

Physical Fitness Through Relays

The various components of fitness can be promoted through careful selection of the movements and distances for each relay. Little equipment is needed, and relays can be selected and varied to meet almost any situation. Relays which demand strength, balance, agility, speed, and coordination have good values for physical fitness.

Relays of this type make good use of fundamental movements, basic stunts, and miscellaneous movement patterns. Relays can employ the entire range of fundamental movements like walking, running, skipping, galloping, hopping, jumping, leaping, sliding, or any combinations thereof. Stunts which require movement like the crab walk, seal walk, puppy run, lamedog walk, rabbit jump, frog jump, and similiar moving stunts make good strength demands on the arms, legs, trunk, and shoulders.

Relays involving stopping and starting or changes of directions offer good developmental possibilities. Obstacle races, potato type relays, figure eight, leap frog, and even carrying relays have good values.

The children must travel far enough in any movement to get value for physical fitness components. This, of course, would depend upon the movement selected for the relay.

Even ball handling relays can be combined with movement to make them more demanding on the individual.

Practical Suggestions

Reference should be made to Chapter 13 for directions with regard to relays for primary children. In addition to the suggestions presented in that chapter, the following should be considered.

1. Be definite in directions. Tell them how and when to start and what is expected of each runner. Be sure the child running last knows how to finish for his team.

2. In many relays, particularly of the

revolving type, it helps to keep things straight if the last player or runner has some kind of identification. Arm bands of crepe paper, hats, pinnies, or colored shirts form good identification. This keeps the leader informed of the progress of the race and allows him to anticipate the finish. The leader can line himself with the finish line so he can make a good judgment of the winner.

3. Appoint a captain for each team. Let him arrange the order, be responsible for the application of the rules, and help keep things under control.

4. Be careful of putting too much emphasis on winning. Too much pressure makes the skilled resent being on teams with those who are less able to perform.

5. Demonstrate a relay just enough so that each team understands the procedures. This can entail a simple demonstration by one individual or having the entire team practice the routine. If the new relay does not seem to be started properly, stop the group and review the instructions.

6. Any dropped or mishandled ball must be retrieved by the person dropping it. It must be started by him in the proper sequence at the point it was dropped.

7. It is important the teams making mistakes or omissions be penalized either by deduction of points, dropping the finish place down one notch, or by disqualification.

8. Make some rules about the handling of supplies. Have a central source and appoint one person from each team to secure and return equipment.

9. A block, bean bag, Indian club, chair, standard, or other definite marker should be used for a turning point. A definite turning point is better than just having the children run to a line and back.

Selected Relays for the Intermediate Grades

Relays should be selected in keeping with the children's previous experience in stunts and skills. Relays have a universal appeal to children which makes it difficult to pinpoint different relays to various grades. However, allocation is desirable so that by following the progression of relays in this guide, the children will experience a varied and interesting group and secure good fitness values.

The relays and formations from the primary grades should be reviewed. Since many of the stunt descriptions are found in the primary program, descriptions will be reviewed only briefly, if at all, in the presentation of the various relays at levels which seem suitable. Additional relays are found in the sports units under the different sports. Good use can be made of these in the teaching of sports skills.

Fourth Grade

1. LANE OR SHUTTLE RELAYS (Simple Movements)

   a. Fundamental Movements. Running forward or backward, hopping forward and backward, jumping.

   b. Stunt Movements. Puppy Dog Run, Rabbit Jump, Crab.

   c. Simple Soccer skills, particularly dribbling.

   d. Variety Movements. Walking on heels, walking heel and toe, alternate double gallops, etc.

2. ATTENTION RELAY

   Formation: Players of each team are facing forward in lane formation about arms distance apart. The distance between teams should be about 10 feet. Two turning points should be placed for each team. One is 10 feet in front and the other 10 feet behind each team.

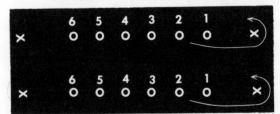

   Procedure: Players on each team are numbered from front to rear consecutively. The teacher calls "Attention." All come to the position of attention. The teacher calls out a number. The player on each team holding this number steps to the right, runs around the front and the back marker, and returns to place. The first team to have all members of the team at attention, including the returning runner, wins a point.

250

Teaching Suggestion: The numbers should not be called in order but all members should be called. Be sure there is enough distance between teams so the runners will not collide in the spaces between them.

Variations:
1. Use different means of locomotion.
2. Organize the teams by pairs and have two run at a time, holding inside hands.
3. <u>Under the Arch.</u> The leader calls two consecutive numbers, for example 3 and 4. Immediately, the numbers 3 and 4 on each team face each other and form an arch by raising both hands. The players in front of the arch (numbers 1 and 2) run forward, go around the front marker, run to the back marker and go around it, and then back to place, passing under the arch. The players behind the arch run under the arch first, run around the front marker, then around the back marker, and back to place. When all have returned to place, the arch players drop hands and resume position. The first team to be at attention is the winner.

Note that the running is always forward at the start. Each player follows the person ahead of him, keeping in place. They go around the front marker, around the back marker, and back to place. At the appropriate time while taking this path, the players pass under the arch.

3. ARCH BALL RELAY

Formation: Lane with the player at the head of each team holding a ball.
Procedure: Each head player, using both hands, hands the ball over his head to the next person and so on down the line. The end man, on receiving the ball runs to the head of the line and the race continues as he passes the ball over his head. Each player has a turn at the head of the line and when the original head returns with the ball to his place at the head of the line, the race is over.
Teaching Suggestion: Each player must handle the ball with both hands.

4. CARRY AND FETCH RELAY

Formation: Lane with a circle 20 inches in diameter 30 feet in front of each team.
Procedure: Each team has a bean bag or block of wood. The first runner carries the object to the circle, runs back, and tags off. The next runner fetches the object back and hands it to the third runner, who carries forward to the circle. The relay continues until each player has either "carried" or "fetched" the object.

5. CORNER FLY (Spry) RELAY

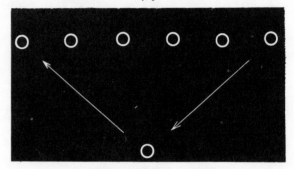

Formation: Leader and line.
Procedure: The players are in a line, facing the leader, who has a ball. He passes to and receives the ball from each player beginning with the player on <u>his</u> left, with the exception of the last player (on his right). When this player receives the ball, he calls out "Corner Fly." He runs forward and takes the leader's spot, who takes a place at the line to <u>his</u> left. In the meantime, all players adjust positions, moving over one place to fill the spot vacated by the new leader. The relay continues with each player becoming the leader in turn. When the original leader returns to his spot with the ball, the relay is over.

6. FIVE IN A ROW RELAY

Formation: Lane. A line is drawn about 20 feet in front of the teams.
Procedure: The front player of each team has five bean bags or blocks. On signal the front player hops forward and places the five objects one at a time reasonably spaced with the last

object placed over the line. He changes
hopping foot and returns hopping over
each object. The second player hops
forward over each object until he reaches
the farthest one. He changes his hopping foot and hops back, picking up the
blocks one at a time. He hands the
blocks to the third player who puts out
the blocks again. Each player in turn
either distributes or gathers the blocks.

Teaching Suggestion: The blocks
should be spaced with the last block
placed beyond the line. The last is important because it determines how far
each player will need to hop.

Fifth Grade

1. **LANE AND SHUTTLE RELAYS** (Simple
Movements)
   a. Fundamental Movements. Continue
   with various locomotor movements.
   Use various combinations. Hop sideward, jump, slide.
   b. Stunt Movements. Lame Dog, Seal,
   Crab sideward and backward, Goofy
   Walk, Toe Tug Walk, Measuring Worm.

2. **CHARIOT**

   Three people run at a time forming a chariot. The chariot is formed by two people
   standing side by side with inside hands
   joined. The "driver" stands behind and
   grasps the hands on the outside of the pair,
   forming the chariot.

3. **KANGAROO**

   First player jumps forward with a ball between his knees held there by pressure.
   He goes the distance and then gives the
   ball to the next person. A bean bag can
   be used instead of a ball.

4. **INDIAN CLUB RELAYS**

   Formation: Lane.
   Procedure: There are a number of relays that can be run using Indian clubs.
   a. All Up, All Down. Three Indian
   clubs are set in a small circle about
   20 feet in front of each team. The
   first player runs forward and puts the
   Indian clubs down. The second runner goes forward and sets the clubs

up one at a time. The clubs must
stand. The next player puts them
down, and so on.
   b. Draw a short (2 feet) line about 20
   feet in front of each team. An Indian
   club is standing on one side of the
   line. Each player must run forward
   and stand the Indian Club on the
   other side of the line, using one
   hand only.
   c. Two adjacent circles are drawn about
   20 feet in front of each team. Three
   Indian clubs are standing in one of
   the circles. Each runner in turn runs
   forward and, using one hand only,
   moves the clubs one at a time so
   they will stand in the other circle.
   The next player moves the clubs
   back one at a time to the original
   circle.
   d. Roll and Set. Each team has a mat
   and an Indian Club. The mat is
   placed lengthwise in front of the
   team, and the club is on the floor
   near the edge of the mat nearest to
   the team. The starting mark is about
   five feet from the edge of the mat.
   The first player runs toward the mat,
   picking up the club. With the club
   carried in his hand, he does a front
   roll and sets the club beyond the far
   edge. He runs back and tags off the
   next player. This player runs to the
   club, picks it up, does a front roll
   on the way back, and sets the club
   in the original spot. The players
   alternate in this fashion until all
   have run. The club must stand each
   time or the player must return and
   make it stand.

5. **OVER AND UNDER**

   Formation: Lane formation.
   Procedure: Each player at the head of
   the line has a ball. The front player
   passes the ball over his head with both
   hands to the player behind him. This
   player passes the ball between his legs
   to the next player. The ball alternates
   over and under down the line. Each back
   player runs to the front and starts the
   over and under passing. When the team
   has returned to original position, it is
   through.
   Variation: Instead of over and under,

the ball can be passed right and left down the line.

6. PASS AND SQUAT

Formation: Lane with one player about 10 feet in front of his team.

Procedure: #1 has a ball. He throws it to #2 who returns the ball to #1. #2 squats down as soon as he has returned the ball to #1 so the throw can now be made to #3. When the last person in line receives the ball he does not return it but carries it forward straddling the members of his team including #1 who has taken a place at the head of the line. The player carrying the ball forward now acts as the passer and receiver. The race is over for a team when the original #1 player receives the ball in the back position and straddles the players back to his original position.

7. RESCUE RELAY

Formation: Lane with the first runner at a line about 30 feet in front of his team.

Procedure: The runner who is in front of his team runs back to the team and takes the first player in line by the hand and "rescues" him to the thirty foot line. The player who has just been rescued runs back and gets the next player, and so on until the last player has been conducted to the line.

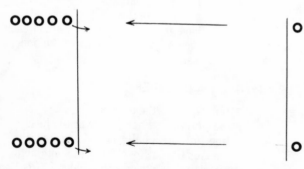

Variation: The first player who runs back to begin the rescue routine, can use either of the following carries to transport the next player. The players should be lined up in decreasing order with respect to their abilities to carry. Generally, the player in front should be the biggest or strongest, and the weights of

the others should be decreasingly lighter with the smallest being carried last.

a. Piggyback Carry (Not Recommended for Girls)

The rider jumps up on the back of the carrier who locks his arms under the knees of the rider. The rider should be as high as possible.

b. Fireman's Carry (Not Recommended for Girls)

The rider takes a wide stride position with his right arm out somewhat to the side. The "Fireman" grasps the right wrist of the rider with the left hand and, crouching down, puts his right arm through the legs of the rider until his shoulder makes contact in the lower abdominal region of the rider. The carrier turns toward the rider's leg and picks up the rider across the back of his shoulders, retaining the hold of the rider's arm with the left hand. The rider should be high on the shoulder, and the lifting movement should be with the legs primarily.

Teaching Suggestion: The carries must be practiced before putting them into relays. Also, the child doing the carrying must release his hold on the rider immediately if he should begin to fall.

8. THREE SPOT RELAY

Formation: Lane. Three parallel lines are drawn in front of the teams at distances of 10, 20, and 30 feet.

Procedure: The three parallel lines in front of the teams provide three spots for each team. Each player is given three tasks to perform, one at each spot. He then runs back and tags off the next player who repeats the performance. Suggestions for tasks are:

Prone (face down on the floor)
Back (lie on back on floor)
Obeisance (touch forehead to floor)
Nose and Toe (touch toe to nose from sitting position)
Do a specified number of hops, jumps, push-ups, sit-ups, etc.
Perform a designated stunt like the Coffee Grinder, Knee Dip, etc.
Rope Jumping with specified turns.

Teaching Suggestions: It must be made

clear that the runner must perform according to the designated directions at each spot. He must complete the performance before moving to the next spot. Many other task ideas can be used. An excellent idea is to have the winning team select the requirements for the next race.

9. BEAN BAG LEG PASS RELAY

Formation: Lane. Each member of the team is on his back, his arms out to the side and his feet and legs perpendicular to the ground. The first player has a bean bag in front of him.

Procedure: The first player picks up the bean bag between his feet and passes it back over his head to the next player who takes the bean bag with his feet, passes it back, and so on. Teams are not permitted the use of hands, as the bean bags must be handled entirely by the feet. The relay is over when the last person places the bean bag on the floor behind him. A little experimentation will determine the distance each player should be positioned from the next in order to pass the bean bag efficiently.

Sixth Grade Relays

The sixth grade program should review and utilize the relays from the previous grades. In addition, the following have value.

1. LANE RELAYS

a. Continue with running, hopping, and jumping relays. Add Sore-toe where a player holds his left foot in front of him with his right hand. At the turning point, the right foot is held with the left hand.

b. Obstacles. Put three or four obstacles in a row in front of each team with the obstacles spaced evenly. Players weave in and out of obstacles. Use with basketball and soccer dribbling techniques.

c. Continue with the various stunt races requiring the use of both hands and feet.

d. Wheelbarrow Race. One person walks on his hands while his partner holds him by the knees, wheeling him down to a mark. Change positions for the return.

e. Horse-and-Rider and Fireman's Carry. These are described under fifth grade relays. Be sure both partners are about

the same size. Have one partner carry the other to a turning point, and then reverse the positions for the return trip.

f. Sedan Carry. Three people run at one time, two to carry and one to ride. To form a seat for the carry, two children face each other. Each grasps his own left wrist with his right hand. The open hand now grasps the wrist of the partner. The person carried sits on the seat and puts his hands around the necks of the carriers.

g. Different Movements. Each runner uses a different locomotor movement when he runs.

2. AROUND THE BASES

Formation: Four bases are laid out in a baseball diamond. Two teams compete at a time, lined up at opposite bases on the inside of the diamond.

Procedure: The lead-off player for each team makes one complete circuit of the bases, followed by each player in turn.

Variation: The same type of relay can be run indoors using chairs or Indian clubs at the four corners. Further variation can be made by requiring the children to run more than one lap or circuit on a turn.

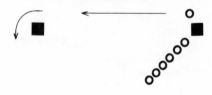

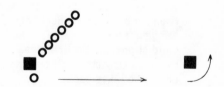

3. CIRCULAR ATTENTION

Formation: Two teams form a circle facing counterclockwise, each occupying one-half the circle. The players of each team are numbered consecutively.

Procedure: The teacher calls the group to attention. Then, a number is called. The children, one on each team, holding this number immediately run forward (counterclockwise) around the circle and back to place, standing at attention. The first to get back at attention scores a point for his team. Call numbers until all have run.

Variation: Circle Leap Frog. All players are crouched down on their knees with their foreheads supported in cupped hands on the floor. When a number is called, the runner straddles or leap frogs all the children around the circle and back to place, resuming the original position. Scoring is the same as in Circular Attention.

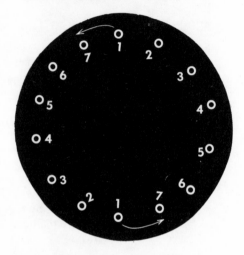

4. HIP HIKING RELAY

Formation: Shuttle Relay with the halves about 10 feet apart.

Procedure: Children take a position sitting on the floor with the legs forward, the weight of the legs on the heels, and the knees bent at about 90 degrees. The arms are crossed in front and held out at shoulder level. Progress is made by reaching out with the heels and then bringing the seat forward. The first child of one shuttle line hikes forward to the other shuttle half tagging off a child who hikes back.

Teaching Suggestions: Hip Hiking Relay has good posture values in the development of the pelvic region. However, it is a strenuous exercise and children during early stages should not hike too far.

5. JACK RABBIT RELAY (Jump Stick Relay)

Formation: Lane. Each runner carries a broom stick 3-1/2 to 4 feet long. A turning point is established about 30 feet in front of each lane.

Procedure: Each player carries the broom stick and rounds the turning point from the right side. The race starts by the first player in line running forward around the turning point and back to the head of the line. In the meantime, the next player takes a short step to the right and gets ready to help with the stick. The runner with the stick is now returning on the left side and shifts the stick to his left hand. The second player reaches out his right hand and takes the other end of the stick at the head of the line. The stick is now carried under the others who must jump up to let the stick go past. When the stick has passed under all the players, the original player releases his grip and remains at the end of the line. The second runner runs around the turning point, and the next player in line helps him with the stick and becomes the next runner when the stick has gone under all the jumpers. Each player repeats until all have run.

Teaching Suggestion: If the children are unfamiliar with the relay, some practice is needed. When the children carry the stick back under the jumpers, it should be quite close to the ground.

6. PONY EXPRESS (Carrying the Mail)

Formation: Lane with a turning point 20 feet in front of each lane.

Procedure: The smallest child of each team is the "mail." The "mail" is carried piggyback by each runner in turn around the turning point and back to the starting line. The race begins with the "mail" in horse and rider position on on the first runner. After the runner finishes his lap, the "mail" is transferred to the next runner without touching the ground. The race is over when the last runner has carried the "mail" back across the finish line.

Teaching Suggestion: The carry should be made high on the back. When the transfer of the "mail" is made, the two runners concerned should stand side by side to make the transfer.

7. POTATO TYPE RELAYS

Formation: Lane with a small box about 1 foot square placed 5 feet in front of each lane. At intervals of 5 feet beyond the box, a total of four 12 inch circles are drawn. This makes the last circle 25 feet from the starting point. Four blocks or bean bags are needed for each team. To start, the blocks for each team are placed in the box in front of it. The first runner goes to the box and takes a single block and puts it in one of the circles. He returns to the box each time and places the blocks one at a time in the circles. When the four blocks are in the circles, he tags off the second runner. This runner brings back the blocks one at a time to the box and tags off the third runner, who returns the blocks to the circles, and so on.

Variation: The race can be run using Indian clubs. Instead of using a box, draw a circle large enough to contain four Indian clubs.

Teaching Suggestions: The use of the box to receive the blocks makes a definite target for the blocks to be placed. When the blocks are returned to the circles, some regulation must be made regarding the placement. The blocks should be considered placed only if they are inside or touching a line. Blocks outside need to be replaced.

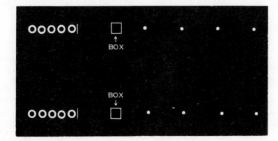

8. PRONE RELAY

Formation: Players are lying face down on the floor in a circle with their heads toward the center of the circle and hands joined.

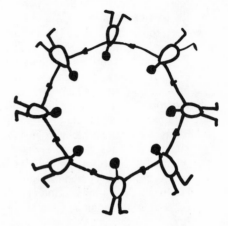

Procedure: Players on each team are numbered consecutively. When a number is called, the player with that number runs around or over the players on his team and back to place in prone lying position with hands joined. The first player back scores a point for his team. Play for a definite score or until all numbers have been called.

Variation:

1. Human Hurdle. Each team forms a small circle sitting with backs to the center of the circle. Otherwise, procedure is the same.

2. Cyclone. This is a team race and the team getting back to the original place first is the winner. At the starting signal, the #1 player gets up and starts around the group. Immediately, after #1 passes him, the second player follows. The third player follows just as soon as #1 and #2 have passed him. The remainder of the players follow in the same manner. When #1 gets back to his place, he takes his original position. Each player in turn goes around until he gets back to his original place.

   Note that the last player cannot move until all the other players have gone by him. Only then does he start his trip around the circle. When he gets back to place, the race is over. This race can be done from the original prone position or from the sitting position.

9. STRIDE BALL RELAY

Formation: Lane.

Procedure: Children stand with a wide stride forming an alley between their legs. The child at the head of each team has a ball. He bends over, rolls the ball between his legs and down the alley to the last man. The last player in line takes the ball to the head of the line, and the routine is repeated in turn by each player. The team which rotates back to original position first wins.

Variation: This relay can be combined with basketball shooting drills. The teams are lined up facing a basket. Instead of the back man merely moving to the front of his team, he dribbles to the basket before proceeding to the head of his team. Many interesting combinations of scoring can be used in this relay.

10.   TADPOLE RELAY

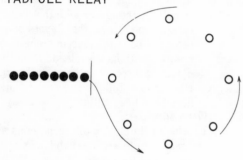

Formation: One team forms a circle facing in and has a ball. Another team is in lane formation with the head of the lane 10 feet from the circle.

Procedure: The objective of the game is see how many times the ball can make complete circuits of the circle by passing to each player while the other team completes a relay. The other team is in lane formation facing the circle and lined up behind a line 10 feet from the circle. Each player in turn runs around the outside of the circle and tags off the next runner until all have run. In the meantime the ball is being passed around the circle on the inside. Each time the ball makes a complete circuit, the circle players count the number loudly. After the relay has been completed and the count established, the teams trade places and the relay is repeated. The team making the highest number of circuits by passing is the winner. The relay gets its name because the formation resembles a tadpole.

Variation: Vary with different types of passes and different methods of locomotion by the running team.

Chapter 22

Classroom Physical Education Activities Intermediate Level

Adapting the Regular Program
Suggested Classroom Activities

There will be times when it is necessary or even desirable to have the physical education period in the classroom setting. When the playroom or gymnasium is not available, or when the playground is not usable, it becomes necessary to use the classroom for physical education. Also, there will be times during the day when a few minutes of physical activity will help children get release from tension and the press of study.

Adapting the Regular Program

Many of the normal run of activities from the gymnasium or playground can be adapted. This is the starting point for classroom physical education. Too often, the social recreation type of activity is the entire program. Some suggestions for activity types are:

Stunts and Tumbling

Stunts not requiring the use of mats can be practiced in a classroom setting. Children can take turns at the head of each row or at other available spaces in the classroom. If the chairs are movable, mats can be brought in and mat type activity carried on.

The balance beams make excellent activity for classrooms. A minimum of space is needed.

Rhythmics

The formations which could be used would depend upon the size of the room and whether or not the desks were movable. If the desks can be moved to the center of the room, circle dances can be conducted in the room around the sides.

Time can be given over to discussions of various aspects of the dance program; the introductions of music, patterns, and formations form the basis of fruitful activity.

Special Fitness Activities

Depending upon the room available, exercises provide good activity for limited areas. Selected elements of movement exploration can be pursued.

Relays

Relays make excellent activity for classroom physical education. Many can be modified to suit the classroom environment. Rows can be used as the competing units. If there is insufficient room, alternate rows can be used for competition. Leader and file types are particularly useful in the classroom. Children should remain seated if not active in a relay and keep feet out of the aisles.

Sports and Related Activities

Rules, strategy, and regulations of the sports activities can be covered during class sessions. Good visual aids illustrating techniques have value for the discussions.

Games

Many of the regular physical education games can be adapted in formation and rules for space limitations peculiar to the particular situation. Many other activities are identified as particularly for the classroom. These vary from social recreation types to reasonably active games.

This source questions a heavy emphasis and reliance on social recreation and intellectual games. The alphabet, sentence, and blackboard games have a place in the program but only a minor role. Movement is the key to physical education and the games should induce movement and/or provide an opportunity to practice skills.

Suggested Classroom Activities

ADD AND SUBTRACT

Playing Area: Classroom

Players: 2-4

Supplies: Two rubber heels or blocks of wood for each player. One is marked with a plus sign and one with a minus sign. Different colored bean bags could be used.

Lay out a nine square diagram with each square 12 inches wide. Each square is numbered 1 through 9. Each player tosses two rubber heels (or bean bags) toward the target on the floor, one at a time. He adds the score made by the plus throw and subtracts the score of the minus throw. Scores are determined where the heel rests on the target. If the heel rests on a line between two squares, the higher value is taken. Any throws falling completely outside the target area are scored minus 10.

The game adapts itself well to the classroom as a target can be drawn at the front of each aisle.

AROUND THE ROW

Formation: Row in a classroom

Players: Whatever number there is in a row

Supplies: None

The game is played by rows with an extra player for each row. The children from a row plus the extra player on the command "March" walk around the row. At a signal they stop marching and attempt to get a seat. One player is left out. The game continues to the next row using the player left out as the extra.

BALLOON VOLLEYBALL

Formation: A rope is stretched across the middle of the classroom

Players: Entire class

Supplies: Two balloons. Extras should be available.

This is an informal game with the children trying to bat the ball back and forth across the rope. Two balloons should be used at once to provide good action. Several variations are possible.

1. All children standing. Rope should be stretched just over their reach.
2. All children sitting on the floor. Rope about 3 feet from the floor.
3. Children in seats that cannot be moved. Rope should be about 5 feet high.

In each case, a system of rotation should be set up. Scoring is done when a side fails to control a balloon and allows it to touch the floor or a wall. The balloon can be batted as often as possible.

Variation: By putting a small marble or button inside the balloon, the balloon will take an erratic path, adding to the interest.

BASKETBALL BOUNCE

Formation: Individual or by team formation.

Players: 2 to 6 for each basket.

Supplies: Basketball, volleyball, or other rubber ball. Wastepaper basket.

Each player on his turn stands behind a line which is 5 to 10 feet from a wastepaper basket. Five chances are allowed to bounce the ball on the floor in such a fashion that it goes in the basket. Score 5 points for each successful "basket."

BOWLING

Formation: File by rows

Players: 2-6

Supplies: Bowling pin or pins. Balls for rolling.

Many bowling games are possible in the

classroom, using the aisles as the "alley." Various kinds of balls can be used for rolling. The target can be a single pin or group of pins.

Competition can be between individuals in a row or between rows.

CHAIR QUOITS

Formation: File

Players: 2 to 6

Supplies: Chair for each group; 5 deck tennis rungs or rope rings.

A line is established about 10 feet from a chair turned upside down so that the legs are pointed toward the thrower. Each throws the 5 rings for the following scores.

    Ringer on back legs   10 points
    Ringer on front legs   5 points

Make a score sheet and keep score for several rounds.

Variation: Fruit jar rings can be used with the chair or with other targets.

FLOOR PING PONG

Formation: Regular table tennis court marked off on the floor.

Players: 2 to 4

Supplies: Table tennis ball; a paddle for each player.

Play as in regular table tennis. Games should be short (10 points) so many children can be accommodated.

HUNTER, GUN, RABBIT

Playing Area: Classroom

Players: Entire class

Supplies: None

The children are divided into two teams which line up facing each other. They can be sitting or standing. Each team has a captain.

Each team goes into a huddle and decides on one of the following three imitations:

    Hunter--bring hands up to the eyes and pretend to be looking through binoculars.

    Gun--bring hands and arms up to a shooting position and pretend to shoot.

    Rabbit--put hands in back of head with fingers pointed up. Move back and forth like moving rabbit ears.

To score, the following priorities have been set up.

1. If one side is the hunter and the other gun, the hunter wins as the hunter shoots the gun.
2. If one team selects gun and the other imitates a rabbit, the gun wins as the gun can kill the rabbit.
3. If one side is the rabbit and the other the hunter, the rabbit wins as it can run away from the hunter.
4. If both teams have the same selection, no point is scored.

The first team scoring ten points wins.

IMITATION

Formation: Children scattered around the room. The leader is in front.

Players: Entire class.

Supplies: Record Player, records.

The game is based on the music phrase length of 8 counts. The leader performs for 8 counts with any kinds of movement he wishes. For the next 8 counts, the children imitate his movements in the same sequence. The leader sets another round of movements and the children imitate.

After a period of imitation, the leader selects another child to be in front as leader.

PUT HANDS

Formation: Students are standing or seated. They can be scattered around the room.

Players: Entire class

Supplies: None

One child is the leader and stands in front of the class. He gives certain directions verbally and tries to confuse the class by doing something else. He can say, "Put your hands on top of your head." He might put his own hands on top of his shoulders. Those who are in error have a point scored against them. Directions he can give, to which he should make other movements are:

"Put your hands on -- shoulders, toes, knees, head, chest, etc."

"Reach out to the -- side, front, back, high."
"Put your right hand (or left) on your shoulder,
   behind your back, etc."

After a short period of time, the leader should
be changed.

SNAP

Formation: Children seated in a circle.

Players: 10 - 15

Supplies: None

   This is a rhythm game involving a three-
count rhythm. The children must practice the
rhythm well before the game can be successful.
The action is as follows:

Count 1	Slap knees
Count 2	Clap hands
Count 3	Snap fingers

   Each child in the circle has a number.
The leader calls a number on the third count
(snap fingers). The player whose number was
called then calls another when he snaps his
fingers. The object of the game is to keep the
precise rhythm and keep the numbers called
back and forth across the circle.

Errors:

Breaking the rhythm.

Not calling another number after yours has been
   called.

Calling when your number has not been called.

Calling a number of a player who has been
   eliminated.

   Players are eliminated after they have
made three errors. The number of an eliminated
player is dead and cannot be called.

WHO'S LEADING

Formation: Children are in a circle formation either sitting in chairs or on the floor.
   They can be standing, but this gets fatiguing.

Players: Entire class.

Supplies: None.

   One child is "It." He steps away from the
circle and covers his eyes. The teacher points
to one child who is the "Leader." The "Leader"
starts any motion he chooses with his hands,
feet, body, etc. All children follow the movements as he does them. The child, who is "It,"
watches the group as they change from one motion to another to try to determine who is leading. Players should cover up for the leader,
who also tries to confuse "It" by looking at
other players.

   "It" gets three guesses. If not successful, he chooses another child to be "It." If he
guesses correctly, he gets another turn (limit
of 3 turns).

OTHER GAMES

   The teacher should examine the sections
on games, both primary and intermediate, for
activities of possible use. Also, the section
with regard to classroom activities for the primary grades should be checked for activities
that intermediate children might enjoy.

Chapter 23
Basketball Activities

An activity so popular as basketball needs little motivation. The fundamentals of the game are to be stressed in physical education classes with emphasis on lead-up activities. Additional opportunity for playing should be provided in a broad intramural program.

Basketball in the elementary schools should not be regarded as a proving ground for future high school stars. It should be an instructional program with the basic purpose the overall development of all children. Ball handling skills should be developed slowly and should be an outgrowth of the instruction in basic skills on the primary level. In the primary grades, the children learn the elements of catching, bouncing, passing, and dribbling many kinds of balls. Later in the intermediate grades, shooting, offensive and defensive play, and rules are added to this base. The suggested program begins in the third grade, and the program for this grade is included in the plan of progression which follows.

Emphasis on Different Grade Levels

Third Grade

Little actual basketball playing is done in the third grade. Concentration should be on the simple basic skills of passing, catching, shooting, and dribbling. The lead-up game, End Ball, permits the youngsters to use their basic skills in a game where the children are more or less stationary.

Fourth Grade

The fourth grade adds to the basic skills acquired in the third grade. The improvement of the skills and the addition of the lay-up shot, more dribbling skills, and different passes comprise the emphasis in this grade. Captain Ball adds the elements of simple defense, jump balls, and critical passing. Basic rules covering traveling and dribbling violations should be taught.

Fifth Grade

In the fifth grade, different kinds of basketball games are introduced. Shooting games, such as Around The Key and Twenty-one, are popular. Side line Basketball and Captain Basketball provide new experiences for the children. Continued practice on all the basic skills previously introduced is necessary for good progression. More basketball skills are added to the already growing group. Selected rules necessary to play the simple versions of basketball should be covered.

Sixth Grade

The sixth grade should continue practice on all skills. Shooting games from the other grades can be continued, and the game of In the Pot can be added. Basketball Snatch Ball, and One Goal Basketball give opportunity to use skills which have been acquired. Regular basketball with its formations, line-up, and other details

GRADE	THIRD	FOURTH	FIFTH	SIXTH

Skills	Passing
	  Chest or Push
	  Baseball
	  Bounce
		Passing
		  Underhand
		  One hand
		  Two hand
			Passing
			  One handed
			    push
			  All passes to
			    moving tar-
			    gets
				Passing
				  Two hand
				    overhead
				  Long passes

	Catching
	  Above waist
	  Below waist
			Catching
			  While moving	

	Shooting
	  Two handed
	    chest
		Shooting
		  Two handed
		    chest
		  Lay-up, right
		    and left
			Shooting
			  One hand push
			  Free throws
				Shooting
				  One hand jump

	Dribbling
	  Standing and
	    moving
		Dribbling
		  Down and back
		  Right and left
		    hands
			Dribbling
			  Figure eight
			
			Pivoting
				Dribbling
				  Practice with
				    eyes closed

			Guarding	Stopping
				  Parallel stop
				  Stride stop
				
				Three man
				  weave

Knowledges	Rules
	  Dribbling
		Rules
		  Violations
		  Dribbling
		  Traveling
		  Out of bounds
			Rules
			  Held Ball
			  Personal fouls
			  Holding
			  Hacking
			  Charging
			  Blocking
			  Pushing
			    etc.
				Rules
				  Conducting the
				    game
				
				  Officiating

Activities	End Ball	Birdie in the
		  Cage
		Captain Ball
			Captain Basket-
			  ball
			Side Line "
			Twenty One
			Around The Key
				One Goal Basket-
				  ball
				Five passes
				Basketball Snatch
				  Ball
				In The Pot
				Three on Three

Skill Tests		Dribble	Figure Eight
			  Dribble
			Wall Test
				Figure Eight
				  Dribble
				Baskets per
				  Minute
				Free Throws

should be covered so that the children can be ready to participate in basketball played as a regular game. Officiating should be taught because it is of value to have children officiate for their scrimmages or games.

Practical Suggestions

1. Many basketball skills, particularly on the third grade level, do not mandate the use of basketballs. Other balls such as volley, playground, and rubber balls can be used with success.
2. The junior size basketball should be used for the elementary school program.
3. If practical, the baskets should be lowered to nine feet as compared with the high school height of ten feet.
4. The program should concentrate on skills with many drills. Basketball offers endless possibilities, and drills should be utilized to give variety and breadth to the instructional program.
5. In the sixth grade, the girls can play against the girls on one end of the floor, and the boys occupying the other.
5. Each child should have an opportunity to practice all the skills. This is not possible when a considerable portion of the class time is devoted to playing the game.

Skills in Basketball

The basic skills in basketball to be covered in the elementary school class program in physical education can be divided into passing, catching, shooting, dribbling, and game skills.

Passing

Chest or Two-Hand Push Pass. The feet may be in an even position or one may be slightly ahead of the other. The ball is held at chest level with the fingers spread slightly above the center of the ball. The elbows are comfortably bent, and the delivery is made with a snap of the wrists. As the arms are extended, the fingers and wrists release the ball. A step is taken in the direction of the throw, or the weight shifts from rear to front foot.

Baseball or One-Hand Pass. Stand with the side toward the direction of the throw. The ball is brought back with both hands to a point over the shoulder or at the side of the head. The ball is now thrown like

a softball using the hand and wrist of the throwing arm for good follow-through.

Bounce Pass. Either of the previously two passes described can be adapted to make a bounce pass. The object is to throw the ball to a teammate on first bounce so the ball comes up to the outstretched hands. It should rebound waist high by hitting the floor four to five feet from the receiver. Do not bounce the ball at the receiver's feet.

Underhand Pass. For the two-hand underhand pass, the ball should be in both hands held near one hip with the elbows bent. The delivery is made with a snap of the wrists and follow through with the elbows. A step is taken in the direction of the throw.

For the one-hand underhand pass, the ball is brought back with both hands (one in front and the propelling hand behind) and thrown like an underhanded toss in softball.

One-Hand Push Pass. One hand is placed in front and one in back of the ball. The pass is made with the wrists and fingers of the pushing hand. A step is taken with the left foot if the right hand propels the ball, and vice versa. The pass later becomes the one-hand set shot, using about the same technique.

Two-Hand Overhead Pass. This pass is used when there is a height advantage. Player stands in short stride position (one foot slightly ahead of the other). The ball is held overhead with both hands with the fingers slightly back of the ball. The action is mostly in the wrist and fingers. The ball should go on a level path and be received high.

Catching

A player should move to meet a basketball when catching it. The fingers should be relaxed and cupped. To receive high pass, the thumbs are together, and the little fingers meet for one caught low. For passes received at waist level, the hands are in a parallel position. A little "give" with the hands and arms to absorb the recoil is important.

Dribbling

The wrist and hand furnish most of the force for the dribble. The dribble is a push with the cupped hand and wrist. The hand should "feel" the ball coming back up just before pushing for the next dribble. The ball should not be batted.

Shooting

Children should start with the two-hand set shot. Later, they can be introduced to the more popular one-hand variety.

<u>Push Shot</u>. The feet may be together or one foot ahead with the knees slightly bent. The hands are placed behind the ball and a little to the side. The wrist action should start when the ball is at eye level. There should be good follow-through.

<u>Lay-Up Shot</u>. From the right side, the shot should be timed so that it can be made taking off the left foot. Carry the ball in both hands until just before shooting. Aim at a spot on the backboard, shooting with the fingertips, arm extended. The shooting hand should be behind the ball and not under it.

<u>One-Hand Push Shot</u>. The shot begins much like the one-hand push pass except the ball is aimed above the basket. The ball is held in front of the body in front of the right shoulder. Dip the right hand slightly and put plenty of wrist and finger flick into the shot.

<u>One-Hand Jump Shot</u>. The ball is held above the head with the left hand in front and the right hand back and under the ball. At the height of a jump, the ball is released by a push of the right hand with good use of finger and wrist motion. The ball is guided with the pads of the fingertips.

Defense

The player should face his opponent with his knees slightly bent and the feet comfortably spread. The weight should be evenly distributed on both feet to allow for movement in any direction. A defensive player should stand about three feet from his opponent and waive one hand to distract or block passes and shots. Movement sidewards is done with a sliding motion. A defensive player should be loose and able to move quickly so as not to be caught flat-footed.

Stopping

To stop quickly, the weight of the body should be dropped to lower the center of gravity and the feet applied as brakes.

In the parallel stop, the body turns sideward, and the feet act together as brakes. The stride stop comes from a forward movement and is done in a one-two count. The stopping begins with one foot hitting the ground with braking action, and the other is firmly planted <u>ahead</u> on the second count. The knees are bent, and the body center of gravity is lowered. From a stride stop--by picking up the front foot and carrying it to the rear and at the same time fading to the rear, the movement becomes a pivot.

Drills in Basketball

With so many different skills which can be put into various combinations, the possibilities of basketball drills are endless. Some of the more common drills are given.

Passing and Catching

Many standard skill formations can be used, particularly the two-line circle, circle and leader, line and leader, shuttle turnback, and the regular shuttle. With only five players in a circle formation, a star drill is particular effective. Players pass to every other one and the path of the ball in a full round forms a star.

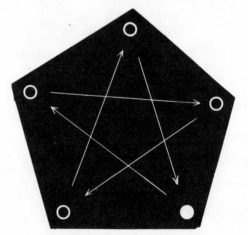

This adapts itself well to a ball passing relay.

Another drill of value is the three-man weave. This drill needs sufficient explanation and must be practiced. It should be remembered that the player in the center always starts the drill. The drill has two other key points. The first to remember is that "you always go behind the player to whom you throw the ball. The

second is that just as soon as you go behind and around the player, head diagonally
across the floor until you receive the ball."
The pass from the center man can start to
either side.

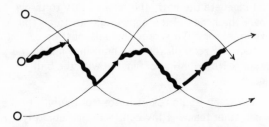

    Dribbling drills feature moving to a
point and back and also weaving in and
around objects. The shuttle formation
makes an excellent drill.

SHUTTLE DRIBBLING DRILL

Formation: Shuttle

Number: 6 to 10

Supplies: Basketball

    Player from one line dribbles up to the
other line, passes or hands the ball, and then
continues to the back of that line. The next
player dribbles the ball back to the starting
point.

FILE DRIBBLING DRILL

Formation: File

Number: 4 to 8

Supplies: Basketball

    Dribble down to a line and back. Player
can dribble right handed going down and left
handed coming back.

DRIBBLE AND PIVOT DRILL

Formation: File

Number: 4 to 8

Supplies: Basketball

    The player at the head of the line dribbles
forward to a prescribed point, stops, pivots to
face the line, and then passes to the next player
who repeats. First player goes to the end of the
file.

FIGURE EIGHT DRILL

Formation: File

Number: 4 to 8

Supplies: Basketball, 3 obstacles (chairs,
   Indian clubs, etc.)

    Players dribble in and around the obstacles.
Be sure that the player changes dribbling hands
each time so that his body is between the ball
and the obstacle, which represents an opponent.

Variation: Have the dribbler circle each
   club once and go to the next, which he circles the other direction, using the other
   hand.

Shooting Drills

    Shooting drills should be practiced both
from a stationary position and from a moving
one.

LAY-UP DRILL

Formation: Double file

Players: 6 to 16

Supplies: Basketball

    One file retrieves the ball and passes to
the player coming in for a lay-up shot. Players
change to the end of the other file each time.
The drill can also be varied by the retrieving
team passing the ball back to the head of the
other file where the player dribbles in. Change
sides and approach the basket from the other
side.

FILE AND LEADER

Formation: File and leader

Number: 6 to 8

Supplies: Basketball

    The player at the head of the line passes
the ball to the leader and then:

1. Runs by him on either side receiving a return pass for a lay-up shot.
2. Stops at a point in front or to the side of
   him and receives a return pass for a set
   shot.

SET SHOT FORMATION

Formation: Semi-circle and leader

Number: 4 to 8

Supplies: Basketball

Players scatter in a semi-circle with the leader acting as the retriever. He passes to each player in succession who takes his shot. Players should start from a close distance and work back. Two, and even three, squads can work on one basket. Rotate shooting areas after a period of practice. Each child should have a chance at the leader's position.

Basketball Activities

Third Grade

END BALL

Players on each team are divided into three groups: forwards, guards, and end men. The object is for a forward to throw successfully to one of his end zone players.

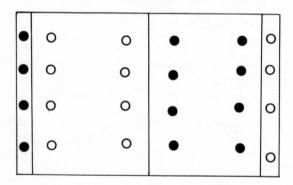

Playing Area: A court 20 by 40 feet is divided in half by a center line. End zones are marked 3 feet wide and completely across the court at each end.

Players: 9 to 15 on each team.

Supplies: Basketball or ten inch rubber playground ball.

· The players from each team are positioned as·follows. The end zone players take a position in one of the end zones. Their forwards and guards then occupy the half of the court farthest from this end zone. The forwards are near the center line, and the guards are back near the end zone of that half.

The ball is started with a center jump between the two tallest opposite forwards. When a team gets the ball, the forwards try to throw over the heads of the opposing team to an end zone player. To score, the ball must be caught by an end zone player with <u>both</u> feet inside the zone. No dribbling or moving with the ball is permitted.

Fouls: Fouls result in loss of the ball to the other team. Play continues immediately. Fouls are:

1. Hold a ball more than five seconds.
2. Step over the end line or step over the center line into the opponents' territory.
3. To walk (travel) with the ball.
4. To push or hold another player.

Out of Bounds: The ball belongs to the team that did not cause it to go out of bounds. The nearest player retrieves the ball out at the sideline and returns it to the guard of the proper team.

Teaching Suggestions: Encourage fast, accurate passing. Players in the end zones must practice jumping high to catch and still land with both feet inside the end zone area.

A system of rotation is desirable. Each time a score is made, players on that team can rotate one person. This means that one end zone player becomes a guard, a guard moves up to the forward line, and one of the forwards goes into the end zone.

Variation:

1. A game which carries the progression one step farther is Free Throw End Ball. The end zone player scores one point when he catches the ball in keeping with the rules.

   He is allotted one free throw which gives him the chance to score an additional point.

2. <u>Corner Ball</u>. This differs from End Ball only in that the scoring zone is located in the corners. A three by three foot square is drawn in each corner which imposes the limitation that only two players from each team are in position to receive the ball, one in each corner on the respective end of the playing area. Otherwise, the play is the same as in End Ball.

Fourth Grade

BIRDIE IN THE CAGE

Formation: Circle with one player in the center.

Players: 8 to 20

Supplies: Soccer ball, Basketball, Volley-ball.

The object of the game is for the center player to try to touch the ball. The ball is passed from player to player in the circle, and the center player attempts to touch the ball on one of these passes. The player who threw the ball that was touched takes the place in the center. Also, in case of a bad pass resulting in the ball leaving the circle area, the player whose fault caused the error changes to the center of the ring.

Teaching Suggestions: The ball should move promptly and rapidly. Passes should not be allowed to a neighboring player. If there is difficulty in touching the ball, a second center player may join the first.

Play can be limited to a type of pass as bounce, two-hand, etc.

CAPTAIN BALL

A team is composed of a captain, three forwards, and four guards. The guards throw the ball into the forwards who attempt to throw the ball to their captain.

Playing Area: 20 by 40 feet. Three two-foot circles are laid out in the shape of a triangle with a fourth circle (for the captain) in the center of the triangle.

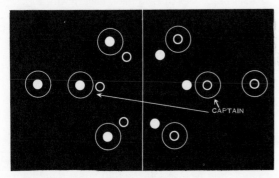

Players: 7 on each side

Supplies: Basketball

The captain and the three forwards are each assigned to respective circles and must keep one foot always inside the circle. Guarding these four players are three guards.

The game is started by a jump at the center line by two guards from opposing teams. The guards can rove in their half of the court but must not enter the circles of the opposing players. The ball is put in play by a center jump after each score.

As soon as a guard gets the ball, he throws it to one of his forwards who is open. The forwards must maneuver to be open. The forward now tries to throw it to the other forwards or into the captain. Scoring is as follows:

2 points -- all three forwards handle the ball and it then is passed to the captain.

1 point -- the ball is passed into the captain but has not been handled by all forwards.

Fouls:

1. Stepping over center line, or stepping into circle by guard.
2. Traveling, running, or kicking the ball.

Penalty: Free throw. Ball is given to one of the forwards who is unguarded and gets a throw to the guarded captain. If successful, scores one point. If not successful, ball is in play.

Out of Bounds: As in basketball. Ball is awarded to the team (guard) which did not cause the ball to go out.

Out of the Circle: If a forward or captain catches a ball with <u>both</u> feet out of his circle, the ball is taken out of bounds by the opposing guard.

Teaching Suggestions:

1. The size of the circle should be determined by the abilities of the players.
2. If more players are to be used, additional circles can be drawn.
3. Teach short and accurate passing. Teach faking with the eyes. Bounce passes work well when mixed with high passes. For the latter pass, the circle players can learn to jump.
4. Rotate the turns at center jump among the guards.

Variation: Play with four guards instead of three. This makes it more difficult for the forwards to move the ball.

Fifth Grade
CAPTAIN BASKETBALL

Captain Basketball is nearer to the game of basketball than Captain Ball. Captain Ball has limited movement of the forwards because of the circle restrictions. Captain Basketball brings in more natural passing and guarding as found in the basketball scrimmage.

Playing Area: Basketball court with center line. A captain's area is laid out by drawing a line four feet out from the end line between the two foul restraining lines. The captain must keep one foot in this area.

Players: 6 or 8 on each team

Supplies: Basketball

The game is played much the same as basketball. A throw by one of the forwards into the captain scores two points. A free throw scores one point.

A team is composed of three forwards; one captain, and four guards. The captain must keep one foot in his area under the basket.

The game is started with a jump ball, and then the players advance the ball as in basketball. However, none may cross the center line. Thus, the guards must bring the ball up to the center line and throw it to one of their forwards. The forwards maneuver and attempt to pass successfully into the captain.

Fouls: As in basketball. Stepping over the center line or a guard stepping into the captain's area draws a free throw.

Free Throw: The ball is given to a forward at the free throw line. He is unguarded and has five seconds to pass successfully to his captain, who is guarded by one player. The ball is in play if the free throw is unsuccessful.

Teaching Suggestions:
1. The game provides a good opportunity to learn both rules and techniques of basketball.
2. While players are required to remain in their own half of the court, they should be taught to move freely in that area.
3. Stress short, quick passes as long passes are not effective.
4. Stress proper guarding techniques.
5. If only 6 play on each team, the team has 3 guards, 2 forwards, and the captain.

SIDELINE BASKETBALL

Playing Area: Basketball court

Players: Class is divided into two teams, each team lining up on one side of the court facing the other.

Supplies: Basketball

The game can be played by three or four active players from each team. The remainder of the team players stand on the sideline and may catch and pass the ball to the active players. They may not shoot nor may they enter the playing floor.

Active players play regular basketball except that they may pass and receive the ball from the sideline players. The game starts with the active players of each team occupying one of the end lines. When the whistle blows, the teacher passes the ball to one of the active players (usually to the team that did not score), and regular basketball is played until one team scores or three minutes have elapsed. When either occurs, the active players take places in the line on the left side of their line and three new active players come out from the right. All other players move down three places.

No official out of bounds on the sides is called. The players on that side of the floor simply recover the ball and put it in play by a pass to an active player without delay or waiting for a signal. Free throws are not awarded; when a player is fouled, the ball is given to the other team for a throw in.

Sideline players may not pass to each other but must pass back to an active player. Sideline players should be well spaced along the side.

TWENTY-ONE

Playing Area: One end of a basketball court

Players: 3 to 8 in each game, with a number of games played on one end of the floor. Players are in file formation.

Supplies: Basketball

Each child is permitted a long shot (from a specified distance) and a follow-up shot. The long shot if made counts two points and the short shot one. The follow-up shot must be made from the spot the ball is recovered from the first shot.

The first player scoring a total of twenty-one is the winner. If the ball misses the backboard and basket altogether on the first shot, the second shot must be taken from the corner.

Variations:

1. For a simpler game, allow dribbling before the second shot.
2. A player continues to shoot as long as he makes every shot. This means if he makes <u>both</u> the long and short shot, he goes back out to the original position for a third shot. All made shots count and he continues until he misses.
3. The game works very well as team competition with each player contributing his total to the team score.
4. Various combinations and types of shots may be used.

AROUND THE KEY

Playing Area: One end of a basketball floor

Number: 3 to 8 players

Supplies: Basketball

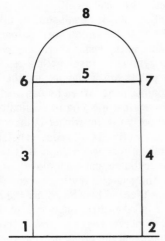

Variation:

Spots are arranged for shooting as indicated in the diagram. A player begins at the first spot and continues as long as he makes the shot. When he misses, he has two choices. The first is to wait for his next turn and continue from the place he missed. The second is to "risk it," which means that he gets another shot from where he missed. If he makes this, he continues. If he misses, he starts over from the beginning on his next turn. The winner is the one who completes the key first or who has made the farthest progress.

In the beginning, it is well to give each child two shots from each spot.

1. Each child shoots from each spot until he makes the basket. A limit of three shots from any one spot should be made. The child finishing the round of nine spots with the lowest number is the winner.
2. The order of the spots can be changed. A player can start on one side of the key and continue back along the line, around the free throw circle, and back down the other side.

Sixth Grade

ONE GOAL BASKETBALL

Playing Area: An area with one basketball goal

Number: Two teams, 2 to 4 on each

Supplies: Basketball

If a gymnasium has as many as four basketball goals, many children can be kept active with this game. If only two goals are present, a system of rotation can be worked out.

The game is played with the regular rules with the following exceptions:

1. The game begins with a jump at the free throw mark with the centers facing the side lines.
2. When a defensive player recovers the ball, either from the backboard or on an interception, the ball must be taken out beyond the foul line circle before offensive play is started and an attempt at a goal can be made.
3. After a basket is made, the ball is taken in the same fashion away from the basket to the center of the floor where the other team starts offensive play.
4. Regular free throw shooting can be observed after a foul, or some play that the offended team takes the ball out of bounds.
5. If an offensive player is tied up in a jump ball, he loses the ball to the other team.

Variation: A system of rotation can be instituted wherein the team that scores a basket "holds" the floor and the losing team must retire in favor of a waiting team. For more experienced players, a score of three or more points can be required for eliminating the opponents.

FIVE PASSES

Playing Area: One-half a basketball floor.

Number: Two teams, four on each team.

Supplies: Basketball

The object of the game is to complete five consecutive passes which scores a point. On one basketball floor, two games can go on at the same time, one in each half.

The game is started with a jump ball at the free throw line. The teams observe regular basketball rules in ball handling, traveling, and fouling. Five consecutive passes must be made by a team which counts out aloud as the passes are completed.

The ball must not be passed back to the person from whom it was received.

No dribbling is allowed. If for any reason the ball is fumbled and recovered, or improperly passed, a new count is started. After a successful score, the ball con be thrown up again at a center jump at the free throw line. A foul gives a free throw which can score a point.

Variation:
1. After each successful point (five passes), the team is awarded a free throw which can score an additional point.
2. After a team has scored a point, the ball can be given to the other team out of bounds to start play again.
3. Dribbling can be allowed but this decreases the premium on passing. Dribbling can be limited to a certain number of bounces.

BASKETBALL SNATCH BALL

Playing Area: Basketball court

Number: Two teams, 6 to 15 on each team

Supplies: Two basketballs

Each team occupies one side of a basketball floor. The players on each team are numbered consecutively, and must stand in this order. The two balls are laid on the center line where it is bisected by the restraining circle for jump balls. When the teacher calls a number, the player from each team whose number is called runs to the ball, dribbles it to the basket on his right and tries to make the basket. As soon as the basket is made, he dribbles back and places the ball on the spot where he picked it up. The first player to return the ball after making a bas-

ket scores a point for his team. The teacher should use some system of keeping track of the numbers so all children will run. Numbers can be called in any order.

Variation: Players can run by pairs with two players from each team assigned the same number. In this case the ball must be passed between the paired players at least three times before a shot can be taken. Three passes are required before the ball is returned to its spot.

IN THE POT

Playing Area: Basket and area near.

Number: 4 to 12 in each game. A number of games can be played on one basket.

Supplies: Basketball

This is a shooting game with emphasis on accuracy. A player is allowed a long and a short shot. If he makes <u>either</u> shot, he adds points to the pot. If he misses, he takes out whatever points are in the pot. A long shot counts two points, and a short adds one to the pot. A player who misses <u>both</u> shots takes out whatever points are in the pot and these are scored against him. When he has accumulated ten points against him, he is eliminated and must drop out until the winner is determined.

No dribbling is allowed. The short shot must be taken from where the ball is recovered from the backboard and each player may take this shot with the one-two rhythm. If the first shot touches neither the backboard nor the basket, the short shot is taken from the corner of the floor.

Each player keeps his own score of points against him, and the group playing keeps track of the points in the pot. If there are more points in the pot than needed to eliminate a player, only sufficient points for the elimination are taken out. The remainder are left in the pot for the next shooter that misses.

THREE ON THREE

Playing Area: One-half of a basketball court

Number: Teams of three, 3 to 5 teams

Supplies: Basketball

An offensive team of three stands just forward of the center line facing the basket. The center player has a basketball. Another team of three is on defense and awaits the offensive team in the area near the foul line.

The remaining teams await their turns and stand beyond the end line.

Regular basketball rules are used. At a signal, the offensive team advances to score. A scrimmage is over when a score is made, or the ball is recovered by the defense. In either case, the defensive team moves to the center of the floor and becomes the offensive unit. A waiting team comes out on the floor and gets ready for defense. The old offensive team goes to the rear of the line of waiting players. Each team should keep its own score.

By using only one-half the floor, two games can be carried on at the same time.

Variation:

1. If the offensive team scores, it remains on the floor and the defensive team drops off in favor of the next team. If the defense recovers the ball, the offensive team rotates off the floor.
2. If a team makes a foul (by one of the players), that team rotates off the floor in favor of the next team.

Basketball Tests

The tests in basketball cover dribbling, passing, shooting, and free throws. For timing, a stop watch is needed.

Straight Dribble. A marker is placed fifteen yards down the floor from the starting point. The dribbler must dribble around the marker and back to the starting position. Allow 3 trials, take best time.

Figure Eight Dribble. Three obstacles (Indian Clubs, bases, etc.) are placed five yards apart and five yards from the starting point. The player must dribble in and out of the markers in the path of a figure eight. Allow 3 trials.

Wall Pass Test. A player stands five feet from a smooth wall. He is given thirty seconds to make as many catches as he can from throws or passes against the wall. Balls must be caught on the fly. Generally, this two-hand or chest pass is used in this test.

Baskets per Minute. A player stands near the basket in any position that he wishes. On the signal he shoots and continues shooting for a period of one minute. His score is the number of baskets he made during the time period.

Free Throws. Score is kept of the number of free throws made from a specified number of tries. Players should be allowed three or four warm up tries.

The Game of Basketball

For elementary school children, the game of basketball is similar to the official game played in the junior and senior high schools, but has modifications in keeping with the capacities of the children. The following represents the basic rules which apply to the game for elementary children:

Teams. A team for boys is made up of five players, composed of two guards, one center, and two forwards. For girls, there are six players on each team consisting of two forwards, two guards, and two roving players. A line is drawn across the center of the court for girls. The forwards and guards of each team must remain in their respective halves of the court and are not permitted to cross the center line. The roving players have no such restriction and may play anywhere on the entire court. One of the roving players jumps at the center circle for the toss-up.

Timing. The game is divided into four quarters, each of which is six minutes in length.

Officials. The game is under the control of a referee and an umpire, both of whom have an equal right to call violations and fouls. They work on opposite sides of the floor and are assisted by a timer and a scorer.

Putting the Ball in Play. Each quarter is started with a jump ball at the center circle. Throughout the game, the jump ball is used when the ball is tied between two players, or when an out-of-bounds ball is uncertain with respect to who caused it to go out.

After each successful basket or free throw, the ball is put in play at the end of the court under the basket by the team against whom the score was made.

Violations. The penalty for a violation is the award of the ball to the opponents at a near out-of-bounds point. The following are violations:

1. Traveling - taking more than one step with the ball without passing, dribbling, or shooting. Sometimes called walking or steps.
2. Stepping out of bounds or causing the ball to go out of bounds.

3. Double dribble - a second series of dribbling without another player handling the ball, palming (not clearly batting) the ball, or dribbling the ball with both hands at once.
4. Stepping on or over a restraining line during a jump ball or free throw.
5. Kicking the ball.
6. Remaining more than three seconds in the area under the offensive basket, bounded by the two sides of the free throw lane, the free throw line, and the end of the court.

Personal Fouls. Personal fouls are holding, pushing, hacking (striking), tripping, charging, blocking, and unnecessary roughness.

When a foul is called, the person who was fouled receives one free throw. If he was fouled in the act of shooting (basket missed), he receives two shots. If the basket was made, the score counts and one free throw is awarded.

Technical Fouls. Technical fouls include failure of substitutes to report to the proper officials, delay of game, and unsportsmanlike conduct.

Disqualification. A player who has five personal fouls called against him is out of the game and must go to the sidelines. Disqualification can occur from extreme unsportsmanlike conduct or a vicious personal foul.

Scoring. A basket from the field scores two points and a free throw, one point. The team that is ahead at the end of the game is declared the winner. If the score is tied, an overtime period of two minutes is played. If the score is still tied after this period, the next team to score (1 or 2 points) is declared the winner.

Substitutes. Substitutes must report to the official scorer and await a signal from the referee or umpire before entering the game. The scorer will sound his signal at a time when the ball is not in play so that the official on the floor can signal for the player to enter the game.

Chapter 24

Football Type Activities

Emphasis on Different Grade Levels
Practical Suggestions
Football Skills
Flag Football Drills
Activities
Testing Football Skills

Touch and flag football are modifications of the game of American Football. A ball carrier is considered down in touch football when he is touched with one hand. Some rules call for a two handed touch, while other rules require a player to wear one or two flags which the opponents must seize in order to down the ball carrier (hence the name, flag football). The shape of the ball makes the skills of ball handling more difficult than that of a soccer or volleyball. This, in turn, means that the teacher must spend sufficient time on football skills if the children are to enjoy the activity.

Flag football has advantages over touch football in that the ball carrier is not stopped by a touch but must lose his flag. This means that there can be more twisting and dodging, making the game more interesting and challenging. In addition, there is little argument over whether or not the ball carrier was downed.

Emphasis on Different Grade Levels

Fourth Grade. Passing, centering and catching should comprise the fourth grade program. Most of the time should be spent on skills. The two lead-up games of Keep-away and Football End Ball make use of the skills listed.

Fifth Grade. The fifth grade should review the skills of the fourth grade level. The emphasis then shifts to passing skills to moving receivers in football drills. Punting and kicking games are introduced.

Sixth Grade. More specialized skills like blocking, carrying the ball, ball exchanges, and football agility skills feature the lead-up work for the game of flag football.

GRADE	FOURTH	FIFTH	SIXTH
Skills	Passing Centering Catching	Stance Pass receiving Punting	Blocking Carrying the ball Running and dodging Ball exchange Lateral passing
Knowledges			Football rules Plays and formations
Tests	Passing for distance Centering -	Punting for distance Passing for distance	Passing for accuracy Passing for distance
Activities	Keep Away Football End Ball	Kick Over Fourth Down	Football Boxball Flag Football Pass Ball

Practical Suggestions

To insure better play in football-type activities, the following suggestions are made.

1. Children should have a chance to practice all skills. In drills, which give opportunity to a number of skills, a system of rotation should be organized so players shift positions automatically and practice all skills.
2. Roughness and unfair play must be controlled by strict enforcement of the rules and good supervision.
3. The junior size football should be used in the elementary grades.
4. Girls, too, like to handle footballs and should have a chance to practice skills. Football End Ball is an excellent game for girls to make use of passing and catching.
5. Play should be organized so that when the boys play flag football, the girls can be playing Football End Ball, soccer, or speedball.
6. Drills should be carried with attention to proper stance and approximating game conditions. Boys should line up in proper stance when going out for passes.
7. Football-type games should be organized so that the play is not dominated by one or two individuals.

Football Skills

Passing. Skillful forward passing is needed in flag football and the lead-up games; this is a potent weapon. The ball should be gripped lightly behind the middle with the fingers on the lace. The thumb and fingers should be relaxed. The left foot should be placed so it points in the direction of the pass, and the body is turned sidewards, when throwing right handed. The ball is raised with two hands up and over the right shoulder. The ball is delivered directly forward with an overhand movement of the right arm with the index finger pointing toward the line of flight.

Lateral Passing. Lateral passing is pitching the ball underhanded to a teammate. The ball must be tossed sideward or backward. The ball should be tossed with an easy motion and no attempt should be made to make it spiral like a forward pass.

Catching. The receiver should keep his eyes on the ball and catch it in his hands with a slight giving movement. As soon as the ball is caught it should be tucked in carrying position. The little fingers should be together for most catches.

Carrying the Ball. The ball should be carried with the arm on the outside, and the end of the ball into the notch formed by the elbow and arm.

Centering. Player takes a position with his feet well spread and toes pointed straight ahead. His knees are bent, and he should be close enough to the ball to reach it with a slight stretch. The right hand takes about the same grip that would be used for passing. The other hand is on the side near the back and merely acts as a guide. Center passing for the T formation is done, however, with one hand. The other arm rests on the inside of the thigh.

Stance. The three-point stance is the one most generally used in flag football. Feet are about shoulder width apart, toes pointing straight ahead, with the toe of one foot even with the heel of the other. The hand on the side of the foot that is back is used for support, resting on the knuckles. The player should look straight ahead and always take the same stance irrespective of the direction he is to move.

Some players prefer the parallel stance wherein the feet, instead of in the heel and toe position, are lined up even. In this case, either hand can be placed down for support.

Blocking. In blocking in flag football, the blocker must stay on his feet. The block should be more of an obstruction than a take-out. He should set with his shoulder against the opponents shoulder or upper body. Making contact in any direction from the rear not only is a foul, but can cause injury.

Ball Exchanges. Children love to work plays where the ball is exchanged from one player to another (a reverse) or even with two exchanges (double reverse). The object is to start the play in one direction and then give the ball to another player heading in the opposite direction. The ball can be handed backwards or forwards. The player with the ball always makes the exchange with the inside hand, the one nearest the receiving player. The ball is held with both hands until the receiver is about six feet away. The ball is then shifted to the hand on that side with the elbow bent and kept partially away from the body. The receiver comes toward the exchange man with his near arm with bent elbow carried in front of his chest with the palm down. The other arm has the palm up and is carried about waist high. As the ball is given (not tossed) to the receiver, he clamps down on the ball to secure it. Then, as quickly as he can, he changes it to normal carrying position.

A fake reverse can be run where the ball carrier fakes the change and keeps the ball.

Punting. Punting should be first practiced with a soccer or playground ball of that size. The kicker should stand with the feet slightly apart, the knees flexed with the kicking foot slightly forward. The fingers should be extended in the direction of the center. The eyes should be on the ball from the time it is centered until it is kicked. The kicker should actually see his foot kick the ball. After the ball is received, the kicker should take a short step with his kicking foot. A second step is taken with the other foot. The kicking leg is swung forward, and at the impact the knee is straightened to provide maximum force. The toes are pointed and the long axis of the ball makes contact high and on the outside of the instep. The leg should follow through well after the kick.

Flag Football Drills

Drill in flag football skills can be organized for a single skill or a combination of skills. Another consideration that is important is the rotation of players during drills so that each child will have an opportunity to practice all skills. A sufficient supply of footballs is a necessity to any efficient drill period in football skills.

BALL CARRYING

Formation: Regular zone flag football field with 20 yard interval lines.

Players: 6 to 12

Supplies: Football, flags for each player

The ball carrier stands on the goal line ready to run. Three defensive players await him at 20 yard intervals, each one stationed on a zone line facing the ball carrier. Each defender is assigned to the zone he faces and must down the ball carrier by pulling a flag while the carrier is still in the zone. The ball carrier runs and dodges, trying to get by each defender in turn without having any of the flags pulled. If one flag is pulled, the runner continues. If both flags are pulled, the last defender uses a two-hand touch to down the ball carrier. After the

runner has completed his run, he goes to the end of the defender line and rotates into the defending positions.

BALL EXCHANGE

Formation: Shuttle with the halves about 15 yards apart.

Players: 10 to 20

Supplies: Football

The two halves of the shuttle face each other across the 15 yard distance. A player at the head of one of the files has a ball and carries it over to the other file, where he makes an exchange with the front player of that file. The ball is carried back and forth between the shuttle files. The receiving player should not start until the ball carrier is almost up to him. A player, after handing the ball to the front player of the other file, continues around and joins that file.

CENTERING

Drill 1.

Formation: Shuttle turnback, 5 yards between halves of the shuttle.

Players: 6 to 8 in each drill.

Supplies: Football

The ball is centered back and forth between the two parts of the shuttle. As soon as a player takes his turn, he goes to the end of his line.

Drill 2.

Formation: Semicircle and leader

Players: 6 to 8

Supplies: Football

The leader centers the ball to each player in turn, who passes or centers the ball back. After one complete round, the leader rotates to one end of the line and a new leader repeats the routine.

COMBINATION

Formation: Regular offensive formation with passer, center, end, and ball chaser

Players: 4 to 10

Supplies: Football

Passing, centering, and receiving skills are combined into one drill. Each player, as soon as he has taken his turn, rotates to the next spot. A minimum of four players are needed. The four positions are:

Center - centers the ball to the passer
Passer - passes the ball to the end
End - receives the pass
Ball Chaser - retrieves the ball if missed by the receiver (end), or takes a pass from the end (if he caught the ball) and carries the ball to the center spot which is his next assignment.

The rotation follows the path of the ball. This means that the rotation system moves from center to passer to end to ball chaser to center. Extra players should be stationed behind the passer for turns.

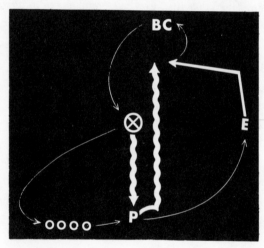

KICKING

Formation: Shuttle turnback, with the two parts kicking distance apart.

Players: 6 to 8 in each drill

Supplies: Football

The emphasis is on kicking skills, but the skill of catching a kicked ball can be practiced. The two halves of the shuttle formation face each other and kick back and forth. Centering the ball can be added to the drill.

ONE-ON-ONE DEFENSIVE DRILL

Formation: Center, passer, end, defender.

Players: 8 to 10

The drill is as old as football itself. A defensive player stands about 8 yards back awaiting an approaching end. The passer tries to complete the pass to the end while the defender tries to stop or intercept the ball. Have one defender practice against all the players and then change defenders.

Variation: Have two ends and two defenders. Passer throws to the end that appears to be the most unguarded.

PASSING AND CATCHING

Formations: Passing and catching can be organized through many different drills, such as line and leader, file and leader, shuttle turnback, double line formation, and others.

Players: 6 to 8

Supplies: Football

The formation will dictate the pattern and rotation of players, if any.

PUNT RETURN

Formation: A center, kicker, two lines of ends, and receivers.

Players: 10 to 20

Supplies: Football, flags for each player

The object of the drill is for the receiver to catch a punted ball and return it back to the line of scrimmage while two ends attempt to pull a flag.

Two ends are ready to run downfield. The center centers the ball to the kicker who punts the ball downfield to the punt receiver. The ends cannot cross the line of scrimmage until the ball is kicked. Each end makes two trips down field as a "tackler" before rotating to the punt receiver position.

A good punter is necessary for this drill. Only selected children with the degree of skill to punt the ball far enough downfield should be permitted to kick. It is also important that the ends wait until the ball is kicked or they will be downfield too soon to give the receiver a fair chance to make a return run.

STANCE

Formation: Squads in extended file formation

Players: 6 to 8 in each file

Supplies: None

The first person in each file performs and when finished with his chore goes to the end of his file. On the command "Ready," the first person in each file assumes a football stance. The teacher can correct and make observations. On the command "Hip," the players charge forward for about five yards. The new players at the head of the line get ready.

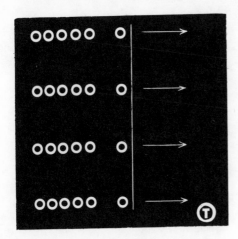

Activities

Fourth Grade

FOOTBALL END BALL

The only difference between this game and basketball end ball is that a football is used. Distances children are to throw from the forwards to the end men should be governed by the capacity of the children. See page 266 for a description of End Ball.

KEEP AWAY

Playing Area: Football field or large play space

Numbers: Two teams, 8 to 12 on each side

Supplies: Football, pinnies or crepe identification marks.

The object of the game is for one team to retain possession of the ball as long as possible, keeping it from the other team. Teams should be marked so that the players can distinguish opponents.

The same body contact rules that govern basketball should be enforced. The defensive team trying to recover the ball may play the ball but is not permitted to push, shove, hold, or otherwise interfere physically with an opponent. Players scatter and one team attempts to retain possession of the ball by passing to teammates. No player can take more than five steps with the ball under penalty of loss to the other team.

Variation:
1. A certain number of <u>consecutive</u> successful passes could score a point. Begin with five passes and if this proves too easy, raise the number.
2. The captain can start the passing and if every player on a team handles the ball, a score is made when the captain again has the ball in his possession. Players could handle the ball more than once but no point could be scored until each member of the team has handled the ball, and it is returned to the captain.

Watch out for roughness. A quick whistle is needed to avoid pile-ups. If there is too much roughness, award the ball to the other team when it hits the ground. Otherwise, the ball should be in play.

Fifth Grade

KICK OVER

Playing Area: Football Field with a ten yard end zone.

Number: 6 to 10 on each team.

Supplies: Football

Teams are scattered on opposite ends of the field. The object is to punt the ball over the other team's goal line. If the ball is caught in the end zone, no score results. If the ball is kicked beyond the end zone on the fly, a score is made regardless whether or not the ball was caught. A ball kicked <u>into</u> the end zone on the fly and not caught also scores a goal.

Play is started by one team with a punt from a point 20 to 30 feet in front of the goal line it is defending. On a punt, if the ball is not caught, the team must kick from the spot of recovery. If the ball is caught, three long strides are allowed to advance the ball for a kick. Players should be numbered and kick in rotation.

Variation: Scoring can be made by only a drop kick across the goal line.

Teaching Suggestions: The player whose turn it is to kick should move fast to the area from where the ball is to be kicked.

FOURTH DOWN

Playing Area: Football field (use only one-half) or equivalent space.

Number: Two teams, 6 to 12 on each team.

Supplies: Football

Every play is a fourth down which means that the play must score or the team loses the ball. No kicking is permitted, and players may pass any time from any spot in any direction. This means that there can be a series of passes on any play either from behind or beyond the line of scrimmage.

The teams line up in an offensive football formation. The ball is put in play by centering. The back receiving the ball can either run or pass to any of his teammates. The one receiving the ball has the same privilege. Passes can be made any time.

To start the game, the ball is placed in the center of the field and the team that wins the toss has the chance to put the ball into play. After each touchdown, the ball is brought to the center of the field, and the team against whom the score was made puts the ball into play.

To down a runner or pass receiver, a two handed touch above the waist is made. The back first receiving the ball from the center has immunity against tagging provided he does not try to run. All defensive players must stay 10 feet away from him unless he runs. The referee should wait a reasonable length of time for the back to pass or run, and if he holds the ball beyond that, the referee should call out, "Ten Seconds." The back must now throw or run within ten seconds, or the defensive players can tag him.

The defensive team players scatter to cover the receivers. They can use a man-to-man defense with each player covering an offensive

man or employ a zone defense.

Since the team with the ball loses possession after each play, rules for determining where the ball is to be placed when the other team takes possession are needed.

If a player is tagged with two hands above the waist, the ball goes to the other team at this spot.

If an incomplete pass is made from <u>behind</u> the line of scrimmage, the ball is given to the other team at the spot where the ball was put into play.

Should an incomplete pass be made by a player while <u>beyond</u> the line of scrimmage, the ball is brought to the spot from which it was thrown.

Variation:

1. The game could be called Third Down and two downs would be allowed to score.

Teaching Suggestions:

1. The team in possession should be encouraged to pass as soon as practical as children become tired from running around to become free for a pass.
2. The defensive team can score by intercepting a pass. Since passes can be made at any time, upon interception, the player should look down the field for a pass to one of his teammates.
3. Some time should be spent showing children how to stay with (guard) an intended receiver. Also, children should be taught how to maneuver to get free to receive a pass.

Sixth Grade

FOOTBALL BOX BALL

Playing Area: Football field fifty yards long. Five yards beyond each goal is a six by six foot square which is the box.

Number: Two teams, 8 to 16 on each.

Supplies: Football, team colors.

The teams should be marked so that they can be distinguished. The object of the game is similar to End Ball in that the team tries to make a successful pass to the captain in the box.

To begin the play, players are onside, which means that they are on opposite ends of the field. One team, losing the toss, kicks off from their own ten yard line to the other team. The game now becomes a kind of a keep-away with either team trying to get and retain possession of the ball until a successful pass can be made to captain in the box. The captain must catch the ball on the fly and still stay with both feet in the box. This scores a touchdown.

Rules: A player may run sidewards or backwards when in possession of the ball. He may not run forward but is allowed his momentum (two steps) if receiving or intercepting a ball. Penalty for illegal forward movement while in possession of the ball--loss of ball to opponents, who take the ball out of bounds.

The captain is allowed the opportunity of only three attempts or to score one goal. If either occurs, another player is rotated to the box.

On any pass or attempt to get the ball to the captain, the team loses the ball. If a touchdown (successful pass) is made, the team brings back the ball to its ten-yard line and kicks off to the other team. If the attempt is not successful, the ball is given out of bounds on the end line to the other team.

Any out of bounds is put in play by the team which did not cause the ball to go out of bounds. No team can score from a throw-in from out of bounds.

In case of a tie ball, a jump ball is called at the spot. The players face in a jump ball as in basketball.

Players must play the ball and not the individual. For unnecessary roughness, the player is sidelined until a pass is thrown to the other team's captain.

On the kickoff, all players must be onside, that is, behind the ball when it is kicked. Penalty is loss of ball to the other team out of bounds at the center line. After the kickoff, players may move to any part of the field.

On the kickoff, the ball must travel ten yards and then it can be recovered by either team. A kickoff outside or over the end line is treated as any other out of bounds.

A ball hitting the ground remains in play as long as it is inbounds. Players may not bat or kick a free ball. Penalty is loss of ball to the other team out of bounds.

Falling on the ball means loss of ball to the other team.

FLAG FOOTBALL

Flag football is an important modification of the game of football. Many versions of flag and touch football exist and are used successfully. Flag football can be played with one or two flags. The flag is a length of cloth which is hung from the belt of each player. A ball carrier is considered down when a defensive player grasps and removes the flag from his belt. In the single flag game, the flag is hung from the back. In the two flag version, each player has two flags which are hunt from the sides at the waist. Sometimes it is difficult for a player to reach around the ball carrier and remove the one flag hung in the back. This leads to a rougher type of game. With two flags, the defensive player has a choice of pulling either flag to stop the play.

Playing Area: A field 30 by 60 yards marked off in 20 yard intervals with lines parallel to the goal line. This divides the field into three zones.

If there is sufficient room, end zones of ten yards can be marked off, defining the area behind the goal in which passes can be caught.

Numbers: 6 to 9 on a team. If 6 or 7 are on a team, four men are required to be on the line of scrimmage. For 8 or 9 players, five offensive men must be on the line.

Supplies: Football, two flags for each player. Flags should be about 3 inches wide and 16 inches long.

Timing: The game shall consist of two halves. A total of 25 plays shall make up each half. All plays count in the 25 except the try for one point after a touchdown and a kickoff out of bounds.

Scoring: Touchdown - 6 points. Point after touchdown - 1 point. Safety - 2 points. A point after touchdown is made from a distance of three feet from the goal line. One play (pass or run) is allowed for the extra point.

Kickoff: The game is started with a kick-off. The team winning the toss has the option of selecting the goal it wishes to defend or choosing to kick or receive. The loser of the toss takes the option not exercised by the first team.

The kick-off is from the goal line, and all players on the kicking team must be on side. The kick must cross the first zone line or it does not count as a play. A kick that is kicked out of bounds (not touched by the receiving team) must be kicked over. A second consecutive kick out of bounds gives the ball to the receiving team in the center of the field. The kick-off may not be recovered by the kicking team unless caught and fumbled by the receivers.

Downs and Yardage: The field is divided into three twenty-yard zones. A team has four downs to move the ball into the next zone or lose the ball. For example, a team that secures the ball in the center has four downs to move the ball into the next zone or score. If the ball is legally advanced into the next zone, then the team now has four downs to score. A ball on the line between zones is considered in the more forward zone.

Time-Outs: Time outs are permitted only for injuries or when called by the officials for any reason.

Substitutions: Unlimited substitutions are permitted. Each must report to the official.

Forward Pass: All forward passes must be thrown from behind the line of scrimmage. All players on the field are eligible to receive or intercept passes.

Huddle: The team in possession of the ball usually huddles to make up the play. After any play, the team has thirty seconds to put the ball into play after the referee gives the in play signal.

Blocking: Blocking is done with the arms close to the body. Blocking must be done from the front or side and blockers must stay on their feet.

Tackling: A player is down if one of his flags has been pulled. The ball carrier must make an attempt to avoid the defensive player and is not permitted to run over or through the defensive player, except in close line play. The tackler must play the flags and not the ball carrier. Good officiating is needed for this point as defensive players may attempt to hold or grasp the ball carrier until they can remove one of the flags.

Punting: All punts must be announced. Neither team can cross the line of scrimmage until the ball is kicked. Kick receivers may run or use a lateral pass. They cannot make a forward pass after receiving a kick.

Fumbles: All fumbles are dead at the spot of the fumbles. The first player who touches the ball on the ground is deemed to have recovered the fumble. No player may kick or

bat a free ball. When the ball is centered to a back, he must gain definite possession of the ball before a fumble can be called. He is allowed to pick up a bad pass from the center or a ball of which he did not have possession.

Touchback: Any kicked ball over the goal line is ruled a touchback and is brought out to the twenty yard line to be put in play by the receiving team. A pass intercepted behind the goal line can be a touchback if the player does not run it out. It is a touchback even if he is tagged behind his own goal line.

Safety: A safety occurs when the team defending a goal line causes the ball to go back over the goal line by fumbling, running, or being caught during a scrimmage behind its own goal line.

Penalties:
Loss of five yards
    Off side
    Delay of game (too long in huddle)
    Failure of substitute to report
    Passing from spot not behind line of scrimmage (also loss of down)
    Stiff arming by ball carrier of not avoiding a defensive player
    Failure to announce intention to punt
    Shortening the flag in the belt. Playing without flags in proper position.
    Faking the ball by the center (he must center the pass on the first motion)
Loss of fifteen yards
    Holding, illegal tackling
    Illegal blocking
    Unsportsmanlike conduct (can be disqualification)

PASS BALL

Pass Ball is a more open game than Flag Football. The game is similar to Flag Football with these differences:

1. The ball may be passed at any time. This means that it can be thrown at any time beyond the line of scrimmage, during an interception, during a kick-off, or during a received kick.
2. Four downs are given to score a touchdown.
3. A two-handed touch on the back is used instead of pulling a flag.

4. If the ball is thrown from behind the line of scrimmage and results in an incomplete pass, the ball is down at the previous spot on the line of scrimmage. If the pass originates otherwise and is incomplete, the ball is placed at the spot from where this pass was thrown.

5. Since the ball can be passed at any time, no downfield blocking is permitted. A player may screen the ball carrier, but cannot make a block. Screening is defined as running between the ball carrier and the defense.

Testing Football Skills

Tests for football skills include the skills of centering, passing, and kicking (punting).

Centering. Each player is given 5 trials centering at a target. The target should be stationed 6 yards behind the center. Targets which can be used are:

1. An old tire suspended from the ground so that the bottom of the tire is about 2 feet from the ground. Scoring: For centering the ball through the tire--2 points, for hitting the tire but not going through it--1 point. Possible total-- 10 points.
2. If a baseball pitching target is used in the softball program, the device is quite suitable also for a centering target. Scoring is the same as with the tire target.
3. A 2 by 3 foot piece of plywood is needed. This is held by a player at the target line in front of his body with the upper edge even with the shoulders. The target is held stationary and not to be moved during the centering. Scoring: For hitting the target--1 point. Possible total--5 points.
    Other targets can be devised.

Pass for Accuracy. Suspend a tire about shoulder height so that it is fairly stable. The tire can be suspended from goal posts or by the use of volleyball standards. Each' player is given five throws from a minimum distance of 15 yards. As skill increases, increase the distance.
    Scoring: for throwing through the tire--2 points, for hitting the tire but not passing through--1 point. Possible total --10 points.

Passing for Distance. Each player is allotted three passes to determine how far he can throw a football. The longest throw is measured to the nearest foot. It is important to reserve the test for a relatively calm day as the wind can be quite a factor (for or against) in the test.

The passes should be made on a field marked off in 5 yard intervals. Markers made from tongue depressors mark the first pass distance. If a later throw is longer, the marker moves to that point. With markers, the members of a squad can complete the passing turns before measuring, which can then be done at one time for all members of a squad.

Kicking for Distance. Punting, place kicking, and drop kicking can be measured for distance with similar techniques described for passing for distance.

FLAG FOOTBALL FORMATIONS

The following formations are based upon a 9 player team, with 4 backs and 5 linemen. The formations would necessarily vary if the number on each team were decreased. A variety of formations can be presented to the children making for a varied and more interesting game. Formations can be right or left. Only the right formation is presented.

Key: Center ⊗   Lineman O
      End   E   Back   B

Offensive Line Formations

Balanced (tight ends)

E   O   ⊗   O   E

Unbalanced Right (tight ends)

E   ⊗   O O   E

Line Over Right (tight end)

⊗   E   O O   E

Right End Out (Can be one or both)

E   O   ⊗   O (5 YD)   E

Right End Wide (can be one or both)

E   O   ⊗   O   (15 YD)   E

Right End Wide, Left End Out (can be reversed)

E (5 YD) O   ⊗   O   (15 YD)   E

Spread (3 to 5 yards between each lineman)

E   O   ⊗   O   E

Offensive Formations

It should be noted that the formations diagrammed can be combined with any of the offensive line formations. For purposes of clarity, a balanced line with tight ends is used for all formations. However, a variety of line formations can be used with each of the backfield formations.

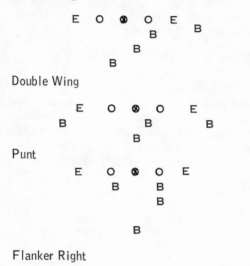

Single Wing.

Double Wing

Punt

Flanker Right

Wing Right, Flanker Left

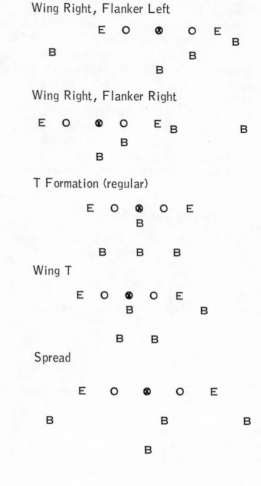

Wing Right, Flanker Right

T Formation (regular)

Wing T

Spread

Pass Patterns

The following pass patterns may be run by the individual pass catcher, be he a lineman or a back. They are particularly valuable to use in practice where the pass receiver will inform the passer of his pattern.

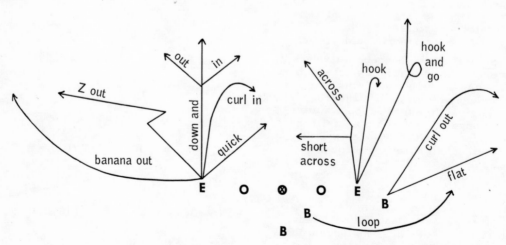

Chapter 25

Soccer

Soccer football is one of the most popular games in the world today, and numbers millions among its participants. However, in the United States, it is overshadowed by American Football as a fall sport.

Soccer is a game for the "educated feet." The purpose is to advance the ball without the use of hands or arms down the field and into the goal. The official goal consists of two goal posts 24 feet apart with a cross bar 8 feet high. The ball must go under the cross bar and between the posts in order to score. However, in the lead-up games, goals are modified so that the ball merely crosses a line below shoulder height or is kicked through a line of defenders.

Success in soccer depends upon how well individual skills are coordinated in team play. Good soccer also stresses position play rather than group of individuals dashing about chasing a ball.

Soccer rates high in its contributions to fitness and offers many opportunities to develop social and emotional qualities.

Emphasis on Each Grade Level

Fourth. Preliminary to the fourth grade, the children should have played Circle Kick Ball and had some experience in kicking skills on an elementary level. Circle Kick Ball is to be reviewed. Fourth grade material stresses kicking primarily and its use in simple lead-up games. Simple rules regarding touching the ball with the hands or arms and what constitutes fouling can be introduced on this level. The toe trap is taught so children can control the ball without the use of hands.

Fifth. Continued emphasis and expansion of kicking skills together with the skills of dribbling and passing make up the bulk of the fifth grade program. Simple elements of team play are brought in. The children should play a modified form of soccer in the fifth grade.

Sixth. Sixth grade children should be introduced to regular soccer with such modifications as needed. The skills designated for the fourth and fifth grade should be reviewed and practiced. A unit of study on soccer as an international game can be scheduled as a class project.

Practical Suggestions

1. Planning soccer experiences is based on the recognition that the skills of soccer must be developed. Few children have opportunities for soccer skills. In addition, the skill of controlling the ball with the feet comes slowly, and sufficient drills together with suitable lead-up activities in progression are important.

2. Soccer, with its attack and defense, can be a rough game. Rough play like pushing, shoving, kicking, and tripping must be controlled. Rules need to be strictly enforced. Good execution of skills leading to good ball control will help eliminate knots of players. Attention to proper heading, blocking, and kicking skills will help eliminate injuries from contacting the ball. Players need to be alert to kicked balls as these may strike players in the face or head unexpectedly. Girls should be taught to fold arms across the chest

GRADE	FOURTH	FIFTH	SIXTH
Skills	Instep Kick Side of Foot Kick Toe kick Toe trap	Heel Kick Outside Foot Kick Dribbling Knee trap Foot trap Passing	Kicking Goals Kick-off (place kick) Punt Volleying Heading
Knowledges	Simple Rules	Ball Control and Passing	The Game of Soccer Team Play and Rules
Activities	Soccer Touch Ball Circle Kick Ball (Review) Circle Soccer Soccer Dodgeball Diagonal Soccer Side Line Soccer Soccer Snatch Ball	Dribble Call Ball Line Soccer Three Line Soccer Modified Soccer	Zone Soccer (coed) Regular Soccer Modified Speed Ball
Tests	Toe Trap Accuracy Kick (Stationary position)	Dribbling Trapping (3 types) Accuracy Kick	Dribbling Punt Place Kick Penalty Kick Accuracy Kick

when stopping the ball. Glasses should be removed when possible or glass guards provided.

3. Children need to be watched carefully for fatigue as soccer is a vigorous game. The teacher should use methods of rotation to help rest players.

4. If soccer is played indoors or on a hard surface, the ball can be deflated enough so it will be confined to the ground. It is difficult for children to keep a lively, bouncing ball in control on a hard surface.

5. Scoring can be modified for children in keeping with their capacities. Scoring must be a challenge but should be neither too easy nor too difficult. To avoid arguments, when the ball is to be kicked through a line of children, the height should be limited to shoulder level or below. This tends to emphasize an important soccer principle of control of the ball on the ground.

Basic Soccer Rules for Lead-up Games

Since lead-up games contain the basic elements of soccer, the rules should show good similarity in many of the activities. There will be variations for the individual games, but the following represent general rules that have a wide application.

1. The ball may not be deliberately played with the hands, forearm, or arm. Mere incidental touch should be disregarded. If the arms are in contact with the body and are used only to block or stop the ball from this position, there is no violation. The free kick is the normal penalty for a touch violation. The ball is placed on the ground with defenders not closer than a specified distance (10 feet, for example) depending on the game. The ball must not be kicked before the referee signals. In some games where the free kick is not practical, a point can be awarded for an illegal touch. A goal cannot be scored from a free kick of this type.

2. The goal keeper is exempt from the illegal touch rule. He may handle the ball within his own area by catching, batting or deflecting with his hands. He may not be charged by the opponents and while holding the ball is limited to four steps by official rules. In elementary school play, the teacher should insist that the goalkeeper get rid of the ball immediately by throwing or kicking. This removes the temptation to play or rough up the goalie. In some lead-up games, a number of students may have privileges of the goalie in handling the ball. The rules need to be clear, and the ball handling should be done within a specified area.

3. For serious fouls like tripping, striking, kicking, holding, or pushing an
opponent, a direct free kick is awarded.
A goal may be scored from such a kick.
In soccer, if the team commits one of
these fouls within its own penalty area
(defensive), a penalty kick should be
awarded. Only the goalkeeper may
defend against this kick which is from
12 yards out. All other players must
be outside the penalty area until the
ball is kicked. In lead-up games, consideration should be given to penalty-
type fouls. These would be committed
in a limited area by the defensive team
near the goal it is defending. A kick
can be awarded or a goal can be scored
for the attacking team for the foul.

4. The ball is out of play, and the whistle
should blow when the ball crosses any
of the boundaries, a goal is scored, or
a foul is called. When a team last
touches or causes the ball to go out of
bounds on the sides, the other team is
awarded the ball. The ball must be
placed near the out of bounds spot and
play is started with a kick. No goal
can be scored from the kick, nor may
the kicker touch the ball again until it
contacts another player.

5. If the ball is caused to go over the end
line, by the attacking side, the defending team receives a kick from any point
desired near the end line of that half of
the field. If the defense last touched
the ball going over the end line, then
the attacking team is awarded a corner
kick. The ball is taken to the corner
on the side where the ball went over
the end line and a direct free kick is
executed. The ball may score from
this kick.

6. The game is started by a kick-off with
both teams on side. In lead-up games,
the kick-off can be used, or the ball
can be dropped for a free ball. In
some games, the teacher may find it
advisable simply to award the ball for
a free kick in the back court to the
team not making the score.

7. Playing time in lead-up games can be
by quarters or by reaching a predetermined score. In a regular soccer,
the play is by quarters.

8. If the ball is trapped or ensnarled
among a number of players or someone
has fallen, a quick whistle is needed.
The ball can be put in play by dropping
it between players of opposite teams.
It can also be rolled in for a start under these conditions.

Soccer Skills

Kicking. Kicking may be done with the instep, the toe, the inside and outside of the
foot, or with the heel. Directions are giv-
en for a right-footed kicker and are to be
reversed for the lefty. Children should
practice kicking with either foot.

Instep Kick. In the kick, the top of the
instep meets the ball as in punting a football. To take the proper position, the left
foot is placed as close beside the ball as
possible without touching it. The body
weight is on a forward lean with the weight
on the ball of the left foot. Keeping the
toe down and foot extended well, the power
comes from the knee by snapping the bent
leg forward. The eye is on the ball which
is contacted with the instep. There is
good follow through with the shift of weight
to the non-kicking foot.

Toe Kick (Kick-Off). The toe kick is not
considered to be as accurate as other kicks
but has use in kicking off and driving the
ball for distance. The technique is similar to the instep kick with the exception of
the position of the feet. The kicking toe
is kept up and the foot is at right angles
with the line of the leg. The force is from
the snap of the knee joint. The non-kicking
foot is kept slightly back of the ball.

Inside Foot Kick. Contact is made with
the inside of the foot. The kick is used
for passing or goal kicking. The knee is
slightly bent, and the leg is swung from
the hip. The kick is used for short distances only.

Outside Foot Kick. This kick is used for
only short distances and for passing or
maneuvering the ball. Contact is made
with the outside of the foot.

Heel Kick. This has value for a short
pass to a teammate behind the player.
Player steps slightly ahead of the ball
and with a short snappy punch of the heel
propels the ball backwards.

Punt. Used by the goalkeeper only, the
punt can be done stationary or on the run.
The ball is held by both hands at waist
height in front of the body. In the stationary position, the kicking foot is forward.
A very short step is taken with the kicking
foot and then a full step on the other leg.
With the knee bent, the kicking foot swings
forward and upward. As contact is made
with the ball at the instep, the knee
straightens and additional power is se-

cured from the other leg through a coordinated rising on the toes or hop.

Trapping. Trapping enables a player to stop or slow down a rolling ball or one on the fly so he can start his own movement. In the elementary school, three types of trapping should be taught. Relaxation and "giving" with the ball are important in all traps.

1. Toe Trap. This is the simplest of all traps and involves stopping a rolling ball by putting the toe on the ball and holding it to the ground.
2. Foot Trap. Using the inside of the foot and giving with the ball, the motion of the ball is stopped by the inside of the foot.
3. Knee Trap. The knee trap can stop both a rolling and a bouncing ball. The ball is smothered with one or both knees. Usually both knees are used.

Dribbling. Dribbling is to move the ball with a series of taps or pushes to cover ground and still retain control of the ball. The best contact point is the inside of the big toe. Both the inside and outside of the foot at times can be used to move the ball.

Volleying. The change of the direction of a ball on the fly is called volleying. This can be done by stiffening a part of the body so the ball will rebound in the desired direction. Volleying can be done with the instep, knee, thigh, hip, or shoulder.

Heading. Heading is a special kind of volleying in which the direction of flight is changed by making an impact with the head. The neck muscles can be used to aid in the blow. The eye must be kept on the ball until the moment of impact which is made at the top of the forehead at the hair line.

Relays. Almost all soccer drills can be organized as relays. Caution is urged to introduce relays only after the children have mastered the skills successfully to have reasonable control of the path of the soccer ball. Insistence of procedure in soccer relays is important. The ball should always be under good control, and a relay should finish with the ball in the possession of the team, not just kicked through or past some line. Touching the ball with the hands or arms should mean disqualification.

Drills for Soccer Skills

The drills for soccer consist of emphasis on kicking, heading, trapping, passing, dribbling, and scoring. Some of the drills concern themselves with only one skill, but the majority offer opportunity to practice a variety of skills. Some of the emphasis in drills centers on the formation and the possibilities which may be developed in the drill formation.

Circle. The circle formation can be used for kicking, passing, and trapping. The ball may be kicked back and forth across the circle or may be passed from player to player in a circular direction. Trapping may be included in the skills.

Circle and Leader. The circle and leader formation lends itself well to the development of soccer skills. The use of the leader in the center allows for more controlled skill practice. The leader passes and receives the ball from each circle player in turn. After completing a round to all the players, the leader takes his place in the circle, and another child becomes the leader.

Two Line Drill. Two lines of three to four children face each other across a ten-yard distance. Players practice kicking, passing, and trapping in this formation. The ball is kicked back and forth in a sequential pattern to include each child.

Shuttle Turnback. The two halves of a shuttle formation face each other about ten yards apart. The first player in line kicks to the first person of the other file who traps the ball and then prepares for his kick. After kicking, the player goes to the end of his file.

Shuttle Dribbling. Dribbling, passing, and trapping can be practiced in the regular shuttle drill. The first player dribbles to the other file. The ball continues to be dribbled back and forth in turn. Each dribbler joins the rear of the file toward which he dribbled.

The player can dribble part way toward the other file and, when about five yards away, pass to the head of the other file.

Circular Dribbling. The players form a large circle standing about three yards apart and facing in. One player starts dribbling the ball around the circle alternating going outside the first player and inside the next in a weaving pattern. After a player completes the round of the circle, he passes to the player ahead of him who continues the drill. Eight players in a circle make a nice number for this drill.

The drill can be used as a relay but considerable control is needed to assure that the path of the ball has been accurate and complete in the weaving movement.

File (lane) Formation Drills. Each team is in a relay formation to practice the skills. A standard or base should be placed about fifteen feet in front of the file. The following patterns of drills illustrate some of the possibilities from this formation.

1. Player dribbles forward, around the base and back to the file.
2. Player dribbles forward, around the base, and from this point passes back to the head of the file.
3. Use three blocks, four yards apart. Player dribbles in and out of the blocks in a weaving motion forming a figure eight pattern.

Passing Drill. A double shuttle formation is used for this drill, which is the equivalent of two teams alongside each other in shuttle formation. The shuttle halves are about 25 to 30 yards apart.

Two players, one from each file, move at a time. One player has the soccer ball. A short dribble is taken forward and then the ball is passed to the other player moving forward with him. The second player takes a short dribble forward and passes the ball back. This continues until they reach the other files where two players repeat the maneuver, returning the ball to its original starting place. The ball is shuttled back and forth by two players at a time.

Heading and Volleying. Two drills are suggested for heading, with 6 to 8 players in a drill formation.

1. Circle and leader. The leader in the center tosses the ball to each in turn for practicing heading or volleying. This is a drill for control and for developing good form.
2. Circle Formation. After the children have some practice in volleying and heading, they can volley or head the ball in a circle formation trying to keep it up continuously.

Goal Kicking. Three stages are suggested for goal kicking drills.

1. A file of players is stationed about 40 feet in front of the goal. A ball chaser awaits behind the goal. Each file player in turn dribbles forward about 10 to 15 feet and attempts to score a goal.

2. A goalie guards the goal while another child is the ball chaser. Each file player in turn advances with the ball and tries to outwit the goalie and score a goal.
3. Three-on-two drills emphasize the need for accurate passing and kicking. Two players are on defense and three offensive players advance with the ball. The object for the three is to advance and score a goal.

Activities

Third Grade

CIRCLE KICK BALL

Formation: Circle with hands joined

Players: 10-20

Supplies: Soccer or 10 inch playground ball

Players kick the ball (with the side of the foot) back and forth inside of the circle. The object is to kick the ball out of the circle under-neath the joined arms of the circle players. A point is scored against each of the players where the ball left the circle. Any player kicking the ball over the joined hands gets a point against him. A variation is to eliminate the offending players instead of scoring points against them.

Fourth Grade

SOCCER TOUCH BALL

Formation: Circle with player in center.

Players: 8 - 10

Supplies: Soccer

Players are spaced around a circle about ten yards in diameter. The object of the game is to keep the player in the center from touching the ball. The ball is passed back and forth as in soccer. If the center player touches the ball, the person who kicked the ball goes to the center. Also, if there is an error like a missed ball, that person exchanges with one in the center.

CIRCLE SOCCER

Formation: A double circle is drawn on the floor.   The outer circle is 20 to 25 feet in diameter and the inner circle is placed so that a two-foot space is available between circles.   A diameter is drawn across both circles.

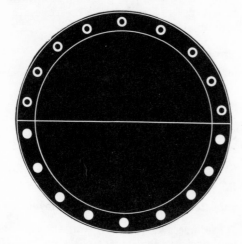

Players: 20 - 30 children divided into two teams.

Supplies: A soccer ball, slightly deflated.

The object of the game is to kick the ball through the defense of the other team.   Each team occupies the space between the circles, one on each side of the diameter.

Scoring: One point is scored for the opponents if:
1. The ball is touched with the hands.
2. The ball goes through the team below the shoulder level.
3. A player steps over the inner circle when kicking.
4. The ball is kicked higher than the shoulders of the smaller of two adjacent players.   A game consists of 21 points.

Dead Ball: If the ball comes to rest in the circle, any player on that side may pass the ball to a teammate.   Any other ball is put into play where it left the circle.   If between two players, the one on the right has the right to play the ball.

Blocking: The ball may be blocked with any part of the body except the hands and forearms.

Rotation: After each score, the players rotate one place to the right.

Teaching Suggestions: Emphasize that girls are to cross arms over the chest when blocking a ball.   Particularly on hard surfaces should the ball be deflated enough to stay on the ground.   Kicking with the side of the foot will also keep the ball low.   Children should be encouraged to trap the ball before returning it.

Variation: The same principle of kicking through the other team in Circle Soccer can be used if the two teams are lined up facing each other about twenty feet apart.   However, two retrievers, one from each team, are needed to return the ball to their own teams.   They roam the center and pass only to their own teammates.   They may compete for the loose ball but cannot block or impede the ball.   A rotation system after each point is needed to include the retrievers.

SOCCER DODGE BALL

Formation: One team forms a circle with the other team grouped in the center.

Players: 20 - 30.

Supplies: Soccer, slightly deflated.

This is a variation of Team Dodge Ball (page 116), except that the ball is kicked instead of thrown at the center players.   Players may not use their hands to control or retrieve the ball.   A point is scored for the kicking team for each time a person in the center is hit.   Hit players can be eliminated or remain to be hit again.   A point is deducted from the team score for every violation by touching with the hands.

The ball should be deflated slightly and kicked with the side of the foot.

DIAGONAL SOCCER

Formation: A square about 30 by 30 feet with a diagonal line from corner to corner.

Players: 20 to 40

Supplies: Soccer Ball

The diagonal line divides the playing area into two team halves; the members of the team line up on the sides of the square in their half. Two players are out on the floor from each team in their own half of the floor.   These are the active players; the others act as line guards.   The active players try to intercept

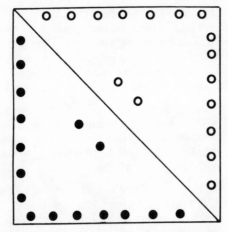

passes and kick through the opposite team's line to score. When a score is made, the active players rotate to the sidelines and two new players take their places.

Players on the sidelines may block the ball with their bodies but cannot use their hands. The team against whom the point was scored starts the ball for the next point.

Scoring: Scoring is much the same as in Circle Soccer in that a point is scored for your opponents if you:

1. Allow the ball to go through your line below shoulders.
2. Touch the ball illegally.
3. Kick the ball over the other team above shoulder height.
4. If an active player steps over the diagonal line to retrieve or kick the ball.

Teaching Suggestions: If the class is large, enlarge the area and use 3 or 4 active players at a time.

SIDE LINE SOCCER

Formation: Square about 40 by 40 feet.

Players: 10 to 15 on each team.

Supplies: Soccer.

The teams line up on the sidelines of the square with the end lines open. Three active players from each team are called for from the end of the team line. These remain active until a point is scored and then are rotated to the other end of the line.

The object is to kick the ball over the end line which has no defenders. The three compete against each other and can be helped by the players on the sidelines. A ball to score must go over the end line at or below shoulder height and counts two points. None of the players may play the ball with the hands. The active players follow the restrictions of no pushing, holding, kicking, or other rough play. This constitutes a foul and causes a point to be awarded to the other team.

The ball must be last kicked by an active player to score. If the ball is out of bounds or does not score, play continues until a point is scored by the group of active players.

Play is started by the referee dropping the ball between two players from opposite teams. Out of bounds is given to the team opposite the one which caused the ball to go out. This is a free kick but cannot score a goal directly from the kick. Violation of the touch rule is also a free kick at the spot of the foul.

Teaching Suggestions: When the ball is dropped, the remaining players should be back protecting their goal.

Variation: If the scoring seems to be too easy, make smaller goals on each end by use of jumping or volleyball standards or other markers.

The distance between goals can also be increased to make more playing area.

SOCCER SNATCH BALL

Formation: Two parallel lines about 30 feet apart.

Players: 6 to 10 on each team.

Supplies: Soccer

Each team is numbered consecutively and is back behind its line. For each number on one team there is a corresponding number on the other team.

The teacher places the ball at a spot midway between the two lines. The teacher calls a number, and the two players, one from each team, run forward. Each tries to capture the ball and kick it back to his own line. A point is scored when the ball is over the line below shoulder level. If over shoulder height, the other team scores a point.

Teaching Suggestion: The teacher varies the order of the numbers but should make sure that every number is called. If the ball goes out on the sides, it can be dropped between the two active players.

Fifth Grade

DRIBBLE CALL BALL

Formation: Circle formation for each team.

Players: 6-10 on each team.

Supplies: Soccer ball for each team.

The players on each team are numbered consecutively. The teams should be equal in numbers. A soccer ball is placed in a two-foot square in the center of each team circle. When the teacher calls a number, each opponent holding this number runs to the center of his circle and dribbles the ball out through the space just vacated, around the circle, and back through the opening to the center area, where he finishes by placing his foot on the ball while it is in the small square. As soon as the winner is determined, he returns to his place and another is called. One point is scored for the winner.

Teaching Suggestions: The game should be played with not over ten children on each team. It is better to have more teams with fewer children on each team. The teacher should stand where he can see the order of teams finishing. The players could sit down in the circle, and the player whose number is called arises and competes. If the players are seated, there is less tendency to make the circle smaller. The game is over when all numbers have been called.

Variation: If as many as four teams are competing as one, scoring can be on the basis of 3 points for first, 2 for second, and 1 for third.

LINE SOCCER

Formation: Two goal lines about 50 feet apart with sidelines 40 to 50 feet wide.

Number: 10 to 20 on each team.

Supplies: Soccer.

Each team stands on one goal line which it is to defend. The referee stands in the center of the field holding a ball. At the whistle two players (three if the teams are large) from the right side of each line run to the center and become the active players. The referee drops the ball to the floor and the players try to kick it through the other team defending the goal line. The players in the field may advance by kicking only. The line players act as goalies and are permitted to catch the ball. The ball must be laid down immediately and either rolled or kicked. It cannot be punted or drop kicked.

Scoring: One point is scored when the ball is kicked through the opponent's goal below shoulder level. One point is also scored in case of a personal foul involving pushing, kicking, tripping, etc.

Penalties: For illegal touching by the active players, a direct free kick from a point twelve yards in front of the penalized team's goal line is given. All active players on the kicking team, except the kicker, must be to one side until the ball is kicked.

Time Limit: A time limit should be set of two minutes for any set of players. If no goal is scored during this time, a halt is called and players are changed.

Out of Bounds: The ball is awarded to the opponents of the team last touching it out of bounds. A free kick from the side line is in order. If the ball goes over the shoulders of the defenders at the end line, any end line player may retrieve the ball and put it in play with a throw or kick.

Teaching Suggestions: Line Soccer should be played with the rules of soccer where possible. If boys and girls are together, girls should complete only against girls as active players. Arrange the rotation so this occurs.

Variations:
1. If there is enough space, the teams can be divided into fourths (1's, 2's, 3's, and 4's.) They need not keep any particular order at the end lines but simply come out as active players when called. By the use of numbers, the teacher can put different groups against each other.
2. An offside line can be used. This is a line parallel to the goal line and five feet from the line. No offensive player can cross the offside line. The object is to keep the charging players away from the defensive line.
3. A regular goal can count two points while a goal from a direct free kick can count only one.
4. Instead of giving a score for a personal foul, a penalty kick can be awarded. For illegal touching, a free kick can be awarded.

THREE LINE SOCCER

Formation: Soccer field 80 to 120 feet long, 60 to 100 feet wide.

Number: 15 to 20 on each team.

Supplies: Soccer.

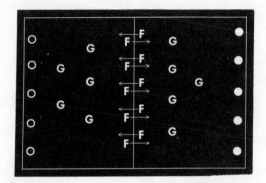

This game follows the same general rules of Line Soccer. Each team is divided into three equal groups and line up as Forwards, Guards, and Goalies. Whenever a point is scored or the time is called, the teams rotate positions.

The forwards stand at the center line for the kickoff and then for play move into the forward (for them) portion of the field. The guards are scattered in the back half of the field and the goalies are on the goal line. Thus forwards compete against guards of the other team while the goalies guard the goal.

The goalies may use their hands to defend their goal but the other players follow regular soccer player rules.

The game is started with a kick-off at the center with all players on side. After each score, the team that did not score get to kick off.

Penalties:
    Free Kick -- For illegal touch and from the spot of the foul.
    Direct Free Kick -- Personal foul by a team in its front court.
    Penalty Kick -- Personal foul by a team in its back court (defense). The ball is placed 12 yards from the goal line and only the goalies may defend.

MODIFIED SOCCER

Formation: Any large area 100 by 150 feet.

Number: 9 to 13 on each team.

Supplies: Soccer.

The game begins to approximate regular soccer play but without position play. Each team has one goalkeeper, and the remainder of the players are divided between forwards and guards. The goal is 24 feet wide and should be marked by jumping standards.

The game follows the same rules as Three Line Soccer except that instead of a full line of goalies, there is only one goalkeeper. One new feature needs to be introduced, the Corner Kick. This occurs when the ball goes over the end line but not through the goal last touched by the defense. If the attacking team last touched the ball, the goalkeeper kick is awarded. The goalie puts the ball down and place-kicks it forward. If the defenders last touch a ball going over the end line, the ball is taken to the nearest corner for a corner kick. This is a direct free kick and a goal can be scored from the kick.

Most soccer rules, previously outlined, apply to this version of the game.

The forwards play in the front half of the field and the guards are in the back half. However, neither are restricted to these areas entirely but may cross the center line without penalty.

Sixth Grade

ZONE SOCCER (Coed)

Playing Area: Soccer field 100 to 150 feet long, 90 to 120 feet wide.

Players: 2 teams of 8 to a side (4 boys and 4 girls)

Supplies: Soccer

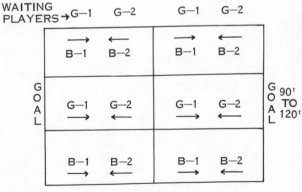

CODE: TEAM 1:   BOYS, B—1;   GIRLS, G—1
         TEAM 2:   BOYS, B—2;   GIRLS, G—2

The field is divided into six zones as illustrated, with a pair of players (one from each team), occupying each zone. At the side of the field (at the top in the diagram) extra players await turn to rotate on to the field. The occupants of any one zone are either both boys or both girls. Players must play a ball only in their zone or on a line bordering the zone. This allows for mixed participation, but boys compete against boys and girls against girls. Also, the size of the teams means that two separate games can be organized in a normal class situation utilizing 32 or more students. The game proceeds as in soccer with the following exceptions.

1. There is no goalkeeper. No players may use the arms and hands to stop or handle the ball.

2. The ball to score must go through the goal at shoulder height or below. Each goal from the field scores 2 points.

3. In addition to the other fouls normally called in soccer, a free kick is declared if a player kicks or interferes with a ball not in his zone. A goal may be scored from such a kick. A score resulting directly from a free kick counts 1 point. On a free kick, the defensive player in the zone where the ball is kicked must be back at least 15 feet. Any foul closer than 15 feet to the goal results in moving the ball out 15 feet in front of the goal with the defender positioned on the goal line.

4. Balls which go outside on the sidelines are placed in play by a stationary kick by the opposite team at the point where the ball went out.

5. Balls which go over the end line, except for a deliberate kick by the defense, are put in play by a free kick by the defense 5 feet in front of the goal line at the point where the ball crossed the goal line. A deliberate kick over its goal line by the defense results in a free kick 15 feet directly in front of the goal by an offensive player.

6. Players rotate after every score or at the end of a fixed time period. A system of rotation is set up so that the sidelined players move into the adjacent zone. The players on the far side after rotating off the field go around to take the place of the original sidelined players who have just moved into the adjacent zone.

7. After a score, the ball is put in play just back of the center line by the team which did not score. A team cannot score _directly_

from this kick. The ball must be passed to another player before a score can result.

REGULATION SOCCER

The Field:

SOCCER FIELD

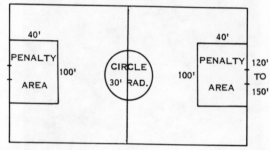

240' TO 300'

Players: 11 on each side, including 5 forwards, 3 halfbacks, 2 fullbacks, and 1 goalkeeper

Duties of Players:

Forwards--Advance the ball into scoring territory and attempt to score.

Halfbacks--Work both as offense and de= fense. Must do a great deal of running. Must back up both offense and defense.

Fullbacks--Primarily defense. Must be skilled in defensive movements.

Goalkeeper--The last line of defense. Must be agile and skillful in blocking the ball. May use hands on defense within own penalty area.

The Kick-off: On the toss of the coin, the winner gets the choice of kicking off or selecting his goal. The loser exercises the option not selected by the winner.

The ball must travel forward about one yard by the kicker, and he cannot touch it again until another player has kicked it. The defensive team must be ten yards away from the kicker. After each score, the team not winning the point gets to kick off. Both teams must be on-side at the kick-off. The defensive team must stay on side and out of the center circle until the ball is kicked.

Scoring: Regular Soccer rules call for scoring by counting the number of goals made.

Playing Time: Elementary School children should play not more than six minute quarters.

There should be a rest period of one minute between periods and ten minutes between halves.

Out of Bounds: When the ball goes out of bounds on the sides, it is put in play with a throw-in from the spot where it crossed the line. No goal may be scored nor may the kicker play the ball a second time until it has been touched by another player. All opponents are to be ten yards back at the time of the throw.

If the ball is caused to go out of bounds on the end line by the attacking team, a goal kick is awarded. The ball is placed in the goal area and kicked beyond the penalty area by a defending player. He may not touch it twice in succession and all defensive players are to be ten yards back.

Corner Kick: If the ball is caused to go out of bounds over the end line by the defensive team, a corner kick shall be awarded. The ball shall be placed one yard from the corner of the field and kicked into the field of play by an attacking player. The ten yard restriction also applies here to the defensive player.

Dropped Ball: If the ball is touched by two opponents at the same time and caused to go out of bounds, a drop ball shall be called. The referee drops the ball between two opponents who cannot kick the ball before it touches the ground. A drop ball is also called when the ball is trapped among downed players.

Fouls: Personal fouls involving unnecessary roughness are penalized. Tripping, striking, charging, holding, pushing, or jumping into an opponent intentionally are forbidden.

It is a foul for any player except the goalkeeper to handle the ball with the hands or arms. The goalkeeper is allowed only four steps and must then get rid of the ball.

Other fouls are:
Playing the ball again when it should be contacted first by another player as in the throw-in, penalty kick, or free kick.
Failure to kick the ball the proper distance on the kick-off or penalty kick.
Goalkeeper carrying the ball or taking more than four steps.
Kicking the ball before it hits the ground on an official drop ball.

Penalties: A penalty kick is awarded if a personal foul is committed by the defense within its own penalty area. The ball is placed 12 yards from the goal and only the goalkeeper can be in the penalty area.

A direct free kick is awarded at the spot for a personal foul and illegal touching. This kick may score a goal.

A free kick is awarded for the other infractions listed. Another player must play the ball after the free kick in order that a goal can be scored.

Teaching Suggestions: Players should be taught to play their positions, staying on their side of the field.

Teams should wear pinnies or shirts so that the teams can be distinguished.

Teams should attempt to develop control and accuracy. The ball is better advanced by passing rather than by long kicking.

The lines should be spread to avoid crowding.

Halfbacks should take most free kicks so the forwards can be in position.

Eye glass protectors must be worn by those with glasses.

MODIFIED SPEEDBALL

Speedball combines the techniques of soccer and basketball. The ball may be advanced as in soccer or by passing as in basketball. Rule departures from the game of soccer are:

1. Any player may catch a kicked ball before it touches the ground. The ball can be advanced by passing as in basketball. As soon as the ball touches the ground, the play is as in soccer, until another kicked ball is caught in the air. A ball which bounces from the ground, even though it is in the air, cannot be caught. It is a ground ball and must be played as such.
2. A player catching the ball is allowed only two steps or traveling is called giving the other team the ball outside. Jump ball may be called as in basketball when the ball is tied up with two opposing players.
3. Fouls follow the same pattern as in soccer. The penalty area in speedball is a line ten yards out from the goal line.
4. One air dribble is allowed in advancing the ball. To make an air dribble, a player throws the ball into the air ahead of himself, runs forward, and catches the ball before it hits the ground. Dribbling the ball by bouncing, as in basketball, is not permitted.

5. For violations for traveling and illegal handling of the ball, the other team is awarded the ball out of bounds for a throw in.

Scoring:

Goal--a ball kicked through the goal as in soccer scores 2 points.

Touchdown--a ball passed over the goal line caught by a teammate scores 1 point.

Tests for Soccer Skills

The tests for soccer skills cover various kinds of kicks, dribbling, and trapping.

<u>Dribbling-Figure Eight</u>. Three obstacles or markers are arranged in line, four yards apart with the first positioned four yards from the starting line. The starting line is four yards wide. A stop watch is used, and the timing is done to the nearest tenth of a second.

Three trials are given each player, with the fastest trial taken as the score. On each trial, the contestant dribbles over the figure eight course and finishes by kicking or dribbling the ball over the four yard finish line, at which time the watch is stopped.

The test is best done on a grass surface, but if a hard surface must be used, the ball should be deflated somewhat so that it can be controlled.

<u>Trapping</u>. The formation is a file plus one. The one in front of the file is the thrower. The thrower stands 15 to 20 feet in front of the file and rolls the ball on the ground to the player at the head of the file. Three trials each for the toe trap, foot trap, and knee trap are given. The ball must be definitely stopped and controlled. A score of 9 points is possible, one point awarded for each successful trap.

The thrower should adopt one type of throw which is to be used for all traps and all players. If the scorer judges that the roll wasn't a proper opportunity, the trial is taken over. For the fourth grade, the only trap taught is the toe trap. Five trials can be allowed with only one trap being tested.

<u>Soccer Punt for Distance</u>. A football or other field marked in gridiron fashion at five or ten yard intervals is needed. One soccer is needed, but if three can be used, considerable time is saved. A measuring tape (25 or 50 feet) plus individual markers round out the supply list.

Each player is given three kicks from behind a restraining line over which

he cannot cross during the kicks. One child marks the kick for distance while one or two other children act as ball chasers.

After the three kicks, the player's marker is left at the spot of his longest kick. This is determined by the point where the ball <u>first touches</u> after the kick. Measurement is taken to the nearest foot.

The squad or small group should all kick before the measurements are taken. The punt must be from a standing, not running, start.

If a child crosses the line during the kick, it is ruled a foul and counts as a trial. No measurement is taken.

<u>Soccer Place Kick for Distance</u>. The directions are the same for this test as for the punt for distance with two exceptions. The ball is kicked from a stationary position. It must be laid on a flat surface and not elevated by dirt, grass, or other means.

The second difference is that the child is given credit for the entire distance of the kick including the roll. The kicking should be done to a grassy surface as the ball will roll indefinitely on a smooth, hard surface. If the surface presents a problem, the test can be limited to the distance the ball has traveled in flight.

<u>Penalty Kick</u>. The child faces a target area from behind a point ten yards out where the ball has been placed. The child stands behind the ball.

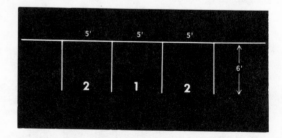

The target area is formed by a rope stretched tight so it will be 6 feet above the ground. Four ropes are dropped from this at distances 5 feet apart. This outlines three target areas 6 feet high and 5 feet wide. The center target area scores 1 point and the side areas 2. This is in keeping with the principle that a penalty kick should be directed away from a goalkeeper toward either corner of the goal.

Each child is allotted 5 kicks at the target. A score of 10 points is possible.

<u>Accuracy Kick</u>. The same target is used for this kick as for the penalty kick. However, the center area scores 2 points and

the side areas 1 each. A balk line is drawn about 20 feet from the target. The child is back another 20 feet for a start. He dribbles the ball forward and must kick the ball as it is moving but before it crosses the balk line. Five trials are given and a score of 10 points is possible.

Variation: The test can also be used with a stationary kick (placekick). The kicking distance would depend upon the capacities of the group.

Chapter 26
Softball

Softball plays an important part in the elementary school program. Too often, however, it is the only activity stressed outdoors.

The major emphasis in softball should be on instruction. Children have adequate opportunity during recess, noon-hour and other times to play the game. In the physical education class, too much of the softball participation is of the "choose-sides-and-let-em-go" variety. Since youngsters are eager for and love softball, a good instruction program should make use of this drive. Softball instruction should begin in the third grade and progress through the sixth. By the time the children are in the fifth grade, they should be playing regular softball, modified for their level.

Since softball experiences vary so much, it is difficult to allocate with sureness the various skills and knowledges for a progressive program. The third grade program is outlined because it is felt that planned instruction in the game should begin on this level. It is recognized that second graders should throw and catch with softballs along with other types of balls. However, the plan of instruction for softball to include the necessary elements begins on the next grade level.

Emphasis on Different Grade Levels

<u>Third Grade</u>. Teaching the basic skills of throwing, catching, and batting is the emphasis on the third grade level. The lead-up games for the third grade are quite simple but do provide an introduction to the game of softball. There is very little emphasis on the pitcher and the catcher. A few basic rules are learned.

<u>Fourth Grade</u>. In the fourth grade, specific skills of pitching, infield play, base running, bunting, and batting provide the material for this portion. Proper pitching techniques in keeping with the pitching rules are important to the budding softball player.

<u>Fifth Grade</u>. The fifth grade student should be provided with the background to play the game of regulation softball designed for his age level. The material for instruction is pointed toward this end. Much of emphasis is an expansion of the fourth grade program. Additional techniques useful in the regular game of softball have been added.

<u>Sixth Grade</u>. The sixth grade program adds Tee-Ball, new pitching techniques, and double play work. Batting, throwing, catching, and bunting skills are continued.

Practical Suggestions

1. Safety is of utmost importance. The following should be observed.
   a. Throwing the bat is a constant danger. The members of the batting team should stand on the side opposite to the batter. For a right-handed batter, the batting team members should be on the first base side, and vice versa.
   b. To control the batter in keeping him from throwing the bat:
      (1) Have the batter touch the bat to the ground before dropping it.
      (2) Call the batter "out" if he throws the bat.
      (3) Have the batter carry the bat to first base.
      (4) Have the batter change ends with the bat before dropping it.

GRADE	THIRD	FOURTH	FIFTH	SIXTH
Skills				
Throwing	Gripping the ball Overhand throw Underhand toss	Continued practice Around the bases	Throw-in from outfield Side arm throw	Continued practice

Catching
and
Fielding
	Catching thrown
	  balls
	Catching fly balls
	Grounders
		Continued practice
		Fielding grounders
		  in infield
		Sure stop for out-
		  field
			Catching flies
			  from fungo
			  batting
			Infield practice
				Flies and infield
				  practice

Batting	Simple skills	Fungo hitting Continued practice	Different posi- tions at plate	Tee batting Bunting
Fielding positions		Infield practice How to catch	Infield positions Backing up other players	Double play

Base
running
	To first base	To first base and
		  turning
		Circling the base
			Getting a good
			  start off base
			Tagging up on
			  fly ball
				Sacrifice

Pitching	Simple underhand	Application of
		  pitching rule
			Target pitching	Curve, drop,
				  slow pitches

Coaching			Coaching at bases	
Knowledges				

Rules	Strike Zone
	Foul and Fair
	  ball
	No lead-off
	Safe and out
		Pitching Rule
		  Position
		  Illegal Pitches
		Foul Tip
		Bunt Rule
		When the batter
		  is safe or out
			Infield Fly
			Keeping Score
			Base Running
				Review all rules
				Situation type
				  quiz

Activities	Throw It and Run
	
	Two Pitch Softball
		Hit and Run
		Kick Softball
		Hit the Bat
		Two Pitch Softball
		  (from 3rd grade)
			Five Hundred
			Bat Ball
			Home Run
			Kick Pin Softball
			Scrub (Work-up)
				Tee Ball
				Twice Around
				Far Base Softball
				Hurry Baseball
				Three Team
				  Softball
				Base Circling
				  Contest

Tests	None	Target Throw
		Throw for distance
			Old Woody
			  (Strike Target)
			Throw for
			  distance
			Circling the bases
				Tee Batting
				Old Woody
				Throw for dis-
				  tance
				Circling the bases

(5) Have the batter place the bat in a three-foot circle before running.

c. Sliding leads to both injury and destruction of clothing. No sliding should be permitted. Runner should be called out.

d. If a catcher is expected to stand up close behind the plate, while catching, he must wear a mask.

e. Colliding while running for the ball can be held to a minimum if players are taught to call for the ball and not to trespass on the other players' areas.

2. Care of equipment is a responsibility of all. The trademark of the bat should be kept up when contacting the ball in the middle of the swing. The bat should be used to bat softballs only. Hitting rocks and sticks with the bat injures the bat and lessens both its effectiveness and life. The bat should be carried from one person to another and not thrown.

3. The spoiler of many games of the softball type is the pitcher-batter duel. If this is prolonged with few hits by the batter, the remainder of the players justifiably become bored from standing around. By having a member of the batting team pitch is one method of eliminating the problem. The teacher needs to give attention to this to see that the pitcher is under control.

4. Players should rotate often. A good rule in physical education classes is that everyone, including the pitcher, should rotate at the start of a new inning.

5. The distance between the bases has a heavy effect on the game. The distance should be lessened or increased according to the game and the capacities of the children.

6. Umpires can be appointed or the team at bat can umpire. A rule that can be followed is that the person who made the last out of the previous inning is the umpire for the coming inning. There should be instruction for all in umpiring. To expect a child to umpire properly without proper instruction is poor teaching.

7. Encourage good players to recognize and give approval to those who are less skillful. Since there are many differences in ability, an opportunity for a lesson in tolerance is present. It is important not to let an error become a tragedy to a child.

8. Each player should run out his hit, no matter how hopeless it seems.

9. Analyze each of the lead-up games for its purpose and practice the needed skills before their inclusion in the game.

10. Insist on conformance to the rules. Copies of the Official Guide for Softball should be available in the classroom.

11. Children need to recognize that perfection in softball skills comes only through good practice sessions.

12. Teach respect for officials and acceptance of the umpire's judgment. The disreputable practice of baiting the umpire should be no part of the child's softball experiences.

Basic Rules for Softball
Third and Fourth Grades

For the few lead-up games and as an introduction to softball, it is necessary to establish certain selected rules of softball for use in the third grade. The following provides a minimum.

1. The nine players on a softball team are the catcher, pitcher, first baseman, second baseman, short stop, third baseman, left fielder, center fielder, and right fielder. The right fielder is the outfielder nearest first base.

2. All pitching is underhand.

3. A pitch to be called a strike must be over the plate and between the knees and shoulders of the batter. A ball is a pitch which does not go through this area.

4. A foul ball is a batted ball that settles outside the foul lines between home and first or home and third. A ball that goes over a base is a fair ball. Also, any fly ball that lands in foul territory beyond first or third base is a foul ball.

5. No lead-off from any base is permitted in softball. The runner must keep his foot on the base until the pitcher releases the ball.

6. The batter is out if a fly ball, either foul or fair, is caught.

7. The batter is safe if he reaches first base before the fielding team can get the ball to the first baseman with his foot on the base.

8. A batter is out if he misses the ball three times. This is called striking out.

9. A run is scored if the baserunner makes the circuit of bases (first, second, third, and home) before the batting team has three outs.

Basic Rules for Softball

Fifth and Sixth Grades

Most sporting goods establishments have copies of the official rules available, and for rules study an official rule guide should be used. However, the following represent some of the basic rules for the game. The rules listed in the section immediately preceding should be reviewed.

Playing Area. The official diamond has 60-foot base lines and a pitching distance of 46 feet. Play in the intermediate grades should be with baselines not over 45 feet and a pitching distance of 35 feet or less.

Number of Players. Nine players make up a team. A few years ago, a tenth man called the short fielder was officially a part of the game, but has since been eliminated.

Batting Order. Players may bat in any order, although at times it is convenient in class play to have them bat according to their positions in the field. Once the batting order has been established, it may not be changed, even if the player changes to another position in the field.

Pitching Rule. The pitcher must observe the following:

1. Face the batter with both feet on the pitching rubber with the ball held in front of him with both hands.
2. He is allowed one step toward the batter and must deliver the ball while taking that step.
3. The ball must be pitched underhanded.
4. He cannot fake a pitch nor make any motion toward the plate without delivering the ball.
5. He cannot roll or bounce the ball to the batter to keep him from hitting it.
6. No quick return is allowed before the batter is ready.

Batting. The bat must be a softball bat. The batter cannot cross to the other side of the plate when the pitcher is ready to pitch. If a player bats out of turn, he is out. A bunt foul on the third strike is out. A pitched ball that touches or hits the batter, entitles the batter to first base.

Base Running. No lead-off is permitted. The runner must hold his base until the ball leaves the pitcher's hands on the penalty of being called out. On an overthrow where the ball goes into foul territory and out of play, runners advance one base beyond the base to which they are headed at the time of the overthrow. On an over-

throw at second base by the catcher with the ball rolling into center field, the runners may advance as far as they can. To avoid being tagged on a base line, the runner is limited to a three-foot distance on either side of a direct line from base to base. A runner hit by a batted ball while off the base is out. The batter, however, is entitled to first base. Base runners must touch all bases. If a runner fails to touch a base, it is an appeal play which means that the fielding team must call the oversight to the attention of the umpire, who will then (and not before) rule on the play.

Fly Ball. Any fly ball, foul or fair, when caught is out. A foul fly, however, must be over the head of the batter or it is ruled as a foul tip. A foul tip caught counts as a strike and the ball is in play. A foul tip, then, caught on the third strike makes the batter out.

Softball Skills for the Third Grade

Overhand Throwing. The ball is held with two fingers on top, third and fourth fingers on one side, and the thumb on the other. The hand is brought back so the hand is well behind the shoulder at about that height. The left side of the body is turned in the direction of the throw, and the left arm is raised and in front of the body. The weight is on the back (right) foot with the left foot advanced with the toe touching the ground. The arm comes forward, and the ball is thrown with a downward snap of the wrist. The weight of the body is brought forward into the throw with the weight shifting to the front foot. There should be good follow-through.

Underhand Toss. The hand and arm are brought back with the palms forward in a pendulum swing. The elbow is held slightly bent. The weight is mostly on the back foot. The arm comes forward almost like a bowling motion and the ball is tossed. The weight shifts to the front foot during the toss.

Pitching. Stand with both feet facing the batter and the ball held in front. As the ball is brought back for the toss the forward step of the left foot begins. When the toss is made, the weight is shifted to the forward (left) foot.

Catching Fly Balls. There are two methods for catching a fly ball.

1. For a low ball, the fielder keeps his little fingers together and forms a

basket with his hands.
2. For a higher ball, the thumbs are together, and the ball is caught just in front of the chin.

There should be "give" with the catching hands. Care should be taken with a spinning ball to provide sufficient squeeze of the hands to stop the spinning.

Fielding Grounders. Always play the ball, don't let the ball play you. Advance on the ball. Try to catch it on a high hop or just as it hits the ground. Feet should be well apart and the eyes on the ball.

The little fingers are together and the hands are lowered with a stooping motion rather than being bent over. For right handers, the left foot should be slightly ahead.

Batting (Right Handed). Stand with the left side of the body toward the pitcher with the feet spread and the weight on both feet. The body should be facing the plate. Hold the bat with the trade mark up such that the left hand (for right handed batters) grasps the bat lower than the right. The bat is held over the right shoulder point both back and up. The elbows are away from the body for free swinging.

The swing begins with a hip roll and a short step forward in the direction of the pitcher. The bat is now swung level with the ground at the height of the pitch. Eyes are kept on the ball until it is hit. After the hit, there is good follow through.

Beginning batters should use the choke grip which is to hold the bat several inches above the small end of the bat.

Base Running. Children should be taught to run directly toward first base and run to a spot past the base. Too often, they run to first base, stop, and put a foot on it.

Softball Skills for the
Fourth to Sixth Grades

Throwing and catching should be continued from the third grade instruction. Additional points to be emphasized are:

Throwing and Catching. Step toward the target and follow through well. Begin at short range and increase distances. Practice getting the ball away quickly.

Add the side arm throw, which is used for short distances and when there is need to throw quickly. The ball is thrown from the hand at shoulder level with a bent elbow and quick snap of the wrist.

In catching, stress relaxation and giving with the ball. Players should keep the eyes on the ball and move quickly in position in front of the path of the ball. Getting the ball away fast after a catch should be emphasized.

In fielding grounders, the body should be crouched with the hands about six inches above the ground. The hands can be lowered or raised depending on the path of the ball.

Infield Practice. Infield practice should be frequently held, from the simple throwing around the bases to a full fledged practice.

Batting. Youngsters should have experience with different grips on the bat -- the end, choke, and modified grips. Stress a light grip on the bat as this relaxes the forearm muscles. The bat should be held back but not on the shoulders. The arms are away from the body. As the ball is delivered, the batter takes a short, low step forward. The hit is made with a free, full, level swing and follow through.

Points the batter should avoid are:

Lifting the front foot high off the ground
Stepping back with the rear foot
Dropping the rear shoulder
Chopping down on the ball or golfing
Dropping the elbows
Crouching or bending forward
Failure to keep eyes on the ball

Bunting. The child turns almost facing the pitcher with his right foot alongside the home plate. As the pitcher releases the ball, the upper hand is run about halfway up the bat. Hold the bat loosely in front of the body and parallel to the ground. Just meet the ball. The ball can be directed down either first or third base lines.

The surprise or drag bunt is done without the squaring around or facing the pitcher. Hold the bat in a choke grip, and, when the pitcher lets go of the ball, run the right hand up on the bat. Direct the ball down either foul line, keeping it inside as near the line as possible.

Sure Stop for Outfield Balls. To keep the ball from going through an outfielder and allowing extra bases, a type of stop can be used which uses the body as a barrier in case the ball is missed by the hands. The fielder turns half right and lowers the left knee to the ground at the point where the ball is coming. The hands attempt to catch the rolling ball, but if missed, the body will generally stop the ball.

Baserunning. Since in softball the runner must hold the base until the pitcher releases the ball, the children should be shown a type of leaning sprint start with the left foot on the bag and the right toes digging in for a start. In running to bases, the children should run at the base and avoid circling.

Pitching. The pitcher should assume his position with both feet on the rubber and facing the batter. The ball is held with both hands in front of the body. As the arm comes forward, the child steps with his left foot. Additional speed can be had from a good stretch to rear before the throw. However, the goal at this stage is accuracy. Good follow through and wrist action are important.

Fielding Positions. In the infield, children should be off the bases in proper fielding positions. Shifts for both the infield and outfield should be made on right and left handed hitters. Players should be taught to straddle the bag when receiving the ball for a tag play.

Drills for Softball Skills

Softball Throwing and Catching Drills

Many drills can be utilized for throwing and catching softballs. The ball can be thrown from one player to another in various formations using normal throwing, pitching, rolling grounders, or throwing fly balls. Leader and class formations have particular value. Groups should be kept small so children will get many turns. For a normal size class, at least four softballs are needed for most drills.

The following formations are suggested.

1. Two line - 3 to 4 children in each line.
2. Around the Bases - 4 to 8. Establish a diamond using the normal base distance for the children. Throw around and across the bases. If more than one child is at a base, they take turns.
3. Shuttle turn back - 4 to 8. Each child after his turn goes to the back of his file.
4. Leader and line or semicircle - 5 to 8. The leader completes on a round of the specified throwing skill and then rotates by going to the end of the line to his left (facing the others). A child from the other end of the line comes forward and the children all move over one place.

If sufficient space is a problem, the leader and file formation can be used. Also, the leader may have a base in his spot to provide a target for throwing or pitching.

Batting Drill. A batter, pitcher, and catcher are in position with the remainder of the players scattered in the field. Each player is allowed a certain number of swings. The pitcher should serve the type of pitch that can be hit easily. The catcher stands back from his regular position and retrieves the balls which are missed by the batter. Not over 10 players should be in any one drill.

An order of rotation will assure each player his turn. Players can be numbered and take turns in that order.

Bunting can also be practiced with a formation of this type. However, only one or two fielders are needed for a bunting drill.

Infield Drill. The children are placed in the normal infield positions of catcher, first, second, third, and shortstop. One child acts as batter and gives directions. The play should begin with practice of throwing around the bases either way. After this, the "batter" rolls the ball to the different infielders beginning with the third baseman and continuing in turn around the infield, with each throwing to first to retire an imaginary batter-runner. Various play situations can be developed.

If the batter is skillful enough, he can hit the ball to the infielders instead of rolling the ball, making a more realistic drill. If a second softball is available, time is saved when the ball is thrown or batted past another infielder.

Pitching Drill. Groups of five or six children can practice pitching skills in these formations.

1. Semi-circle and leader. The leader stands behind a base and acts as the catcher for the other children who stand in a semi-circle facing him and stationed the pitching distance (35 feet) away. Each in turn pitches to the leader.
2. Pitching, catching, umpiring. The three skills are combined into a drill which can be done with a minimum of four players. A pitcher is in position in front of a home plate at regular pitching distance. Another player stands as the batter but does not strike at the ball. A catcher is behind the plate and an umpire behind him. Extra players line up behind the pitcher to take turns.

The pitcher should observe all legal restrictions for his position. The pitcher should pitch to a defined number of "batters," or be given a set number of pitches. The umpire observes good practice in his position and calls the balls and strikes

Activities

Third Grade

THROW IT AND RUN SOFTBALL

Playing Area: Softball diamond reduced in size.

Numbers: Two teams of 7 to 11 each. Usually 9 players are on a side.

Supplies: Softball or similar ball.

The game is played very much like softball with the following exception. With one team in the field at regular positions, the pitcher throws the ball to the "batter" who instead of batting the ball, catches it, and immediately throws out into the field. The ball is now treated as a batted ball and regular softball rules prevail. However, no stealing is permitted and the runners must hold bases until the "batter" throws the ball. A foul ball is out.

Variation:
1. Under Leg Throw. Instead of having the batter throw directly, have him turn to the right, lift his left leg, and throw the ball under the leg into the playing field.
2. Beat Ball Throw. The fielders instead of playing regular softball rules, throw the ball directly home to the catcher. The batter, in the meantime, runs around the bases. He gets one point for each base he touches before the catcher gets the ball and calls out "Stop." There are no outs, and each batter gets a turn before changing sides to the field. A fly ball caught would mean no score. Similarly, a foul ball would score no points but count as a turn at bat.

TWO PITCH SOFTBALL

Playing Area: Softball Diamond

Numbers: Regular softball teams but the numbers can vary.

Supplies: Softball, bat.

This introductory game is played like regular softball with the following changes:

1. A member of the team at bat is the pitcher. Some system of rotation should be set up so every child takes a turn as pitcher.
2. The batter has only two pitches in which to hit the ball. He must hit a fair ball on either of these pitches or he is out. He can foul the first ball, but if he fouls the second he is out. There is no need to call balls or strikes.
3. The pitcher, because he is a member of the team at bat, does not field the ball. A member of the team at field acts as the fielding pitcher.
4. If the batter hits the ball, regular softball rules are followed. However, no stealing is permitted.

Variation: Three Strikes
In this game, the batter is allowed three pitches (strikes) to hit the ball. Otherwise, the game proceeds as in Two Pitch.

Fourth Grade

TWO PITCH SOFTBALL

Described in the third grade program, the game should be emphasized in the fourth grade also.

HIT AND RUN

Playing Area: Softball Field, Gymnasium

Players: Two teams, 6-15 players on each team.

Supplies: Volleyball, soccer, or playground ball. Home plate and base marker.

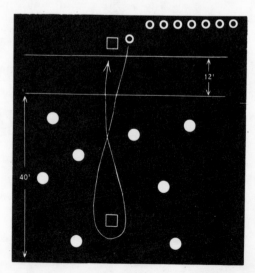

One team is at bat and the other scattered out in the field. Out of bounds must be established but the area does not need to be shaped like a baseball diamond. The batter stands at home plate with the ball. In front of him 12 feet away is a short line, over which the ball must be hit to be in play. In the center of the field about forty feet away is the base marker.

The batter bats the ball with his hand or fist so it crosses the short line and lights inside the area. He then attempts to run down the field, around the base marker, and back to home plate without being hit by the ball. The members of the other team field the ball and attempt to hit the runner. The fielder may not run or walk with the ball but may throw to a teammate closer to the runner.

A run is scored for each successful run around the marker and back to home plate without getting hit with the ball. A run is also scored if a foul is called on the fielding team for walking or running with the ball.

The batter is out if:

1. A fly ball is caught.
2. When hit below the shoulders with the ball.
3. If the ball is not hit beyond the short line.
4. If the team touches home plate with the ball before the runner does. This may be used only when the runner stops in the field and does not continue.

The game can be played in innings of three outs each, or a change of team positions can be made after all have batted from one team.

Variation: Five Passes.
The batter is out if:

1. A fly ball is caught.
2. The ball is passed among five different players of the team in the field with the last pass to a player at home plate, beating the runner to the plate. The passes must not touch the ground and must be among five different players.

Teaching Hint: The distance the batter runs around the base marker may need to be shortened or lengthened, depending upon the ability of the children.

KICK SOFTBALL

Playing Area: Regular softball field with a home base three feet square.

Numbers: Regular softball teams but numbers can vary.

Supplies: Soccer or other ball to be kicked.

Batter stands in the kicking area three-foot square home plate. Batter kicks the ball rolled on the ground by the pitcher. The ball should be rolled only with moderate speed. An umpire calls balls and strikes. A strike is a ball which rolls over the three foot square. A ball is one that rolls outside this area. Strike-outs and walks are called the same as in softball. The number of foul balls allowed should be limited.

Otherwise, the game is played as in softball with no stealing permitted.

Variation:
1. The batter can kick a stationary ball. This saves time as there is no pitching.
2. Punch Ball. Using a volleyball, the batter can hit a ball as in a volleyball serve or he can punch a ball pitched by the pitcher. The latter punch sometimes causes some pain if the pitch is too hard.

HIT THE BAT

Playing Area: Open field for fungo batting.

Numbers: 3-10 children.

Supplies: Softball, bat.

Children, except the batter, are scattered in the field. The batter tosses the ball to himself and hits the ball to the fielders. The object of each fielder is to become the batter. The fielder becomes the batter if

1. He catches three flies from the present batter.
2. He can hit the bat with the ball.

To become eligible to throw to the bat, the fielder must field the ball cleanly. The batter lays the bat down on the ground facing the throw so it presents the largest possible target. From where he caught the ball, the fielder throws at the bat and tries to hit it.

Variations:

1. If hitting the bat seems to difficult, count a throw as successful when the ball goes directly over the bat.
2. Two balls caught on first bounce can count as one fly ball caught.
3. Catching three fly balls can be ruled out and the following substituted.

If a fielder catches a fly ball, he gets ten steps toward the bat from where he caught the ball. If he catches the ball on first bounce, he gets five steps. This makes it easier to hit the bat.

Variation: The batter is not put out if he can catch the ball on the fly after it rebounds from the bat after being hit by a rolling ball.

Fifth Grade

FIVE HUNDRED

Playing Area: Field big enough for fungo hitting.

Number: 3 to 12, although more can play.

Supplies: Softball, bat

There are many versions of this old game. A batter stands on one side of the field and bats the ball out to a number of fielders who are scattered. The fielders attempt to become batter by reaching a score of five hundred. To do this, the fielder is granted points for the following:

Points
200 Catching a ball on the fly
100 Catching a ball on first bounce
50 Fielding a grounder cleanly

Whenever a change of batters is made, all fielders lose their points and must start over.

Variation:

1. The fielder must total exactly 500.
2. Points are subtracted from the fielder's score if he fails to handle a ball properly. Thus, if he drops a fly ball, he loses 200 points. Similarly with the other scores.

BATTER BALL

Playing Area: Softball diamond lines as in diagram.

Numbers: Two teams, 8 to 12 on each.

Supplies: Softball, bat, mask

Batter Ball involves batting and fielding but no base running. It is much like batting practice but adds the element of competition.

A line is drawn directly from first to third base. This is the balk line over which a batted ball must travel to be fielded.

Another line is drawn from a point on the foul line 3-1/2 feet behind third base to a point 5 feet behind (in line with home plate) second base. Another line connects this point with a point on the first base line 3-1/2 feet behind that base. The shaded space is the infield area.

Each batter is given three pitches by a member of his own team to hit the ball into fair territory across the balk line. The pitcher may stop any ground ball he wishes before it crosses the balk line. The batter then gets another turn at bat.

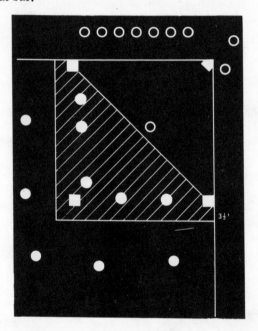

Scoring:

1. Successful grounder - 1 point. The batter scores one point when an infielder fails to handle cleanly his grounder within the infield area. Only one player may field the ball. If the ball is fielded properly, the batter is out.
2. Line Drive in infield area - 1 point. A ball from the bat which lands first in the infield area can be handled only on first bounce for an out. If it bounces in front of the balk line, it is classed as a grounder and can be handled on any bounce. Any line drive caught on a fly is out.
3. Fly ball in infield area - 1 point. Any fly

ball in the infield area must be caught or the batter scores one point. The ball must be caught legally by the first person touching it.

4. Two-bagger - 2 points. Any fly ball, line drive or not, that lights fairly without being caught in the outfield area scores two points. If caught, the batter is out.
5. Home run - 3 points. Any fly ball driven over the heads of the farthest outfielder in that area scores a home run.

Three outs can constitute an inning or all batters may be allowed one turn and then change to the field.

A new set of infielders should be in place for each inning. The old set goes to the outfield. Pitchers should be limited to one inning. They take a turn at bat.

Teaching Suggestions: Many games of this type take special fields either rectangular or a narrowed angle type. This game was selected because it uses the regular softball field with the added lines. The lines can be drawn with a stick or can be marked with regular marking.

The pitcher has to decide whether or not he should stop a ball. If the ball goes beyond the restraining line, even though he touched it, the ball is in play.

HOME RUN

Playing Area: Softball diamond. First base only is used.

Players: 4 - 10

Supplies: Softball, bat.

This game can be played with as few as four children. The needed players are a batter, catcher, pitcher, and one fielder. The other players are fielders, although some can take positions in the infield.

The batter hits a regular pitch and on a fair ball must run to first base and back to home before the ball can be returned to the catcher.

The batter is out when:

1. A fly ball, fair or foul, is caught
2. He strikes out
3. On a fair ball, the ball beats him back to home plate

To keep skillful players from staying in too long at bat, a rule can be made that after a cer-

tain number of home runs, the batter automatically must take his place in the field.

A rotation (work-up) system should be set up. The batter should go to right field, moves to center, and then to left field. The rotation continues through third baseman position, shortstop, second base, first base, pitcher, and catcher. The catcher becomes the next batter. Naturally, the number of positions is dependent upon the number of players in the game.

If there are sufficient numbers, there can be an additional batter waiting to take his turn.

The game actually can be played with three youngsters eliminating the catcher. With only one fielder, the pitcher would cover home plate.

The first base distance should be far enough to be a challenge but close enough so a well hit ball will score a home run. The distance would be dependent on the number playing and the capacity of the children.

Variation:
1. It is possible to play this game more like softball allowing the batter to stop at first if another batter is up.
2. A fly ball caught by a player puts the fielder directly to bat. The batter then takes his place at the end of the rotation, and the other players rotate up to the position of the fielder who caught the ball. The rule may cause children to scramble and fight for fly balls which is a situation not desired in softball. It should be ruled that the ball belongs to the player into whose territory it falls.

KICK PIN SOFTBALL

Playing Area: Softball diamond
45 foot base distances
20 foot pitching distance

Numbers: Two teams, 8 to 12 on a side.

Catcher, pitcher, three basemen and the rest fielders.

Supplies: One soccer ball, four Indian Clubs.

The Indian Clubs are placed on the outside corner of each base and in the middle of home plate. The batter kicks a ball rolled by the pitcher who aims at the Indian Club on home plate. The kick must be a fair ball. The batter <u>circles around</u> the outside of the bases and finally touches home plate. In the meantime the fielders retrieve the ball and pass it successively to the basemen on first, second, third, and then home. As each baseman receives the ball he kicks the pin down and passes to the next base.

The batter is out when:

1. A pitched ball knocks down the pin on home plate.
2. The ball is caught on the fly by a fielder.
3. The batter knocks over any pin during his time at bat.
4. A second foul ball occurs any time at bat.
5. If the ball, in its rotation from first base to the other bases in succession, gets ahead of the runner and the baseman kicks the pin down.

The batter scores a run only on a home run beating the ball to home plate.

The game can be played by innings with three outs or it can be played so each player of the team at bat gets a turn before changing to the field.

Teaching Suggestions: Indian clubs stand outside with difficulty. A three by three inch square of plywood screwed to the bottom will make them stand easily.

Old bowling pins can generally be secured from the local bowling alley. The industrial arts department can aid in restoring a flat bottom for better standing.

The pitcher should use judgment in rolling the ball. The fun comes in the kick and the resultant run and not the duel between the batter and the pitcher. This can be controlled somewhat by the addition of a rule that if a certain number of balls (not hitting the club if the batters let the ball go by) are thrown, the batter gets a free kick. The kick would be a place kick with the ball placed just to the left of home place where the batting box for the right handed batter is located.

Variation:

1. Hit Pin Softball is about the same game except that instead of kicking the pin, the pin is knocked over with the ball held in the hands.
2. Instead of counting home runs, a point can be given for each base rounded before the pin is kicked by the baseman holding the ball. A home run scores four points under this counting system.

SCRUB (Work-up)

Playing Area: Softball field.

Number: 7 to 15.

Supplies: Softball, bat.

The predominant feature of Scrub is the rotation of the players. The game is played with regular softball rules with each individual more or less playing for himself. There are at least two batters and generally three. A catcher, pitcher, and first baseman are essential. The remainder of the players assume the other positions. Whenever the batter is out, he goes to a position in right field. All other players move up one position with the catcher becoming a batter. Thus, the first baseman becomes pitcher, the pitcher moves to the catcher, and all other move up one place in a predetermined shift.

Variations:

1. If there are only two batters, then one base is sufficient. The runners use only first base and return back to home plate.
2. If a fly ball is caught, the fielder and batter can exchange positions.

Sixth Grade

TEE BALL

Playing Area: Softball field.

Number: Two regular softball teams, but numbers can vary.

Supplies: Softball, Bat, Batting Tee.

The game is an excellent variation of softball and is played under its rules with the exception of the pitching and the pitcher.

Instead of hitting a pitched ball, the batter hits the ball from a tee. The catcher places the ball on the tee. After the batter hits the ball, the play is the same as in softball. With no pitching, there is no stealing. A runner stays on the base until the ball is hit by the batter.

A fielder occupies the position normally held by the pitcher. His primary duty is to field bunts and any ground balls he can reach, and to back up the positions in the field on throws as a pitcher would normally position himself.

Teams can play regular innings for three outs or change to the field after each player has had a turn at bat.

A tee can be purchased or made from radiator hose. If the tee is not adjustable, it would be better to have three different sizes available.

Tee Ball has many advantages. There are no strike outs, every child hits the ball, there is no waiting for the pitcher-catcher duel, and there are many opportunities for fielding.

The batter should take his position far enough back of the tee so that in stepping forward to swing the ball will still be hit slightly in front of the batter.

TWICE AROUND

Playing Around: Softball infield.

Numbers: Two teams, 4 to 8 on each team.

Supplies: Softball.

Twice around provides competition and practice for throwing around the bases and base running. It should be used only after instruction has been held in both skills.

One team is stationed in the field with at least one player near each base. As a minimum, a catcher and three basemen are needed in the field. The extra players in the field are assigned to bases so some bases, including home plate, will have two fielders. When two fielders are at a base, one takes the first throw and the other takes the second time around.

A player from the team at bat stands with one foot on home plate and ready to run to first base. His task is to make one complete circuit of the bases and tag home plate. The ball starts in the catcher's hands. At the signal "Go," he throws the ball to first base from where it is thrown to second, third, and then home. It continues for another round which gives the game the name of "Twice Around."

The object of the game is to have the ball beat the batter back to home plate on its second round, with the batter making only one circuit.

The capacity of the children will determine the ideal base distance. The teacher should start with a 45 foot distance and then vary according to the level of the children to run, throw, and catch.

The fielders must not interfere with the runner and should stand back from the base unless catching the ball. Each fielder must throw with one foot on the base or touch the base while the ball is held in his hands. If the ball is missed at a base, it must go back to that base and be in touch before continuing.

If the batter is being put out continually, a delay in the throwing cycle can be put in by having the batter roll or throw the ball to a pitcher, The pitcher would then throw the ball to the catcher, and the twice around travel would then start.

FAR BASE SOFTBALL

Playing Area: Softball field with a Far Base. The far base is three by six feet and is located just to the first base side of second base.

Players: Regular softball teams but the number can vary.

Supplies: Softball and bat.

First and third bases are used only to determine foul balls. The batter hits the pitched ball and runs to the far base. He must reach the base before the ball or before he is tagged with the ball. He may stay there or try to return home. However, if he leaves the base, he cannot return except for a caught fly ball. Several runners may be on the far base as long as a batter is left. The batter remains at bat until he hits the ball. A limit should be placed on the number of fouls that can be hit.

Each team is allowed three outs. Outs are made by catching a fly ball, by striking out, by the ball getting to the far baseman before the runner, and the runner tagged by the ball when off the base.

Variation: The game can be played by having the batter run on any kind of a hit, foul or fair. This means that no strikes should be called, and the batter stays at bat until the ball touches the bat. This has the advantage of allowing the poor batter a chance to run as there are no strikeouts. However, it violates a principle by having the batter run after hitting a foul ball or a foul tip.

HURRY BASEBALL

Playing Area: Softball diamond. Shortened pitching distance.

Players: Two teams, 8 to 12 on each side.

Supplies: Softball, bat.

Hurry Baseball demands quick and rapid changes from batting to fielding and vice versa. The game is like regular softball with the following exceptions.

1. The pitcher is from the team at bat. He must not interfere with or touch a batted ball on the penalty of the batter being called out.
2. The team coming to bat does not wait for the fielding team to get set. Since it has its own pitcher, the pitcher gets the ball to the

308

batter just as quickly as the batter can grab and get ready. The fielding team has to hustle to get out to their places.

3. Only one pitch is allowed to a batter. He must hit a fair ball or he is out. The pitch is made from about two-thirds of the normal pitching distance.
4. No stealing is permitted.
5. No bunting is permitted. The batter must take a full swing.

The game is good fun and provides fast activity in the fast changes that need to be made immediately when the third out has been made. Teams in the field will learn to put the next hitter as catcher, so he can immediately take his place in the batter's box when the third out is made. Batters must bat in order. Scoring follows regular softball rules.

THREE TEAM SOFTBALL

Playing Area: Softball diamond.

Players: 12 to 15

Supplies: Mask, ball, bat

This version of softball works well with 12 players, a number considered too few to divide into two effective fielding teams. The players are divided into three teams. The rules of softball apply with the following exceptions.

1. One team is at bat, one team covers the infield (including the catcher), and the third team provides the outfielders and the pitcher.
2. The team at bat must bat in a definite order. This means that instances, due to the few batters on each side, could occur when the person due to bat is on a base. He must be replaced by a player not on base so he can take his turn at bat.
3. After three outs, the teams rotate with the outfield moving to the infield, the infield taking a turn at bat, and the batters going to the outfield.
4. An inning is over when all three teams have batted.
5. The pitcher should be limited to pitching one inning only. A player may repeat as pitcher only after all members of his team have had a chance to pitch.

BASE CIRCLING CONTESTS

Playing Area: Softball diamond

Players: 4 squads (entire class)

Supplies: None

Children love to run around the bases and contests employing this are popular with children. The contest lends itself well to a class of four squads. Each squad takes a position beyond one of the bases far back enough so not to interfere with the runners. Each captain can arrange his runners in any order for running that he wishes, but once arranged all must run in this order.

Scoring: 1st - 4, 2nd - 3, 3rd - 2, 4th - 1. Players must touch all bases on penalty of disqualification. Each player scores points for his team as he finishes in his heat.

The bases need to be fastened securely to avoid inequities and falls. Having bases painted on a black or hard top surface is an excellent solution.

Variation: If four split-second stop watches were available, each child could be timed and other means of scoring devised.

Tests for Softball Skills

Tests for softball skills include throwing (accuracy and distance), fielding grounders, circling the bases, and pitching.

Throw for Accuracy. A target with three concentric circles of 18, 36, and 54 inches is drawn on a wall. Scoring is 3, 2, and 1, respectively, for the circles.

Five throws are given to each child for a possible score of 15. Balls hitting a line score for the higher number.

Instead of the suggested target, a tire could be hung. Scoring would allow 2 points for a throw through the tire and 1 point for just hitting the tire. A maximum score of 10 points is possible with this system.

Throw for Distance. The softball throw for distance is a part of the fitness testing program recommended by this text and is found in that section on page 172.

Fielding Grounders. A file of players is stationed behind a restraining line. A thrower is about 30 feet in front of this line. Each player in turn fields five ground balls. His score is the number of balls he fields cleanly.

It is recognized that there will be inconsistencies in the throw and bounce of the ground balls served up for fielding. If the opportunity obviously was not a fair one, the child should get another chance.

Circling the Bases. A baseball diamond with four bases is needed plus a stopwatch for timing. The object is to time the runner circling the bases. Two runners can run at one time by starting from opposite corners of the diamond. Two watches would be needed with this system.

Variation: The batter can bunt a pitched ball and run around the bases. The timing starts with the bunt and finishes when the batter touches home plate.

Pitching. Pitching is one of the easier skills to test in softball, and certainly is one of the most popular with children. There are two basic methods used for testing:

1. Allow a certain number of pitches at a target. Scoring is on the basis of the number of strikes which can be thrown out of a designated number of pitches.
2. Regular pitching, as if to a batter, counting balls and strikes. "Batters" would be either struck out or walked. The test score would be how many "batters" the child was able to strike out from a given number at bat. This

could be expressed in a percentage.

A target is needed and should be 20 inches wide and 36 inches high. This can be devised a number of ways. It can be outlined temporarily on a wall with chalk, or a more permanent means would be to use paint. The lower portion of the target should be about 16 inches above the ground or floor. The target could be constructed from plywood or wood. Some means of support or hanging would be needed.

Scoring would be based upon whether or not the pitch entered the strike zone as typified by the target. The boundaries of the target should be counted as good. The pitching distance should be normal (35 feet), and regular pitching rules should be observed.

Old Woody. Old Woody is the name of a pitching target which is in the form of a stand that can be moved from school to school. The target size is as outlined above. A sturdy frame holds the target and allows it to be used in most any spot. The contest is based upon the number of strikeouts a pitcher can throw to an imaginary batter. He continues pitching until he "walks" the batter. Other variations could be used.

Chapter 27

Volleyball and Related Activities

Volleyball is an excellent recreational activity, is important in the program because it is one of the few sports in which boys and girls can participate together, and can accommodate reasonably large numbers of children in a small area. The introduction to the game begins in the program with simplified Newcomb and proceeds through a simplified version of the regular game of volleyball in the sixth grade. Simple Newcomb is played in the third grade.

Emphasis at Each Grade Level

Fourth Grade. In the fourth grade, the serve is introduced, the underhand type. The children should practice a simple return which emphasizes merely batting the ball over the net with both hands. Both Modified Newcomb and Bounce Volleyball employ the serve and use regular rules of scoring. A system of rotation is to be used in the games.

Fifth Grade. Students in this grade will learn to handle the high and low passes. They will be introduced to the regular game and should learn the basic rules so they can play. They should review the serve and polish up on this skill. The first two games, Keep It Up and Wall Volley, employ skills of passing. Cage Volleyball follows the scoring rules but uses some modifications. The regular game with modifications should be introduced in the fifth grade level.

Sixth Grade. Students in this grade should add the concepts of set-up, spiking, and blocking. Game rules which affect these phases of the game should be covered. An introduction to elementary strategy should be a part of the instruction.

General Suggestions

For any particular class of about thirty students, two volleyball courts are

GRADE	FOURTH	FIFTH	SIXTH
Skills	Serve-Underhanded Simple Return	Chest Pass Underhand Pass	Set Up Spiking Blocking
Knowledges	Simple Rules Rotation	Basic Game Rules	Game Strategy Additional Rules
Activities to be stressed	Modified Newcomb Bounce Volleyball Shower Serve Ball	Keep It Up Wall Volley Cage Volleyball Volleyball	Set-Up Newcomb Three-and-over
Testing	Simplified Serve Test	Simplified Serve Test Wall Passing Test	Serve Scoring Test Wall Passing Test

needed. Not more than 12 to 14 children can play profitably in volleyball games.

A court should be 25 by 50 feet with a net height of 6-1/2 to 7 feet. If no net is available, one may be improvised by using a rope as a substitute. A line should be drawn on the floor down the center of the court directly under the net. This is called the center line.

Regular volleyball rules call for one chance to serve the ball over the net <u>without</u> touching the net. In learning stages, the teacher can modify the rules to allow a second chance, or permit other players to assist to help the ball over. Another possible modification is to move the server forward from his base line to a point where he can serve the ball over the net easily.

At the net, the players should stand an arm's length away for best play. Other players should play their positions rather than "ganging up" on the ball.

Rotation should be introduced in the fourth grade and used in all lead-up games.

To save time, children should be taught to roll the ball to the server. Other players should let the ball roll on the floor quickly to its destination.

The use of the fist to hit the ball on volleys causes poor control and interrupts the play. Children should normally use both hands to hit the ball. If difficulty occurs with the enforcement of this, the teacher can rule hitting with the fist a foul, causing loss of point.

A referee should be appointed for the games as violations of rules occur in the heat of the game. Particularly difficult for a player to detect and call on himself are such violations as reaching over the net, stepping over the center line, and lofting (not batting) the ball. A referee can call these violations effectively when positioned near the net.

The ball should be a volleyball or one of similar size and be properly inflated. To use a heavy, flabby ball takes much away from the game.

Basic Rules

Officially, six players make up a team under men's rules and eight under the rules of the game for girls. However, any number from six to nine make suitable teams for elementary schools.

To begin the first game, captains toss a coin for the order of choices. The winner can select either to serve or take his choice of courts. Whichever option he selects, the other captain takes the other option.

At the completion of any game, the teams change courts, and the losing side serves.

To be in position to serve, the player must have both feet behind the right one-third of the end line. He must not step on the end line during the serve. The server is in what is known as "right back" position.

Only the serving team scores. The server retains his serve, scoring consecutive points, until his side loses and is put out. Members of each team take turns serving, the sequence being determined by the plan of rotation.

Official rules allow the server only one serve to get the ball completely over the net and into the opponent's court. Even if the ball touches the net (net ball) and goes into the correct court, the serve is lost.

The lines bounding the court are considered to be in the court. Balls landing on the lines are counted as good.

Any ball that touches or is touched by a player is considered to be "in", even though the player who touched the ball was clearly outside the boundaries at the time. He is considered to have played the ball if he touches it.

The ball must be returned over the net at least by the third volley, which means that the team has a maximum of three volleys to make a good return.

Chief violations causing loss of the point or serve are:

1. Touching the net during play.
2. Not clearly batting the ball. This is sometimes called palming or lofting the ball.
3. Reaching over the net during play.
4. Stepping <u>over</u> the center line. Contact with the line is not a violation.

A ball going into the net may be recovered and played provided no player touches the net.

The first team to reach a score of fifteen points wins the game <u>provided</u> the team is at least two points ahead of the opponent. If not, play continues until one team secures a two point lead.

Only players in the front line may spike but all players may block.

Not player may volley the ball twice in succession.

Description of Skills

<u>Underhand serve</u>. There are many different serves in volleyball but best results are obtained if the instruction is

concentrated on the relatively simple and easy underhanded serve. The description is for a right-handed player. Stand with the left foot forward and pointed toward the net with most of the weight on that foot. The ball is held in the palm of the left hand with the arm across the body so the ball may be struck with the right hand moving straight forward. The right hand forms a partial fist with the knuckles toward the ball. Swing the right hand forward in an underhanded motion striking the ball out of the left palm. The ball is not tossed into the air but remains in contact with the left palm until struck by the right hand.

An alternate method is to use the cupped hand to strike the ball.

Chest Pass or Return. Receive the ball about chest height using cupped hands with finger tip control. One foot is slightly ahead with the knees bent. The palms face forward and the elbows are up somewhat. A player should maneuver to a position directly under the ball with his eyes on the ball. The return is made by making forcible contact with the hands and adding the thrust of the knees and body.

Underhand Pass or Return. This is definitely a second choice and is used to handle a ball below the waist. Players should use the chest pass whenever possible. Feet should be in easy comfortable position with the knees slightly bent. The hands are cupped with the palms up and the little fingers together. The motion is a lifting motion from slightly bent elbows adding the power of the knee and the forward thrust of the hips. The ball, however, must be clearly batted and not lofted.

Set-Up. The name applies to a pass which sets up the ball for a possible spike. The object is to raise the ball with a soft, easy pass to a position one or two feet above the net and about one foot from the net. The set-up is generally the second pass in a series of three. A chest pass is used for the set-up. It is important that the back line player, who has to tap to the setter, makes an accurate and easily handled pass.

Spike. Spiking is the most effective play in volleyball and, when properly done, is extremely difficult to return properly. It is dependent a great deal upon the ability of a teammate to set it up properly. On the elementary level, spiking should be done by jumping high into the air and striking the ball above the net, driving it into the opponent's court. It is the "kill" shot in volleyball. Experienced players may back up for a little run. However, the jump must be made straight up so as not

to touch the net, and the striking hand must not go over the net.

Drills for Volleyball Skills

Serving, passing (chest and underhand), setting up, and spiking are the volleyball skills for which the drills are organized.

Serving
1. Formation: Shuttle turnback

Six to 9 players are in each drill, divided between the two halves of the shuttle formation. The children serve back and forth from a short distance. The second step is to have them serve back and forth over a net, positioned about in the middle of each court. As skill increases, gradually move the service back until the serve can be made from behind the base line.
2. Formation: Two teams face each other from opposite sides of a volleyball court. All players serve from behind the base lines. The ball is served back and forth across the net. There should be some semblance of taking turns but a rigid order is not required. Two or more volleyballs should be used in the drill.

Passing (Chest and Underhand)
1. Formation: Circle with leader

Leader in the center tosses ball at proper height to each player for a chest pass. Player returns ball to leader with a pass. After tossing to all players in the circle, a new leader takes the place. Repeat for underhand passes.
2. Formation: Circle

Six to 9 players in a small circle volley back and forth without regard to any particular order except that players should not volley back to the person from whom the ball was received.
3. Formation: Double line

Players stand in two lines facing each other at a distance of about ten feet. The ball is volleyed back and forth from one line to the other.
4. Formation: File and leader

After the players have had sufficient preliminary practice, volleying across the net is introduced. The leader stands on one side of the net with the file players in position on the other. Both the leader and the child in front of the file are about five feet from the net. The leader tosses the ball over the net to the front player of the file who volleys the ball back over to him. This player goes to the rear of the file. The leader tosses the ball over to the next player, and so on. After one full round, the leader is changed. After volleying skill has been developed, the leader can volley the ball back, rather than catching and tossing it back.

Wall Volley

Formation: File in front of a smooth wall.

A line is drawn on the wall 6-1/2 feet from the floor and parallel to it.

One player from each file begins by throwing the ball above the line and attempting to keep it in play by volleying. Change after a short period.

Set-up and Spike Drill

Formation: Leader and file

The leader stands close to the net and tosses the ball up (set-up) for spiking. Each player in turn practices spiking.

A second stage of this drill is the addition of the set-up player. The ball is tossed to the set-up player who sets up the ball for the line of spikers. Rotate the positions after the line of spikers has completed one round.

Activities

Third Grade

NEWCOMB

Playing Area: Volleyball Court

Players: Two teams, 8 to 10 on each

Supplies: Volleyball

Each team occupies one side of the court. The children may be positioned in two or three lines of players, depending upon the number of children and the size of the court. There is no rotation system, and service is informal.

The object of the game is for one team to throw the ball underhanded over the net in such a fashion that it will not be caught. The game starts by a member of one team throwing the ball into the opposite court. The ball is thrown back and forth until an error is committed. Each time a team commits an error, a point is scored for the opposite team. Errors are: (1) failure to catch a ball, (2) not throwing the ball across the net successfully, and (3) throwing the ball so it falls out of bounds on the other side of the net. The first team reaching a score of 15 is the winner.

There is no formal rotation, but the teacher can change the lines from front to back at times. The child nearest to the ball which touched the floor or went out of bounds starts the play with a throw. The ball may be passed from one player to another before it is thrown across the net.

Fourth Grade

MODIFIED NEWCOMB

Playing Area: Volleyball Court

Players: Two teams, 6 to 9 on each

Supplies: Volleyball

This introductory game is played on the same size court and uses the same net height as in volleyball.

Directions:

1. Players are positioned in two or three lines depending upon the number playing.
2. The game starts with a regular volleyball serve, but after that the ball is caught and thrown back and forth.
3. All throwing must be underhanded, and no child may hold a ball longer than 5 seconds.
4. The object of the game is to throw the ball into the opponents' court so that a player there misses it or it touches in fair territory.
5. Regular volleyball scoring is used and a system of rotation of positions should be worked out.

Teaching Suggestions:

1. Players should play position and not monopolize play.
2. The game is interesting only if the player gets rid of the ball immediately.
3. Rather than throw directly over the net, back line players should pass the ball forward to teammates.

Variations:

1. A football, softball, or deck tennis ring can be used.
2. Overhand throwing can be allowed if a restraining line is drawn five feet from and parallel to the net on each side, providing an area from which no ball can be thrown. Players may enter this zone to catch the ball. The purpose of the zone is to avoid the situation where a player can move to the net, jump up and throw the ball directly down into the other court making it difficult,

if not impossible, to catch. The five-foot distance can be varied with the capacity of the children.

ONE-BOUNCE VOLLEYBALL

The game can be taught utilizing the formations and rules of Modified Newcomb. The positions, formation, and rotation are the same as in Newcomb. The play starts out similarly with a serve by the right back player.

Directions:
1. The ball is not to be caught and thrown but is to be batted (volleyed).
2. The ball may be played as in volleyball or the team can allow the ball to bounce once and then pass or return it. The ball can bounce between hits or passes. There can be any number of hits or bounces before the ball goes over the net. However, a ball may not bounce twice between hits.
3. Scoring is as in volleyball.

Variation: Allow only three players to handle the ball before it must be returned across the net.

SHOWER SERVICE BALL

Formation: Two volley ball teams, each occupying its respective court. Players are scattered in no particular formation. A line, parallel to the net, is drawn through the middle of each court.

Players: 8-12 on each team

Supplies: 3 to 6 volleyballs

The game involves the skills of serving and catching. To start the game, the volleyballs are divided between the teams and are handled by players in the serving area. The serving area is between the base line and the line drawn through the middle of each court.

Balls may be served at any time in any order just so the server is in the serving area (back half) of his court. Any ball that is served across the net is to be caught by any player near the ball. The person catching or retrieving a ball hitting the floor moves quickly to his serving area and serves. A point is scored for a team whenever a served ball hits the floor in the other court or is dropped by a receiver. Two scorers are needed, one for each side.

Teaching Suggestion: The line through the middle of each court should be moved nearer the base line after serving skill becomes better. Later, the game can be played without the line, with all serves from back of the base line of each court.

Fifth Grade

KEEP IT UP

Playing Area: Playground, gymnasium

Players: 5 to 8 players on each team

Supplies: Volleyball for each team

Each team forms a small circle of not more than eight players. The object of the game is to see which team can make the greatest number of volleys in a specified time or which team can sustain the ball in the air for the greatest number of consecutive volleys.

Directions:
1. Game is started with a bat by one of the players on the signal "Go."
2. Balls are volleyed back and forth with no specific order of turns.
3. A child may not volley a ball twice in succession.
4. The ball cannot be returned to the player from whom it came.
5. Any ball touching the ground does not count.

WALL VOLLEY

Playing Area: For each team, an area with a smooth wall.

Players: 2-6 on each team. As many teams as there are areas available.

Supplies: One volleyball for each team.

Formation: The first player from each team takes his place in front of the wall and back of a line drawn 4 feet from the base of the wall.

Each player is given a specified time (30 seconds) to volley the ball against the wall as many times as he can, staying behind the restraining line. A good hit is one that is made from behind the line and which hits the wall on the volley. After the time period, the second player comes forward and repeats the performance. The team score is the total of the individual members.

Variation: Each player must stop when he misses. Those with no misses continued throughout the time period.

CAGE VOLLEYBALL

Cage volleyball is a variation of regular volleyball. The ball used is a cageball, 24 inches in diameter.

Directions:
1. In serving, toss the ball into the air, propel it with both hands.
2. Assistance may be given on the serve to get the ball over the net.
3. Any number of hits may be made in any combination or order by the players, but the ball must be clearly batted and not lofted or carried.
4. Scoring and rotation follow volleyball rules.

VOLLEYBALL

The game is started with a serve by the right back player of the team winning the toss, standing outside his end line in the serving area. He gets only one attempt to make a successful serve. Following the serve, the ball is volleyed back and forth until one team commits an error. Points can be scored only by the serving team. The server retains his serve, scoring points until his team commits an error. The ball then goes to other team for the serve. The team winning the serve must rotate when beginning the serve of any one player. The rotation is done clockwise and positions the player from the right forward position to the right back position as the server.

The ball may be touched only three times before it must be returned to the court of the other team. No player may hit the ball twice in succession.

The referee generally has two calls. These are:

1. Side out--The serving team fails to return the ball successfully to the other court or one of the members is guilty of a rule violation.
2. Point--The receiving team in this case fails or is guilty of a rule violation.

However, when there are fouls on both teams, the official may call "Double Foul" in which case the point is replayed and no score or side out results.

Other rules are listed in the general discussions of this unit.

Sixth Grade

SET-UP NEWCOMB

The purpose of this variation of Newcomb is to emphasize the set-up and spike. The game starts the same as in Newcomb with the ball served over the net and the receiving team catch-ing it. The game differs in the following details.

1. After the ball is caught it is thrown to a player in the front line who tosses the ball up for a spike by his teammate. The receiving team must catch the spike and follow the same pattern of set-up and spike.
2. The player catching the ball must toss it up immediately for the spike. No waiting is permitted.

THREE-AND-OVER VOLLEYBALL

This game follows the regular rules of volleyball with the exception that the ball must be played three times before going over. The object is to establish the concept of team volleyball with the routine of pass, set-up, and spike. The team loses the serve or point if the ball is not played three times.

Tests for Volleyball Skills

Serving and volleying are the skills to be tested in volleyball. Serving is tested in two ways, one with a simple serve, and one with an accuracy score.

Simplified Serve Test. The child to be tested stands in the normal serving position behind the end line on the right side. He is given a specific number of trials in serving. His score is the number of times he serves successfully out of his trials (10). The serve must clear the net without touching and land in the opponents' court. A ball touching a line is counted as good.

Serve Accuracy Test. A line is drawn parallel to net through the middle of one

of the courts. Each half is further subdivided into three equal areas by lines
parallel to the side lines. This makes a
total of six areas, which correspond to the
six positions of members of a volleyball
team. The areas are numbered from 1
to 6.

Each child is allotted one service attempt to serve the ball into the each of the
six areas in turn. Scoring is as follows:
  2 points -- serving into the desig-
               nated court area
  1 point -- missing the designated
               area but landing in an ad-
               jacent area to the target
               area
  0 points -- failing to serve into the

target or adjacent area

Wall Test for Volleying. A child stands
behind a restraining line 4 feet away from
a wall. A line is drawn on the wall parallel to the floor and 6-1/2 feet up, representing the height of the net. A player is
allowed 30 seconds to make as many volleys
as he can above the 6-1/2 foot line, while
keeping behind the restraining line. A
counter is assigned to each testing station
to count the successful volleys.

To start, the child makes a short
toss to himself for his first volley. If time
permits, more than one opportunity can be
allowed, and the best count from any of the
30 second periods is his score.

ROTATION SYSTEMS

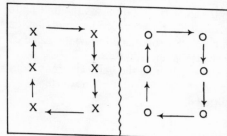

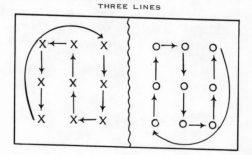

Chapter 28
Track and Field Activities

Emphasis on Different Levels
Practical Suggestions
Track and Field Events

Youngsters by nature love to run and jump. In the intermediate grades, this interest makes track and field activities quite popular. Children are motivated by competition with others and with themselves. However, the compeititve aspects of these activities must not be over-emphasized.

The program for the elementary grades in track and field is composed of short sprints (40 to 60 yards), running and standing broad jumps, the high jump, and jump combinations. Distance running has little place in the program in the elementary school. Children may jog for distances above the sprinting distances, but this must be at a moderate place and without competition.

Emphasis on Different Levels

Fourth Grade. The fourth grade should stress running short distances. The children should be introduced to the sprint start and the two broad jumps.

Fifth Grade. The fifth grade begins more serious efforts in form. To the fourth grade program is added the high jump. Scissors form should be used in learning.

Sixth Grade. Relays, both the shuttle and the regular track type, are to be experienced in the sixth grade. No child should run farther than 60 to 75 yards on his leg of the relay. The children should be taught a method of passing the baton. In the field events, the jump combinations add interest. In the high jump, both the regular and modified western rolls can be shown. The squad method can well be utilized with squads practicing different events on a rotation basis.

Practical Suggestions

1. Care must be exercised in controlling distance running for children of this age.
2. Form should be stressed at all times. Children should be brought to the realization that results in track and field are based on good form and proper practice.
3. The amount of activity should be built up slowly. A period of conditioning should precede any competition or all-out performance.
4. Children should warm up with bending and stretching exercises.
5. Pits with loose sand, dirt, or sawdust are needed for the jumping events.

GRADE	FOURTH	FIFTH	SIXTH
Skills	40 yard dash Sprinter's start	50 yard dash Sprinter's start	60 yard dash Sprinter's start Baton passing Relays
	Running broad jump Standing broad jump	Running broad jump Standing broad jump High jump	Running broad jump Standing broad jump High jump Hop, step, and jump

6. It is not desirable to have the children wear track shoes since only a few children will be able to afford them.

Track and Field Events

Running form. The body leans forward somewhat. The arms swing in opposition to the legs, that is, when the right leg comes forward, there is a thrust of the left arm. The arms are bent at the elbows and swing from the shoulders so the hands come up almost to shoulder height in front of the body. The arms should swing in the forward-backward plane and not across the body. The knee is lifted sharply forward and upward and brought down with a vigorous pushing motion, the toes pushing off the ground the moment they touch.

In coaching running form, concentrate on the following:
The quality of lightness
The quality of looseness
Good foot and ankle movement
Good knee action
Proper body position
Proper length of pace

Sprint Start. To take the "on the mark" position, the toe of the front foot is placed from 4 to 10 inches from the starting line. The fingers are spread and the weight on the tips of the fingers. The knee of the rear leg is placed just opposite the ankle of the leg already down.

On the "get set" command, the knee of the rear leg is raised so that the knee is level with the ankle of the other leg. The back is level with the ground, and the eyes are focused at a point six to eight feet ahead of the starting line. The weight is evenly distributed between the hands and the feet.

On the signal to start, a sharp drive is given with both feet, with the front leg straightening when the back leg comes forward for a step. The body should rise gradually and not "pop up" right after the start.

Baton Passing. The runner exchanges the baton from his left hand to the right hand of the runner ahead. The runner should carry the baton like a candle when passing. The receiver reaches back with his right hand and begins to move ahead when the coming runner is three to five yards back of him. He grasps the baton and immediately shifts it to his left hand while moving. The exchange should be made on the move with the front runner timing his start and increase of speed to the pace of the runner coming in. If the baton is dropped, it must be picked up or the team is disqualified.

Standing Broad Jump. In both the standing and running broad jump, the measurement is made from the take-off board or line to the nearest point on the ground touched by the jumper. It is important that the children do not fall or step backward after making the jump. In the standing broad jump, the performer toes the line with the feet flat on the ground and fairly close together. His arms are brought forward in a preliminary swing and then swung down and back. The jump is made with both feet as the arms are swung forcibly forward to assist in lifting the body upward and forward. While in the air the knees should be brought upward and forward with the arms forward to sustain balance.

Running Broad Jump. A short run is needed and should be planned so that the toes of the jumping foot will contact the board in a natural stride. The jumper takes off with one foot and should strive for height. The landing is made on both feet after the knees have been brought forward. The landing should be made in a forward direction, not sidewards.

Each contestant is given a certain number of trials (jumps). If a person runs into the pit or steps over the scratch line while jumping, this counts as one of the trials.

Measurement is from the scratch line to the nearest point of touch.

The pit for the broad jump should be filled properly and the sharp edges covered or leveled with sand. The take-off board should be adjusted to the jumping ability of the poorer jumpers in the group. Early jumping should be done for form. Distance can come later.

The pit must be clear before the next jumper takes his turn.

High Jump--Scissors Style. The high jump bar is approached from a slight angle. The take-off is from the outside leg (the one farthest from the bar). The front leg is lifted and goes over first, followed quickly by the rear leg in a looping movement. There should be a good kick upward with the front leg, together with an upward thrust of the arms. The knees should be straightened at the highest point of the jump. The landing is made on the leading foot followed by the rear foot.

High Jump--Western Roll. An approach at an angle of 45 degrees is used. The take-off is with the inside foot with the outside foot swung forward and upward.

The body lies parallel to the bar in crossing the bar. The hands and the take-off foot hit the ground about the same time.

High Jump--Western Roll--Modified. This form is sometimes called the straddle jump because the body in crossing the bar is face down to the bar. The take-off is the same as in the normal Western Roll. The landing is made on the swing-up foot and the hands. This jump is popularly termed the "Belly Roll." High jumping should be started at a low height and increased gradually with emphasis on form as opposed to a contest to see who is the best jumper.

Hop, Step, and Jump. This event is increasing in popularity, particularly so because it is included in Olympic competition. A take-off board and a jumping pit are needed. The distance from the take-off board to the pit should be of a distance that the poorer jumpers can make. The event begins with a run, similar to the broad jump. The take-off is with one foot and the jumper must light on the same foot to complete the hop. The jumper then takes a step followed by a jump. The event finishes like the broad jump by lighting on both feet. The jumper must not step over the take-off board in his first hop, under penalty of fouling. Distance is measured from the front of the take-off board to the closest place where the body touches. This is usually a mark made by one of the heels, but could be an arm or part of the body if the jumper landed poorly and fell backwards toward the take-off board.

Jump Combinations. Different jumping combinations can be set up to challenge the children. Combinations like two or three standing broad jumps, and up to five hops in succession can be used.

Chapter 29

Individual and Dual Activities for all Grades

Individual Rope Jumping
Long Rope Jumping
Tether Ball
Other Activities

This sections several activities which are difficult to allocate to specific grade levels because allocation would depend in many cases upon previous experience. This section includes individual rope jumping, long rope activities, Tether Ball, Sidewalk Tennis, and several miscellaneous activities.

Individual Rope Jumping

Rope jumping makes excellent contributions to physical fitness. The space requirements are small and the cost of materials negligible.

Rope jumping as a rhythmic activity has been presented previously on pages 202 to 205. There is some repetition in the material which follows, but the emphasis on the activity is using it on an individual basis without music. However, the activity is enhanced with music and suitable rhythms can make the activity more enjoyable. With or without music, the carry-over values are excellent, and the children should get an opportunity to practice and learn both ways.

Rope Length. When the player stands on the rope with both feet, the rope should come up to his arm pits. Sash cord, 3/8 inch, makes suitable material for ropes. Yellow plastic rope (not nylon) with a tight weave of 3/8 inch diameter makes an excellent rope. The ends can be melted and sealed permanently with a burner or match.

General Suggestions. The jumper should develop a sense of rhythm. The rope should turn at a constant rhythm. The rope should be turned with centrifugal force with a quick easy motion of the hands. All steps can be done from a single time jump meaning that the rope makes a complete turn for every jump. During the double time jump, the performer can execute two steps between swings or a little preliminary hop and a step. The rope is turning at half the speed of the single time jump. The single time method is more strenuous and leads to better fitness values.

Learning the Single Time Rhythm. Take both ends of the rope in one hand (usually the right) and turn the rope forward but at the side of the body. Work on the rhythm of the turn, gradually adding a bounce of the body by the toes. The rope should slap the floor lightly on each turn. Coordinate the bounce of the body with the turn of the rope so the body is in the air when the rope slaps the floor.

After sufficient practice, change to normal rope jumping position and attempt to apply the learned rhythm with the rope going under the feet.

The rope should be held in each hand, primarily with the thumb and first two fingers.

Rope Routines
1. Basic step -- Keep feet together, knees slightly bent, and jump over rope.
2. Alternating feet -- Shift the weight from one foot to another, alternating the feet in jumping.
3. Hopping on one foot -- Hop a number of times on one foot and the same number on the other.
4. Straddle Hop -- Alternate from a feet together position on one jump to a straddle position on the next jump.
5. Front and Back -- Alternate right and left foot forward.
6. Cradle -- With the weight on the back foot (the other is in front), rock from

back foot to front foot on each jump.

7. Progress forward by running, skipping, jumping, hopping.
8. Crossed Hands Forward -- When the rope is above the head, cross the hands in front of the chest far enough so the hands are to the side. On the next jump, return to position.
   Different combinations can be done. Make two jumps before changing. Try four and eight before changing.
9. Double Turn -- The rope passes under the feet twice before the jumper lands. The jump must be higher than normal and the rope speeded up.
10. Backward Jumping -- Most skills can be done with the rope turning backward.
11. Forward to Backward (and Return) -- Just as the rope starts downward, instead of letting it go under the feet, the child swings both arms to the left (or right) and makes a half-turn in that direction. The rope should now be turning backwards for him. Continue until a change is desired and repeat, returning to a forward jump.
12. Partner Jumping -- Partner runs in and both jump over the same rope.
13. See how fast one can turn the rope for 15, 30, or 60 seconds. Count the number of successful turns.

Long Rope Jumping

Groups of 5 make a convenient group for practicing long rope skills. Two of the group are turners and the others jumpers. The children should rotate between turning and jumping. The rope should be 16 to 18 feet long.

Introductory Skills

1. Hold the rope 6 inches from the ground. Children jump over and back and forth. Raise the rope a little each time. Be sure to hold the rope loosely in the hands.
2. The Ocean Wave is another stationary jumping activity. The turners make waves in the rope by moving the arms up and down. The children try to time so as to jump over a low part of the "wave."
3. Snake in the Grass. The holders stoop down and wiggle the rope back and forth. Children try to jump over the rope and not touch it as it moves.
4. Swing the rope in a pendulum fashion.

Children jump the rope as it passes under them.

5. Have the child stand in the center between the turners. Carefully turn the rope in a complete arc over the jumper's head. As the rope completes the turn, the jumper jumps over it. He immediately exits in the same direction as the rope turned.
6. While the rope is being turned, the jumper runs in and jumps once. He runs out immediately. The rope must be coming toward the jumper (front door).
7. Run through the turning rope without jumping.

Intermediate Skills

1. Front Door -- When rope is turned forward toward the jumper, it is called the front door.
2. Back Door -- The rope is turned away from the jumper.
3. With line at a 45 degree angle try the following:
   Run into front door, out back door.
   Run in front door, jump once, run out.
   Run in back door, jump once, run out.
   Run in front or back door, increase the number of jumps, run out.
   Run in front or back door, jump any number of times, but do 1/4, 1/2, 3/4, and full turns in the air.
4. Hot Pepper -- Turners turn the rope with increased speed with the jumper trying to keep up with the rope.
5. High Water -- The rope is turned so that it is gradually higher and higher off the ground.
6. Use doubles, triples, or four at a time. After some skill has been reached, the children can run in, jump a specified number of times, and run out keeping hands joined all the time.
7. Circling with doubles, triples, or four at a time. Start as a small circle, run in and jump in a circle. Keep the circle moving in one direction or the other. Run out as a circle.
8. Have the rope held at high jumping height. Practice high jumping skills -- scissors, western roll, modified western (belly) roll. Jump for form and not for height. Be sure the rope is held loosely. If mats are available, these are a help. Since the jumping is not for competition, these are not mandatory.
9. Bounce a ball while jumping. Toss a ball back and forth to a partner standing outside

the turning rope. Toss a ball back and forth to a partner jumping with you.

10. The jumper jumps using an individual rope while jumping under the long rope. Both ropes should be turned the same way. Later the long rope can be turned in the opposite direction.

Two Ropes

1. Double Dutch -- Two ropes are turned alternately, rope near the jumper is turned front door, rope away from jumper is turned back door.
2. Double Irish -- Two ropes are turned alternately, the ropes moving the opposite of Double Dutch.
3. Egg Beater -- Two large ropes are turned at right angles simultaneously with four turners.
4. Fence Jumping -- Two ropes are held motionless about 2 feet apart, parallel to each other and each about 12 inches above the ground. Have the players jump or hop in and out of the ropes in various combinations. The children can devise many different methods.
5. Try two rope combinations with the jumper using an individual rope. Jumper must jump single time with the individual rope.

Rhymes

As the jumpers become proficient, they can make use of many familiar rhymes which are used for long ropes. For example -

Teddy Bear, Teddy Bear, turn around
Teddy Bear, Teddy Bear, touch the ground
Teddy Bear, Teddy Bear, show your shoe
Teddy Bear, Teddy Bear, you better skidoo

For Red Hot Pepper--
Mabel, Mabel, Set the table
Bring the plates if you are able
Don't forget the salt and
Red Hot Pepper!

On the words "Red Hot Pepper" the rope is turned as fast as possible until the jumper misses.

For counting a definite number of turns --

Bulldog, poodle, bow wow wow
How many doggies have we now?
One, two, three, etc.

The rope is turned a specified number of turns, after the jumper exits from the rope.

Tether Ball

Tether ball is a popular game and is a natural where space is limited. The equipment consists of a pole and a tetherball attached to the pole by a length of rope. Pole assemblies are generally put in permanently with a concrete installation.

Two to four players can participate, but the game is generally played by two children.

The first server is picked by lot. One player stands on each side of the pole. Server puts ball in play by tossing it in the air and hitting it in the direction he chooses. The opponent must not strike the ball on the first swing around the pole. On the second time around the pole, he hits the ball back in the opposite direction. As the ball is hit back and forth, each player tries to hit the ball so that the rope winds completely around the pole in the direction he has been hitting the ball. The game is won by the player who succeeds in doing this or whose opponent forfeits the game by making any of the following fouls:

1. Hitting ball with any part of the body other than the hands or forearms
2. Catching or holding the ball during play
3. Touching the pole
4. Hitting the rope with the forearm or hands
5. Throwing the ball
6. Winding the ball around the pole below the five foot mark

After the opening game, winner of the previous game serves. Winning four games wins the set.

Other Activities

SIDEWALK TENNIS

Playing Area: On any sidewalk, four cement squares in a row can be used. Areas can be drawn on the gymnasium floor or other surfaced area.

SIDEWALK TENNIS

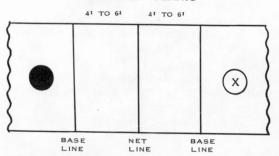

Players: 2

Supplies: Tennis ball or other rubber ball which bounces well.

The game is between two players, one in each court. The object is for the server to serve the ball over the net line into the other court. The server must bounce the ball behind the base line and hit the ball underhanded into the opponent's court. The receiver must let the ball bounce and then return it with the open palm. Points are only scored by the server. If he fails to make a good serve or a good return he loses the serve. Points are scored when the receiver fails to make a good return.

It is a foul and loss of serve if the server steps over the base line when serving. It is out of bounds if the ball at any time lights beyond the baseline. Any ball lighting on a line bordering a court is considered to have lighted in that court.

The first player scoring eleven points wins providing he is two points ahead. If either player does not have a two point advantage when his score totals eleven, the game continues until one player is two points ahead.

Variation: The game can be played as doubles. Partners alternate on returns.

STEP TARGET

Playing Area: Set of porch steps with a sidewalk in front and a restraining line 8 to 10 feet back from the steps marked on the sidewalk.

Players: Only one can play at a time but there can be other children waiting turns.

Supplies: Sponge, rubber, or tennis ball.

A child stands back of the restraining line with the ball. He throws the ball against the steps in such a manner that he can catch it on the fly or first bounce. He continues to throw and score as long as he catches the returns on the fly or on first bounce. When he misses, the next child takes the turn.

Scoring is done as follows:

100 points Catching ball hitting the stair <u>edge</u>

10 points Catching any other ball on the fly

5 points Catching any ball on first bounce

First player to reach the score of 500 is the winner.

HOPSCOTCH

Playing Area: Diagram as drawn on a hard surface area

Players: Not more than 4 or 5 to any one game

Supplies: A lagger for each player. A stone is ideal.

Each player has a lagger. The first player starts the game by tossing the lagger into the number one box. He then hops <u>over</u> the first box into the second box. He then hops into box #3 on the same foot. The general rule is to hop on one foot in the single boxes and both feet (one in each) into the double boxes. When he reaches boxes 7-8, he turns around completely in place with a jump exchange of the feet into the opposite boxes. He hops back with a jump into boxes 4-5. When he reaches box 2, he reaches over and picks up his lagger, hops into box 1 and out. He now tosses his lagger into box 2 and repeats the routine. He continues into the other boxes with his lagger until he has covered all eight. Certain rules are basic.

1. The player may not hop into the box where his lagger is tossed. He picks up the lagger on the way back by stopping in the box immediately front. After he has picked up the lagger, he can hop into the box.
2. A player loses his turn if his lagger fails to be tossed into the correct box or rests on a line.
3. Stepping on a line, missing a box, falling, or stepping into a box where the lagger rests are fouls and stop the turn at that point.
4. After a player has gone completely through the boxes (through the "eighties"), he may write his name in any box, and no one but that player may step in that box. The player whose name is in the most boxes wins.

There are innumerable forms of hopscotch and each area has its favorites. Hopscotch formations take the forms of simple lines of boxes, crosses, squares, snail, and other varied figures. It is truly an international game played in almost every country.

KICK SHUFFLE

Playing Area: Diagram as illustrated on a
hard surface

Players: 2 - 4

Supplies: 3 kicking blocks (2" x 4" x 4")

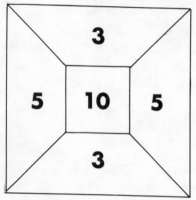

The target can be laid out permanently with paint or temporarily with chalk. The blocks are made from regular 2 x 4 inch lumber. These should be cut a little short of 4 inches in order to match the width of the lumber.

The first player stands at a kicking line drawn about 15 feet from the front of the target. He stands at the line with one foot, and with the other slides or kicks the blocks, one at a time, at the court. He scores the points as listed if the block rests in a particular space. If the block is on a line <u>between</u> two spaces, he scores the lower figure. If the block stops on an outside line, it scores nothing.

The game can be played by two or three players who take turns at a target. With larger numbers or using partners, it would be better to lay out a court with two targets, one at each end, similarly to shuffle board courts.

Other diagrams could be arranged.

The Oregon Motor Fitness Test

The Oregon Motor Fitness was developed cooperatively by the University of Oregon, Oregon State University, physical educators through the public schools, and the Department of Education for the State of Oregon. The test is presented by permission of the Department of Education.

The test is a valuable tool for measuring physical fitness qualities because of its simplicity. It uses simple equipment and can be given to a class usually in one class period. Like most tests on the elementary level, the testing program begins in the fourth grade. The tests are different for boys and girls.

DIRECTIONS FOR ADMINISTERING THE BOYS' TEST BATTERY
(Grades 4, 5, and 6)

PUSH-UPS

Starting Position: The pupil assumes a front-leaning rest position with the body supported on hand and toes. The arms are straight and at right angles to the body.

Action: The pupil dips or lowers the body so that the chest touches or nearly touches the floor, then pushes back to the starting position by straightening the arms, and repeats the procedure as many times as possible.

Rules: The chest, no other part of the body, must touch or nearly touch the floor with each dip. The arms must be completely extended with each push-up. The body must be held straight, with no bend in the hips, throughout the exercise.

Scoring: The number of times the body is correctly pushed up. If the body sags, if the hips rise, or if the pupil does not push completely up or go completely down, no credit is given for each push-up.

STANDING BROAD JUMP

Starting Position: A take-off line is drawn on the floor or mat. At a distance that all can jump, additional lines are drawn parallel to the take-off line and two inches apart to a point exceeding the farthest jump anticipated. The first line should be an even number of feet from the take-off line. The pupil toes the take-off line with both feet, but with feet slightly apart, prior to each jump.

Action: Taking off from both feet, the pupil jumps as far as he can. In jumping, he crouches slightly and swings the arms to aid in the jump.

Rules: The pupil must take off from both feet and land on both feet. The start must be from a stationary position.

Scoring: The distance to the nearest inch from the take-off line to the closest heel position. If the pupil falls back, he should re-take the test. Record the best of three trials.

KNEE-TOUCH SIT-UPS

Starting Position: The pupil lies on his back on the floor, knees straight, feet approximately 12 inches apart, with hands clasped behind head. A scorer kneels on the floor and holds the soles of the feet against his knees, pressing firmly.

Action: The pupil performs the following movement as many times as possible: (a) Raise the trunk, rotating it somewhat to the left, and bend forward far enough to touch the right elbow to the left knee. (b) Lower the trunk to the floor. (c) Sit up again, but rotate the trunk to the right and touch the left elbow to the right knee. (d) Again lower the trunk to the floor.

Rules: The knees may be slightly bent as the subject sits up. The pupils must not pause during the test; the movement must be continuous either when leaning forward to touch the knee or when lowering the trunk to the floor. Bouncing from the floor is not permissible.

Scoring: One point is given for each complete movement of touching elbow to knee. No score should be counted if the subject unclasps hands from head, rests on the floor or when sitting, or keeps knees bent when lying on the back or when beginning the sit-up.

OREGON MOTOR FITNESS TEST SCORE CARD—BOYS GRADES 4, 5, AND 6

NAME ....

SCHOOL .... COUNTY ....

DATE	Month Sept. 19......			Month 19......			Month 19......			Month 19......			Month 19......			Month 19......			Month 19......			Month 19......			Month 19......		
GRADE																											
AGE																											
HEIGHT																											
WEIGHT																											
OBJECTIVE TESTS	Test Score	Rat-ing	Std. Pts.	Test Score	Rat-ing	Std. Pts.	Test Score	Rat-ing	Std. Pts.	Test Score	Rat-ing	Std. Pts.	Test Score	Rat-ing	Std. Pts.	Test Score	Rat-ing	Std. Pts.	Test Score	Rat-ing	Std. Pts.	Test Score	Rat-ing	Std. Pts.	Test Score	Rat-ing	Std. Pts.
Standing Broad Jump																											
Push-Ups																											
Sit-Ups																											
TOTAL STAND-ARD POINTS																											

RATING NORMS FOR BOYS GRADES 4, 5, AND 6

TEST ITEMS	Superior	Good	Fair	Poor	Inferior	Grade
Standing Broad Jump	69-Up	62- 68	52- 61	42- 51	12- 41	
Push-Ups	25-Up	18- 24	7- 17	1- 6	0	4
Sit-Ups	64-Up	47- 63	22- 46	1- 21	0	
Standing Broad Jump	73-Up	66- 72	56- 65	46- 55	16- 45	
Push-Ups	22-Up	16- 21	7- 15	1- 6	0	5
Sit-Ups	70-Up	52- 69	22- 51	2- 21	0- 1	
Standing Broad Jump	77-Up	70- 76	59- 69	49- 58	18- 48	
Push-Ups	24-Up	18- 23	9- 17	4- 8	0- 3	6
Sit-Ups	75-Up	55- 74	25- 54	1- 24	0	
TOTAL STANDARD POINTS	204-Up	180-203	144-179	112-143	111-Down	

DIRECTIONS FOR RECORDING AND SCORING TESTS

1. Record the actual test score for each item in the column marked "Test Score" on this side of the score card.
2. Using test score, check rating norms and record superior, good, fair, poor, or inferior for each test item in the rating column.
3. Find standard point score corresponding to each actual test score in the "Scoring Table" on the back of the card and record in column marked "Standard Points"
4. Add "Standard Points" for all test items and record total at bottom of card in space on line marked "Total Standard Points".
5. Using total standard points, check rating norms to determine fitness rating of superior, good, fair, poor, or inferior. Record this rating in the space provided at the bottom of the rating column.
6. Repeat the test at the end of the school year; it is recommended that a mid-year test also be given. Below-standard individuals should be tested more frequently.

SCORING TABLE
FOR BOYS GRADES 4, 5, AND 6

Std. Pts. Based on T-Score	Standing Broad Jump in Inches			Number of Push-Ups			Number of Sit-Ups		
	4th	5th	6th	4th	5th	6th	4th	5th	6th
100	97	100	106	55	43	39	131	153	158
98	95	99	104	53	41	37	127	148	153
96	93	97	102	51	40	36	123	143	147
94	91	95	100	50	39	35	118	138	142
92	90	94	98	48	37	34	114	133	137
90	88	92	97	46	36	33	110	128	132
88	86	90	95	44	34	32	106	123	127
86	85	88	93	42	33	30	102	118	122
84	83	87	91	40	32	29	97	113	117
82	81	85	90	38	30	28	93	108	112
80	80	83	88	36	29	27	89	103	107
78	78	82	86	35	27	26	85	98	102
76	76	80	84	33	26	25	81	93	97
74	74	78	83	31	25	23	76	88	92
72	73	77	81	29	23	22	72	83	87
70	71	75	79	27	22	21	68	78	81
68	69	73	77	25	21	20	64	73	76
66	68	72	75	23	19	19	60	68	71
64	66	70	74	22	18	18	56	63	66
62	64	68	72	20	16	16	51	58	61
60	63	66	70	18	15	15	47	53	56
58	61	65	68	16	13	14	43	48	51
56	59	63	67	14	12	13	39	43	46
54	57	61	65	12	11	12	35	38	41
52	56	60	63	10	9	10	30	33	36
50	54	58	61	9	8	9	26	28	31
48	52	56	60	7	6	8	22	23	26
46	51	55	58	5	5	7	18	18	21
44	49	53	56	3	4	6	14	13	16
42	47	51	54	1	2	5	9	8	11
40	46	49	53		1	3	5	4	6
38	44	48	51			2	1	1	2
36	42	46	49			1			
34	41	44	47						
32	39	43	45						
30	37	41	44						
28	35	39	42						
26	34	38	40						
24	32	36	38						
22	30	34	37						
20	29	33	35						
18	27	31	33						
16	25	29	31						
14	24	27	30						
12	22	26	28						
10	20	24	26						
8	18	22	24						
6	17	21	23						
4	15	19	21						
2	13	17	19						
1	12	16	18						

GENERAL INSTRUCTIONS TO TEACHERS

. The motor fitness tests are to be taken by only those individuals who are physically able to participate in the regular program of physical education.

. In no instance should pupils be permitted to perform any test more than is necessary to get one hundred points. Performance should be stopped on any test if, in the opinion of the instructor, the pupil is overtaxing himself.

. Individuals should be acquainted with the tests in advance of the testing period and sufficient practice should be allowed for thorough understanding of the execution of the tests.

Time should be provided for a few minutes warm-up at the beginning of each test period.

. All equipment and facilities necessary for the administration of the tests should be prepared before the testing period begins.

. Establish a policy of strictly enforcing all rules and regulations in scoring and administering the test.

DIRECTIONS FOR ADMINISTERING THE GIRLS' TEST BATTERY
(Grades 4, 5, and 6)

HANGING IN ARM-FLEXED POSITION

Equipment: A horizontal bar or similar support parallel to the floor; a stop watch, or a watch with a second hand; a stool or bench.

Starting Position: The student stands on a stool or table placing the hands shoulder width apart, palms outward on a one-inch standard horizontal bar or ladder with elbows flexed to permit chin to be level with the bar.

Action: The support is removed. The student holds her chin at the level of the bar as long as possible.

Rules: The legs should remain extended throughout.

Scoring: The number of seconds the student is able to maintain some flexion in the elbow, preventing the upper arm from straightening.

STANDING BROAD JUMP

Starting Position: A take-off line is drawn on the floor or mat. At a distance that all can jump, additional lines are drawn parallel to the take-off line and two inches apart to a point exceeding the farthest jump anticipated. The first line should be an even number of feet from the take-off line. The student toes the take-off line with both feet, but with feet slightly apart, prior to each jump.

Action: Taking off from both feet, the student jumps as far as she can. In jumping, she crouches slightly and swings the arms to aid in the jump.

Rules: The student must take off from both feet and land on both feet. The start must be from a stationary position.

Scoring: The distance to the nearest inch from the take-off line to the closest heel position. If a student falls back, she should re-take the test. Record the best of three trials.

CROSSED-ARM CURL-UPS

Starting Position: The student assumes a lying position on the back with knees bent at approximately a right angle, soles of the feet flat on the floor, arms folded and held against the chest. The feet of the student tested should be held down firmly by a partner. The feet are hip width apart.

Action: The student rises to an erect sitting position and returns to a back lying position as many times as possible without stopping.

Rules: The feet must remain on the floor throughout the test. The elbows must be kept down, and the arms are not used to help the body sit up. Bouncing from the floor is not permissible. Resting during any phase of the performance is not allowed.

Scoring: The number of times the student raises herself correctly to a sitting position.

OREGON MOTOR FITNESS TEST SCORE CARD—GIRLS GRADES 4, 5, AND 6

NAME ....

SCHOOL .... COUNTY ....

DATE	Month Sept. 19......			Month 19......			Month 19......			Month 19......			Month 19......			Month 19......			Month 19......			Month 19......			Month 19......		
GRADE																											
AGE																											
HEIGHT																											
WEIGHT																											
OBJECTIVE TESTS	Test Score	Rat-ing	Std. Pts.	Test Score	Rat-ing	Std. Pts.	Test Score	Rat-ing	Std. Pts.	Test Score	Rat-ing	Std. Pts.	Test Score	Rat-ing	Std. Pts.	Test Score	Rat-ing	Std. Pts.	Test Score	Rat-ing	Std. Pts.	Test Score	Rat-ing	Std. Pts.	Test Score	Rat-ing	Std. Pts.
Hanging in Arm-Flexed Position																											
Standing Broad Jump																											
Crossed-Arm Curl-Ups																											
TOTAL STAND-ARD POINTS																											

RATING NORMS FOR GIRLS GRADES 4, 5, AND 6

TEST ITEMS	Superior	Good	Fair	Poor	Inferior	Grade
Hanging in Arm-Flexed Position	30-Up	20- 29	5- 19	1- 4	0	
Standing Broad Jump	65-Up	58- 64	49- 57	39- 48	0- 38	4
Crossed-Arm Curl-Ups	66-Up	50- 65	26- 49	2- 25	0- 1	
Hanging in Arm-Flexed Position	31-Up	22- 30	10- 21	2- 9	0- 1	
Standing Broad Jump	75-Up	68- 74	57- 67	46- 56	0- 45	5
Crossed-Arm Curl-Ups	68-Up	52- 67	28- 51	4- 27	0- 3	
Hanging in Arm-Flexed Position	37-Up	27- 36	12- 26	1- 11	0	
Standing Broad Jump	73-Up	66- 72	55- 65	44- 54	0- 43	6
Crossed-Arm Curl-Ups	71-Up	55- 70	31- 54	1- 30	0	
TOTAL STANDARD POINTS	204-Up	180-203	144-179	112-143	111-Down	

DIRECTIONS FOR RECORDING AND SCORING TESTS

1. Record the actual test score for each item in the column marked "Test Score" on this side of the score card.
2. Using test score, check rating norms and record superior, good, fair, poor, or inferior for each test item in the rating column.
3. Find standard point score corresponding to each actual test score in the "Scoring Table" on the back of the card and record in column marked "Standard Points".
4. Add "Standard Points" for all test items and record total at bottom of card in space on line marked "Total Standard Points".
5. Using total standard points, check rating norms to determine fitness rating of superior, good, fair, poor, or inferior. Record this rating in the space provided at the bottom of the rating column.
6. Repeat the test at the end of the school year; it is recommended that a mid-year test also be given. Below-standard individuals should be tested more frequently.

SCORING TABLE
FOR GIRLS GRADES 4, 5, AND 6

Std. Pts. Based on T-Score	Arm-Flexed Hang in Seconds			Standing Broad Jump in Inches			Number of Crossed-Arm Curl-Ups		
	4th	5th	6th	4th	5th	6th	4th	5th	6th
100	69	65	77	91	104	102	130	120	149
98	66	63	75	89	103	101	126	117	145
96	64	61	72	87	101	99	122	114	140
94	61	59	70	86	99	97	118	110	136
92	59	56	67	84	97	95	114	106	131
90	57	54	62	83	95	93	110	103	127
88	54	52	62	81	93	91	106	99	122
86	52	50	60	79	92	89	102	95	118
84	49	48	57	78	90	87	98	92	113
82	47	46	55	76	88	85	94	88	109
80	44	44	52	75	86	84	90	84	104
78	42	42	50	73	84	82	86	81	100
76	40	40	47	71	82	80	82	77	95
74	37	38	44	70	81	78	78	73	91
72	35	35	42	68	79	76	74	70	86
70	32	33	39	67	77	74	70	66	82
68	30	31	37	65	75	72	66	63	77
66	27	29	34	63	73	70	62	59	73
64	25	27	32	62	72	68	58	55	68
62	23	25	29	60	70	67	54	51	64
60	20	23	27	59	68	65	50	48	60
58	18	21	24	57	66	63	46	45	55
56	15	19	22	55	64	61	42	41	51
54	13	16	19	54	62	59	38	38	46
52	10	14	17	52	61	57	34	34	42
50	8	12	14	51	59	65	30	30	37
48	5	10	12	49	57	53	26	27	33
46	3	8	9	47	55	51	22	23	28
44	1	6	7	46	53	50	18	19	24
42		4	4	44	51	48	14	16	20
40		2	1	42	50	46	10	12	16
38				41	48	44	6	8	11
36				39	46	42	3	4	6
34				38	44	40	1	1	1
32				36	42	38			
30				34	41	36			
28				33	39	35			
26				31	37	33			
24				30	35	31			
22				28	33	29			
20				26	31	27			
18				25	30	25			
16				23	28	23			
14				22	26	21			
12				20	24	19			
10				18	22	18			
8				17	20	16			
6				15	19	14			
4				14	17	12			
2				12	15	10			
1				11	14	9			

GENERAL INSTRUCTIONS TO TEACHERS

1. The motor fitness tests are to be taken by only those individuals who are physically able to participate in the regular progr of physical education.
2. In no instance should pupils be permitted to perform any test more than is necessary to get one hundred points. Performa should be stopped on any test if, in the opinion of the instructor. the pupil is overtaxing himself.
3. Individuals should be acquainted with the tests in advance of the testing period and sufficient practice should be allowed thorough understanding of the execution of the tests.
4. Time should be provided for a few minutes warm-up at the beginning of each test period.
5. All equipment and facilities necessary for the administration of the tests should be prepared before the testing period beg
6. Establish a policy of strictly enforcing all rules and regulations in scoring and administering the test.

Sources for Records for the Rhythmic Program in the Elementary School

The following sources, in most cases, handle a variety of records. It is suggested that you write and ask for descriptive literature. The request should include the type of rhythmic program and the grade level for which the records are intended.

American Squares
1161 Broad Street
Newark 14, New Jersey

Canadian F. D. S.
Educational Recordings
605 King Street
W. Toronto, 2B, Canada

Chartwell House
Box 166, Bowling Green Station
New York 3, New York

Cheviot Corporation, Dept. J.
9844 Everest Street
Downey, California

Children's Music Center
2858 W. Pico Boulevard
Los Angeles 6, California

Dance Record Center
1161 Broad Street
Newark 14, New Jersey

David McKay, Inc.
119 West 40th Street
New York 18, New York

Educational Activities, Inc.
Box 392
Freeport, New York 11520

Educational Dance Recordings, Inc.
P. O. Box 6062
Bridgeport 6, Connecticut

Freda Miller Records for Dance
Department J., Box 383
Northport, Long Island, New York

Hoctor Records
Waldwick, N. J.

Honor Your Partner Records
Box 392
Freeport, New York 11520

Kimbo - U.S.A. Records
Box 55, Deal, New Jersey

Merrbach Records Service
P. O. Box 7308
Houston, Texas

RCA Victor Education Dept. (J)
155 E. 24th Street
New York 10, New York

Record Center
2581 Piedmont Road N. E.
Atlanta, Georgia 30324

Russell Records
P. O. Box 3318
1403 Callens Road
Ventura, California

Stanley Bowman Co., Inc.
12 Cleveland Street
Valhalla, New York

Source for Bode Gymnastic Records
(Dr. Rudolf Bode, Germany)
Gretal Dunsing (Distributor for USA
and Canada)
5315 Drexel Ave.
Chicago, Illinois

Record--Chicken Fat (Fitness Song)
Available at U. S. Junior Chamber
of Commerce
Tulsa, Oklahoma

Bibliography and Related Materials Resource

The bibliography is divided into subject areas. Addresses of the publisher can be secured from most libraries. In particular, addresses are listed in the Publisher's Trade List Annual and Books in Print. Attempt was made to include only those materials which were both pertinent and available. Included also is a listing of card packets available in games, rhythms, and stunts.

The term "AAHPER" refers to the American Association for Health, Physical Education and Recreation, 1201 Sixteenth Street, N.W., Washington, D.C. The address of the National Recreation Association is 8 West Eighth Street, New York 11, New York. Both agencies will supply lists of available publications.

In some cases, publications are listed without a publication date, as the author was unable to find dates for the manuscripts in question. Also, it should be noted that titles in some instances include more than one area. However, these were classified under the area of greatest emphasis.

The bibliography is organized under the following headings:

1. Curriculum in Elementary School Physical Education
2. Fitness and Exercise
3. Games and Similar Activities
4. Rhythms, Songs, and Dances
5. Stunts, Tumbling, and Apparatus
6. Health, Safety, and Posture
7. General and Miscellaneous
8. Card Packets for Games, Rhythms and Stunts

1. Curriculum in Elementary School Physical Education

Andrews, Sauborn, and Schneider. *Physical Education for Today's Boys and Girls*. Boston: Allyn and Bacon, 1960.

Athletic Institute. *Physical Education for Children of Elementary School Age*. Chicago: The Athletic Institute, 1951.

Bauer, Lois M. and Barbara A. Reed. *Dance and Play Activities*. Vol. 1 for Grades 1-3, Vol. 2 for Grades 4-6. New York: Chartwell House, 1951.

Bucher, Charles A., and Evelyn M. Reade. *Physical Education and Health in the Elementary School*. New York: The Macmillan Co., 1964.

Clarke, H. Harrison and Franklin B. Haar. *Health and Physical Education for the Classroom Teacher*. Englewood Cliffs, N. J.: Prentice-Hall Co., 1964.

Curtiss, Mary L., and Adelaide B. Curtiss. *Pyysical Education for Elementary Schools*. Milwaukee: The Bruce Publishing Co., 1957.

Davies, M. B. *Physical Education Games and Athletics for Training Colleges*. London, England: George Allen and Unwin, Ltd., 1959.

Department of Education, N. S. W. *Physical Education in Primary Schools*. Sydney, N. S. W., Australia: Minister for Education, N. S. W.

Detroit Public Schools. *It's All in the Game--About Children in Play.* Detroit: The Board of Education of the City of Detroit, 1961.

Espenschade, Anna S. *Physical Education in the Elementary Schools* (#27 of the Series, *What Research Says to the Teacher*). Washington, D. C.: National Education Association, 1963.

Evans, Bacon, Bacon, and Stapleton, *Physical Education for Elementary Schools.* New York: McGraw-Hill Book Co., Inc., 1958.

Fait, Hollis, F. *Physical Education for the Elementary School Child.* Philadelphia: W. B. Saunders Co., 1964.

Farina, Furth, and Smith. *Growth Through Play.* Englewood Cliffs, N. J.: Prentice-Hall, Inc., 1959.

Fraser, Bransford, and Hastings. *The Child and Physical Education.* Englewood Cliffs, N. J.: Prentice-Hall, Inc., 1956.

Greene, Arthur S. *Physical Activities for Elementary Schools.* Minneapolis: T. S. Dennison Co., 1963.

Halsey, Elizabeth and Lorena Porter. *Physical Education for Children, A Developmental Program.* New York: Henry Holt and Co. (Dryden Press), 1963.

Humphrey, James H. *Elementary School Physical Education.* New York: Harper and Bros., 1958.

Jones, Morgan, and Stevens. *Methods and Materials in Elementary Physical Education.* Yonkers-on-Hudson, N. Y.: World Book Co., 1959.

Jones, P. and A. Bilbrough. *Physical Education in the Primary School.* London, England: University of London Press, Ltd., 1963.

Kruse, Charles. *Physical Education in the Elementary Schools.* St. Petersburg, Fla.: Kruse Publishing Co., 1959.

Larson, Leonard A., and Lucille Hill. *Physical Education in the Elementary School.* New York: Henry Holt and Co. (Dryden Press), 1957.

LaSalle, Dorothy. *Guidance of Children Through Physical Education.* New York: The Ronald Press, 1957.

Miller, Arthur G., and Virginia Whitcomb. *Physical Education in the Elementary School Curriculum.* Englewood Cliffs, N. J.: Prentice-Hall, Inc., 1963.

Neilson, N. P. and Winifred Van Hagen. *Physical Education for Elementary Schools.* New York: The Ronald Press, 1964.

O'Keefe, Pattric Ruth, and Anita Aldrich. *Education Through Physical Activities.* St. Louis: C. V. Mosby Co., 1959.

Ontario Department of Education. *Physical Education -- Junior Division.* Toronto, Ontario: Canadian Association for Health, Physical Education, and Recreation (515 Jarvis St.), 1960.

Pearson, C. Eric. *A Classroom Teacher's Guide to Physical Education.* New York: Bureau of Publications, Teachers College, Columbia Univ., 1958.

Roberts, Nan H., et al. *Physical Education Handbook for Elementary School Teaching.* San Antonio, Texas: Naylor Co., 1957.

Salt, Fox, and Stevens. *Teaching Physical Education in the Elementary School.* New York: The Ronald Press, 1960.

Smalley, Jeanette. *Physical Education Activities for the Elementary School.* Palo Alto, Calif.: National Press Publications.

Van Hagen, Dexter, and Williams. *Physical Education in the Elementary School.* Sacramento, California: State Department of Education, 1951.

Vannier, Maryhelen, and Mildred Foster. *Teaching Physical Education in Elementary Schools.* Philadelphia: W. B. Saunders Co., 1963.

2. Fitness and Exercise

Available at the AAHPER

Children and Fitness. 1960.
Cycling in the School Fitness Program. 1963.
Exercise and Fitness (Statement by the American Medical Association and the AAHPER).
    1964.
Fitness Test Dial (Boys).
Fitness Test Dial (Girls).
Fitness Test Manual. 1961.
Your Child Can't Sit and Keep Fit. 1961. (Brochure. Available in quantities.)
Your Child's Health and Fitness. (Brochure. Available in quantities.)
Your Child's Health and Fitness Filmstrip.
Youth and Fitness. 1959.

Also, available from the AAHPER is a variety of fitness materials, including record
    forms, certificates, emblems, and bar patches. Write for descriptive literature.

Available from the President's Council on Physical Fitness. Write to Superintendent of
    Documents, U. S. Government Printing Office, Washington, D. C.

Adult Physical Fitness. 1963.
Vim. (Fitness program for girls.) 1964.
Vigor. (Fitness program for boys.) 1964.
Youth Physical Fitness. Suggested Elements of a School Centered Program, 1961.
Physical Fitness Elements in Recreation. 1963

Available from the President's Council on Physical Fitness, Room 4820, GAO Building,
    441 G. Street NW, Washington, D. C. 20548.

Physcial Fitness for a Strong America (A Circuit Training Program.) 1964.
Bender, Jay and Edward J. Shea. *Physical Fitness: Tests and Exercises.* New York:
    The Ronald Press, 1964.
Nelson, Dale O. *Special Exercises for Physical Fitness.* Logan, Utah: Dept. of Health,
    P. E., and Rec. Utah State University, 1964.
Prudden, Bonnie, *Is Your Child Really Fit?* New York: Harper and Brothers, Pub-
    lishers, 1956.
Royal Canadian Air Force. *Exercise Plans for Physical Fitness.* New York: Pocket
    Books, Inc., 1962.
Vermes, Hal G. *The Boy's Book of Physical Fitness.* New York: Association Press,
    1961.
Vermes, Jean C. *The Girl's Book of Physical Fitness.* New York: Association Press,
    1961.
Walsh, John E. *The First Book of Physical Fitness.* New York: Franklin Watts, Inc.,
    1961.

3. Games and Similar Activities

AAHPER. *After-School Games and Sports: Grades 4-5-6.* 1964.
AAHPER. *Group Games for Girls and Women.* 1957.
AAHPER. *How We Do It Game Book.* 1963.
AAHPER. *Learning About the World Through Games and Dances.* 1964.
AAHPER. *Recreational Games and Sports* (Girls). 1963.

AAHPER. *Values in Sport*. 1963.

Anderson, D. *Games for Boys and Girls*. Grand Rapids, Mich.: Zondervan Publishing House, 1955.

Athletic Institute. *How to Improve Your Track and Field for Elementary School Children and Junior High School Girls*. Chicago: Athletic Institute.

Bancroft, Jessie H. *Games*. New York: The Macmillan Co. Revised.

Bell, R. C. *Board and Table Games from Many Civilizations*. New York: Oxford University Press, 1960.

Borst, Evelyne. *The Book of Games for Boys and Girls: How to Lead and Play Them*. New York: The Ronald Press, 1953.

Borst, Evelyne and Elmer D. Mitchell. *Social Games for Recreation*. New York: The Ronald Press, 1959.

Depew, Arthur M. *The Cokesbury Game Book*. Nashville: Abingdon Press, 1960.

Donnelly, Richard J., Helms, William G. and Elmer D. Mitchell. *Active Game and Contests*. New York: The Ronald Press, 1958.

Forbush, William B. and Harry R. Allen. *Book of Games*. Holt, Rinehart and Winston, Inc., 1946.

Frankel, Lillian and Godrey. *Games for Boys and Girls*. New York: The Sterling Publishing Co., Inc.

Froh, Alfred and Margaret King. *Games for Young People*. Minneapolis: Augsburg Publishing House.

Gardner, Grace H. *Games We Like to Play*. New York: Williams-Frederick Press, 1959.

Geri, Frank. *Illustrated Games, Rhythms and Stunts for Children* (Upper Elementary). Englewood Cliffs, N. J.: Prentice-Hall, Inc., 1957.

Geri, Frank. *Illustrated Games and Rhythms for Children* (Primary Grades). Englewood Cliffs, N. J.: Prentice-Hall, Inc., 1955.

Harbin, E. O. *Games of Many Nations*. Nashville: Abingdon Press, 1954.

Harbin, E. O. *Games for Boys and Girls* (Gr. 3-5). Nashville: Abingdon Press, 1951.

Hindman, Darwin A. *Complete Book of Games and Stunts*. Englewood Cliffs, N. J.: Prentice-Hall, Inc., 1956.

Hindman, Darwin A. *Handbook of Indoor Games and Stunts*. Englewood Cliffs, N. J.: Prentice-Hall, Inc., 1955.

Hofsinde, Robert. *Indian Games and Crafts*. New York: William Morrow and Co., Inc., 1957.

Hunt, Sarah E. *Games and Sports the World Around*. New York: The Ronald Press, 1964.

Joseph, Helen. *The Family Book of Games and Sports*. Chicago: Popular Mechanics Press, 1954.

Kemmerer, James and Eva May Brickett. *Games and Parties for All Occasions*. Minneapolis: T. S. Dennison and Co., 1962.

Kohl, Marguerite and Frederica Young. *Games for Children*. New York: Hill and Wang, Inc., 1953.

Kraus, Richard. *The Family Book of Games*. New York: McGraw-Hill Book Co., 1960.

Kraus, Richard. *Play Activities for Boys and Girls*. New York: McGraw-Hill Book Co., 1957.

Latchaw, Marjorie and Jean Pyatt. *A Pocket Guide of Games and Rhythms for the Elementary School*. Englewood Cliffs, N. J.: Prentice-Hall, Inc., 1958.

Leeming, Joseph. *Real Book of Games*. New York: Doubleday and Co., Inc., 1953.

Macfarlan, Allan and Paulette. *Fun With Brand-New Games*. New York: Association Press, 1961.

Macfarlan, Allan A. *Book of American Indian Games*. New York: Association Press, 1958.

Macfarlan, Allan A. *More New Games for 'Tween-Agers*. New York: Association Press, 1958.

Millen, Nina. *Children's Games from Many Lands*. New York: Friendship Press, 1951.

Mulac, Margaret E. and Marian Holmes. *School Game Book*. New York: Harper and Row, Publishers, 1950.

Nagel, Charles. *Play Activities for Elementary Grades*. St. Louis: The C. V. Mosby Co., 1964.

National Recreation Assn. *Games for Quiet Hours and Small Spaces*, 1948.

Recreational Activities for the Elementary Classroom and Playground. Darien, Conn.: Teacher's Publishing Co.

Settle, Geraldine Webb. *Easy Games for Youngsters*, Minneapolis: T. S. Dennison and Co.

Smith, Charles F. *Games and Game Leadership*. New York: Dodd, Mead and Co., 1953.

Stuart, Frances R. *Classroom Activities*. Washington, D. C.: AAHPER, 1963.

Tedford, Jack. *The Giant Book of Family Fun and Games*. New York: Franklin Watts, Inc., 1958.

Wackerbarth, Marjorie and Lillian S. Graham. *Games for All Ages and How to Use Them*. Minneapolis: T. S. Dennison and Co.

Webb, Marion A. *Games for Younger Children*. New York: William Morrow and Co., Inc., 1947.

Young, Wilham P., and Horace J. Gardner. *Games and Stunts for All Occasions*. Philadelphia: J. B. Lippincott Co., 1957.

4. Rhythms, Songs, and Dances

AAHPER. Materials for Teaching Dance, Vol. 1. *Modern Dance and Children's Dance*. 1962.

Andrews, Gladys. *Creative Rhythmic Movement for Children*. Englewood Cliffs, N. J.: Prentice-Hall, Inc., 1954.

Ashton, Dudley. *Rhythmic Activities -- Grades K-6*. Washington, D. C.: AAHPER, 1964.

Barr, Lillian J. *Motion Songs for Tots*. Minneapolis: T. S. Dennison and Co.

Bley, Edgar S. *Best Singing Games for Children of All Ages*. New York: Sterling Publishing Co., 1959.

Buttree, Julia M. *The Rhythm of the Redman--in Song, Dance and Decoration*. New York: The Ronald Press, 1930.

Carabo-Cone, Madeleine. *Playground as Music Teacher*. New York: Harper and Row, Publishers, 1959.

Driver, Ann. *Music and Movement*. New York: Oxford University Press, 1936.

Duggan, Schlottmann and Rutledge. *The Folk Dance Library* (five volumes). The Teaching of Folk Dance, Folk Dances of Scandinavia, European Countries, British Isles, United States and Mexico. New York: The Ronald Press, 1948.

Durlacher, Ed. *Teacher's Manual #1 for Nursery, Kindergarten, 1st, 2nd, and 3rd Grades*. Freeport, N. Y.: Square Dance Associates, Inc.

Durlacher, Ed. *Teacher's Manual #2 for Intermediate Elementary Grades 4, 5, and 6*. Freeport, N. Y.: Square Dance Associates.

Evans, Ruth. *40 Basic Rhythms for Children*. Putnam, Conn.: U. S. Textbook Co., 1958.

Flood, Jessie B., and Cornelia F. Putney. *Square Dance U. S. A.* Dubuque, Iowa: Wm. C. Brown Co., 1955.

Fox, Grace and Kathleen G. Merrill. *Folk Dancing*. New York: The Ronald Press, 1957.

Hall, J. Tillman. *Dance! A Complete Guide to Social, Folk, and Square Dancing*. Belmont, Calif.: Wadsworth Publishing Co.

Harris, Pittman and Waller. *Dance-A-While*. Minneapolis: Burgess Publishing Co., 1964.

Heaton, A. *Fun Dances*. Dubuque, Iowa: Wm. C. Brown Co., 1959.

Hughes, Langston, *First Book of Rhythms*. New York: Franklin Watts, Inc., 1954.

Jackson, Grace Rogers, and Jeanette Pruyn Reed. *Sing It and Do It*. Albuquerque, N. M.: University of New Mexico Press, 1942.

Kraus, Richard G. *Folk Dancing: A Guide for Schools, Colleges, and Recreation Groups*. New York: The Macmillan Co., 1962.

Kraus, Richard G. *Square Dances of Today and How to Teach and Call Them*. New York: The Ronald Press, 1950.

Kulbitsky and Kaltman. *Teacher's Dance Handbook No. 1*. Newark, N. J.: Folkraft, 1959.

LaSalle, Dorothy. *Rhythms and Dances for Elementary Schools*. New York: The Ronald Press, 1951.

Lunt, Lois. *Hop, Skip and Sing*. Minneapolis: T. S. Dennison and Co., 1959.

Lunt, Lois. *Mix, 'Em and Match 'Em*. Minneapolis: T. S. Dennison and Co., 1961.

Mason, Bernard S. *Dances and Stories of the American Indian*. New York: The Ronald Press, 1944.

McIntosh, David S. *Singing Games and Dances*. New York: Association Press, 1957.

Metz, Louis L. *Action Songs and Rhythms for Children*. Minneapolis: T. S. Dennison and Co., 1962.

Murray, Ruth Lovell. *Dance in Elementary Education*. New York: Harper and Row Publishers, 1963.

National Recreation Assn., Virginia Musselman, Editor. *Mixers to Music for Parties and Dances*.

Pitcher, Gladys. *Playtime in Song*. New York: M. Whitmark and Sons, 1960.

Ryan, Grace L. *Dances of our Pioneers*. New York: The Ronald Press, 1939.

Seeger, Ruth Crawford. *American Folk Songs for Children*. New York: Doubleday and Co., Inc., 1948.

Sehon Elizabeth and Lou O'Brien. *Rhythms in Elementary Education*. New York: The Ronald Press, 1951.

Sheehy, Emma D. *Children Discover Music and Dance*. New York: Holt, Rinehart and Winston, Inc., 1959.

Taylor, Loren. *Dramatics for Children*. (9 volumes). Minneapolis: Burgess Publishing Co., 1965.

Tobitt, Janet. *Red Book of Singing Games and Dances from the Americas*. Evanston, Ill.: Summy-Birchard Publishing Co.

Tobitt, Janet. *Yellow Book of Singing Games and Dances From Around the World*. Evanston, Ill.: Summy-Birchard Publishing Co.

Wiltrout, Dorothea. *Let's Sing and Play*. Chicago: Children's Press, Inc.

5. Stunts, Tumbling, and Apparatus

Bedard, Irving. *Gymnastics for Boys*. Chicago: Follett Publishing Co., 1962.

Burns, T. and T. Micoleau. *Tumbling Techniques Illustrated*. New York: The Ronald Press, 1957.

Cotteral, Bonnie and Donnie Cotteral. *The Teaching of Stunts and Tumbling*. New York: The Ronald Press, 1936.

Harris, Rich. *Introducing Gymnastics*. Napa, Calif.: Physical Education Aids, 1964.

Horne, Virginia Lee. *Stunts and Tumbling for Girls*. New York: The Ronald Press, 1943.

Kripner, Joseph. *Visual Aids for Physical Education*. (A set of four charts with illustrations for stunts, tubmling, pyramids, self-testing activities.) Chicago 20: Joseph Kripner, 1709 W. 83rd St.

LaPorte, William R. and A. Renner, *Tumbler's Manual*. Englewood Cliffs, N. J.: Prentice-Hall, Inc., 1938.

Lokken, Newton C. *Tumbling*. New York: The Sterling Publishing Co., Inc.

McClow, L. L. *Tumbling Illustrated*. New York: The Ronald Press, 1931.

Provasnik and Zabka. *Gymnastic Activities with Hand Apparatus for Girls and Boys*. Minneapolis: Burgess Publishing Co., 1965.

Rodgers, M. A. *A Handbook for Stunts*. New York: The Macmillan Co., 1928.

Ryser, Otto E. *Teacher's Manual for Tumbling and Apparatus Stunts*. Dubuque, Iowa: Wm. C. Brown Co.

Szypula, G. *Tumbling and Balancing for All*. Dubuque, Iowa: Wm. C. Brown Co., 1957.

Willee, A. W. *Small Apparatus for Primary School Physical Education*. New York: Cambridge University Press, 1955.

6. Health, Safety, and Posture

AAHPER. *Answers to Health Questions in Physical Education*.

AAHPER. *Health Appraisal of School Children*. 1961.

AAHPER. *The Physical Education Instructor and Safety*.

AAHPER. *Physical Growth Chart for Boys*. 1960.

AAHPER. *Physical Growth Chart for Girls*. 1960.

AAHPER. *Safety Education in Physical Education for the Classroom Teacher*. 1961.

AAHPER. *Suggested School Safety Policies: Accident Prevention in Physical Education Athletics, and Recreation*. 1964.

AAHPER. *Teaching Safety in the Elementary School* (Classroom Teachers Series). 1962.

Darrow, May Goodall. *The Posture Problem Up To Date*. New York: The Vantage Press, 1959.

Davies, Evelyn A. *The Elementary School Child and His Posture Patterns*. New York: Appleton-Century-Crofts, Inc., 1958.

Gold, Ruth E. *Book Mechanics Charts (4), Elementary Level*. Philadelphia: C/O author.

Kelley, Ellen Davis. *Teaching Posture and Body Mechanics*. New York: The Ronald Press, 1949.

Lowman, Charles, and Carl Haven Young. *Postural Fitness: Significance and Variances* Philadelphia: Lea and Febiger, 1960.

Smith, Helen N. and Mary E. Wolverton. *Health Education in the Elementary School*. New York: The Ronald Press, 1959.

Walker, Herbert. *Health in the Elementary School--The Role of the Classroom Teacher*. New York: The Ronald Press, 1955.

Wells, Katherine F. *Posture Exercise Handbook*. New York: The Ronald Press, 1963.

7. General and Miscellaneous

AAHPER. *Audio-Visual Materials in Physical Education*. 1957.

AAHPER. *Classroom Activities*. 1963.

AAHPER. *Desirable Athletic Competition for Children*. 1952.

AAHPER. *Equipment and Supplies for Athletics, Physical Education and Recreation*. 1960.

AAHPER. *Planning Facilities for Health, Physical Education and Recreation*. 1956.

Allen, Catherine. *Fun For Parties and Programs*. Englewood Cliffs, N. J.: Prentice-Hall, Inc., 1956.

Athletic Institute and AAHPER. *Equipment and Supplies for Athletics, Physical Education and Recreation*. 1960.

Butler, George D. *Recreation Areas--Their Design and Equipment*. New York: The Ronald Press Co., 1958.

Carter, Joel W. *How To Make Athletic Equipment*. New York: The Ronald Press, 1960.

Cratty, Bryant J. *Movement Behavior and Motor Learning*. Philadelphia: Lea and Febiger, 1964.

Doll, Edgar A. *Oseretsky Motor Proficiency Tests*. Minneapolis: American Guidance Services, Inc., 1946.

Hartley, Ruth E., and Robert M. Goldenson. *The Complete Book of Children's Play*. New York: Thomas Y. Crowell Co., 1957.

Ledermann, Alfred and Alfred Trachsel. *Creative Playgrounds and Recreation Centers,* New York: Frederick A. Praeger, Inc., 1959.

Menke, Frank G. *The Encyclopedia of Sports*. New York: A. S. Barnes and Co., 1953.

National Recreation Association, *Make Your Own Games*.

National Recreation Association. *Successful Play Activities*. 1948.

Sapora, Allen V., and Elmer D. Mitchell. *The Theory of Play and Recreation*. New York: The Ronald Press, 1961.

Smith, Anne Marie. *Play for Convalescent Children in Hospitals and at Home*. New York: A. S. Barnes and Co.

Taylor, Margaret Fisk. *Time for Wonder*. Philadelphia: Christian Educational Press, 1961.

U. S. Department of Health, Education and Welfare, Elsa Schneider, Specialist. *Physical Education in Urban Elementary Schools,* Washington, D. C.: Supt. of Documents, U. S. Govt. Printing Office, 1959.

Ward, Winnifred. *Play Making with Children*. New York: Appleton-Century-Crofts, Inc., 1957.

8. Card Packets for Games, Rhythms, and Stunts

Berger, H. Jean. *Program Activities for Camps*. Minneapolis: Burgess Publishing Co., 1961.

Fischer, Hugo and Dean Shawbold. *Individual and Dual Stunts*. Minneapolis: Burgess Publishing Co., 1950.

Gibson and Jervey. *Holiday Funfest (Games, Grades 1-6)*. Minneapolis: Burgess Publishing Co., 1964.

Frederick, A. Bruce. *Gymnastic Action Cards*. Minneapolis: Burgess Publishing Co., 1965.

Harris, Jane A. *File-o-Fun*. (card file for social recreation). Minneapolis: Burgess Publishing Co., 1962.

Richardson, Hazel A. *Games for the Elementary School Grades*. Minneapolis: Burgess Publishing Co., 1951.

Richardson, Hazel A. *Games for Junior and Senior High Schools*. Minneapolis: Burgess Publishing Co., 1957.

Stuart, Frances R., and John S. Ludlam. *Rhythmic Activities, Series I* (K-3). Minneapolis: Burgess Publishing Co., 1963.

Stuart, Frances R., and John S. Ludlam. *Rhythmic Activities, Series II* (4-6). Minneapolis: Burgess Publishing Co., 1963.

Stuart, Frances R., and Virginia L. Gibson. *Rhythmic Activities, Series III* (5-8). Minneapolis: Burgess Publishing Co., 1961.

Stuart, Frances R., Gibson, Virginia L., and Arden Jervey. *Rhythmic Activities, Series IV* (1-9). Minneapolis: Burgess Publishing Co., 1963.

Index

EXERCISES

GAMES

HORIZONTAL LADDER

RELAYS

RHYTHMICAL ACTIVITIES

ROPES, CLIMBING

STUNTS AND TUMBLING